M

THRESHOLD
EDITIONS

MERCURY
RADIO ARTS

OTHER BOOKS BY GLENN BECK

THRESHOLD EDITIONS

MERCURY RADIO ARTS

NEW YORK   LONDON   TORONTO   SYDNEY

GLENN BECK
ARGUING WITH SOCIALISTS

WRITTEN & EDITED BY:

GLENN BECK

CONTRIBUTORS

JUSTIN HASKINS
DONALD KENDAL
STU BURGUIERE

ART & DESIGN

ALEXANDER SOMOSKEY
JACOB THOMPSON

ILLUSTRATIONS

BRYNDON EVERETT

TO ALL THOSE SEARCHING FOR TRUTH AND REFUSING TO SURRENDER YOUR SENSE OF HUMOR. HONEST AND BOLD QUESTIONS ARE ALWAYS BETTER THAN BLINDFOLDED FEAR.

THRESHOLD EDITIONS

MERCURY RADIO ARTS

Threshold Editions/Mercury Radio Arts
An Imprint of Simon & Schuster, Inc.
1230 Avenue of the Americas
New York, NY 10020

First Threshold Editions/Mercury Radio Arts hardcover edition April 2020

THRESHOLD EDITIONS and colophon are trademarks of Simon & Schuster, Inc.

GLENN BECK is a trademark of Mercury Radio Arts, Inc.

For information about special discounts for bulk purchases, please contact Simon & Schuster Special Sales at 1-866-506-1949 or business@simonandschuster.com.

The Simon & Schuster Speakers Bureau can bring authors to your live event. For more information, or to book an event, contact the Simon & Schuster Speakers Bureau at 1-866-248-3049 or visit our website at www.simonspeakers.com.

Designed by Alexander Somoskey
Illustrated by Bryndon Everett

Manufactured in the United States of America

10 9 8 7 6 5 4 3 2

Library of Congress Cataloging-in-Publication Data
Names: Beck, Glenn, author.
Title: Arguing with socialists / written and edited by Glenn Beck; contributors, Justin Haskins, Donald Kendal, Stu Burguiere, Alexander Somoskey, Jacob Thompson, Bryndon Everett.
Description: New York : Threshold Editions, 2020. | Includes bibliographical references. | Summary: "In Arguing With Socialists, New York Times bestselling author Glenn Beck arms readers to the teeth with information necessary to debunk the socialist arguments that have once again become popular, and proves that the free market is the only way to go"–Provided by publisher.
Identifiers: LCCN 2019060240 (print) | LCCN 2019060241 (ebook) | ISBN 9781982140502 (hardcover) | ISBN 9781982140519 (trade paperback) | ISBN 9781982140526 (ebook)
Subjects: LCSH: Socialism–Political aspects. | Communism. | Capitalism. | Free enterprise.
Classification: LCC HX73 .B423 2020 (print) | LCC HX73 (ebook) | DDC 335–dc23
LC record available at https://lccn.loc.gov/2019060240
LC ebook record available at https://lccn.loc.gov/2019060241

ISBN 978-1-9821-4050-2
ISBN 978-1-9821-4052-6 (ebook)

ACKNOWLEDGMENTS

I hate these things because I always forget too many people. Let me start with my agents at United Talent Agency: Brent Weinstein, Jay Sures, and Byrd Leavell. They are the very best and have always believed in me, even when I didn't. Thanks to Tyler Cardon, a miracle worker, who saw my vision, didn't try to change it, but instead made it better. Justin Haskins and Donald Kendal, who have rocked this book. It has been a fun journey. I have learned a lot. Thanks for making me look good :] Stu Burguiere, whose contributions were brilliant, as always. Here's to another twenty years! Pat Gray, here's to another thirty! We used to laugh so hard we'd pee our pants. Just think, thirty years from now, we won't need the laughter to pee and crap our pants. Alexander Somoskey, who was mocked relentlessly in college because he had the balls to say out loud that his goal was to work for me someday. They mocked, I hired, and I've enjoyed our creative collaboration ever since. Thanks to Bryndon for the illustrations and Jake for the design work. Thank you for putting up with the insane hours and never bitching when we didn't get to sleep.

Thank you to my radio team, TV team, and the entire Blaze Media family. Rikki, Booey, Sara, Sarah, Marissa, Adam, Kase, Clayton, Kyra, Jay, the social media team, you all rock! To Rob and the floor crew, producers, and directors, who always make me look good even when I change everything at the last minute. Thanks to all of the Blaze Media talent. I am honored to call you coworkers and friends. Together, we truly are greater than the sum of our parts. Together we can change the world. Thanks to all of my writers and researchers: Jason, Nathan, Larry, Justin. You guys are the best. Thanks to my social media team. Thanks to Chelsea Cardon, whom I first met as she worked on my "Man in the Moon" stage show in 2013. I almost killed her with work. Thanks for never giving up and always overdelivering.

Thanks to my family for never saying a negative word when "I have to go off to write" every year for weeks on end. Tania, Mary, Hannah, Raphe, Cheyenne, Tim, Lorelei, Coen and Uno, I love you. Tania, I need you more than ever. Bishop Lance for keeping me from going too far off the path. Your friendship has saved me from myself. Robert, Colleen, and family. Matthew, thanks for asking me to officiate at your wedding. It meant a ton – you bum:) Mark and Rick of Gavin de Becker & Associates and my detail Chad and Caesar (good with a gun, but deadly with a hair dryer). I will never understand why you would take a bullet for me, and let's make sure we never have to see if you actually would. Thank you to my Scottish Executive Assistant at MRA Craig Poole–yeah, yeah, the Scots invented everything, including freedom, apparently. But it took Americans to get it done and our leader didn't need face paint or a skirt. Long live the queen.

Finally thank you to Carolyn Reidy and the whole team at Simon & Schuster. Thanks for believing and pushing me over the years. 14 years and 13 #1 best sellers and, what, 7 or 8 others in the top five? I have lost count... It has been a great run. Thank you for the support.

See, you have been scanning for your name and it isn't here. "That bastard! He forgot me." I know that's what it looks like but your name isn't here because I didn't want to embarrass you with my fawning. You are far too modest and humble :-) Finally, dear reader, thank YOU. You have changed my life. You are part of the best audience one could hope for. Stay strong. Have faith. He is in charge.

HOW TO USE THIS BOOK

TABLE OF
CONTENTS

SETTING THE STAGE

FINAL
APPROVED
-GB

"THIS IS THE MOST IMPORTANT ELECTION OF OUR LIFETIMES."

Sound familiar? It should. Not an election year goes by without swarms of media personalities, activists, "community organizers," and politicians screeching at the top of their lungs about the threats of the present age and how if their side loses—enter the political party of your choice here—it would be the end of human civilization as we know it. This is my tenth consecutive "most important election," and I think it's a safe bet that the next one will be just as dire.

AUTHOR'S NOTE

TODAY'S ELECTIONS CAN BE SUCH AGONIZING PROCESSES THAT THE END OF HUMAN CIVILIZATION DOESN'T SEEM LIKE SUCH A BAD OPTION.

I'm not trying to minimize the problems Americans are facing today or the important choices we're going to have to make over the next few decades if we're going to survive the twenty-first century. We really are living in a remarkable, disruptive, *and* dangerous time.

When Donald Trump says that many "skilled craftsmen and tradespeople and factory workers have seen the jobs they loved shipped thousands of miles away," and that in some parts of the country, whole communities have been "plunged into depression-level unemployment," he's right.[1]

When Bernie Sanders laments that "half of the country lives paycheck to paycheck as tens of millions of our people are an accident, a divorce, a sickness, or a layoff away from economic devastation," he's right, too.[2]

Ted Cruz is right when says that "every student deserves a great education," but that "too many young Americans are denied those opportunities" because America's school system is in "grave" shape.[3]

And Elizabeth Warren is right when she says, "Families are getting crushed by health costs," and that because of high health insurance deductibles, health insurance for many "is like a car with the engine missing. It looks fine sitting on the lot, but it is inadequate if they actually need to use it."[4] (Thanks, Liz, for outlining some of the failures of Obamacare so eloquently.)

But if you think for even one moment that many of these problems will be solved if we elect the "right" party in the next election—whether Republican or Democratic—then you haven't been paying attention. We could elect the "right" party every election for the next dozen "most important elections" and we would still end up with more crises than we started with. Political parties are equal opportunity offenders when it comes to creating crises.

This isn't because the challenges we're facing are insurmountable. I don't wake up each morning in despair. Technically, I wake up every morning in a SpongeBob onesie, a lengthy discussion of which was cut by the publisher.

We can make America better than it has ever been. But not if we put our faith in politicians, or any human being, for that matter. America has been able to survive endless switching between Team Red and Team Blue (even Team Whig), and yet it has still managed to become the most successful nation in the history of the world. Washington elites want you to believe their alleged brilliance is the only reason America has been as successful as it has, and that they can save you if only you were willing to give them more power over your life, *but that's just not true.* Our nation thrives not because of its politicians, but in spite of them.

 Neal DiCaprio-Cortez @GreenNewNeal*
.@glennbeck, I can't believe I'm saying this, but you're right. Politicians won't fix these problems by maintaining the status quo. We need to completely change our entire system. That's why millions of people like me are calling for socialism.

 ANY SIMILARITY OF THE FICTIONAL TWITTER HANDLES USED IN THIS BOOK TO ANY ACTIVE TWITTER HANDLE IS COINCIDENTAL AND UNINTENTIONAL.

LAWYER'S NOTE
LEGAL DOCUMENT

Ah, there you are—my friend. I'm so glad we agreed to have this conversation, and I'm looking forward to meeting the comrades you've brought with you throughout our dialogue.

I know it's tempting to jump right into it, but before we can have a truly meaningful conversation, we need to define our terms. Far too often, important discussions—no matter how sincere the participants are—end up devolving into screaming matches, or, at best, people just end up talking past each other. And in many cases, our disagreements result from people using the same terms but defining them differently.

We see this all the time when people talk about the "far left" or the "far right." To many on the left, when they think of the "far right," they conjure up images of neo-Nazi rallies or fascist dictators. But if you ask someone who identifies as a conservative what they consider "far right," they are much more likely to think of people who believe in extremely limited government—people like Ayn Rand and other libertarians who think government should be so small that it can't even build roads, never mind throw millions of people into concentration camps.

How can we have a useful conversation about right-left politics if one side thinks the "far right" is akin to Nazism and the other side thinks "far right" is best epitomized by *Atlas Shrugged*'s libertarian town of Galt's Gulch? You can't.

So, before we get into details about socialism, communism, and capitalism, we need a common understanding of what these words mean. In Chapters 2 and 3, we'll go into much greater detail about all of these concepts, and we'll cite heavily from people who actually claim to be socialists and communists. But for now, let's quickly go over some very basic definitions of our terms.

socialism *noun*

[so·cial·ism | \ ˈsō-shə-ˌli-zəm \]

"any of various economic and political theories advocating collective or governmental ownership and administration of the means of production and distribution of goods."[5]

SOCIALISM DEFINITION

In a socialist economy, the society as a whole collectively owns and manages property, taking the power out of the hands of individuals and granting it instead to the wider community, often by giving more control over property to government

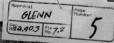

agencies. This goes over very well with humans. Just try taking toys away from one child and "sharing" them with others in the same room. Let me know how that works out.

Marx describes socialism as a pit stop (emphasis on the *pit*) on the glorious road toward communism. Technically, socialism is a "transitional social state between the overthrow of capitalism and the realization of Communism"—the phase when capitalism must be discredited and destroyed, along with all those who stand in the way of the people's progress or revolution.

DEMOCRATIC SOCIALISM DEFINITION

democratic socialism *noun*

[pred·a·tor·y | \ ˈpred-*uh*-tawr-ˌee \] · [so·cial·ism | \ ˈsō-shə-ˌli-zəm \]

features the same system of collective ownership and management of property inherent in every other socialist system, along with all of its problems. The only difference is its adherents also pinky swear that they'll never support any form of government other than one in which elections are *democratically* held, as if democracy magically guarantees there won't be tyranny.

(ASK AFRICAN AMERICANS WHO LIVED IN THE JIM CROW SOUTH OR JAPANESE AMERICANS WHO WERE FORCED TO LIVE IN GOVERNMENT-RUN INTERNMENT CAMPS DURING WORLD WAR II HOW WELL DEMOCRACY WITHOUT PROTECTIONS FOR INDIVIDUAL RIGHTS WORKS OUT.)

SOCIALIST CHEAT SHEET:

IF IT'S UNPOPULAR TO SAY YOU'RE A COMMUNIST, SAY YOU'RE A SOCIALIST.

IF IT'S UNPOPULAR TO SAY YOU'RE A SOCIALIST, SAY YOU'RE A DEMOCRATIC SOCIALIST.

IF IT'S UNPOPULAR TO SAY YOU'RE A DEMOCRATIC SOCIALIST, SAY YOU'RE A DEMOCRAT.

Although many of America's most prominent "democratic socialists" say their system is entirely different from the socialist horror stories we've seen in numerous countries over the past century, the truth is, democratic socialism is nothing more than socialism with a better PR department.

MORE
DEFINITIONS

swedish-style socialism *noun*

[swe·dish | \ "swidɪʃ \] · [so·cial·ism | \ ˈsō-shə-ˌli-zəm \]

is a mythical creation invented by socialists desperately looking for proof that socialism works. When they examined history and couldn't find any examples of socialism working— not a single one—they fabricated the Scandinavian socialism myth.

communism *noun*

[com·mun·ism | \ ˈkom-yuh-niz-uhm \]

is "a system in which goods are owned in common and are available to all as needed."[6] In the Marxist sense, communism is the most extreme form of socialism. In a communist utopia, *all* property, including many kinds of personal property, is collectively owned and managed. According to actual communists, this has never been achieved. In its most idealistic form, communism does not include an all-powerful, centralized government, but rather people sharing, working, and living for the common good.

real-world communism *noun*

[reel | \ ree-uhl \] · [world | \ wurld \] · [com·mun·ism | \ ˈkom-yuh-niz-uhm \]

like many forms of socialism, results in misery, death, despair, and authoritarianism— everything communists say they oppose while fomenting revolution but can't seem to avoid when they come into power.

CAPITALISM DEFINITION

capitalism *noun*

[cap·i·tal·ism | \ ˈka-pə-tə-ˌliz-əm \]

is "an economic system characterized by private or corporate ownership of capital goods, by investments that are determined by private decision, and by prices, production, and the distribution of goods that are determined mainly by competition in a free market."[7]

Or, put in really simple terms: In real, free-market capitalism, I own personal property, you own personal property, and we're able to exchange that property by using money or bartering.

Free-market capitalism is very different from the corrupt, crony brand of "capitalism" commonly found today. Under our current system, large corporations and other special interests work with government agencies and politicians to heavily tilt the scales in their favor, stifle competition, and establish a regulatory and taxing structure that favors many wealthy, powerful businesses over smaller ones.

FREE-MARKET CAPITALISM DEFINITION

Free-market capitalism with a "safety net" *noun*

[cap·i·tal·ism | \ ˈka-pə-tə-ˌliz-əm \]

is a market-based, capitalistic economy that includes publicly funded social safety nets for those who are unable to support themselves. This is the system utilized by countries such as Sweden, which has a largely free market; few regulations, making it easy to start a business; a tax-friendly atmosphere; and laws that protect honest businesses and their owners.

Free-market capitalism with a "safety net" is a market-based, capitalistic economy that includes publicly funded social safety nets for those who are unable to support themselves. This is the system utilized by countries such as Sweden, which has a largely free market; few regulations, making it easy to start a business; a tax-friendly atmosphere; and laws that protect honest businesses and their owners.

Free-market capitalism with a "safety net" is *not* a socialist system. It is the free market that allows countries like Sweden to be able to raise enough in tax revenue to provide generous benefits in their welfare programs. Most of these countries, as you will see in upcoming chapters, eventually scale their welfare states back as they become financially impossible to maintain (*cough, cough, Social Security*). The biggest difference between a free-market capitalist system with a safety net and a completely free-market model is the latter depends on the private social structure—churches, Lions Clubs, PTAs, soup kitchens, Jerry Lewis telethons, etc.—to assist people who are incapable of supporting themselves.

There are obviously extreme differences between these concepts that carry with them important real-world consequences. If Americans move further down the road to socialism and communism, there's no question that things will change—and radically so. Americans will especially love the bare grocery store shelves and rolling power outages. But, we are not merely looking for something *different*, we're looking for something *better*. We agree that America is facing difficult challenges, like high health care costs and college loan debt, millions of people trapped in a cycle of poverty, out-of-control corporations in bed with government agencies, as well as economic disruption caused by automation.

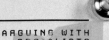

SOCIALIST FUN FACT!

No truly socialist system could come up with the brilliance of Ikea, a place that somehow has built a business model selling both furniture and Swedish meatballs. However, the incomprehensible directions they utilize to "help" you put the furniture together absolutely had to be the handywork of a completely incompetent and borderline masochistic socialist bureaucrat.

Where we disagree is on the *solutions* to these problems. Socialists believe that we can make the world a better place by taking property and wealth away from the people who have it and centralizing economic, political, and social power. But I believe America is at its best when individuals are empowered with the freedom to pursue their own hopes and dreams—whatever that might mean to you—while strengthening cultural traditions that teach and encourage the individual to help, heal, and promote the general welfare.

Maybe you're an auto mechanic who hopes to one day open your own shop. Or maybe you're a nurse who spends your free time studying to become a doctor.

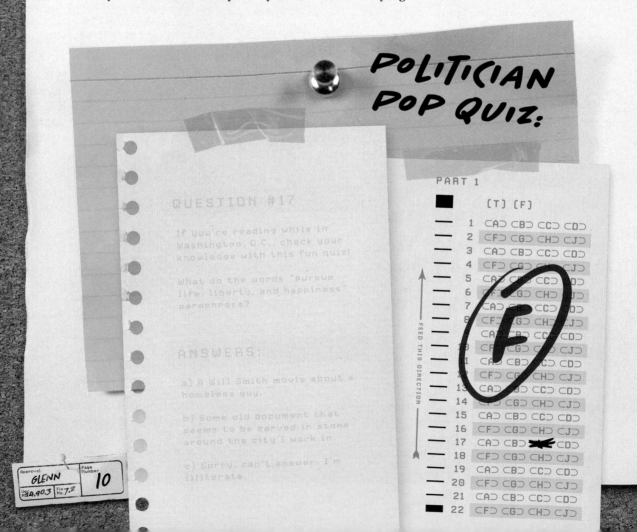

POLITICIAN POP QUIZ:

QUESTION #17

If you're reading while in Washington, D.C., check your knowledge with this fun quiz!

What do the words "pursue life, liberty, and happiness" paraphrase?

ANSWERS:

a) A Will Smith movie about a homeless guy.

b) Some old document that seems to be carved in stone around the city I work in.

c) Sorry, can't answer. I'm illiterate.

Or maybe you work for a massive multi-national corporation but secretly aspire to start your own small bakery one day. Whatever it is that drives you, that makes you feel excited about life—that's your "American dream," and I believe that when we're free to pursue our own unique passions and goals for life, we're all better off.

All Americans want to send their children to high-quality schools. We all want a lower-cost health care system that works. We all want an increased standard of living and better job opportunities. And we all want to live in peaceful, stable communities. (Okay, maybe not Antifa members, but everyone else does.) In essence, we all want to pursue life, liberty, and happiness.

So, the real question isn't, "Who should we elect?" or "How do we beat the other side?" It's, "What ideas and policies are most likely to create (or conserve) an America where her citizens are able to pursue life, liberty, and happiness—and have a good chance at achieving it?" Throughout this book, I'm going to do my best to prove that socialism, democratic or otherwise, is not the answer, and I'm going to give you the tools you need to convince others of that reality.

If you happen to be someone who identifies as a socialist, or even just someone who thinks socialism has a valuable role to play in America's future, there's a good chance you're reading this because a friend or family member put this book in your hands with the hope that you can be convinced to reverse course before you and your comrades destroy the country. I don't know who that person is, but I know he or she is *really* smart. (And you can tell your friend or family member I said so!) If you're a socialist, there will be times as you're reading this book that you will feel surprised or skeptical. There may even be moments when you want to slam the book shut after I take a particularly harsh jab at Bernie Sanders. That's okay. Important conversations that challenge our existing ideas and force us to rethink concepts we thought we understood can be frustrating. (Plus, Bernie almost certainly deserved it.)

But please keep in mind as you read through this important "conversation"—whatever your thoughts are about socialism—that despite the book's cartoons, jokes, and other entertaining elements, my goal here is to teach people that the socialist reforms commonly put forward as "solutions" to all of society's ills would actually cause significant harm to everyone, *especially* to those Americans who are already struggling.

Don't take my word for anything I say throughout the book. *Do your own homework.* And don't forget that in most cases, Americans agree on the problems we face, it's the proposed *solutions* to the problems that divide us. We all agree that America has a long way to go before it reaches its full potential. On that point, we all stand firmly on common ground.

END OF CHAPTER 1

CAPITALISM: BABY OR BATHWATER?

LOOKS GOOD!
APPROVED
-GB

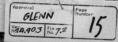

"AND SO I DO THINK THAT RIGHT NOW WE HAVE THIS NO-HOLDS-BARRED, WILD WEST HYPER-CAPITALISM. WHAT THAT MEANS IS PROFIT AT ANY COST. CAPITALISM HAS NOT ALWAYS EXISTED IN THE WORLD, AND IT WILL NOT ALWAYS EXIST IN THE WORLD."[1]

— ALEXANDRIA OCASIO-CORTEZ

A cigar-smoke-filled room full of old white men laughing as they light bucketloads of cash on fire, just for the fun of it—for countless Americans, especially those who spend their evenings watching CNN and MSNBC, that's what they imagine when they think about capitalism. They think capitalism is an outdated idea that needs to be replaced with something innovative, a new and revolutionary way of thinking. It's a corrupt, broken model that worked when people were riding around on horseback, but it can't possibly manage the complexities of the modern, technologically advanced world.

Or, as self-described socialist and media darling Rep. Alexandria Ocasio-Cortez, D-N.Y., claimed, "capitalism is irredeemable."[2]

"Capitalism is an ideology of capital—the most important thing is the concentration of capital and to seek and maximize profit," Ocasio-Cortez also said, adding later that "we should be scared right now because corporations have taken over our government."

Sen. Bernie Sanders, I-Vt., another self-described socialist, says America has become an "oligarchy," a government ruled by the wealthiest few.

According to Sanders, "The simple fact is that in the United States today, at a time of unprecedented income and wealth inequality, we have a very small number people—multi-billionaires who comprise less than one/one hundredth of 1 percent of our population—who exercise extraordinary power over our economic, political, and social life. ... The oligarchy in this country, whose greed is insatiable, is ... moving us toward a government of the few, by the few, and for the few. And that is a direction we must oppose with every fiber of our being."[3]

CAPITALISM IS AN IDEOLOGY OF CAPITAL
– AOC

Looking back on the past few decades, it's not hard to see how we ended up here, in a world where cartoon characters like Comrade Bernie Sanders and Alexandria Ocasio-Cortez—people who would have been laughed out of the room when I was growing up—have

- TECHNICALLY, BERNIE HAD ALREADY BEEN LAUGHED OUT OF THE ROOM LONG BEFORE I WAS BORN. MORE RECENTLY, HE HAS LAUGHED HIS WAY INTO MULTIPLE VACATION HOMES.

Every year, tens of thousands of people flock to Austin, Texas, to attend the South by Southwest festival—an event where people gather to appreciate music, film, and art.

During one of the nights during the 2019 South by Southwest event, attendees gathered together, their beer cups overflowing and smartphones in hand, to listen to Alexandria Ocasio-Cortez explain that "capitalism is irredeemable."

The evening was dripping with irony. Only in America can a democratic socialist attending an event full of relatively wealthy Millennials endlessly disparage the very economic system that made the event possible in the first place.[a]

WHAT A COUNTRY!

managed to become the faces of the new Left in the United States. Many Americans, especially those in the working class, are realizing that the current system isn't working as advertised.

Millions of people pay one-third of their income or more in taxes, and they get almost nothing in exchange for it. Some work their entire lives—40 years or more—and end up with nearly as much in the bank as able-bodied Americans who spent decades relying on welfare programs when they could have had a job.

When economic times get tough, thousands of business owners, including many small businessmen and businesswomen, lose everything they have built while well-connected, multi-billion-dollar corporations get handouts and bailouts from their friends in Washington, D.C.

Some entrepreneurs struggle to find funding to help make the next big idea a reality, while others with close friends or family members in the right places get access to lucrative government grants.

After spending years in America's failing public school system, many college students arrive on campus less prepared for the real world than ever before, and they often end up graduating with tens of thousands of dollars in student loan debt, far more than their parents ever did. And then when they finally enter the workforce, they quickly realize their degree in women's studies or art history isn't going to help them get a job—even though their high school teachers and professors promised them all they'd need to do is graduate from college and they would be set for life.

For decades, millions of jobs have been shipped overseas to countries that hate American values. Whole communities, especially in many parts of the Midwest, have been totally decimated, and because cities like Youngstown, Ohio, and Buffalo, New York, don't have the same political clout as Alexandria, Virginia, they don't end up with equal economic opportunities. Too often, businesses go wherever they can get the best government pay-off, not where the market would ordinarily lead them. This is not free-market capitalism. This is crony capitalism, a problem that can only exist when big government tries to control markets.

"SO YOU KNOW THE GOVERNMENT IS TAKING 40% OFF MY TAXES AND UNCLE SAM, I WANT TO KNOW WHAT YOU DO WITH MY F****** TAX MONEY BECAUSE, YOU KNOW WHAT I'M SAYING LIKE, WHEN YOU DONATE TO A KID FROM A FOREIGN COUNTRY, THEY GIVE YOU UPDATES OF WHAT THEY'RE DOING IN ANOTHER NATION.

"I WANT TO KNOW WHAT TO DO WITH MY F****** TAX MONEY BECAUSE I'M FROM NEW YORK AND THE STREETS IS ALWAYS DIRTY. IT WAS VOTED THE DIRTIEST CITY IN AMERICA. WHAT IS YA'LL DOING? THERE'S STILL RATS ON THE DAMN TRAINS. … WHAT IS YA'LL DOING WITH MY F****** MONEY, I WANT TO KNOW. I WANT RECEIPTS, I WANT EVERYTHING. I WANT TO KNOW WHAT YA'LL N****** DOING WITH MY F****** MONEY … UNCLE SAM, I WANT TO KNOW WHAT THE F*** YOU'RE DOING WITH MY MOTHER****** MONEY."[b]

LIKE...
WHAT
THE F*CK?

— CARDI B.

THIS MEGA-GENIUS WOUND UP SUPPORTING BERNIE SANDERS FOR PRESIDENT, APPARENTLY BELIEVING THE ONLY THING BETTER THAN PAYING 40% OF YOUR MONEY FOR NOTHING, IS PAYING 90% OF YOUR MONEY FOR NOTHING.

As a certain reality-TV star turned president would say, the system is "rigged"—and Americans know it. What they aren't so sure about, however, is what can be done to fix these problems.

For years, Americans have been trudging off to the polls on the second Tuesday in November, electing the people who have promised to have their backs. But then, year after year, surprise! It turns out politicians don't really care about fixing *your* problems. Things have gotten so bad, even colonoscopies and root canals are more popular than Congress.[4]

So, Americans started to wander through the Ideas Desert, desperate for anything that might provide a solution. But no matter how far they trekked, there was no water to be found.

The mainstream news media, which is supposed to act as a check on the power of government, has transformed from a watchdog to a lapdog. Instead of asking tough questions about the United States' future, they feed Americans an endless stream of garbage: "Wait, what's that? You want a story about the nation's whopping $23 trillion debt, or how that means every single taxpayer now owes $186,000 to the Federal Reserve and foreign countries like China. Sorry, we've a got a breaking story on Donald Trump's latest tweet, followed by a story about Donald Trump's hair, followed by a report on Trump's ice cream consumption—can you believe he actually got two scoops?[5] And then we've got more 'news' on Russian collusion, and then an in-depth report on Twiggy the water-skiing squirrel . . . and his expertly considered opposition to Donald Trump."

It's in this environment that millions of Americans, desperate for solutions to the world's problems, worried and confused about the future, have started to take socialism seriously. Unlike many Democrats and Republicans, socialists are promising people something entirely different, a totally new world. Their vision is big, expansive, and yeah, to a lot of people it sounds too good to be true, but for many of those who are tired of being lied to and misled by politicians and supposedly "unbiased" news networks, it's worth taking a shot on something, anything that hasn't been done before.

Of course, socialism has been tried before—over and over and over again. But if you're under the age of 40, you probably don't remember much about the socialism of the Soviet Union. You weren't alive to understand the dangers of the Cold War, and you didn't experience Vietnam or Mao's China, either. To many young people, socialism is idealistic, democratic, and peaceful. It's not gulags, Nazis, and prison camps.

Socialists are selling snake oil, but they're successful because they're selling their "cure" to a people desperate for healing. And when people get desperate, they're often willing to try just about anything. Socialism is the fast-acting diet pills or hair restoration tonics of the political philosophy world. It sounds great in theory, but in the end, those who try these "fine products" end up just as fat and bald as they were before—if they survive at all.

When I tell people the only way to fix our country's problems is by embracing free markets, not giving an unlimited amount of power to government bureaucrats who couldn't manage their way out of a paper bag, some people—many people, in fact—laugh or scoff or write me off as just another crazy member of the "vast right-wing conspiracy." They say I'm greedy, selfish, and heartless. They say that if I really cared about the world, I'd support single-payer health care, the Green New Deal, and a long list of other socialist policy programs.

ONE DROP OF THIS AND YOU'LL BE RICH, HEALTHY AND READY TO TAKE ON THE BOURGEOISIE!

BERNIE THE SNAKE OIL SALESMAN

But none of that is true. I oppose socialism because it hurts the poor, eliminates individual freedom, and destroys economic opportunities for everyone. I reject high taxes because I believe, based on mountains of evidence, that when people are empowered with the ability to control their own wealth, they use it more wisely than George Bush, Barack Obama, or John Q. Bureaucrat, who works in some gigantic government building in Washington, D.C., in a job that's almost impossible to fire him from. I oppose the tens of thousands of pages of federal government regulations because I believe fewer regulations makes it easier for small business owners, entrepreneurs, and innovators to change the world and create products that improve life for everyone.

I love free-market capitalism, not the funhouse-mirror distortion of "capitalism" we see today. I love the kind of capitalism that embraces free enterprise and free people. I'm talking about the kind of capitalism and innovation that led to the creation of the modern computer and the proliferation of the countless millions of new ideas, products, and services made possible by the internet. Also, the one that came up with the McGriddle.

When socialists and progressives think of capitalism, they imagine Rich Uncle Pennybags—the Monopoly man—a chubby, white, mustachioed rich guy sporting a top hat and monocle. But that's not the face of free-market capitalism. It's the millions of small business owners who work tirelessly every single day in the pursuit of providing people with goods and services they need to live better lives. It's family-run restaurants that feature the best darn ice cream you've ever had. It's innovators tinkering away in their garages on the next great invention that will change the world. It's immigrants who arrive on America's shores with nothing in their pockets but a heart full of passion to pursue a life of peace, freedom, and hard work.

THE MYTH OF THE ROBBER BARONS

ONE OF THE MOST PERSISTENT MYTHS ABOUT CAPITALISM IS THE MODERN ARCHETYPE OF THE "ROBBER BARON." INDUSTRIALISTS LIKE JOHN D. ROCKEFELLER, CORNELIUS VANDERBILT, AND ANDREW CARNEGIE ARE ROUTINELY DEMONIZED AS CUTTHROAT CAPITALISTS WHO WOULD STOP AT NOTHING TO EARN AN EXTRA BUCK.

IN REALITY, AS MISES INSTITUTE SENIOR FELLOW THOMAS DILORENZO PUTS IT, "THIS IS A DISTORTION OF THE TRUTH."

AS DILORENZO EXPLAINS IN HIS BOOK HOW *CAPITALISM SAVED AMERICA*, PEOPLE FAIL TO MAKE THE DISTINCTION BETWEEN "MARKET ENTREPRENEURS" AND "POLITICAL ENTREPRENEURS." YES, SOME BUSINESS OWNERS USED THEIR POLITICAL LINKS TO TIP THE SCALES IN THEIR FAVOR - LIKE LELAND STANFORD, WHO "USED HIS POLITICAL CONNECTIONS TO HAVE THE STATE PASS LAWS PROHIBITING COMPETITION FOR HIS CENTRAL PACIFIC RAILROAD." THESE ARE THE "POLITICAL ENTREPRENEURS."

THE MARKET ENTREPRENEURS, HOWEVER, LEVERAGED THEIR OWN HARD WORK TO GET A LEG UP ON COMPETITION. "ROCKEFELLER PAID METICULOUS ATTENTION TO EVERY DETAIL OF HIS BUSINESS, CONSTANTLY STRIVING TO CUT HIS COSTS, IMPROVE HIS PRODUCT, AND EXPAND HIS LINE OF PRODUCTS," WROTE DILORENZO. "HIS BUSINESS PARTNERS AND MANAGERS EMULATED HIM, WHICH DROVE THE COMPANY TO GREAT SUCCESS."[c]

Our current system isn't even remotely close to a truly free market. It's overregulated, designed to favor big corporations and well-connected special interests, and it's full of corruption and sweetheart deals between policymakers and business owners who will do anything to make a quick buck. That's not capitalism. That's *crony* capitalism, and it can only exist in a society in which government officials are extremely powerful. After all, you can't buy off a powerful government official if there aren't any.

America is facing some very serious and important problems, but centralizing authority and putting government in charge of virtually every aspect of our lives won't fix them. It would only make things much worse.

Neal DiCaprio-Cortez @GreenNewNeal
Oh, @glennbeck, come on. We've heard this all before. Anyone with even half a brain knows that capitalism isn't working. After everything that happened with the 2008 financial crisis—the corruption, predatory lending, bailouts—it's apparent that we need to radically transform our economy. Capitalism had its chance, and it failed. It's time to finally give socialism a shot in the United States.

♡ 1   ⇄   ♡

I'm so glad you brought up the 2008 financial crisis. I couldn't think of a more perfect example of how government's involvement in our economy has distorted markets and caused massive and far-reaching economic problems. The 2008 crisis and subsequent economic crash aren't examples of capitalism run amok, they are proof that politicians and government bureaucrats—no matter how well-intentioned they might be—are *terrible* central planners who often cause a lot more harm than good.

According to socialists and progressives, the 2008 financial crash began when banks started to engage in "predatory lending" practices, offering mortgages to people who had no business getting large loans. The story goes that bankers, who were supposedly emboldened after the George W. Bush and Clinton administrations reduced financial regulations, were looking to earn as much money as possible, so they did whatever they could to trick and coerce unsuspecting consumers into agreeing to take on increasingly bigger mortgages. Bankers then packaged those

SOCIALIST
DICTIONARY

predatory lending *noun*

[pred·a·tor·y | \ ˈpred-*uh*-tawr-ˌee \] · [\ ˈlend \]

the horrific and criminal action taken by a bank or financial institution in which feeble peasants are hunted down and targeted to receive large amounts of money they ask for.

ponzi scheme *noun*

[pon·zee | \ ˈpɒn-zi \] · [skeem | \ ˈskim \]

a form of fraud in which belief in the success of an enterprise is fostered by the payment of quick returns to the first investors from money invested by later investors. Also see "entitlement programs."

mortgages together and sold them on Wall Street as securities. In many cases, Wall Street bankers then repackaged those mortgages and sold them again. Because housing prices were continuously rising, everyone was making money, but once housing prices crashed, the whole Ponzi scheme came tumbling down.

While there's certainly some truth to this narrative, it's hardly a complete picture of what really happened in the lead-up to the 2008 crash. As with so many other events that have occurred throughout history, the roots of the crisis stem back much further—all the way to the 1990s, a magical time featuring the birth of the modern internet, cinematic wonders like *Jurassic Park*, and the impeachment of a certain Democratic Party president who was more interested in screwing around with the new White House intern than he was killing Osama bin Laden.

During the 1990s, the cost of owning a personal computer that could be used at home dropped dramatically, allowing tens of millions of American families to purchase their first personal computer, as well as all the software that was needed to operate it. This created a huge new market, both in the consumer electronics industry and online. During this period, a slew of Wall Street investors and millions of others who were overly optimistic about the potential for new internet-based companies to turn big profits invested far too much wealth in companies that were unlikely to succeed, creating the "DotCom Bubble." Who would have guessed that websites like Pets.com and Boo.com were not worth the tens of millions of dollars many investors said they were?

When the bubble burst in the year 2000, the Federal Reserve—America's government-created and government-led central bank—lowered interest rates under the leadership of then-Chairman Alan Greenspan.[6] Lowering interest rates makes lending easier, thereby flooding the economy with more cash and spurring investment, especially in real estate. Instead of allowing the economy to grapple with the mal-investments of that era, the Fed's "easy-money" policies, along with other government actions, essentially replaced the DotCom bubble with an even bigger one: the housing bubble, which grew increasingly large and unsustainable until it popped in late 2007, directly leading to the 2008 crash.

Peter Schiff—a stockbroker, financial commentator, author, economist, and the founder of Euro Pacific Capital—is best known for predicting the collapse of the housing market. For years prior to the 2008 recession, Schiff warned that the Fed's easy-money policies were fueling a massive bubble in the real estate market that was destined to burst. Of course, almost no one in power listened to him. Why would they? Government officials were happy that housing prices were going up and the economy was expanding, and many bankers were making money in the growing real estate market. It was a win-win—well, at least until the economic chaos ensued.

In the aftermath of the recession, Schiff, reflecting on the Left's narrative of Wall Street gone wild, said, "In one of [President Bush's] speeches, [he] said that Wall Street got drunk and he was right. They were drunk. So was Main Street. The whole country was drunk. But what he doesn't point out is where they got the alcohol. Why were they drunk? Obviously, Greenspan poured the alcohol. The Fed got everybody drunk and the government helped out with their moral hazards and the tax codes and all the incentives and disincentives they put in all the various ways that they interfered with the free market and removed the necessary balances that would have existed, that would have kept all this from happening."[7]

SHOTS!!
SHOTS!!

Instead of allowing the economy to sober up after the DotCom Bubble, Greenspan lowered interest rates. This signaled to Wall Street that the party was still going. "Relax and have another drink, everyone. In fact, bring in the funnels and togas!"

As Schiff noted, although one of the root causes of the 2008 financial crisis was the Fed's easy-money policies, the housing bubble didn't result from these policies alone. It was also caused by other market distortions created by the formation of really stupid, politically motivated government policies.

One such "really stupid" policy began in 1992, when U.S. Rep. Barney Frank (D-Mass.) successfully pushed through reforms that imposed "affordable housing" requirements on Fannie Mae and Freddie Mac, government-sponsored enterprises that were created to keep cash "flowing to mortgage lenders in support of homeownership and rental housing."[8] Despite their innocuous names—which sound like they could be lovable characters in Andy Griffith's charming town of Mayberry—Fannie Mae and Freddie Mac facilitated and exacerbated the housing bubble by agreeing to purchase millions of high-risk loans from banking institutions, encouraging them to make even more high-risk loans. Sticking with Schiff's analogy, these policies were the equivalent of offering half-priced shots.

Peter Wallison is the Arthur F. Burns fellow in financial policy studies at the American Enterprise Institute and a member of the Congressional Financial Crisis Inquiry Commission that was created by Congress to determine the primary causes of the 2008 financial crisis. In a 2011 article for *The Atlantic*, Wallison noted that prior to Frank's 1992 reforms, Fannie Mae and Freddie Mac "had been required to buy only mortgages that institutional investors would buy—in other words, prime mortgages—but Frank and others thought these standards made it too difficult for low income borrowers to buy homes. The affordable housing law required Fannie and Freddie to meet government quotas when they bought loans from banks and other mortgage originators."[9]

At first, Fannie and Freddie's quota for high-risk, subprime loans was 30 percent, but over time, the federal government sharply increased those quotas. In 1995, it was 42 percent. In 2000, it was 50 percent. By 2007, the quota reached a stunning 55 percent. Fannie Mae and Freddie Mac were literally being forced by law to make and rely upon absolutely horrible investments—investments so bad most people would never even dream of making them. Even though the market was already half in the bag, these quotas ensured even more intoxication—like a comedy club's two-drink minimum.

Although Fannie and Freddie did not originate the subprime mortgages themselves, the quotas they were forced to meet created a significant incentive in the mortgage lending industry to originate as many loans as possible. After all, the banks originating the loans weren't going to be the ones stuck with them at the end of the day. They knew most of their subprime loans would end up in the hands of quasi-government agencies that were required to buy up bad loans.

As one report by the American Enterprise Institute, which was co-authored by Wallison, put it, "when Fannie and Freddie began to increase significantly their commitment to affordable housing loans, they found it easy to stimulate production

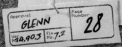

in the private sector by letting it be known in the market that they would gladly accept loans that would otherwise be considered subprime."[10] Another round, everybody!

People who previously wouldn't have been able to get $300,000 of financing for a home were suddenly getting access to mortgages worth half-a-million dollars or more. Payments for adjustable rate mortgages were extremely low because the Fed-created interest rates were low. Many people even started to buy second and third homes to "flip," because housing prices were rising so rapidly that people could buy a home one year, do nothing to it, and then sell it the following year for a big profit.

> **"BY 2008 19.2 MILLION OUT OF THE TOTAL OF 27 MILLION SUBPRIME AND OTHER WEAK LOANS IN THE U.S. FINANCIAL SYSTEM COULD BE TRACED DIRECTLY OR INDIRECTLY TO U.S. GOVERNMENT HOUSING POLICIES."**
>
> **— PETER WALLISON**
> MEMBER OF THE CONGRESSIONAL
> FINANCIAL CRISIS INQUIRY COMMISSION

Wallison notes that as a result of these bad economic policies, "by 2008 19.2 million out of the total of 27 million subprime and other weak loans in the U.S. financial system could be traced directly or indirectly to U.S. government housing policies." And according to Wallison, the other 7.8 million high-risk loans would not have been originated if it were not for the massive bubble created by Fannie Mae, Freddie Mac, and the federal government's absurd and irresponsible housing mandates. Isn't powerful, centralized government just swell?

Wallison went so far as to say that "the financial crisis would not have occurred if government housing policies had not fostered the creation of an unprecedented number of subprime and otherwise risky loans immediately before the financial crisis began."[11]

IN 2010, before the commission tasked with determining the causes of the 2008 financial crisis could issue its final report, Congress passed the Dodd-Frank Act to supposedly "fix" the systemic problems that led to the crash. As former Obama chief of staff and Chicago mayor Rahm Emanuel once said, "You never want a serious crisis to go to waste."

When the bubble slowed and then started to deflate, the foundational cracks that had previously been obscured ruptured—and they ruptured in spectacular fashion. This is why the so-called Great Recession happened in 2008. The market finally had one too many drinks, stumbled out of the bar, ralphed all over itself, and then promptly passed out in a pile of trash on the street.

Did some of the actions made by greedy bankers and Wall Street financial corporations contribute to the crash? Absolutely. But everyone wanted free drinks without consequences. Wall Street rewarded the market's drunk drivers. The only ones that ultimately paid were the pedestrians with tire marks on the back of their heads.

Those actions would never have occurred—at least not anywhere to the extent they did—without government's "easy-money" lending and "affordable housing" policies. The 2008 financial crisis isn't a cautionary tale about the dangers of free markets, it's a horror story about what can happen when government officials put politics above sound economic policies while crony capitalists risk your money, livelihood, and home, all to their own benefit. You lost yours, but they were bailed out.

POVERTY

Professor Tweed @checkurprivilegeplz
Maybe government did play a role in the 2008 financial crisis, but you admitted Wall Street's greed also played a role, and if we look at the big economic picture, it's clear that capitalism is to blame for many of our problems, including in areas you can't blame government. For example, it's 2019, and America is the richest country in the world, and yet, we still have extreme poverty.

 1

Yes, America is the richest country in the world. And the reason Americans are so wealthy is that for centuries they have enjoyed relatively free markets and personal liberties. That's why people from around the world have been able to come to our shores and achieve incredible things with nothing more than a strong work ethic and a commitment to freedom. No one looking for economic opportunity or individual liberty is banging down the doors of socialist Cuba or Venezuela. In fact, capitalist nations have had to work hard to establish and manage complex immigration systems because millions of people desperately try to cross their borders every year—often illegally. Meanwhile, socialist regimes around the world work tirelessly to keep people from escaping.

If there's so little economic opportunity in the United States, why is our history full of entrepreneurs who started out poor or in the middle class but who then ended up amassing huge fortunes? Oprah Winfrey grew up in an impoverished single-parent household in Mississippi. As a young boy, Starbucks Chairman and CEO Howard Schultz's family was poor and lived in government-subsidized housing. Larry Ellison, the billionaire founder of tech giant Oracle, spent much of his youth in a working-class neighborhood in Chicago's South Side.[12] Donald Trump was just a lowly dishwasher before . . . okay, so some of them did grow up rich.

The United States, despite all of its problems, is still known throughout much of the world as the "land of opportunity." That's not despite free markets, it's because of free markets. You think the Krispy Kreme donut just *happened*? Thanks to free enterprise and individual liberty, some of the poorest communities in America live better than most people currently walking the Earth. Many Americans simply don't know how rich they really are.

According to research by Gautam Nair, who relied on additional research by Branko Milanovic, the former lead economist for the World Bank's Research Department and author of *Global Inequality: A New Approach for the Age of Globalization*, the average person living in the United States believes the median global income is $20,000, even though it's actually much lower, about $2,100.[13] Further, as Nair wrote in an article for the *Washington Post*, "Americans typically place themselves in the top 37 percent of the world's income distribution. However, the vast majority of U.S. residents rank comfortably in the top 10 percent."[14] That means most Americans live better than 90 percent of the world's population.

"AMERICANS TYPICALLY PLACE THEMSELVES IN THE TOP 37 PERCENT OF THE WORLD'S INCOME DISTRIBUTION. HOWEVER, THE VAST MAJORITY OF U.S. RESIDENTS RANK COMFORTABLY IN THE TOP 10 PERCENT."

THIS PARAGRAPH WOULD WORK WELL IN A TOBY KEITH SONG.

Although no one should be satisfied with the existing level of poverty in the United States, there's no denying that being "impoverished" in America is better than being middle class or even "wealthy" in much of the rest of the world. The Heritage

Foundation's senior research fellow in domestic policy, Robert Rector, notes, "According to government surveys, the typical family that Census identifies as poor has air conditioning, cable or satellite TV, and a computer in his home. Forty percent have a wide screen HDTV and another 40 percent have internet access. Three quarters of the poor own a car and roughly a third have two or more cars."[15]

Forget about flat screen televisions and cars. Do you have any idea how many billions of people around the world would kill to have regular access to clean running water, indoor plumbing, and electricity? About 3 billion people worldwide still cook their food and heat their houses using an open fire, a necessary but extremely dangerous activity. According to the World Health Organization, every year "close to 4 million people die prematurely from illness attributable to household air pollution from inefficient cooking practices using polluting stoves paired with solid fuels and kerosene."[16] Can you imagine having the entire populations of Wyoming, Vermont, North Dakota, South Dakota, and Rhode Island die every year from home cooking and heating? Well, you don't need to imagine it because it's already happening around the world. We're just so protected by the wonders of the free market that it's hard to see.

The United States, despite having a much smaller population than many other countries, has become much wealthier than nearly every other nation. The prosperity and quality of life for those in America's middle class continues to grow. And although much is said about America's "shrinking middle class," the truth is that the reason the middle class is getting smaller is that more people born into the middle class are becoming significantly more wealthy, not because middle class families are becoming poorer.[17] And a big part of that success—the biggest part, in fact—is that Americans have for centuries enjoyed personal economic freedoms that other people around the world can only dream about.

I want to live in an America where *everyone* is much richer than they are today, but we're not going to get there by giving more power to government, which is already keeping tens of millions of people trapped in a cycle of poverty. During the Obama administration, numerous changes made by federal regulatory agencies allowed states to roll back welfare provisions designed to prevent dependency. The Obama administration argued that removing these protections was necessary because of the slow economic recovery. However, this decision, coupled with other Obama-era laws like the Affordable Care Act, resulted in gigantic increases in the number of people enrolled and trapped in welfare programs.

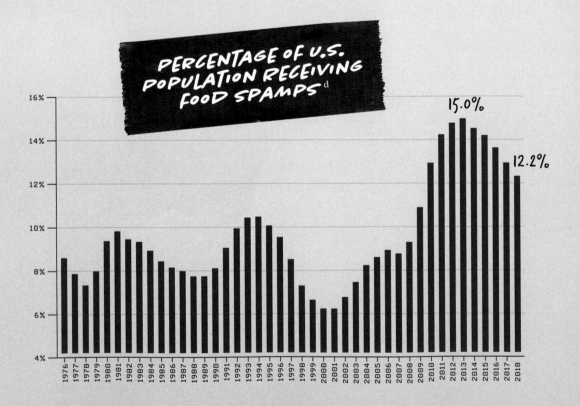

PERCENTAGE OF U.S. POPULATION RECEIVING FOOD SPAMPS [d]

15.0%

12.2%

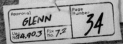

In 2009, enrollment in the Supplemental Nutrition Assistance Program (SNAP), commonly called "food stamps," increased by 5.2 million, to 33.49 million. In 2010, the number of people enrolled soared to 40.3 million. Enrollment then continued to rise annually, even in the midst of the recovery, until it reached an all-time high of 47.63 million in 2013.[18]

Although enrollment has steadily declined since 2013, with the most significant improvements coming under the Trump administration, which encouraged states to reinstitute requirements for able-bodied adults to work or enter job training programs in order to continue receiving benefits, food stamp enrollment remains extremely high. Even in a booming economy, average SNAP participation totaled at least 39.6 million in 2018, 13 million more than it was in 2007, one year before the 2008 financial crisis and subsequent recession. Imagine what those numbers will look like in our next financial downturn.

Medicaid enrollment has increased even more dramatically. In 2009, Barack Obama's first year as president, 52.1 million Americans were enrolled in Medicaid or the Children's Health Insurance Program (CHIP).[19] In 2019, more than 72 million were enrolled in these two welfare programs, an increase of about 38 percent.[20]

Why were so many people enrolled in Medicaid and receiving food stamps when the U.S. economy was experiencing one of its best periods in two decades? In 2019, unemployment for African Americans, Hispanics, women, and individuals with two years of college or less hit historic lows or near-historic lows. Wage growth was at its highest point since the 2008 recession.[21] And the U.S. Bureau of Labor Statistics reported there were more than 7 million available jobs.[22]

The reason so many people remain stuck in entitlement programs isn't that there aren't any economic opportunities for them—it's obvious from the economic data available that there are plenty of good jobs available—it's that government has

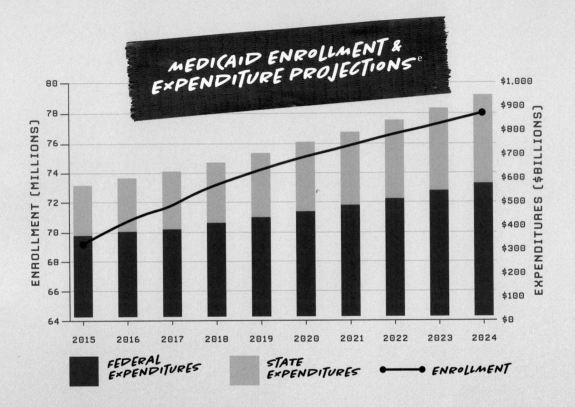

MEDICAID ENROLLMENT & EXPENDITURE PROJECTIONS[e]

■ FEDERAL EXPENDITURES   ▨ STATE EXPENDITURES   ●—● ENROLLMENT

designed many welfare programs in such a way that they are extremely difficult to leave. Our government has actually spent your tax dollars in recruitment advertising for food stamp recipients. We are literally spending money to find new people to spend money on. This is not a winning strategy.

Imagine you work at a fried chicken restaurant, where you earn a few dollars more than your state's minimum wage. You're one of the restaurant's top workers. You can fry chicken with the best of them, and your biscuit skills are legendary. People from all over the region travel to the restaurant to have a meal cooked by you.

Despite all your hard work, the restaurant doesn't offer health insurance to many of its employees, and you have two kids who need health coverage. So, you enroll in Medicaid, which only requires you to pay a small monthly fee. Sure, the coverage sucks, you have a hard time finding access to a doctor, but it's better to have some health care coverage than no coverage, right?

The owner of the restaurant—let's call him Chris Christie, because, you know, I'm guessing Chris Christie *really* likes fried chicken—takes notice of your cooking skills and offers you a big raise. You're excited about the opportunity, but you're concerned that you might lose access to your Medicaid benefits and aren't sure that your raise will outweigh the additional health care costs you'd need to incur. So, you take the rest of the day off from work and head down to the state's Department of We Don't Remember Your Name Because You're Just a Number to Us to find out what your salary increase will mean for you and your family. Unfortunately, it's 11:30 a.m. and half the office is out to lunch, so the line is a mile long. You decide to come back at 3:30 p.m., only to find everyone has already gone home for the evening.

You take the next day off from work and arrive early at the Department of Health and We Don't Remember Your Name Because You're Just a Number to Us headquarters. You meet briefly with Mr. Bureaucrat, who informs you that with your raise, you'll no longer be eligible for Medicaid and will now have to purchase your own health insurance in the Obamacare individual marketplace. "But don't worry," Mr. Bureaucrat assures you, "the state offers big health insurance subsidies for those with your new projected income, but to find out exactly how much you'll get, you will need to meet with Kathy I. Don't Give a Crap at the Department of Insurance and We Can Barely Function as Human Beings, which isn't open today, because they are too busy celebrating Ernesto "Che" Guevara's birthday.

You reluctantly take the next day off too, your third in as many days, marking your longest "vacation" since working at the chicken restaurant. You spend two hours waiting to meet with Ms. Don't Give a Crap at the Department of Insurance and We Can Barely Function as Human Beings and she tells you that you will be eligible for a large Obamacare health insurance subsidy. At first, this sounds like great news, because there's no way you could afford to pay the several hundred dollars per month it would cost to buy an unsubsidized Obamacare plan, but Ms. Don't Give a Crap reminds you that, like everyone else, you'll still be required to cover the cost of your health insurance deductible when you use health care services, which for the cheapest Obamacare plan you can find will cost about $12,000 per year.[23] This presents a big problem for you and your family, because one of your children has a costly health care problem that requires frequent trips to the doctor's office.

By the time you do the math, it turns out your "raise" will end up costing you $4,000 per year, which you can't afford. So, instead of taking the promotion of becoming head chef at Chris Christe's Crispy Chicken Cafe, you decide you're better off in poverty.

To varying degrees, this problem exists throughout the country. Many hardworking people are trapped in one of the federal government's more than 80 welfare programs because of "benefit cliffs" like the one described above. In some cases, people have become too comfortable in their poverty, and there's no incentive for them to work. Why get a job if the government is all too willing to give you free housing, internet, cell phones, bus passes, education, food, and health care? Government's attempts to end poverty often keep people trapped in poverty and discourage people from working.

"THE GOVERNMENT IS GOOD AT ONE THING. IT KNOWS HOW TO BREAK YOUR LEGS, AND THEN HAND YOU A CRUTCH AND SAY, 'SEE IF IT WEREN'T FOR THE GOVERNMENT, YOU WOULDN'T BE ABLE TO WALK.'"

- HARRY BROWNE

Edward Glaeser, a professor of economics at Harvard University, wrote in *City Journal* that in 1967, "95 percent of 'prime-age' men between the ages of 25 and 54 worked. During the Great Recession, though, the share of jobless prime-age males rose above 20 percent."[24] Today, despite tremendous recent economic growth, prime-age labor force participation is still less than 90 percent.

The reduction in labor force participation for all men has been even more dramatic. From 1948 to 1970, the male participation rate rarely dropped below 80 percent, but after decades of decline, the rate now hovers around 69 percent.[25]

In recent years, some states have successfully reformed their welfare programs to encourage more people to enter the workforce. For example, in 2016 Arkansas reinstated work requirements for childless adults enrolled in the state's food stamps program, requiring adults to work or volunteer at least 20 hours per week or to enter a job training program. The results have been nothing short of remarkable. Food stamp enrollment for able-bodied adults without children dropped by 70 percent, and incomes for those leaving the program tripled within two years.[26]

As the results in Arkansas show, one of the best ways to reduce poverty is to create systems that help and encourage people to become self-sufficient. When government gets out of the way, everyone is better off.

Rashida Resistance @AOC_2024_Squad4Life
So, what you're saying is you want to get rid of all welfare programs, is that it? Without social safety nets, people would be even worse off than they are now.

💬 1   🔁   🤍

Not at all. I believe social safety nets are important. But safety nets, like those hung beneath a tightrope walker, are only meant to catch those who fall as a form of temporary aid. Tightrope walkers who fall into their safety nets are supposed to immediately roll out of them; they don't become permanent residents of the safety net, squatting there for months or years later.

And I know this might shock you, but there are good reasons to believe people would actually be much better off if many of the existing bloated and poorly managed government-run social welfare programs were scaled back or significantly reformed to promote, rather than discourage, self-sufficiency. Millions and millions of people are trapped in poverty because of the government programs that are supposedly meant to help them escape poverty. If the prime-age work participation rate were the same today as it was 50 years ago, it's likely there would be, at minimum, hundreds

of thousands of additional workers and potentially millions of additional people living out of poverty.

President Lyndon Johnson—who was, by the way, a truly racist and generally terrible person and one of our country's worst presidents—launched a "War on Poverty" during his 1964 State of the Union address. During the address, Johnson, who proposed a long progressive wish list of new social programs, declared that "our joint federal-local effort must pursue poverty, pursue it wherever it exists—in city slums and small towns, in sharecropper shacks or in migrant worker camps, on Indian Reservations, among whites as well as Negroes, among the young as well as the aged, in the boom towns and in the depressed areas. Our aim is not only to relieve the symptom of poverty, but to cure it and, above all, to prevent it."[27]

AUTHOR'S NOTE:

SEE LBJ'S LONG AND WELL-DOCUMENTED HISTORY OF RACIST EPITHETS AND RECKLESS ECONOMIC POLICIES

After a half-century of Johnson's "Great Society" welfare programs, along with numerous others instituted by progressives in the years since Johnson's administration, the national poverty rate is about the same as it was in the 1960s, despite more than $20 trillion of government spending that targeted impoverished individuals and communities.[28] Many of the cities with the worst rates of extreme poverty have been run by progressives who have instituted additional costly and far-reaching welfare programs, including Buffalo, Camden, Detroit, New York City, and Philadelphia, among many others.[29] You say things would be significantly worse if we were to roll back welfare programs, but have you been to the South Side of Chicago? It doesn't get much worse than that.

If building and expanding government-run welfare programs is the key to alleviating poverty, why haven't the progressives who endlessly promote this mythology been successful at ridding America of poverty after decades of trying this approach? Must be because evil Uncle Pennybags is still beating down America's poor with his gold-plated cane.

Some states have shown that it's possible to create social safety nets that take care of those who truly need help—like children and those with severe disabilities—without trapping people in poverty. But even in these cases, there are many times when relying on private charities would be a better option, because government has proven itself to be incapable of managing just about anything effectively (have you tried to renew your driver's license recently?).

THE POWER OF PRIVATE CHARITY

NO EXAMPLE OF PRIVATE CHARITY IS MORE ILLUSTRATIVE OF THE POWER OF VOLUNTARY ACTION THAN THAT OF THE BLACK FRATERNAL ORGANIZATIONS OF THE EARLY TWENTIETH CENTURY. CATO INSTITUTE SENIOR FELLOW MICHAEL TANNER WRITES ABOUT THESE GROUPS IN HIS BOOK *THE POVERTY OF WELFARE: HELPING OTHERS IN CIVIL SOCIETY.*

BECAUSE OF THE EXTREMELY DIFFICULT PLIGHT OF AFRICAN AMERICANS AT THE TIME AND THEIR INABILITY TO ACCESS CERTAIN WELFARE PROGRAMS, A NETWORK OF CHARITIES—COMMONLY CALLED "BLACK LODGES"—DEVELOPED ACROSS THE COUNTRY. THIS NETWORK PROVIDED MUCH-NEEDED SUPPORT.

"IN ADDITION TO LIFE INSURANCE, FRATERNAL ORGANIZATIONS PROVIDED 'LODGE-PRACTICE MEDICINE,' AN EARLY FORM OF HEALTH INSURANCE," TANNER WROTE. "MEMBERS WOULD PAY THE LODGE A PREMIUM OF ONE OR TWO DOLLARS PER MONTH. THE LODGE, IN TURN WOULD CONTRACT WITH A DOCTOR WHO WOULD AGREE, FOR A FLAT MONTHLY OR YEARLY FEE, TO TREAT ALL LODGE MEMBERS."

THE NETWORK WAS MASSIVELY EFFECTIVE. AS TANNER EXPLAINS, "AS A RESULT OF THE WIDESPREAD INFLUENCE OF BLACK FRATERNAL ORGANIZATIONS, AFRICAN AMERICANS WERE MORE LIKELY TO BE INSURED THAN WERE WHITES DURING THE EARLY YEARS OF THE 20TH CENTURY."

Government programs are extremely inefficient ways to help the impoverished, because they require a gargantuan amount of unnecessary spending on things like big government buildings, bloated salaries for bureaucrats, and pensions. Federal welfare programs are also notoriously difficult to reform, and perhaps most importantly, you can't easily fire the vast majority of federal bureaucrats, even if they are terrible at their jobs. As John York, a policy analyst for the Heritage Foundation, notes, "Holding federal employees accountable is essentially impossible. They have the highest job security of any sector of the economy. In fact, out of a federal non-military workforce of 2.1 million, only 11,046 persons—or 0.5 percent—were fired in 2017."[30]

By contrast, those who work in the private sector are three times more likely to have their employment terminated.[31]

York added, "One reason for this is the cumbersome process managers must endure to fire a single employee. Multiple appeals involving as many as four separate agencies, as well as union representatives, are not uncommon. This process can last years even in the most cut-and-dry cases."

On the other hand, charities waste less money and often provide services to people at a fraction of the cost. And when they don't, then people can simply stop giving their money to them—unlike the government, which confiscates much of people's salaries regardless of whether government agencies are wasting cash.

One of the most successful anti-poverty charities is the Doe Fund's Ready, Willing, & Able program. The Doe Fund was started by George McDonald, a garment industry executive in New York City. After spending more than two years handing out sandwiches and clothing in Grand Central Terminal, McDonald realized that his efforts weren't making nearly the impact he hoped.

As the Doe Fund explains, "Although the men and women George helped were grateful for the meal, they expressed their desire for a job so that they could afford a room of their own and support themselves. It was becoming increasingly clear that food and clothing were not enough to bring about real change."

So, in 1990, McDonald did something remarkable: He created the Ready, Willing, & Able program, which helps men—mostly the formerly incarcerated and homeless—escape poverty through the power of work and self-reliance. Since 1990, this one program alone has helped more than 22,000 individuals transition from poverty—in many cases, extreme poverty—to self-sufficiency. Today, it serves thousands of people daily, and much more effectively than many government anti-poverty programs.[32]

According to the Doe Fund's annual report, New York City taxpayers save $3.60 for every $1 spent on the Ready, Willing & Able program, and nearly three-fourths of those who complete the program reported that they had maintained employment three months after graduating.

Other charities have found similar success emphasizing work, rather than merely handing out cash. For instance, the Cincinnati Works program pairs members "with an employment coach who serves as a guide during the job search, helping Members find leads and prepare for interviews." It also offers members access to computers at no cost, so that members can search or apply for jobs, which they often do with a staff member who can help them with their applications. Many of the members in the Cincinnati Works program are at-risk youths and individuals who are "in (or at risk of falling into) a life of crime and violence."

Cincinnati Works provides financial literacy courses, job training resources and workshops, and numerous support services to help people move out of poverty. Thanks to this wildly successful program, thousands of people in the Cincinnati

area have moved out of poverty. In 2018, more than 64 percent of those employed through the program were employed above the poverty level, and the program's job placement and retention rate often exceeds 80 percent.[33,34] This is good news, which the area truly needs considering all of the Bengals football they are forced to endure.

Many government programs have continuously failed to match the success rates of the Doe Foundation and Cincinnati Works. For example, Howard Husock, the vice president for research and publications at the Manhattan Institute, notes, "Of those enrolled in programs supported by the Workforce Investment Act, which provides publicly-funded services to around 7 million annually (typically through government contractors), just slightly over half (56 percent) found jobs—of which another 20 percent lost their (newly acquired) jobs within six months."[35]

If government were to do more to encourage charitable giving, organizations like the Doe Foundation and Cincinnati Works would expand, and thousands of new programs just like them would almost certainly develop. Instead, government confiscates and wastes billions of dollars taken from millions of people who would rather voluntarily give their hard-earned money to charities they trust and that promote their values. In a truly free-market system, this would never happen.

Neal DiCaprio-Cortez @GreenNewNeal
What about the wealth gap, @glennbeck? America is full of income inequality, and it's destroying the country and making life significantly worse for the poor.

♡ 1   ⟲   ♡

Socialists love to obsess over income inequality, and I can understand why. Most people assume that if income inequality is growing, that means poverty is getting more extreme or that people's quality of life is worsening. But history has proven repeatedly—both in the United States and around the world—that just because the rich are getting richer, doesn't mean the poor are getting poorer, or that life isn't improving for the poor.

As we already discussed, the poverty rate in the United States in the 1960s was about the same as it is now, and over that period, the rate has only varied slightly. However, the wealth gap between the richest Americans and poorest Americans has grown steadily, disproving the notion that income inequality in the United States results in greater poverty.

China has experienced similar results over the past few decades. From 1990 to 2009, income inequality in China grew substantially. But as Cato Institute Senior Fellow Michael Tanner noted, "At the same time, the proportion of the [Chinese] population living below $1.25 a day (adjusted for purchasing power parity), the measure usually used for international poverty lines, fell from 60.18 percent in 1990 to only 11.8 percent in 2009."[36] This seems like good news to me. But, if income inequality increased in this period, how can it be?

Even more importantly, there is no correlation between wealth inequality and *living standards* for the poor. In many countries with relatively high wealth inequality, like the United States, those considered to be "impoverished" have enjoyed an increasingly higher quality of life over the past century, even as the wealth gap has grown. In 1900, life expectancy at birth

SIDE NOTE

"I DO NOT THINK A FOCUS ON WEALTH INEQUALITY AS A BASIS FOR BEING CONCERNED ABOUT A MORE JUST SOCIETY IS TERRIBLY WELL DESIGNED."

FORMER DIRECTOR OF THE NATIONAL ECONOMIC COUNCIL UNDER PRESIDENT BARACK OBAMA

LAWRENCE SUMMERS

for the average American was just 47 years. By 1950, the number soared to 68. Today, the average life expectancy at birth is about 78 years, and it's not uncommon for many people to live into their 90s.[37]

In the early 1900s, only the wealthiest Americans could afford to own automobiles and have electricity, and many impoverished families didn't even have access to indoor plumbing. Today, car ownership is common among lower-income earners, and virtually everyone has electricity and indoor plumbing.

At the turn of the century, many Americans were still growing and eating their own food for survival. As researcher Jayson Lusk noted for the Mercatus Center, "In 1900, just under 40 percent of the total US population lived on farms, and 60 percent lived in rural areas."[38] Today, anyone—rich or poor—can go to a grocery store and purchase products from almost every corner of the globe for a fraction of an individual's paycheck, and only about 1 percent of Americans live on farms.

In 1984, only 8.2 percent of U.S. households owned a computer, and only the wealthiest families could afford one. In 2016, 89 percent of households had a computer, and today, it's common for people to walk around with a supercomputer ("smartphones") in their back pocket.[39]

In 1997, just 18 percent of Americans had access to the internet at home. By 2000, the number jumped to 41.5 percent. Today, it's greater than 80 percent. Where would we be without Al Gore's creation?

A.D.D. MOMENT

THE LIBERALIZATION OF CHINA'S ECONOMY

Before you start thinking about giving the Chinese Communist Party credit for China's large reduction in poverty, note that it was government getting out of the way that allowed this prosperity to develop.

Starting in 1978, China began to benefit from a rash of bottom-up reforms that served to liberalize Chinese markets. Among these reforms were the development of private businesses and the creation of Special Economic Zones.

While still a far cry from truly free markets, these reforms introduced market forces and concepts of property rights into a nation that historically had been almost entirely controlled by a centralized government.[g]

Just 150 years ago, not even the world's wealthiest kings could have imagined many of the modern luxuries now enjoyed by Americans of nearly every income group. Americans are now living longer, better, healthier lives than human beings ever have before, and all while income inequality has increased.

Of course, there have been many countries during the past century in which there has been a great deal of wealth equality—like in the former Soviet Union, communist Cambodia, and in modern-day North Korea and Venezuela. But in those countries, the only reason there hasn't been much of a wealth gap is that their populations have been equally *poor*—except, of course, for the tyrants who rule over their subjects from luxurious palaces and mansions while surrounded by armies of soldiers and servants. (Spoiler alert. This is the inevitable outcome for countries experimenting with socialism.)

The truth is, wealth inequality doesn't matter so long as life is improving for everyone, and it unquestionably is improving by leaps and bounds in the United States and many other capitalist countries. Capitalism is driving those improvements. Take away capitalism, and history shows you'll end up with more poverty and a lower quality of life for everybody.

Clay Guevara @coffeeshopcommie
Ok, but America's millionaires and billionaires don't deserve their wealth. They are rich in part because of what others have achieved who came before them, so they should be forced to give their wealth to the rest of society.

♡ 1   ⟲   ♡

Ah, here it is. I've been waiting for this one. It's the whole "you didn't build that" argument, right?

YOU DIDN'T BUILD THAT!

— OBAMA

Yes, every single person today—rich, poor, or middle class—is benefiting from the achievements, innovations, and successes of others who have come before them. And it's true that the wealthiest business owners nearly always have a team of people who work for them, and that without their talents, these business owners wouldn't have achieved nearly as much as they have. But it's not like any of these people were robbed by the wealthy in the process—you know, like the government does when it takes people's hard-earned wealth without giving equal value back in return.

In a free market, people frequently work together to accomplish great things, and in nearly all cases, everyone ends up getting compensated for their efforts. In some instances, workers receive a greater share of the total profits than in other situations, but when workers are paid less, it's not because they were forced to earn less; it's because they voluntarily agreed to accept a certain amount of compensation. In a free market, compensation is determined entirely by what people are willing to pay and be paid. There are no coercive actions, slavery, or price controls in free markets. If you get paid a tiny fraction of the profits, it's because that's what you voluntarily chose to accept as your compensation. No one forced you to agree to those terms; you agreed to them because you believed it was in your best interests to do so.

And everyone benefits from the innovations produced by these arrangements. Has your life or the lives of others around you been made worse or better because of the work of Bill Gates, Steve Jobs, and Google? (Don't ask this question out loud, because all the devices they designed will hear you questioning their authority.)

Socialists' idea that the whole society deserves to share in the wealth produced by a small group of people is—well, dumb. Socialists argue that because everyone who works contributes in some way to the economy, the wealth produced in that economy should be shared equally, according to people's needs, but why? Not all economic activity is equally valuable, and not all economic contributions are equally important.

So, if Elon Musk invents a new technology that can generate electricity for pennies on the dollar compared to what's currently available, he should have to share his wealth equally or disproportionately with someone who "contributed" to the economy by being a telemarketer who hawks Cutco knives? And someone who creates a successful restaurant in Des Moines, Iowa, should share his or her profits with someone who goes door to door selling vacuum cleaners in California?

And what about all the people who don't actually contribute to society? What about the millions of able-bodied adults who have chosen to be reliant on the welfare state rather than work full-time jobs? Why do they *deserve* to share in the profits made by others who did choose to work? Socialists have built much of their movement on the argument that people who spend their days on their mom's couch eating Fruit Loops their mom paid for while watching reruns of *Judge Judy* have in some way *earned* the right to take away the wealth generated by others. Judge Judy would throw that case out of her courtroom in a flash.

I've got to hand it to you socialists: it's pretty impressive you've convinced millions of people to believe in principles that should appear to anyone with common sense to be completely nuts. If this whole overthrow-the-capitalist-system thing falls apart, you should consider a job in marketing (just be forewarned that this would like come with a "salary," and you then might have to deal with the problem of "expendable income").

Clay Guevara @coffeeshopcommie
But capitalism is a system created to exploit people. That's why such a small proportion of Americans control most of the country's wealth. They didn't do anything to work for that wealth. They just sat around and let the dollars earned by others roll in.

 1   ⇄   ♡

In free-market capitalism—not the phony capitalist systems in which corrupt business owners and corrupt politicians engage in secret deals to benefit one another—it's literally impossible for anyone to be "exploited." When you boil it down to its foundation, free-market capitalism is simply an economic system of voluntary exchange: You have property, I have property, and we have the ability to exchange our property freely, either by bartering or by using money. Free-market capitalism and freedom go hand in hand. You can't have individual freedom without free enterprise, and you can't have free enterprise without individual freedom.

This holds true even in the era of American sweatshops. Were people in the early twentieth century duped into taking hard labor jobs because they were too stupid to know any better? No. They voluntarily decided that working at a meat-packing plant or a textile factory was the best way to provide for themselves and their family members. Over time, Americans who were unhappy with their work conditions demanded better wages and working standards, and they eventually received them. It is their efforts that generated the wealth and economic growth that we enjoy today.

You say that business owners and investors don't deserve the money they earn because they often don't contribute any labor themselves; they aren't the ones working on assembly lines or selling products directly to consumers. But the truth is, many business owners do engage in these activities, especially small business owners. You know that small family-owned pizza joint down the street that you love so much? There's a good chance the owner works his or her butt off to make it a success, or at least that he or she did at some point in the past. And although there are a lot of people who have inherited their wealth, the vast majority do not. More than 70 percent of America's billionaires did not inherit their fortune.[40] In many of the cases in which people have inherited wealth, their parents were the ones who amassed it. The idea that most people with huge fortunes belong to families like the Bushes or Kennedys, who have been wealthy for multiple generations, simply isn't true.

But even in the instances where wealthy business owners and investors engage in absolutely no labor at all, they still had to provide the wealth necessary to start the business or to keep it running, not knowing for certain that they would ever get a return on their investment. In fact, every year, wealthy individuals and families lose their fortunes because investments they made don't result in any profits. For that reason alone, they deserve to benefit more than others when a business is successful. After all, they are the ones incurring most of the risk, not the workers. If a business closes, workers don't lose anything but their salary. They can find another job, and often quickly. If a business owner goes bankrupt trying to keep a company afloat, the owner could lose all of his or her wealth and may never get it back.

There *are* regular folks getting exploited—and, quite frankly, screwed—in America's economy today. But those people are suffering because powerful government agents and politicians have interfered with the free market and given dishonest, corrupt business owners a way to tilt the system in their favor. There's a reason that there are so many expensive neighborhoods in the suburbs of Washington, D.C. All the backroom dealings, unfair regulatory schemes, government handouts to millionaires and billionaires, political favors, etc. are examples of *crony capitalism*—not a free market. And as I have already explained, those problems can only exist in a society where government is powerful enough to engage in these corrupt activities. Without a corrupt government, it isn't possible to have crony capitalism.

EDUCATION

Rashida Resistance @AOC_2024_Squad4Life
Well, poverty isn't the only issue. Thanks to greedy capitalists, millions of young people are buried in student loan debt.

💬 1   🔁   ♡

Actually, you can blame the government for this one too. Most of the student loans issued in the United States over the past decade have been by the federal government, so it makes no sense to blame "capitalists" for a problem that is being perpetuated by government bureaucrats.

The rising costs of student lending can be traced back to the creation of the Federal Family Education Loan (FFEL) program in 1965[41] — another one of President Lyndon Johnson's mind-numbingly stupid reforms. Under the FFEL program, the federal government agreed to pay subsidies to private banks issuing college loans. The federal government also agreed to "guarantee" the loans for banks, meaning that if a student were to default on the loan, the government would pick up the tab, not the bank.[42]

SIDE NOTE

DID I MENTION LYNDON JOHNSON WAS ONE OF OUR WORST PRESIDENTS? AND A DISGUSTING RACIST?

At first, like most government programs, the Federal Family Education Loan program was meant to help lower-income people gain access to affordable loans they otherwise wouldn't be able to obtain, but over time, the federal government expanded the program to virtually everyone.

It's not hard to imagine how this program distorted the student lending industry. With a full guarantee from the federal government, banks didn't need to worry about losing their investments. They simply offered loans to virtually every student in the country, regardless of whether they had the financial means to pay the loans back. Schools, realizing that banks would agree to lend out more money than ever, started increasing their tuition rates and the cost of attending college. The incentives to keep costs down and make college more affordable were quickly evaporating.

But progressives weren't done there. In the 1980s and early 1990s, they successfully campaigned to create a pilot direct student lending program, which they promised would save taxpayers billions of dollars. They argued that by cutting out the middle men—the banks—they could reduce costs significantly, freeing up more funding for education programs that provide aid directly to lower-income families.

THE DEPARTMENT OF EDUCATION REPORTS THAT 92% OF ALL CURRENT STUDENT DEBT IS OWED TO THE FEDERAL GOVERNMENT![h]

The pilot direct lending program, which was created by a Democrat-led Congress and signed into law by Republican George H. W. Bush, was later expanded dramatically by congressional Democrats and President Bill Clinton.[43] Over time, the number of students participating in the direct student loan program grew. By 2006, about 20 percent of federally guaranteed loans were offered to students directly by the federal government.[44]

Spurred by the 2008 financial crisis, the Obama administration made another giant progressive leap forward. In 2010, President Obama signed into law legislation that made the federal government the nation's largest student lender, a move he promised

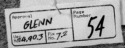

would make higher education more "affordable." Instead of merely guaranteeing many students loans and providing student loans directly to a minority of students, the Obama-era law made 100 percent of federal government guaranteed loans direct student loans, pushing private banks almost entirely out of the lending industry.

Obama and congressional Democrats also expanded the "income-based repayment plans" first created on a bipartisan basis in 2007, which allows students to structure their student loan payments based entirely on their income and lets students who work for a nonprofit organization—including charities, colleges, and even government agencies—have their student loans forgiven after 10 years of making income-based repayments. Yes, you read that correctly. Every American student with direct student loans can have their entire student debt load wiped out by working full-time for the government—for only 10 years. *Indentured servitude*, anyone?

Have you amassed $150,000 in student loan debt pursuing a physical education degree at a ridiculously overpriced liberal arts college? Or maybe you spent $100,000 getting a graduate or undergraduate degree in eighteenth-century French women's poetry or "Canadian studies" or "exercise and movement sciences" or "puppet arts"? (Yes, these are all real majors.) No problem. Just work for your local DMV for 10 years and it will all magically disappear—and by "magically disappear," I mean other people will be forced to pay for the four years you spent in college getting hammered at your puppeteer frat house.

Taken together, these policies—the government-guaranteed loans, direct federal lending, public service loan forgiveness, and more—have created numerous market distortions and have encouraged and even rewarded poor economic decision-making. Many students are no longer incentivized to choose an affordable college. They know that the federal government will give them almost any amount of money a school charges, and many of those who plan to work in public service know they'll never have to pay back most of the money they loan out. Similarly, college administrators know they can continuously raise tuition rates, fees, and the cost of room and board, because the federal government will guarantee to provide the funding needed— even to students with little or no money.

Does this sound familiar? It should. These perverse incentives and market manipulations are eerily similar to those that caused the 2008 recession. If the government knows how to do one thing, it's pouring economic alcohol to get a marketplace drunk.

Presidents Johnson, George H. W. Bush, Clinton, George W. Bush, and Obama— Democrats and Republicans—all contributed to the present student debt crisis, which seems to worsen every single year. Students now have more than $1.6 trillion in outstanding student loan debt, and the cost of attending college has risen astronomically in recent years. According to data from the National Center for Education Statistics (NCES), the average cost of attending a four-year college— including tuition, fees, and room and board—increased by 12 percent in inflation-adjusted dollars from the 1963–64 school year to 1983–84. From 1983–84 to 2003–04, costs skyrocketed by 78 percent. And from 2003–04 to 2017–18, they increased by more than 30 percent.[45]

What has happened with student lending and higher education cost increases in the United States over the past half-century isn't proof of the failure of free-market economics, it's additional evidence that politicians will do absolutely anything to get elected and that government routinely spends money like drunken sailors. And no, I'm not talking girls' trip to Napa Valley drunk, I'm talking all-night bender, fall asleep in a dumpster, puppeteer frat drunk. It's also proof that politicians rarely think or care about the long-term consequences of their actions. They have much more important things to do, after all—like win elections. (Yeah, I know, you didn't need more "proof" of that one.)

In a free market, student loans are investments. Students and their families take on student loan debt if they believe the costs are outweighed by the benefits. Students don't loan out tens of thousands of dollars to become puppet masters; they find apprenticeships or other lower-cost opportunities to learn a new trade. Tuition costs are limited because they are determined based on what students are willing and able to pay.

But in a crony system, banks and government institutions grant loans to students they know are unlikely to ever pay back the loans. Schools charge increasingly higher rates because they know government will give students virtually unlimited student loan debt. This is the model America's political class has been building for decades. Does this make a whole lot of sense to you?

If so, are you drunk?

Professor Tweed @checkurprivilegeplz
Even if government is to blame for much of the increased costs, it doesn't matter, because college should be free.

💬 1   ♻   ♡

There's no such thing as "free" college. Someone is going to pay for it. By saying you want "free" college, you're actually insisting everyone else should pay for your college education, even if they don't want to and even if you don't make good use of your education. Now, that sounds pretty "greedy" to me. Why should others be forced to pay for a degree that only benefits you?

Professor Tweed @checkurprivilegeplz
Universal tuition-free college guarantees people have access to better economic opportunities. It's an investment in our future. That's why so many of the world's most successful countries do it.

💬 1   ♻   ♡

Even if you think it's a good investment, it's still immoral and, frankly, unfair to take other people's hard-earned money—including from many people who never went to college and people who did go to college but paid for it themselves—so that others can get a "free" college degree.

And it's simply not true that using tax dollars to pay for college tuition always improves economic opportunities. In many cases, students in countries with "free" higher education get student loans anyway. For example, Sweden has a "free" college tuition program, but Swedish students often end up spending tens of thousands of dollars on other costs related to college. For example, about 70 percent of Swedish students take out student loans—about the same proportion of American students who get loans to pay for college—and Swedes graduate with about $20,000 in student loan debt, compared to about $30,000 for Americans students.[46]

Universal college education programs also don't necessarily lead to there being a greater proportion of a country's population with a college degree. Higher-education rates in countries like Denmark and Sweden are slightly lower than in the United States. France, which has a highly subsidized college system, also has a lower rate.[47]

"Free" college education doesn't reduce indebtedness overall, either. Because countries that have highly subsidized or no-cost college education programs also typically have extremely high taxes, people have less disposable income and are often forced to pay more for just about everything, including expensive things like housing and motor vehicles. Household debt, relative to disposable income, is actually much higher in countries like Denmark, Finland, Norway, and Sweden— despite their "free" higher-education systems.[48]

We should be working toward making our higher-education system more affordable. Shackling tens of millions of students with tens of thousands of dollars in debt puts

them at great financial risk and slows economic growth in other parts of the economy, especially the housing industry. But the best way to make college more affordable isn't to continue the same failing strategies that have created the high costs that are pervasive throughout the United States today, it's to create significantly more competition in the higher-ed marketplace.

Some colleges are already providing people with low-cost certifications and college courses online, thanks mostly to the technological advancements made by internet entrepreneurs. Through platforms like Coursera and edX, students can enroll in courses at some of the leading universities around the world, including numerous Ivy League colleges like Harvard and Yale, often for less than $100.[49] Liberty University—the world's largest Christian college—has utilized the power of the internet to grow from a relatively small college in rural Virginia to one of the largest universities on Earth. Liberty's enrollment now tops 100,000, an achievement directly related to Liberty's low-cost, technology-focused model.[50]

Making higher education more affordable is already possible, and as Liberty University has shown, it can be accomplished on a large scale. The reason it hasn't become widespread is that the government takeover of the student lending industry has removed most of the free-market elements from the higher-education decision-making process. Students aren't as concerned as they should be about tuition costs—because it's easy to borrow money from the federal government—and colleges know that the government will loan students the money they need no matter how high the

$FREE.99

FREE COLLEGE'S RETURN ON INVESTMENT

What sours the deal even further for students living in a country that offers "free" college is the degree's return on investment.

Using OECD numbers, Matt Palumbo, author of *The Conscience of a Young Conservative* and *In Defense of Classical Liberalism*, shows that students in America can look forward to 65 percent higher earnings after completing a post-secondary education. Our Swedish counterparts should only expect a 9 percent pay increase. The deal is even worse in Norway, where post-secondary graduates only average 2 percent higher pay.[i]

costs, so colleges continue to increase their tuition rates. If higher-ed institutions were required to compete in a free market, costs would be significantly lower and college would be within reach for nearly everyone.

Professor Tweed @checkurprivilegeplz
Well, maybe kids wouldn't need to worry about college if capitalists hadn't ruined our K–12 education system with school choice programs and low tax rates. If government schools had the funds they need to be successful, then our kids would be much better prepared for the future.

💬 1   ♻   ♡

I agree that our children are not being prepared at the K–12 level—for college, the workplace, or life in general. After all, I hear untold numbers of them now eat Tide Pods for amusement. But who runs K–12 education in the United States? It's not billionaire corporations or greedy bankers. It's local and state governments—the same so-called "experts" you want to give even more money and authority to. And they've been doing it for generations, with spectacularly bad results.

Even though the United States spends more than just about any country on Earth on education, U.S. students continue to fall behind most other wealthy countries—including many of America's most important economic rivals. As *The Guardian* reported in September 2018, "According to the Washington thinktank the National Center on Education and the Economy (NCEE), the average student in Singapore is 3.5 years ahead of her US counterpart in maths, 1.5 years ahead in reading and 2.5 in science. Children in countries as diverse as Canada, China, Estonia, Germany, Finland, Netherland, New Zealand and Singapore consistently outrank their US counterparts on the basics of education."[51] According to the mother country, we're so dumb we can't even spell "math" correctly.

✓ *NOT A TYPO*

There's also no correlation between state spending on education and education quality. Many of the states with the highest per-pupil education expenses have some of the worst government-run school districts in the country. For instance, the two biggest spenders on per-pupil education are New York and Washington, D.C., both of which have numerous failing and crime-ridden schools. Further, Colorado ranks in the bottom 15 of states in education spending and teachers' salaries, but it ranks among the top five in ACT scores.[52,53]

The best way to improve educational outcomes in America isn't to keep throwing more money at an already very costly problem. To fix the U.S. education system, we need to introduce competition, freedom, and choice and allow parents to move their children out of government-run schools. A 2016 analysis by EdChoice of 100 empirical studies of school choice programs found educational freedom improves outcomes and/or lowers costs.[54]

Once again, government—not capitalism—has proven to be a bigger problem than it is a problem-solver.

HEALTH CARE

Clay Guevara @coffeeshopcommie
But education isn't the only problem. Health care and health insurance costs have been increasing for decades because of capitalists' greed, too, and this problem isn't the result of government failures.

◯ 1   ⇅   ♡

You won't hear any arguments from me about how expensive the health care system is, or how frustrating it can be to work through the health insurance industry's burdensome, time-consuming processes. But if you think that the problems plaguing the U.S. health care system are primarily being caused by health care providers or insurance companies, then you haven't put much thought into how America's health care model works.

The U.S. health care and health insurance systems are already some of the most highly regulated industries in the world. According to a report by the American Hospital Association (AHA), "Health systems, hospitals and PAC [post-acute care] providers must comply with 629 discrete regulatory requirements across nine domains," costing more than $39 billion annually in additional administrative activities alone. AHA also reports that "an average size community hospital" must dedicate so many hours to regulatory compliance that it amounts to the equivalent of 59 full-time staff members.[55]

And that's just the start. Federal and state rules have led to numerous problems that continue drive up costs and limit inefficiencies. For example, the Affordable Care Act (ACA)—which has been anything but "affordable" for people forced to buy insurance in ACA exchanges—effectively required everyone purchasing health insurance to buy a "qualifying" health insurance plan that includes "essential health benefits." Essential health benefits significantly increase costs because they force insurers to offer plans that include coverage many people don't want or need.

For example, every health insurance plan must cover "maternity and newborn care," even if the recipient is biologically incapable of having children or isn't married and not looking to have kids. All insurance plans must also cover behavioral health services, like alcohol and drug treatments. Some people are alcoholics and drug abusers, but why should everyone have to pay to have these diseases covered when most people will never use treatment services?

The Affordable Care Act also requires mental health coverage, even though the vast majority of Americans don't suffer from a serious mental illness—except socialists, of course. (Okay, before we continue, let me apologize for that last remark. Not all socialists have a serious mental illness. Some just have an ordinary mental illness. Just kidding again—although, have you actually listened to Maxine Waters speak? If that's not an example of mental illness, I'm not sure what is.)

The ACA also requires every health insurance plan to include a variety of "preventative care" services, even though many people don't use them and many more use them but could afford to pay health care practitioners out of pocket for these relatively minor expenses, cutting out the health insurance middlemen.

The Affordable Care Act also effectively eliminated most forms of health insurance underwriting, which means insurers can't charge patients more money who have health conditions normally associated with higher health care costs, passing those costs along to everyone else. For example, health insurers can't charge someone who weighs 400 pounds and eats five meals a day at McDonald's more money than those people who run 10 miles a day just for the fun of it. (By the way, please know that I'm not in any way condoning those who enjoy running every day. Like socialists, these weirdos would also benefit from mental health coverage. Seriously, if you're a running nut, please immediately seek help.) I hate running, but if I did run, I know I would live a longer, healthier life. It's my choice to stay at home eating potato chips instead of going to the gym. Why should you pay for it?

Perhaps worst of all, the Affordable Care Act stops health insurers from denying coverage based on a preexisting condition, no matter how expensive the condition is. This essentially means that much of America's health insurance system no longer exists. The whole point of insurance is to gain coverage *before* you get sick. If people can wait until after they develop a serious illness to buy coverage, then the whole insurance model breaks down—and that's exactly what has happened.

We do need charities and state government programs that offer health coverage to people with serious preexisting conditions like cancer or heart disease. Programs helping those with preexisting conditions have worked effectively in the past. But forcing health insurance companies to provide so-called "insurance" to people who are already sick—and forcing lower-income and middle-income people to pay for their illnesses in the form of higher health insurance costs—is downright dumb. Not only is it extremely costly, it encourages and even rewards irresponsible, dangerous behavior.

It's also worth mentioning that the whole "preexisting conditions crisis"—which, in many ways, led to the passage of the Affordable Care Act—was mostly caused by government in the first place. Prior to the 1940s, most people who had health insurance coverage bought it privately, although because receiving advanced health care services was still relatively rare, many people didn't bother purchasing it. Once the United States entered World War II, everything changed. President Franklin Roosevelt—one of my least favorite presidents—signed an executive order creating the Office of Economic Stabilization, which soon froze wages across the country.

This market manipulation put businesses in an extremely tough situation. Without the ability to offer employees and prospective employees more money, how could business owners compete in the labor market? One of the most successful and popular ways was to start offering employees health insurance coverage and other benefits, marking the creation of our modern employer-sponsored health insurance system.

In 1943, the Roosevelt administration solidified this model, by excluding health insurance provided by employers from taxation, making it significantly less expensive to get health coverage through an employer than on the private market.[56] This created significant demand for health insurance that previously had not existed.

The health insurance coverage rate in 1940 was just 9 percent, but by 1950, more than half the country had health insurance.[57] Employer-provided health insurance remains the most important and expensive benefit offered by employers today, and the tax benefits for providing coverage to employees have increased in the years since World War II.

Although there are some benefits to this model, one of the most significant drawbacks is that when people lose their jobs, they often lose their health insurance coverage. That left a lot of people in extremely difficult situations. For example, John might be enrolled in a good health insurance plan, which he needs because his wife doesn't work and has cancer. But if John lost his job under the pre-Obamacare model, he could end up in a situation where he was unable to find health insurance again, because health insurers might deny coverage based on a "preexisting condition."

This problem was entirely avoidable, however, and fixing it didn't require forcing insurers to provide coverage to people who were already sick and hadn't been contributing to the health insurance pool. For example, if government had changed the tax system so that employers received a tax break for funding a health insurance account that individuals would use to buy their own health insurance plans, then when employees lost their jobs, they would still have health coverage. Further, if government were to alter its health insurance regulations so that any group of individuals could get together and buy a plan—not only through an employer, but through a private association as well—then much of the health insurance market could break away from the labor market altogether and costs would be significantly lower, too. This isn't rocket science. These are commonsense solutions.＊

FUN FACT!

＊THIS IS THE FIRST TIME SOMEONE HAS SAID THIS WHEN NOT REACHING FOR YOUR GUNS.

Government created a system that virtually guaranteed a preexisting conditions problem, then, for decades, it did nothing to fix it. And when it finally did provide a so-called solution—Obamacare—it ended up causing substantial health insurance cost increases.

THE CYCLE OF BIG GOVERNMENT

ARE YOU STARTING TO SEE A PATTERN HERE? COVERED IN THIS CHAPTER ARE SEVERAL EXAMPLES OF PROBLEMS CAUSED BY GOVERNMENT INTERFERENCE AND MEDDLING. AND WHEN THE PROBLEM GETS BIG ENOUGH, DOES THE GOVERNMENT GET OUT OF THE WAY? NO, THE "SOLUTION" IS OFTEN TO DOUBLE DOWN ON THE SAME INTERFERENCE AND MEDDLING THAT CAUSED THE PROBLEM IN THE FIRST PLACE.

Thanks to all the provisions included in the Affordable Care Act—not just the preexisting conditions clause—health insurance premiums in the individual market doubled within just five years of the ACA health insurance exchanges opening, and insurance deductibles have increased by so much that for many people, health insurance plans have become too costly to actually use.[58] The average family health insurance deductible for an ACA-exchange Bronze Plan—the lowest-tier ACA plan—was more than $12,000 in 2019.[59]

Although there's no question President Obama's Affordable Care Act has been a complete disaster, the federal government's involvement in the health insurance industry—under both Democratic and Republican leadership—has been causing dramatic health care price increases for more than two decades. Data compiled by the U.S. Bureau of Labor Statistics show from 1998 to 2016, the cost of "Medical Services" doubled—a 100.5 percent increase—and prices for "Hospital and Related

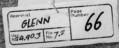

Services" nearly tripled—a 177 percent increase—over the same period.[60] These health care cost increases far outpaced the rate of general inflation, about 47 percent.

Professor Tweed @checkurprivilegeplz
.@glennbeck, you can't blame these cost increases on government. These increases are the result of capitalist greed.

💬 1   🔁   ♡

If these health care cost increases really are the result of heartless, greedy health care providers and insurers, then we should expect to see the same rise in prices in sectors of the health care industry that have not been nearly as distorted by government influence, like cosmetic surgery, which is typically not covered by insurance, requiring patients to pay out of pocket for services. However, research shows the opposite is true. The less government is involved, the more likely it is health care costs have increased at a lower rate.

According to data from the American Society for Aesthetic Plastic Surgery, the average price for the 20 most common cosmetic procedures in the United States rose by only 32 percent from 1998 to 2016, significantly *below* the rate of general inflation and the massive health care cost increases experienced in health care sectors that are more heavily regulated and tied to health insurance. *SEE CHART ON NEXT PAGE* ⟶

If freer markets can make facelifts and breast implants more affordable, they can do the same for other medical services too.[61]

Rashida Resistance @AOC_2024_Squad4Life
So, you want to further privatize the health care industry? That means you want a health care system that lets drug companies jack up prices for sick and dying patients. Wow, @glennbeck, you really are heartless.

💬 1   🔁   ♡

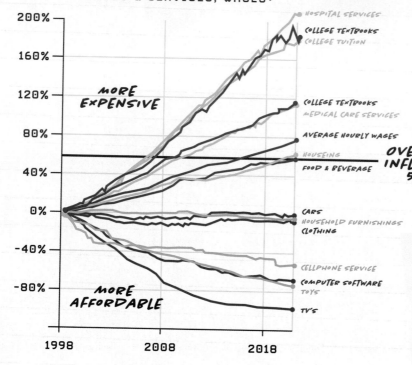

PRICE CHANGES

SELECTED U.S. CONSUMER GOODS & SERVICES, WAGES†

- 200%
- 160%
- 120%
- 80%
- 40%
- 0%
- -40%
- -80%

MORE EXPENSIVE

MORE AFFORDABLE

HOSPITAL SERVICES
COLLEGE TEXTBOOKS
COLLEGE TUITION

COLLEGE TEXTBOOKS
MEDICAL CARE SERVICES

AVERAGE HOURLY WAGES

OVERALL INFLATION 56%

HOUSEING
FOOD & BEVERAGE

CARS
HOUSEHOLD FURNISHINGS
CLOTHING

CELLPHONE SERVICE
COMPUTER SOFTWARE
TOYS

TV'S

1998   2008   2018

IN FACT, AS THIS CHART SHOWS— THE MORE AN INDUSTRY IS TIED TO GOVERNMENT, THE MORE COSTS INCREASE. THE OPPOSITE IS ALSO TRUE.

No, I want a health care system that encourages and rewards innovation, not a system run by slow-moving, inefficient, mostly disinterested bureaucrats. That's never going to happen so long as government is managing nearly every aspect of the health care industry. I'm glad you brought up the pharmaceutical industry, though. It's another prime example of how the federal government is basically King Midas in reverse: everything it touches turns to crap.

Because of the U.S. Food and Drug Administration's (FDA) massive, burdensome, bureaucratic drug approval process, it takes about 12 years and $2.9 billion for a new drug to go from a pharmaceutical lab to the market.[62] And that doesn't include the billions spent by pharmaceutical companies to produce the many drugs that never make it into the hands of consumers. With these huge development costs, is it any wonder that pharmaceutical companies charge high prices for new drugs?

Drug companies only own the patent rights for a new drug for 20 years,[63] which means they have to make as much money as possible on the drug while they own the patent rights to recoup their losses incurred while developing the drug and so that they can earn enough money for their investors. Once the 20 years is up, drug prices often plummet and become extremely affordable for most consumers.

I won't defend the few drug-company scumbags that have unnecessarily increased the cost of drugs people need in the final years of a patent or when no one else in the marketplace is selling a particular product. But those problems, despite the fact they get huge amounts of media coverage, are relatively rare and isolated.

A much bigger problem, however, is that every day, people die waiting for drugs to be approved by the FDA. And in many cases, people suffer waiting for drugs that have already been deemed to be safe and effective but are held up by FDA's mountain of red tape or waiting for later trials to be completed. If I am dying with a deadly disease like cancer, with little or no hope of surviving, shouldn't I have the right to use any treatment my doctor believes has the potential to save or extend my life?

Solutions to fix this problem have been around for years, like Free to Choose Medicine, an FDA reform proposal that would provide suffering patients with access to drugs that have passed some of the most important FDA trial phases but that haven't yet completed all of FDA's arduous process.[64] Or Sen. Ted Cruz's RESULT Act, which would require FDA to approve an application submitted by a drug or medical device company within 30 days if that drug or device has already been sanctioned by another country with a long track record of ensuring efficacy and safety.[65]

These are commonsense reforms that shouldn't be controversial. They are the sort of thing that everyone should be in favor of—Democrats, Republicans, Libertarians, independents, and even your crazy, granola-eating, Birkenstock-wearing hippie uncle Moon Star. But because politicians are—well, politicians—and have benefited from the crony-capitalist system they built, change has been agonizingly slow, and mostly bad, too.

Do pharmaceutical companies, health care providers, and health insurance companies deserve to share in the blame for some of the problems we're seeing now? Sure. But in most cases, they are simply reacting to the changes and processes imposed by governments at the federal and state levels. As the kids say these days, don't hate the player, hate the game—or something like that. And the "game" is unquestionably controlled by government and often to government's benefit.

Clay Guevara @coffeeshopcommie
All right, I agree that when government mixes with markets, some problems arise. But that's not because of government, it's because of capitalism.

💬 1   ⟲   ♡

As I've said throughout this chapter, if you're talking about crony capitalism, then you're right, Mr. Guevara, but if you're referring to the free-market capitalism myself and millions of other Americans support, then nothing could be further from the truth. When coupled with protections for individual rights, free enterprise has liberated more people from poverty than any other economic system in human history. In fact, if the past 50 years has proven anything, it's that even a drop of free-market capitalism can radically improve otherwise completely broken socialist economies.

Take China, for example. In the early 1980s, after decades of socialist-created death, starvation, and misery, China's agricultural system was decollectivized,

and the government soon started creating "Special Economic Areas" that allowed the Chinese to experiment with market-based ideas. Encouraged by the success of China's new experiments in free(ish) enterprise, the Chinese Communist Party eventually transitioned the country to one in which private property ownership is tolerated, markets are much freer, and people have much more economic liberty than they did under Communist hardliners like Mao Zedong, who spent most of his life brutally murdering people whom he deemed to be impediments to building his perfect socialist utopia. (You can read more about China's socialist horror stories in Chapters 4 and 6.)

The effects of China's decision to permit private property ownership and to increase some economic freedoms have turned the country into a global economic powerhouse. From 1960 to 1990, China's GDP increased by $300 billion, or about 500 percent. From 1990 to 2018, China's GDP grew by $13.2 trillion, a 3,680 percent increase.[66] Hundreds of millions of people have been lifted from poverty as a result of these policies, and hundreds of millions more will see their lives improve in China if the country's ruling class finally does agree to completely end its seven-decades-long failed experiment in collectivist economics.

 Neal DiCaprio-Cortez @GreenNewNeal
As long as we have capitalism, we'll have poverty and suffering. That's why we need something completely different. We need socialism.

 1   ♡

Socialism? Oh, you mean the system that has led to the murder, imprisonment, or exile of more than 100 million people? The system that kills individual liberty and has failed, to varying spectacular degrees, in dozens of countries around the world? The same system embraced by the Nazis, Mao's China, and the murderous regimes of Soviet Russia? Yeah, let's talk about socialism . . .

*END OF
CHAPTER 2*

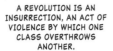

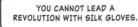

IS SOCIALISM JUST "SHARING & CARING"?

COPY EDITS
ON PAGE 80
—GB

Approval
GLENN
Use 84.90.3 | Fix No. 7.2 | Page Number 73

"THE CHAMPIONS OF SOCIALISM CALL THEMSELVES PROGRESSIVES, BUT THEY RECOMMEND A SYSTEM WHICH IS CHARACTERIZED BY RIGID OBSERVANCE OF ROUTINE AND BY A RESISTANCE TO EVERY KIND OF IMPROVEMENT. THEY CALL THEMSELVES LIBERALS, BUT THEY ARE INTENT UPON ABOLISHING LIBERTY. THEY CALL THEMSELVES DEMOCRATS, BUT THEY YEARN FOR DICTATORSHIP. THEY CALL THEMSELVES REVOLUTIONARIES, BUT THEY WANT TO MAKE THE GOVERNMENT OMNIPOTENT. THEY PROMISE THE BLESSINGS OF THE GARDEN OF EDEN, BUT THEY PLAN TO TRANSFORM THE WORLD INTO A GIGANTIC POST OFFICE. EVERY MAN BUT ONE A SUBORDINATE CLERK IN A BUREAU. WHAT AN ALLURING UTOPIA! WHAT A NOBLE CAUSE TO FIGHT!"[1]

— LUDWIG
VON MISES

Socialism. It's such a nice-sounding word, isn't it? Who doesn't like being "social" or sharing their favorite cute dog picture on "social" media? And "ism"—well, that means it must be an important word. In the English language, you haven't made it until you've become an "ism." There's "abolitionism," "feminism," "prohibitionism," "spiritualism," "pacificism," and everyone's favorite "ism"—"activism." (The opposite of "activism" is "sedentarism," defined as not only as engaging in too little exercise, but also engaging in too much sitting. I am a strict adherent.)

But here's the problem with "ism" ideas, movements, and groups: they often end up meaning many things to a variety of different people, creating confusion-ism (not to be confused with *Confucianism*). Go ahead, ask someone you know what "activism" means and you'll get all sorts of answers. To some, activism means fighting for an important and worthy cause. To others, it conjures up vivid images of jackboot-wearing Antifa protesters hurling bricks through the front window of a Starbucks.

If you slap "judicial" in front of "activism," you'll find about half the country will recall instances when courts triumphantly enshrined some important left-wing idea into law as a new "right," while the other half of America will angrily insist that judicial activism, especially involving cases regarding the Constitution, isn't only wrong, it's illegal. (I'm still in need of regular therapy to recover from the whole John Roberts–Obamacare debacle.)

In our time, there isn't a single "ism" that has garnered more attention or created more confusion than socialism. Despite all the yelling and screaming about socialism that has occurred over the past few years on radio, cable news networks, and on the campaign trail, I'm convinced that most people still have absolutely no clue what socialism really means. And how can we have important, potentially

world-changing conversations about ideas like socialism without first agreeing on a common meaning? We're all just talking past each other, and it's led to a lot of misunderstandings.

Neal DiCaprio-Cortez @GreenNewNeal
.@glennbeck of course people know what socialism is. It's literally one of the most widely talked about topics in the United States today, and really throughout the entire world.

💬 1   ↻   ♡

Really? Before we go any further, consider the following findings from a 2018 Gallup survey that asked Americans what they thought "socialism" means. The answers were, well, *interesting*—yeah, let's go with "interesting."

According to the Gallup report, 10 percent of respondents said "socialism" means "benefits and services—social services free, medicine for all."[2] Six percent said "modified communism, communism"—without giving any explanation of what "communism" means. Another 6 percent replied socialism should be defined as "talking to people, being social, social media, getting along with people," and 3 percent said "restriction of freedom—people told what to do." The most popular answer, the choice selected by nearly one-quarter of respondents (23 percent), was that socialism is "equality—equal standing for everybody, all equal in rights, equal in distribution."

These responses could easily drive one to another dangerous *ism*—alcoholism.

Perhaps most interestingly, only 17 percent of those surveyed by Gallup said socialism is "government ownership or control, government ownership of utilities, everything controlled by the government, state control of business." (By the way, when Gallup

Approval
GLENN
Up
no 34.90.3 | Fix
no 7.2

Page
Number
76

LIFE MOVES
PRETTY FAST

BUELLER
RATION

asked the same question in 1949, 34 percent of respondents selected that answer, a plurality in that year's survey.)

I could talk all day about what I think these results mean. I could probably devote an entire radio segment to any one of these answers. (I mean, seriously, do 6 percent of Americans really think socialism means "being social" or "social media"? Then you spend five seconds on social media and you realize this is entirely plausible.) But this conversation isn't about me. It's about you and the future of the free world.

I believe—no, I *know*—that socialism is one of history's most dangerous ideas. It has resulted in death, destruction, and mayhem everywhere it has ever been attempted on a large scale. More than 100 million people were killed, imprisoned, or exiled by socialist and communist parties in the twentieth century alone.

"I DO HAVE A TEST TODAY, THAT WASN'T BULLSH*T. IT'S ON EUROPEAN SOCIALISM. I'M NOT EUROPEAN, NOR DO I PLAN ON BEING EUROPEAN, SO WHO GIVES A CRAP IF THEY'RE SOCIALISTS?"

- CELEBRATED AMERICAN PHILOSOPHER, FERRIS BUELLER

No matter how well you to try to wrap the American flag around socialism and insist that it's going to allow the workers of the world to escape the so-called "tyranny" that's supposedly being imposed on them by millionaires, billionaires, and giant corporations, socialism only results in the elimination of individual rights. That's the inevitable result of socialist systems, no matter how well-intentioned socialists are.

GLENN
BECK

And although many socialists and those who are sympathetic to socialist ideas believe collectivism creates "equality," the truth is that equality is completely impossible to achieve under a socialist system, because people's individual rights must give way to the will of the collective. Under socialism, it's true everyone theoretically ends up with relatively similar amounts of wealth—although the amount is usually "none"—but their freedoms vary widely. The ruling-class elites running society never have to worry about standing in bread lines, for example. They're too special to live like the rest of us.

But before we can have a detailed discussion about the alleged merits of socialism or its long history of failure, we need to agree about what "socialism" actually is. I'm not talking about the false characterizations of socialism promoted by the right or the left—I'm talking about the well-established, historical meaning of socialism.

So, Clay Guevara, what is socialism?

Clay Guevara @coffeeshopcommie
Socialism is the most equitable, fair, and just way to organize society. It eliminates poverty, improves life for the poorest among us, and ensures no one is left to die penniless in the street. Socialism is all about fairness. In socialism, everyone has equal opportunity and rights.

💬 1   🔁   ♡

Well, if that is your definition, no wonder you are attracted to socialism.

You're right that these are some of the primary goals for socialists, but the pathway to achieve those goals have been presented in many different ways throughout history.

(PARAPHRASED)

"LIFE MOVES PRETTY FAST. IF YOU DON'T STOP AND LOOK AROUND ONCE IN A WHILE, YOU COULD MISS IT. PARTICULARLY IF YOUR SYSTEM OF GOVERNMENT WINDS UP MURDERING YOU AND ABOUT 100 MILLION OF YOUR CLOSEST FRIENDS."

- CELEBRATED AMERICAN PHILOSOPHER, FERRIS BUELLER

BUELLER? BUELLER? BUELLER?

To some extent, socialism is a big-tent ideology, just like conservatism and liberalism. But in the same way virtually all "conservatives" have certain foundational principles in common, socialists of every kind share important philosophical foundations, too, and many of those ideas can be traced back to one man, Karl Marx, history's most influential socialist and originator of the hipster beard trend.

Karl Marx was born on May 5, 1818, in the Prussian city of Trier, located on the banks of the Moselle River in modern-day Germany, close to the border of Luxemburg. Marx's father, Heinrich, was a successful and wealthy lawyer who, ironically, believed in many classical liberal ideas. As one biographer puts it, "Marx's father was a deist who found his God in Locke, Newton, and Leibniz."[3] Boy, sometimes the apple sure falls pretty far from the tree. So basically, our current socialist menace in America all goes back to Marx's daddy issues.

Marx studied at the University of Bonn, University of Berlin, and eventually earned a doctoral degree from the University of Jena. While studying at the University of Berlin, Marx joined the "Young Hegelians," a group that was highly interested in the writings of radical thinker Georg Wilhelm Friedrich Hegel, one of the fathers of the modern "progressive" movement. Hegel was a prominent Prussian academic who believed that humanity had progressed to the point that it could be led by "enlightened" experts, giving rise to the conception that the most ideal nation would be led by a vast bureaucracy of administrators who would rely on science, rather than philosophy, to guide decision-making for the whole populace.[4]

Soon after graduating, Marx became engaged in activist journalism, and he spent most of his life traveling from one part of Europe to the next, writing, editing, and developing his radical ideas about economics and political philosophy, eagerly awaiting a vast European workers' revolution that would never come during his lifetime.

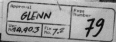

GHOST OF KARL MARX.

"HELLO COMRADES, I BELIEVE I CAN BE OF ASSISTANCE HERE. IN THE *COMMUNIST MANIFESTO*, MY MOST MAGNIFICENT AND FAMOUS WORK FOR WHICH I HAVE BEEN PRAISED ENDLESSLY, I WROTE, 'THE HISTORY OF ALL HITHERTO EXISTING SOCIETIES IS THE HISTORY OF CLASS STRUGGLES. FREEMAN AND SLAVE, PATRICIAN AND PLEBEIAN, LORD AND SERF, GUILD-MASTER AND JOURNEYMAN, IN A WORD, OPPRESSOR AND OPPRESSED, STOOD IN CONSTANT OPPOSITION TO ONE ANOTHER, CARRIED ON AN UNINTERRUPTED, NOW HIDDEN, NOW OPEN FIGHT, A FIGHT THAT EACH TIME ENDED, EITHER IN A REVOLUTIONARY RE-CONSTITUTION OF SOCIETY AT LARGE, OR IN THE COMMON RUIN OF THE CONTENDING CLASSES.' GOD, I LOVE TO HEAR MYSELF TALK."[6]

Marx's ideas have heavily influenced every socialist and socialist movement of the past century, including the various socialist movements and parties that have arisen throughout the history of the United States, even to the present age. For example, the Democratic Socialists of America—the largest socialist organization in the United States whose membership roster includes Congresswomen Alexandria Ocasio-Cortez, D-N.Y., and Rashida Tlaib, D-Mich.—cites and endorses Marx's work throughout its website and frequently discusses Marx's influence during the organization's numerous conferences and meetings.[5]

Throughout Marx's works, one of the most important central themes is class warfare, an idea that serves as the foundation for all modern socialist movements. According to Marx, nearly all of society's conflicts stem from "struggles" between groups of people with varying amounts of wealth.

Marx believed that the only way to resolve these "class struggles" was for wealth and property to be equally redistributed and cooperatively managed, giving rise to the famous Marxist slogan, "From each according to his ability, to each according to his needs." Marx reasoned that

GHOST OF KARL MARX

"THE HISTORY OF ALL PAST SOCIETY HAS CONSISTED IN THE DEVELOPMENT OF CLASS ANTAGONISMS, ANTAGONISMS THAT ASSUMED DIFFERENT FORMS AT DIFFERENT EPOCHS. BUT WHATEVER FORM THEY MAY HAVE TAKEN, ONE FACT IS COMMON TO ALL PAST AGES, VIZ., THE EXPLOITATION OF ONE PART OF SOCIETY BY THE OTHER."

A.D.D. MOMENT

HEARD THAT ONE BEFORE

"By over-all planning, we mean planning which takes into consideration the interests of the 600 million people of our country. In drawing up plans, handling affairs or thinking over problems, we must proceed from the fact that China has a population of 600 million people, and we must never forget this fact."[a]

-Mao Zedong

without collective property ownership, there would always be wealth disparities, which means there would always be at least one class of people "exploiting" another.

Although modern socialist groups have different ideas about how much property should be collectively owned, they generally agree that socialism is only possible with collective ownership. For example, the Socialist Party of Great Britain declares on its website that "common ownership" of property is the "central meaning of socialism."[7]

Collective ownership is not the only distinguishing marker for modern socialists, however. Like Marx, socialist parties, groups, and politicians agree that collective property management is also an essential part of socialism. Again, the Socialist Party of Great Britain writes, "In practice, common ownership will mean everybody having the right to participate in decisions on how global resources will be used. It means nobody being able to take personal control of resources, beyond their own personal possessions."[8]

Similarly, the Socialist Party USA notes, "Socialism is not mere government ownership, a welfare state, or a repressive bureaucracy. Socialism is a new social and economic order in which workers and consumers control production and community residents control their neighborhoods, homes, and schools."[9]

You might be wondering how, exactly, we could transition from a world in which property is not collectively owned to one in which most wealth is owned publicly. According to Marx and modern socialists, wealth should be seized by a powerful ruling class and redistributed to the rest of society.

 Professor Tweed @checkurprivilegeplz
.@glennbeck, you already admitted socialism's primary goal is to eliminate all classes, including "ruling classes." Looks like someone isn't paying attention.

💬 1   ⟲   ♡

If alarm bells aren't going off in your head, get your head examined, because you might be suffering from severe confusion-ism. Throughout history, socialists have been telling the world their plan is to eliminate "classes" and "exploitation," while at the same time insisting they want to use political power to steal wealth from others. I don't know about you, but that sounds an awful lot like "exploitation" to me.

Some modern socialists have a hard time acknowledging that their ideology demands and requires tyranny—at least for a while. Some of them say that someday we'll all live in a world where everyone *voluntarily* chooses to share their wealth. That way, there won't be any need for an oppressive ruling class. But if you actually believe that, then I've got a big, beautiful bridge in Brooklyn that I'd like to sell you. (Cash preferred.)

This isn't rocket science, or even regular science. If you plan to redistribute everyone's wealth, then you're going to need to take it first, and the only way to do that is to seize control of societal institutions and then force people to give up their wealth.

Even Karl Marx acknowledged this sort of "despotism"—his word, not mine—would be needed for the world to "progress" toward a socialist utopia. Marx repeatedly said that the workers of the world, the proletariat, would need to "rule" over the bourgeoisie, those who control wealth and property.

GHOST OF KARL MARX

"THAT'S RIGHT, GLENN. AS I HAVE SAID BEFORE IN THE MOST EMINENT FASHION, 'THE FIRST STEP IN THE REVOLUTION BY THE WORKING CLASS … IS TO RAISE THE PROLETARIAT TO THE POSITION OF RULING AS TO WIN THE BATTLE OF DEMOCRACY. THE PROLETARIAT WILL USE ITS POLITICAL SUPREMACY TO WREST, BY DEGREES, ALL CAPITAL FROM THE BOURGEOISIE, TO CENTRALISE ALL INSTRUMENTS OF PRODUCTION IN THE HANDS OF THE STATE, I.E., OF THE PROLETARIAT ORGANISED AS THE RULING CLASS; AND TO INCREASE THE TOTAL OF PRODUCTIVE FORCES AS RAPIDLY AS POSSIBLE.'"[10]

See, even Ghost Karl gets it, and he's dead. Marx understood, as have the vast majority of his ideological successors, that workers must first become a ruling class before they can steal away the property of others. Marx elaborated on this point elsewhere in *The Communist Manifesto*, noting there is no way to remake the world into a socialist paradise "except by means of despotic inroads on the rights of property, and on the conditions of bourgeois production; by means of measures, therefore, which appear economically insufficient and untenable, but which, in the course of the movement, outstrip themselves, necessitate further inroads upon the old social order, and are unavoidable as a means of entirely revolutionizing the mode of production."[11]

TOP 3
EXAMPLES OF
TEMPORARY
DICTATORSHIPS
WHERE THE
DICTATOR
VOLUNTARILY
RELINQUISHED
POWER:

1.

2.

3.

There it is, plain as day. To enact his revolution of society, it is "unavoidable" that the worker-led ruling class make "despotic inroads on the rights of property." Now, it's true Marx and other socialists say these oppressive actions would only be temporary. Once workers become the ruling class and "wrest . . . all capital from the bourgeoisie," they would then supposedly redistribute the property equally and give up their authoritarian, despotic powers, sharing those powers equally with everyone, including those from whom they just stole their wealth and property (which will totally happen, by the way, and I'm disappointed in you for even questioning it).

I don't mean to be insulting, but you'd have to be bat-crap crazy to buy this garbage Marx is selling. And it's even more nuts to think those who just had their wealth, businesses, and lives destroyed by this new supposedly benevolent socialist ruling class would want to share their property with these tyrants in the future. Yet, Bernie Sanders indeed honeymooned in Soviet Moscow. Go figure.

Imagine you're a business owner who spent decades building a company you love, toiling away day and night to develop innovative new ideas, risking everything you had to pursue your passion. Then, a Marxist socialist government comes to power and begins confiscating your property, at first through a variety of new taxes. Soon, it will take the entire business and transfer ownership to the local community in the name of "fairness." You've lost everything you worked for in the span of just a few months, and now, you're just supposed to continue working and living like it never happened? This is *never* what occurs in the wake of socialist revolutions.

DOES THIS SOUND LIKE "EQUALITY" TO YOU?

At first, many socialist movements start with large-scale, bottom-up revolutions that are favored by a large proportion of the population. But it doesn't take long before the socialist masses choose leaders to "get" the people who are supposedly responsible for all of that society's problems: the farmers, educated, bureaucrats, Jews—whoever the scapegoat happens to be. Once those leaders are in power, they are the ones who get to determine whom to "get."

Although the details—names, national history, ethnic differences, and cultures—vary from one socialist country to the next, the end results of socialist revolutions are always tyranny and often violence. There are many reasons for this, but one of the biggest is that the principles of socialism are so incredibly unjust for those losing their wealth—which, it must be noted, often includes many in the middle class—that society can't function anymore without a strong-man government at the top forcing people to work "for the good of the collective." When you make an omelet, you have to break a few eggs—especially when you're rolling over them with tanks.

When confronted with the seemingly endless list of examples of societal collapse in the wake of socialist policies, some socialists say that we can't use historical accounts of socialism's failure, because humans are always "progressing" and advancing toward a more harmonious, "collective" future, and this "progress" makes socialism both possible and even ideal for today's world. But this ignores the many failing socialist policies and governments in existence *today*. Take Venezuela, for example. It was once one of the most prosperous nations in the entire world, and now, it's a socialist hellhole thanks entirely to the radical policies of its democratically elected socialist tyrants.

Neal DiCaprio-Cortez @GreenNewNeal
Ah, here comes the right-wing fearmongering about Venezuela. You radio talk show hosts just love talking about Venezuela and how it proves socialism is destined to fail in the United States. There's only one problem,@glennbeck: It's not a socialist country.

💬 1   ⟲   ♡

Venezuela isn't the utopia Marx, Bernie Sanders, and others have in mind when they talk about socialism, but it is the inevitable result of what happens when Comrades Karl and Bernie get their way. Socialism always starts out great. People are optimistic, media laud "tough" and "innovative" new socialist leaders, who often enjoy widespread support, and a grand vision for reshaping society energizes many people who had previously felt disenfranchised and disconnected. But socialism *always* eventually leads to destruction, chaos, and despair.

> "WITHIN RUSSIA'S IMMENSE DISORDERLINESS, STALIN FACED THE FUNDAMENTAL PROBLEMS OF PROVIDING ENOUGH FOOD FOR THE PEOPLE AND IMPROVING THEIR LOT THROUGH 20TH-CENTURY INDUSTRIAL METHODS. HE COLLECTIVIZED THE FARMS AND HE BUILT RUSSIA INTO ONE OF THE FOUR GREAT INDUSTRIAL POWERS ON EARTH. HOW WELL HE SUCCEEDED WAS EVIDENT IN RUSSIA'S WORLD-SURPRISING, STRENGTH IN WORLD WAR II. STALIN'S METHODS WERE TOUGH, BUT THEY PAID OFF."[b]

FROM "JOSEPH STALIN: TIME PERSON OF THE YEAR 1942," TIME MAGAZINE, JANUARY 4, 1943.

The chaos in Venezuela—more on this below—is a perfect illustration of what happens when you try to impose socialist ideas. The utopian vision of socialism so many on the left think we're headed for has never existed anywhere in the entire history of the world, and there are really good reasons for that, which we'll come back to later in our conversation. (See Chapter 7.)

The reason so many socialists want to distance themselves from Venezuela, aside from the fact that living there means you're probably eating your pet poodle for dinner, is that protecting the socialist future depends on erasing its past. If Americans learn about how socialists have destroyed that country's once-booming economy, it's unlikely they would be willing to go down a similar road. It's the ultimate "inconvenient truth" for those on the Left who want the world to adopt collectivist policies.

Venezuela's story is remarkable for a number of reasons, but perhaps the most important is that before the rise of socialism, it wasn't just an economic success, it was one of the wealthiest nations in the world. Despite the political chaos of the 1940s and 1950s, Venezuela's vast oil reserves provided its citizens with tremendous riches. Venezuela's proven oil reserves top 300 billion barrels. To put that in perspective, Saudi Arabia's reserves total 269 billion barrels. The United States' oil reserves total just 36 billion barrels.[12]

Thanks in large part to these reserves, in 1950 Venezuela had the fourth highest per capita gross domestic product in the world. Venezuelans were four times richer than Brazilians and the Japanese, who were still in the midst of recovering from World War II, and about 12 times wealthier than the Chinese.[13]

Visiting Venezuela's largest city, Caracas, in 1950 was truly a sight to behold. Caracas was unlike just about anywhere else in Latin America at the time—a truly modern, wealthy city, featuring large highways with thousands of the world's best cars, hundreds of brand-new buildings, and modern consumer goods. You would have thought you had died and went to . . . America.

But from the 1950s to 1980s, everything changed in Venezuela. In 1958, the oppressive dictatorship of Marcos Pérez Jiménez was overthrown by a popular opposition movement, which had won the support of the nation's air force and navy.[14] In the following decades, various left-wing factions competed for control of the country, each promising to improve life for Venezuela's poorest citizens and to root out the corruption that had plagued much of the country's government throughout the period.[15]

To win political favor, numerous welfare programs were created in the 1970s and 1980s, and government nationalized important industries, including natural gas, iron ore, and, most importantly, the petroleum industry. The more government seized control of the economy, the more the economy declined, although by 1982, Venezuela was still the wealthiest country in Latin America, and its workers earned some of the highest wages.[16]

Venezuela's economy declined dramatically in the 1980s and 1990s, however, creating yet another opportunity for radical change. In 1998, socialist Hugo Chavez, who had previously been arrested for his part in a failed military coup, was elected president of Venezuela and soon managed to garner enough political support to rewrite the country's constitution.[17]

SOCIALIST FUN FACT!

ADOLF HITLER, WHO WAS ALSO A SOCIALIST (MORE ON THAT LATER), WAS ARRESTED FOR HIS PART IN A FAILED COUP.

Chavez created hundreds of new reforms, government projects, and welfare programs meant to solidify support among the country's poorest voters and grant to government a greater control of the economy. Chavez's policies were designed to redistribute wealth and collectivize as many businesses as possible. Throughout his time in power, Chavez nationalized numerous energy companies—pushing oil giants Exxon Mobil and ConocoPhillips out of the country—as well as huge sectors of the agriculture, finance, manufacturing, steel, gold, telecommunications, and power industries.[18] And all this was done in the name of socialism and wealth redistribution.[19] The Democratic Socialists of America would have been so proud.

Chavez even nationalized parts of the tourism industry. As Reuters noted in a 2012 report, "In October 2011, Chavez said his government would seize private homes on the Los Roques archipelago in the Caribbean and use them for state-run tourism. The islands are among the nation's favorite and most expensive tourist spots, with pristine white beaches and coral reefs that teem with sea life."[20]

Thanks to high oil prices, Chavez's programs didn't immediately lead to the country's economic collapse, which many progressives and socialists in the United States used as "proof" that socialist policies work. Many even endorsed Chavez's regime, despite his openly authoritarian tendencies. For example, Bernie Sanders's Senate office distributed a newspaper editorial that declared the "American dream is more apt to be realized in South America, in places such as Ecuador, Venezuela and Argentina . . . Who's the banana republic now?"[21]

David Sirota, a speechwriter for Sanders's 2020 campaign, wrote a lengthy article in 2013 for the left-wing publication *Salon* arguing that Hugo Chavez performed an "economic miracle" in Venezuela.[22]

Democratic congressman Jose Serrano said after Chavez's death in 2013 that the Venezuelan president was "a leader that understood the needs of the poor. He was committed to empowering the powerless."[23]

Hollywood actor Sean Penn also lamented Chavez's death, saying, "Today, the people of the United States lost a friend it never knew it had. And poor people around the world lost a champion. I lost a friend I was blessed to have."[24]

SOCIALIST FUN FACT!

MADONNA ACTUALLY SURVIVED A MARRIAGE TO SEAN PENN. SOMEHOW, SEAN PENN ALSO SURVIVED.

What none of Chavez's American admirers knew at the time was that Venezuela's already fragile economy would soon collapse, sending the nation into an economic death spiral it still hasn't recovered from.

After Chavez died, another socialist, Nicolas Maduro, continued his legacy. Soon after coming to power, however, the price of oil dropped substantially, leaving the Venezuelan government with a difficult choice: Would it cut the socialist services that helped keep Chavez—and now Maduro—in power, or would it print money in an attempt to keep its social welfare programs afloat while the government waited for oil prices to recover? Maduro chose the latter, creating economic chaos.

It's important to note that while Maduro didn't help the situation, Chavez had lit the wick to the economic bomb many years before. Socialist revolutions often benefit from the sugar rush of confiscation of private property early in their life cycles, but things inevitably fall apart. Venezuela had already begun to collapse before Maduro; he just helped it along—by continuing, expanding, and doubling down on the socialist policies of Chavez.

More than 4 million Venezuelans left the country, many of whom were the victims of Maduro's socialist policies, especially his government's confiscations of businesses and wealth.[25] Price and labor controls were instituted, including 26 minimum wage increases. In 2019 alone, the minimum wage increased by 300 percent.[26]

The value of the Venezuelan currency, the bolivar, collapsed. The government's commitment to printing currency to pay for services it couldn't afford caused hyperinflation, with the inflation rate surpassing 100,000 percent in 2018. By the start of 2019, the currency had inflated by more than 1 million percent. In the second half of 2019, hyperinflation hit 10 million percent.[27]

Shortages of electricity, clean water, food, and basic consumer goods have become common. Some Venezuelans have become so desperate that they have resorted to killing zoo animals like buffalo and wild boar for food.[28] The country has even endured multiple toilet paper shortages. Now, I don't know about you, but it seems like massive toilet paper shortages is about as good of a reason as any to get the heck out of Venezuela. Killing zoo animals for food is bad enough, but if I have to start growing leafy trees in my own backyard to use as homemade toilet paper, I'm out.

In addition to the economic mayhem in Venezuela, there has been unprecedented political unrest, spurred in large part by a corrupt presidential election in 2018 that has been denounced as illegitimate by the overwhelming majority of democratic nations throughout the world, including the United States. At the time of this writing, the world is still not sure who Venezuela's president will be this time next year.

Attempted coups, widespread violence, and massive protests mark the new "normal" in Venezuela, and it all stems directly from socialist policies like price controls, confiscation of property, the nationalization of private industries, and runaway debt. (Boy, that sounds like the platform for the Democratic Party in 2020.)

Americans need to understand that the elimination of individual rights that we've seen in Venezuela, including property rights, is a hallmark of socialist governments everywhere, even ones that are better managed than the Maduro regime. The reason for this is simple: Under a socialist model, when most of the wealth has been squandered, all that remains as tools to control populations are corruption, authoritarianism, and brute force. Socialist governments use what little cash they have left to bribe voters and military officials to maintain control, and everyone ends up suffering as a result.

A.D.D. MOMENT

VENEZUELA'S "RABBIT PLAN"

To help grapple with the rampant hunger and starvation sweeping through the country, Venezuelan president Nicolas Maduro instituted the so-called "Rabbit Plan," which encouraged citizens to raise and breed rabbits for their "animal protein." In some cases, the government supplied rabbit kittens to communities to help kick-start the scheme.

The plan quickly ran into setbacks due to supposed "cultural problems." Minister of Urban Agriculture Freddy Bernal explained he found that the people started to treat the animals like pets, even putting bows on their new rabbits. "A lot of people gave names to the rabbits, they took them to bed," said Bernal.

To rectify this problem, Bernal suggested an education campaign to make the Rabbit Plan effective. "We need a publicity campaign on radio, TV, in newspapers, in cartoons, everywhere, so that the people understand that rabbits aren't pets but two and a half kilos of meat."[c]

If Americans pursue the same socialist policies, they should expect similar results. And if you think the United States is "too big to fail," you should remember that a lot of Venezuelans thought the same thing in 2010.

 Neal DiCaprio-Cortez @GreenNewNeal
I'm not saying the socialist government of Venezuela has done everything right. Obviously, it hasn't. But you're totally wrong to say that socialist governments always take away individual rights. Some economic "rights" might have to be eliminated under a socialist system, but that's just the cost of creating a society in which people are truly free from billionaire oligarchs. When it comes to other freedoms, like freedom of speech and religious rights, socialism has even stronger protections than many capitalist countries.

 1

Throughout history, Karl Marx's socialist ideas have often been presented alongside false guarantees of personal freedom. The overwhelming majority of socialist and communist parties in the West today claim to support many traditional American values, such as free speech, free association, religious liberty, and equal justice under the law for all people. Yet, as any student of history will note, whenever followers of Marx's ideology have gained significant power, whether through force or through free elections, they have inevitably taken great strides to eliminate personal freedoms, especially free speech and religious freedom.

Although some socialists might say that collectivist governments who have silenced free speech have abandoned traditional socialist ideas, the truth is that the reason free-speech rights seemingly always crumble whenever socialists gain power is that at its foundation, socialism is primarily concerned with empowering the "collective," not the individual. People are nearly always guaranteed "rights" in socialist systems, but those rights are meaningless, because in socialism, the rights of the individual never supersede what's considered to be for the good of the collective. And who decides that? The collective, of course—or, more accurately, a vast bureaucratic administrative state that claims to be operating on behalf of the collective.

But don't take my word for it. Socialists have a long track record of making these very same arguments—all while paying lip service to "free speech" and "religious liberty." For example, these ideas were expressed clearly in a 2017 article by Jonah ben Avraham in the *Socialist Worker*, a publication of the International Socialist Organization.[29] In his article, titled "Looking Closer at Free Speech," ben Avraham wrote that "we must also not make the mistake, as many on the liberal left do, of fetishizing the call for freedom of speech for all . . . Our ultimate goal is to smash fascism, along with capitalism, and build a new world in which racist, sexist and any number of other oppressive conclusions are unthinkable."

A.D.D. MOMENT

MAO'S "HUNDRED FLOWERS CAMPAIGN"

In 1956, the Chinese government under Mao Zedong began a campaign to enhance freedom of speech, inviting criticism of the Chinese Communist Party and their policies. Invoking language from Chinese classical history, "Let a hundred flowers bloom, and a hundred schools of thought contend," it appeared as though freedom of speech was being encouraged. However, this did not last long.

Criticism of the party grew, critical literature and posters spread, and the openness to free expression faded. Mao signaled that the criticism had started to go too far, and retribution soon followed. Mao's political opponents were silenced. Many lost their jobs; others were forced into manual labor or even prison.[d]

"Our freedom of speech is a freedom of speech that helps us accomplish that goal," he added.

For this writer of the *Socialist Worker*, personal freedoms are intricately tied to socialists' goal of liberating the world from the alleged tyranny created by free markets—as strange as that sounds. In other words, the purpose of individual rights is to accomplish the goals of the collective, all at the expense of at least some individuals.

The writer expands on this concept even more clearly when addressing the specific question of whether governments should silence "hate speech":

> ONE COMMON ANSWER IS "NO PLATFORM FOR FASCISTS."
> FASCISTS, THE ARGUMENT GOES, POSE AN EXISTENTIAL THREAT
> TO NOT ONLY THE LEFT, BUT OPPRESSED PEOPLE, AND MUST
> THEREFORE BE STOPPED AT EVERY TURN FROM HAVING ANY
> HEARING. BY THIS LOGIC, ANY ACTION THAT SHUTS DOWN THE
> RIGHT-BE IT AN INDIVIDUAL ACT OF TERRORISM, THE ACTIONS
> OF A SMALL CLIQUE OF ANARCHISTS OR THE MOBILIZATION OF A
> LARGE MASS OF PEOPLE-IS A VICTORY FOR THE LEFT.
>
> THERE IS MUCH TO BE SYMPATHETIC TOWARD IN THIS ARGUMENT.
> THE THOUGHT THAT "FREEDOM OF SPEECH," A RIGHT MEANT
> TO PROTECT THE ABILITY OF MINORITIES TO ADVOCATE FOR
> THEMSELVES EVEN UNDER AN UNFRIENDLY GOVERNMENT, COULD
> APPLY TO NEO-NAZIS LIKE RICHARD SPENCER WHO OPENLY CALL
> FOR ETHNIC CLEANSING IS REPULSIVE.
>
> INDEED, AS SOCIALISTS FIGHTING TO PROTECT FREE SPEECH,
> OUR TASK IS NOT TO DEFEND HATE SPEECH AS AN ACT OF
> PROTECTED POLITICAL SPEECH. WHILE LIBERAL ORGANIZATIONS
> LIKE THE ACLU MAY FIND THE MOST PRESSING TASK OF THE
> DAY TO BE THE LEGAL DEFENSE OF THE NEXT KKK RALLY, WE
> SHOULD SPEAK AGAINST THE RIGHT OF GENOCIDAL SPEAKERS OR
> POLITICAL AGENTS TO HAVE THEIR MESSAGE HEARD.[30]

This is a particularly good description of what many socialists believe about free speech, and it helps to explain why so many on the left are working hard today to silence conservative voices on college campuses, social media platforms, and in other public spaces. For many socialists, "free speech" means you have the power to speak freely—if your goals align with theirs. If you are working to advance capitalism or some other goal deemed to be "racist" or "oppressive," which could be just about anything these days, then they believe you shouldn't be allowed to express your views publicly, because doing so is perceived to be a threat to the collective.

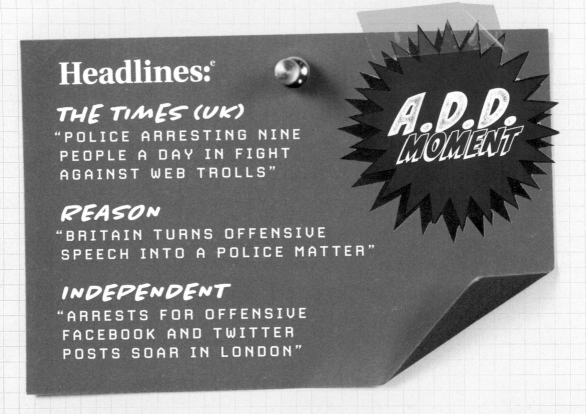

Headlines:[e]

THE TIMES (UK)
"POLICE ARRESTING NINE PEOPLE A DAY IN FIGHT AGAINST WEB TROLLS"

REASON
"BRITAIN TURNS OFFENSIVE SPEECH INTO A POLICE MATTER"

INDEPENDENT
"ARRESTS FOR OFFENSIVE FACEBOOK AND TWITTER POSTS SOAR IN LONDON"

A.D.D. MOMENT

This distorted understanding of individual liberty was codified in the Soviet Union's constitution, which not only promised to protect rights like freedom of speech and religious liberty, but also guaranteed "rights" to all sorts of goods and services. Article 35 of the 1977 Soviet Constitution guaranteed equal rights for women. Article 40 promised a guaranteed job. Article 41 guaranteed a "right to rest and leisure." Article

42 guaranteed "free, qualified medical care provided by state health institutions." Article 43 promised that the state would take care of all elderly citizens, as well as those suffering from illnesses, "partial disability," and even when there is a "loss of the breadwinner." Article 44 guaranteed a right to housing. Article 45 promised free education. And Article 50 promised "freedom of speech, of the press, and of assembly, meetings, street processions and demonstrations."[31]

I could go on, but I think you get the point. On paper, Soviet citizens were guaranteed numerous "rights." How, then, did the Soviets justify committing mass murder, imprisoning dissenters, silencing free speech, and cracking down on religious expression? Well, as any good lawyer will tell you, you've got to read the fine print. Article 39 reads, "Citizens of the USSR enjoy in full the social, economic, political and personal rights and freedoms proclaimed and guaranteed by the Constitution of the USSR and by Soviet laws. The socialist system ensures enlargement of the rights and freedoms of citizens and continuous improvement of their living standards as social, economic, and cultural development programmes are fulfilled."

As a socialist, this probably sounds peachy, right? Free health care, guaranteed job with a living wage, free education, and free speech—what's not to like? But here comes the killer. At the end of Article 39, the Constitution states, "Enjoyment by citizens of their rights and freedoms must not be to the detriment of the interests of society or the state, or infringe the rights of other citizens."

Silly Soviet citizens, you probably thought your constitutional "rights" were real, but it turns out, there was a big, fat, ugly asterisk: Your rights "must not be to the detriment of the interests of society or the state." And who decides whether your individual rights are "to the detriment" of the interests of the larger society or state? Why, the government, of course. It's like going to an all-you-can-eat buffet, only to find out everything is tofu, vegan, and gluten-free because serving steak and ham is seen as a "detriment" to society. *AUTHOR'S NOTE—* *THIS BUFFET SCENARIO WILL HAPPEN SOONER THAN LATER IN AMERICA IF THE AOCS OF THE WORLD HAVE ANYTHING TO SAY ABOUT IT!* →

AOC

You see, in socialism, the idea that individuals have inalienable, eternal rights is a giant myth, comparable to the Loch Ness monster or Big Foot. People hear stories, see faded black-and-white photographs, and think, "Yeah, sure, why can't Big Foot be real?" But sooner or later, people realize that the Big Foot that lurked around town was really just Crazy Cousin Cletus in a bear costume after having one too many six-packs of Pabst Blue Ribbon.

The ideas presented by the writer in the *Socialist Worker* and those espoused in the Soviet Constitution aren't cherry-picked examples, either. They show a nearly universal understanding of what individual liberty means in a socialist society, where the collective is always the primary focus. It's not that all socialists hate freedom per se, or that they all want to force people to violate their religious beliefs; it's that they know the only way to make a socialist industry or society run is if everyone gives up his or her individual rights. Collective property ownership and management requires all people to be working and living cohesively. Dissent can only get in the way of the goals of the majority. Just one regular Joe endowed with inalienable rights from nature—or, even more problematic, from God—poses a risk to the entire socialist way of life.

Some socialists might object and say that freedom of speech is possible in a socialist model and that many modern socialist parties and groups in the West adamantly support free speech. That's true, but so did the Soviets. And so did Hugo Chavez and the other socialists in Venezuela—before he started confiscating the nation's radio stations to spew propaganda. Socialists *always* promise that they will protect individual rights, but, as the Soviet Constitution makes clear, not if those rights get in the way of some other, supposedly more important societal goal.

Rashida Resistance @AOC_2024_Squad4Life
Ok, but @glennbeck, that's the Soviet Union and Venezuela. That's not America. Socialists and progressives in America don't believe in limiting religious freedom and freedom of speech.

💬 1   🔁   ♡

That's what they'll tell you, sure, but American liberals and progressives have a long history of taking away individuals' rights in order to accomplish some larger "collective" goal.

CALIFORNIA ALIEN LAND ACT

In 1913, California governor Hiram Johnson, Theodore Roosevelt's 1912 Progressive Party vice presidential running mate, signed into law the California Alien Land Act, which essentially made it impossible for Japanese immigrants who had yet to become American citizens to own land in the state of California. Any Japanese immigrant caught illicitly owning real property was forced to transfer ownership to the state.[32] Johnson's justification for the bill was that he claimed it would benefit the majority population of California, white American citizens, especially white farmers.

INTERNMENT OF JAPANESE AMERICANS

During World War II, progressive president Franklin Delano Roosevelt forced nearly 120,000 people of Japanese descent, including many American citizens, into government-run internment camps.[33] How did he justify these ruthless actions? Roosevelt insisted they were necessary because in the wake of the Pearl Harbor attacks, people of Japanese descent posed a threat to the country at large. In other words, taking away these Japanese Americans' rights was considered to be good for the collective.

Progressive California attorney general Earl Warren, who would later become the chief justice of the U.S. Supreme Court, supported Roosevelt's internment of Japanese Americans. As the Franklin Roosevelt Presidential Library and Museum

notes, Warren's support for the measure was due in part because he believed "there was no way to distinguish loyal and disloyal Japanese Americans."[34]

A.D.D. MOMENT

JAPANESE AMERICANS, INTERNMENT, DEMOCRACY, & THE U.S. GOVERNMENT

"Camps helped cripple Japanese business well beyond the end of the war, since as Douglas Carey noted: 'Over 110,000 Japanese civilians were detained in this way. Not one of them had been accused of any crime. After the war was over, the majority of those detained went home to find their property looted and destroyed.'

"In a democracy, this is of course a win-win situation for the majority. The democratic system ensured that the Japanese, as a small minority, possessed virtually no political power either on the West Coast or nationally, and were therefore at the mercy of the state. The few politicians who provided even mild resistance to stripping the Japanese of all rights, such as Colorado governor Ralph Carr, were promptly voted out of office.

"The U.S. government has never repudiated the legal principle behind concentration camps, and maintains the legal right to use them again."[f]

PRESIDENT JOHNSON'S REAL CIVIL RIGHTS RECORD

Another example is found when examining progressive hero President Lyndon Johnson's career. Johnson fought against every single civil rights bill that had been proposed during his first two decades serving in Congress.[35,36] It was only late in his political career, when Johnson recognized there were important political advantages to supporting civil rights legislation, that he shifted course and officially backed the 1964 Civil Rights Act, which he privately referred to as "the nigger bill."

RELIGIOUS LIBERTY AND THE AFFORDABLE CARE ACT

Another example is the Affordable Care Act (ACA), the signature piece of legislation for progressive President Barack Obama, who had deep ties to radical socialists. The ACA included provisions that forced businesses to pay for contraception coverage, including birth control pills, even if those services violated the religious beliefs of the business owners providing coverage. In 2014, the Supreme Court struck down that provision in a variety of circumstances in *Burwell v. Hobby Lobby Stores*. The Obama administration argued that the provisions should be upheld because allowing business owners to deny coverage for birth control pills and other contraceptives would put employees at these companies at a disadvantage, a view the progressive justices of the court like Ruth Bader Ginsburg agreed with and espoused in the Court's dissenting opinion.

Or, put more simply, the Obama administration and progressive wing of the Supreme Court believed the importance of providing women with morning-after pills was greater than the religious rights of individuals. Here again, we can see that "rights" only exist when they don't get in the way of some larger progressive or socialist goal.

A.D.D. MOMENT

He [Lyndon Johnson] once asked his African-American chauffeur Robert Parker if he would prefer to be called by his name rather than some pejorative term such as "boy," "nigger," or "chief." When Parker had the temerity to say he preferred to be called by his own name, Johnson reportedly responded: "As long as you are black, and you're gonna be black till the day you die, no one's gonna call you by your goddamn name. So no matter what you are called, nigger, you just let it roll off your back like water, and you'll make it. Just pretend you're a goddamn piece of furniture."

FROM PG. 131 IN MY BOOK LIARS →

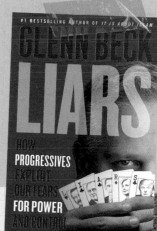

#1 BESTSELLING AUTHOR OF *IT IS ABOUT ISLAM*

GLENN BECK

LIARS

HOW PROGRESSIVES EXPLOIT OUR FEARS FOR POWER AND CONTROL

SINGLE-PAYER ABORTION

Additionally, all of the Democratic Socialists—eh, we can just say Democrats—running in the 2020 presidential primary have said they support imposing a government-run health care system or greatly expanding government health care programs, and that in either case, government would use taxpayer dollars to fund abortion services. Democrats are promoting taxpayer-funded abortions despite the fact more than 100 million Americans oppose abortion. And these are the religious beliefs of a huge percentage of Americans, not some small religious subset. Xenu help you if you're a Scientologist trying to defend your religious beliefs against the government collective.

And let's not forget that the call to eliminate Americans' Second Amendment right to own firearms—a view nearly all modern progressives and socialists hold in common—is based *entirely* on the belief that those individuals' right to possess a firearm for their protection and the protection of their communities should be outweighed by society's interests to limit gun violence.

The debate over gun rights is possibly the clearest example of how under a collectivist view of the world, perception is everything. Facts don't determine what is and isn't a right in socialism, and the elimination of individual rights doesn't need to be based on hard data or scientific studies. There is a mountain of evidence showing that there is no connection between legal gun ownership and crime. In fact, about two-thirds of all gun-related deaths are suicides,[37] and of the remaining 12,000 annual deaths, most are linked to illegal gun ownership. In many cases, they are also associated with gang violence.

Further, in an article for that notorious right-wing rag *The Washington Post*, statistician Leah Libresco, a self-described opponent of widespread gun ownership,

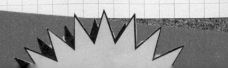

explained that research shows clearly gun control laws simply don't work, no matter how strict they are. "I researched the strictly tightened gun laws in Britain and Australia," Libresco wrote, "and concluded that they didn't prove much about what America's policy should be. Neither nation experienced drops in mass shootings or other gun-related crime that could be attributed to their buybacks and bans. Mass shootings were too rare in Australia for their absence after the buyback program to be clear evidence of progress. And in both Australia and Britain, the gun restrictions had an ambiguous effect on other gun-related crimes or deaths."[38]

Perhaps even more importantly, at minimum, *hundreds of thousands* of Americans have defended themselves using guns over the past decade. A 2013 study of firearm violence conducted by the U.S. Department of Justice's Bureau of Justice Statistics found surveys show from 2007 to 2011, there were at least 235,700 instances in which a victim of a criminal offense "used a firearm to threaten or attack an offender."[39] In another 103,000 instances, victims of property crimes used firearms to defend themselves.

Similarly, a 2013 study conducted by the National Academies' Institute of Medicine and National Research Council, at the request of the U.S. Centers for Disease Control and Prevention, found, "Almost all national survey estimates indicate that defensive gun uses by victims are at least as common as offensive uses by criminals, with estimates of annual uses ranging from about 500,000 to more than 3 million, in the context of about 300,000 violent crimes involving firearms in 2008."[40]

With all of this data, it's clear there is no scientific basis for the claim that legal gun ownership should be abolished or even significantly restricted, but that's exactly what socialists and others want to do. And if they had it their way, it wouldn't matter who has the best arguments or data. All that would matter is that a majority of people believe legal gun ownership causes more problems than it solves. That's why it has historically been so important for socialist regimes to control the press. If you can

DEMOCRATIC SOCIALISTS OF AMERICA HATE THE 2ND AMENDMENT

In an article posted on the Democratic Socialists of America's official website, titled "The Second Amendment Is a Threat to Us All," the authors make their case for the repeal of the Second Amendment. The authors even go so far as to write a new amendment, which would read:

SECTION 1. The second article of amendment to the Constitution of the United States is hereby repealed.

SECTION 2. The manufacturing, transportation or importation in or into any State, Territory, or possession of the United States for delivery or use therein of pump-action, semi-automatic or automatic firearms is hereby prohibited.

SECTION 3. This article shall be inoperative unless it shall have been ratified as an amendment to the Constitution by conventions in the several States, as provided in the Constitution, within ten years from the date of the submission hereof to the States by the Congress.

The authors clarify what this would mean for citizens of the United States, writing:

"In other words, you can have a gun, provided it is manually loaded. That means one bullet loaded in the gun, by hand, at a time. We think the compromise should satisfy amateur and hobbyist gun-owning constituencies. Hunters, sport-shooters and private individuals will still retain their right to access enough firepower to pursue their hobbies or to protect themselves."[g]

twist, turn, and manipulate the "facts" at will, you can add or eliminate so-called "rights" at will, giving the government significant power over society.

There has literally *never* been a country attempting to adopt a truly socialist model that has also maintained a commitment to individual rights. Eventually, the majority dismantles the rights of the minority, often by empowering a small, powerful group to rule over the rest of society as a representative of the collective. This was illustrated perfectly in a fine American documentary film, *Star Wars*, when democratically elected Chancellor Palpatine "reorganized" the Galactic Republic into an empire in order to ensure a "safe and secure society." And he did it with the consent of the majority. As Senator Amidala noted, "So this is how liberty dies, with thunderous applause." (And before you say it, yes, I apologize for using a *Star Wars* prequels reference. But at least I didn't use a Jar Jar Binks reference. I'll fit in an Original Trilogy callback by the end of the book, I promise.)

Marx would never say the elimination of every individual liberty is an essential characteristic of his utopian socialist model. (He opposed some calls to have government control speech in his lifetime.) But it's clear from history that socialist systems inevitably result in the destruction of virtually all individual rights. It's not only a necessary consequence of granting too much power to the majority in society, a core element of every socialist model ever created, but also a necessary part of having an economy in which all or most property is owned collectively and economic decisions are made by the majority at the expense of the minority population.

GHOST OF
KARL MARX

"YOU ARE HORRIFIED AT OUR INTENDING TO DO AWAY WITH PRIVATE PROPERTY. BUT IN YOUR EXISTING SOCIETY, PRIVATE PROPERTY IS ALREADY DONE AWAY WITH FOR NINE-TENTHS OF THE POPULATION; ITS EXISTENCE FOR THE FEW IS SOLELY DUE TO ITS NON-EXISTENCE IN THE HANDS OF THOSE NINE-TENTHS. YOU REPROACH US, THEREFORE, WITH INTENDING TO DO AWAY WITH A FORM OF PROPERTY, THE NECESSARY CONDITION FOR WHOSE EXISTENCE IS THE NON-EXISTENCE OF ANY PROPERTY FOR THE IMMENSE MAJORITY OF SOCIETY. IN ONE WORD, YOU REPROACH US WITH INTENDING TO DO AWAY WITH YOUR PROPERTY. PRECISELY SO; THAT IS JUST WHAT WE INTEND."

Karl, maybe you don't realize it—because, you know, you're dead—but a lot has changed over the past two centuries, and most of it completely contradicts some of your most important claims, including the one that capitalism makes it virtually impossible for working-class people to own property and move out of poverty. Over the past 55 years, the American home ownership rate has never been lower than 62.9 percent, the rate in 1965 and the lowest point following the 2008 financial crisis.[41] That means six in 10 Americans own real property in the United States, not one in 10, the figure you claimed was common in capitalist economies.

It's also worth noting that the vast majority of businesses in the United States are small businesses, not gigantic, multi-billion-dollar corporations. According to the U.S. Small Business Administration, there were 30.2 million small businesses in America in 2018, representing 99.9 percent of all businesses. And nearly half of all U.S. workers, about 47 percent, worked for a small business in 2018.[42]

Some socialists think these "small businesses" are only owned by millionaires and wealthy families, but that's also not true. The Small Business Administration reports, "The median income for individuals self-employed at their own incorporated businesses was $50,347 in 2016." Facts are often very inconvenient for socialists.

As these figures clearly show, the Marxist idea that the U.S. economy is controlled by a handful of billionaires simply isn't supported by any of the available data—which is particularly important to keep in mind because that narrative is one of the key justifications used by socialists when they call for seizing people's property, imposing huge wealth and income taxes, and restricting or even eliminating people's individual rights. "We have to do it," they say, "because if we don't, the ultra-powerful millionaires and billionaires will control all of society. Taking away their rights, wealth, and property is the only way to fix the problem."

Of course, history shows it never "fixes" anything. It destroys economies and leads to death and widespread misery. But hey, at least there's a "chicken in every pot," right? (Or, in some cases, I guess it's a rabbit with a bow tie.)

Rashida Resistance @AOC_2024_Squad4Life
Taking land, authoritarian dictators, the elimination of personal freedoms—this sounds like communism, not socialism. And I'm definitely not a communist!

💬 1   🔁   ♡

What I'm about to say might "trigger" you, but it's really important you try to hang with me. I know you think you're not a "communist," but it certainly sounds like you're a communist to me—a big, red, Marx-loving communist.

Rashida Resistance @AOC_2024_Squad4Life
.@glennbeck, how can you say that? I've told you countless times I don't support ruling classes or big authoritarian governments or gulags or anything like that. I'm a socialist. I believe in sharing wealth and collective property ownership, but I don't believe in big authoritarian states. You're just trying to red-bait me and other socialists who want to make the world a better place.

💬 1   🔁   ♡

Well, you took that about as well as I thought you would. I know a lot of socialists get upset when conservatives throw around the "C" word, but that's just proof that many people don't really understand the difference—or lack thereof—between socialism and communism. The reality (and unfortunate analogy) is that socialism and communism are kissing cousins.

Now, what I'm about to say is going to blow your mind, but by the time I'm finished, I believe the unthinkable is going to happen: You're going to agree with me, Glenn Beck, about communism.

One of the biggest problems people face in modern America is that they're always talking past each other, especially when it comes to politics and political philosophy. To many on the Left, everyone who votes for Donald Trump, or even has something nice to say about a policy he helped to put into place, is a "Nazi." And to many on the right, every Democrat is a "communist." The constant "us" versus "them" battles we're always fighting aren't helpful for a number of reasons, but one of the biggest is that no one ever bothers to take the time to *think*—I mean really think—about their terms, rendering them almost completely meaningless. I might as well just call you a ruthless authoritarian and you might as well call me a heartless, selfish, moral monster. After all, that's what most people mean when they say "communist" or "Nazi" today.

So, if we're going to have a real conversation about socialism, communism, or just about anything else, we need to be on the same page. When I say that you're a "communist," I don't mean that you're an authoritarian dictator who wants to murder everyone who doesn't agree with you. Yes, I think socialism and communism often lead to that, but I know that's not really what *you* want. What I mean by "communist" is that you support the ideological principles handed down by Marx and his followers—the same principles outlined in *The Communist Manifesto*. As we've already discussed, Marx was primarily interested in getting rid of ruling classes—and eventually all classes. He wanted all wealth to be controlled collectively throughout the entire world, because he believed that would be the only way to solve the world's problems and end "exploitation."

Marx didn't believe the final stage of human progress—communism—would involve dictators, prison camps, or any of the other tyrannical things that became associated with communist parties in the twentieth century. He thought people would be freer than ever, because they'd have all the wealth they'd need to live without having to toil away in fields or factories for 100 hours per week. He also thought people would be much happier, because they wouldn't have to worry about starving, losing access to health care services, or being unable to pay their bills. Marx and many other communists believed they were building a world without big, powerful institutions, militaries, or even money. (Yes, that's right, money. If everyone shares all of their wealth collectively, there's no reason to have money. Everyone just gets what they need.) So, in its final form, I think you can say Marxism is for wildly idealistic utopian kooks—no offense, of course—but certainly not tyrants.

 Rashida Resistance @AOC_2024_Squad4Life
Well, that certainly sounds more in line with what I believe, but how do I know what you're saying is accurate? I've never heard anyone talk about communism in this way. Why should I trust that you've got it right?

 1 ♡

Here's another thing we can agree on: You shouldn't. Don't take my word for it. You should do your own homework. But don't be lazy about it. It's really easy to find bad, misleading, inaccurate information about "communism."

In the interest of time, here are a few important examples of socialists talking about communism and the difference between their ideology in communism. Maybe you don't trust *me*, but shouldn't you trust their own words?

In 2019, *Jacobin* magazine, perhaps the most popular and influential socialist publication in the United States, interviewed Paige Kreisman, a socialist who ran for Oregon's 42nd House District in 2020, and their discussion covers the whole "socialism vs. communism" question better than just about anything I've seen in recent years.[43] Kreisman is a transgender woman and a member of the Democratic Socialists of America—the largest socialist organization in America—as well as the Communist Party. So, Kreisman is literally a communist *and* a socialist, and the revealing interview is conducted by a notable socialist publication. We couldn't possibly get further away from "Glenn Beck" than this interview.

At one point during the interview, *Jacobin* asked Kreisman, "Do you see any difference terminologically between socialist and communist?" The following is Kreisman's answer, *exactly* as published by *Jacobin*: "It means different things to different people, you know, it varies. I typically don't lead with 'I'm a communist.' I don't have it in my literature that I'm a communist, though I'm open about it. I call myself a democratic socialist, not just because it has less stigma, but also, I think it's more accurate."

"I'm a Marxist," Kreisman added, "so in dialectical materialism, communism is a mode of production after socialism, characterized by a classless, stateless, currency-less society. That's something that in my mind might as well exist only in theory. Maybe it's possible for us to get there someday, but it's not something that I think we should be worrying about right now. Right now, we need to get to socialism. I don't think we're ever going to be fighting to get from socialism to communism in my lifetime."

So, where does socialism fit into all of this? If socialism involves the collective ownership and management of wealth and communism also involves the collective ownership and management of wealth, then what the heck is the difference? Truthfully, *not much.*

> "IN THEORY SOCIALISM MAY WISH TO ENHANCE FREEDOM, BUT IN PRACTICE EVERY KIND OF COLLECTIVISM CONSISTENTLY CARRIED THROUGH MUST PRODUCE THE CHARACTERISTIC FEATURES WHICH FASCISM, NAZISM AND COMMUNISM HAVE IN COMMON. TOTALITARIANISM IS NOTHING BUT CONSISTENT COLLECTIVISM, THE RUTHLESS EXECUTION OF THE PRINCIPLE THAT 'THE WHOLE COMES BEFORE THE INDIVIDUAL' AND THE DIRECTION OF ALL MEMBERS OF SOCIETY BY A SINGLE WILL SUPPOSED TO REPRESENT THE 'WHOLE.'"[h]

-HAYEK

As Kreisman notes, communism is essentially a final stage of socialism, one "characterized by a classless, stateless, currency-less society." That doesn't necessarily mean it's a different society, though, just a more "advanced" version of a society that has embraced collectivist principles. Marx's communism is the utopian end goal for most of today's socialists. They don't necessarily think it will happen, because, well, people don't want to live in a "classless, stateless, currency-less society," but many socialists hope that we'll eventually get there. And Marx didn't just believe we could get there; he believed it was inevitably going to happen.

Like I mentioned previously, socialism is a big-tent ideology, just like "liberalism" and "conservatism." And in the same way you can have a lot of different kinds of "conservatives"—fiscal conservatives, hawks, doves, social conservatives, libertarian conservatives, etc.—there are many shades of "socialism," and communism is, in many ways, a type of "socialism." In its final stage, communism is a utopian, more "perfect" version of socialism.

But if communism is really just a more advanced stage of socialistic thinking, why wouldn't people like Kreisman choose to regularly call themselves "communists"? Kreisman answered that question later in the *Jacobin* interview, explaining, "The Communist Party used to be a really strong and deeply embedded with the revolutionary movement and the antiwar movement in the seventies. But through the Reagan years, and through the nineties and after the dissolution of the Soviet Union, the party really took a big hit and our membership dipped, and our tactics shifted very drastically. Now we're starting to come back."

Translation: The Soviet Union's failure made "communism" a *really* unpopular word in the United States, even among self-described communists. Huh. I guess even communists don't like being associated with losers. *Rocky IV* must have been a trying experience for American commies.

Kreisman isn't alone in her understanding of socialism and communism. In fact, Kreisman's view is supported by socialist and communist literature. In a 1978 article for the *Socialist Standard*, a publication of the Socialist Party of Great Britain, Adam Buick addressed the differences between "socialism" and "communism" in detail.[44] According to Buick, one of the primary reasons so many are confused about the two terms is that Vladimir Lenin and the radical Bolsheviks of revolutionary-era Russia incorrectly started treating the terms "communism" and "socialism" as though they involved completely separate societies, even though they had previously had a much closer meaning.

"The word communism (which Marx preferred as the word to describe future society) has . . . come to be associated with the State capitalist police dictatorships in Russia, China and other such countries," Buick wrote. "This goes back to a decision of the Bolsheviks in 1918 to change the name of their party from Social Democratic to Communist Party. They did this to distinguish themselves from the Social Democratic parties of the rest of Europe which had so shamefully betrayed the working class over the war [World War I]. From then on communist has been used to describe supporters of Russia, inaccurately since it is not communism in its original sense of common ownership . . ."[45]

Later in the same article, Buick says Lenin's use of "socialism" and "communism" was a "gross distortion" of what Karl Marx had written and what socialists and communists had advocated for during the previous decades. Buick wrote, this "innovation . . . was to make 'socialism' and 'communism' thus defined successive societies after the abolition of capitalism and to attribute this view to Marx (a gross distortion since Marx made no such distinction: he only distinguished a 'first phase' of 'communist society' when there would still have to be some restrictions on individual consumption . . . from a 'higher phase' when the principle 'from each according to his abilities, to each according to his needs' would apply, but these were phases of the same society based on common ownership and democratic control and not successive, separate societies)."

SOCIALISM

I CAN'T BELIEVE IT'S NOT COMMUNISM!

"LOOKS LIKE DEMOCRACY! SPREADS LIKE CANCER."

NEW LOOK, SAME UNBELIEVABLE POLITICS

I can't believe it's not **Communism**

IMPROVED

This view appears to be supported, at least in part, by the writings of Fredrick Engels, who co-authored *The Communist Manifesto* with Marx. If ever there were anyone you should trust to help us understand the differences between communism and socialism, it's Engels.

In 1888, five years after Marx died, an English translation of *The Communist Manifesto*—titled *Manifesto of the Communist Party*—was published in Chicago. This "authorized" English version of the *Manifesto* had been edited by Engels himself, who also wrote the preface. In the preface, Engels, quite revealingly, suggests that *The Communist Manifesto* should be considered a form of "Socialist literature," strongly indicating he believed communism to be well within the sphere of socialist thinking.[46]

"Thus the history of the *Manifesto* reflects, to a great extent, the history of the modern working-class movement," Engels wrote, adding, "at present it is undoubtedly the most widespread, the most international production of all Socialist literature, the common platform acknowledged by millions of working men from Siberia to California."

Interestingly, Engels also explained in the preface why he and Marx didn't adopt the use of the term "socialist" at the time they wrote the first edition of *The Communist Manifesto*. According to Engels, socialism was considered to be too "utopian" and often consisted of "quacks" who were more interested in social causes than the plight of the working class.

"Yet, when it [*Communist Manifesto*] was written," Engels wrote, "we could not have called it a Socialist Manifesto. By Socialists, in 1847, were understood, on the one hand, the adherents of the various Utopian systems: Owenites in England, Fourierists in France, both of them already reduced to the position of mere sects, and gradually dying out; on the other hand, the most multifarious social quacks, who, by all manners of tinkering, professed to redress, without any danger to capital and profit, all sorts of social grievances, in both cases men outside the working class movement, and looking rather to the 'educated' classes for support. . . . Thus, Socialism was, in 1847, a middle-class movement, Communism a working-class movement. . . . And as our notion, from the very beginning, was that 'the emancipation of the working class must be the act of the working class itself,' there could be no doubt as to which of the two names we must take."

In the latter half of the nineteenth century, the goals of Europe's "socialist" parties and movements again shifted to be more in line with the views of Marx and Engels, leading to Engels again classifying himself as a "socialist." But the truth is, the commitment to collective property ownership had never changed between the two camps. They *always* shared nearly identical goals.

All right, enough history. Let's boil all of this down into a few helpful definitions we can agree upon:

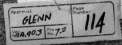

CAPITALISM
DEFINITION

capitalism *noun*

[cap·i·tal·ism | \ ˈka-pə-tə-ˌliz-əm \]

is "an economic system characterized by private or corporate ownership of capital goods, by investments that are determined by private decision, and by prices, production, and the distribution of goods that are determined mainly by competition in a free market."[47]

Or, put in simple terms: In free-market capitalism, I own personal property, you own personal property, and we're able to exchange that property by using money or bartering.

FREE-MARKET CAPITALISM
DEFINITION

Free-market capitalism with a "safety net" *noun*

[cap·i·tal·ism | \ ˈka-pə-tə-ˌliz-əm \]

is a market-based, capitalistic economy that includes publicly funded social safety nets for those who are unable to support themselves. Free-market capitalism with a "safety net" is *not* a socialist system. It is the free market that allows countries with safety nets to be able to raise enough in tax revenue to provide generous benefits in their welfare programs.

socialism *noun*

[so·cial·ism | \ ˈsō-shə-ˌli-zəm \]

is an economic system in which property is, to varying degrees, collectively owned and managed, and wealth is distributed to people according to their needs, not their desires.

LISM
DEFINITION

It's a big-tent political and economic philosophy that includes many different ideas, but they all hold two things in common: property is collectively owned and decisions are made collectively, destroying the rights of individuals.

The Socialist Party USA's (SPUSA) definition of socialism is in line with this view. In its "Statement of Principles," the SPUSA says that in its socialist model, "the people own and control the means of production and distribution through democratically controlled public agencies, cooperatives, or other collective groups. The primary goal of economic activity is to provide the necessities of life, including food, shelter, health care, education, child care, cultural opportunities, and social services."[48]

communism *noun*

[com·mun·ism | \ ˈkom-yuh-niz-uh m \]

is one of several different socialist systems. In the final stage of communism, nearly all property is collectively owned and managed, and wealth is distributed to people according to their needs, not their desires.

COMMUNISM
DEFINITION

This reflects the views espoused by Marx and Engels, who wrote in *The Communist Manifesto*, "The distinguishing feature of Communism is not the abolition of property generally, but the abolition of bourgeois [those who control capital] property. But modern bourgeois private property is the final and most complete expression of the system of producing and appropriating products, that is based on class antagonisms, on the exploitation of the many by the few. In this sense, the theory of the Communists may be summed up in the single sentence: Abolition of private property."

Put simply, the only real difference between communists and socialists is that virtually all Marxist communists eventually want their societies to become "classless, stateless, [and] currency-less," although they don't necessarily believe that will happen soon, just as Kreisman stated in the *Jacobin* interview. Many socialists also want a "classless, stateless, currency-less society," and can thus fairly be called communists, but not necessarily all socialists believe this; some socialists would say we shouldn't take collective property ownership and management to Marx's final stage of "development." It's also worth noting the early stages of communism—before all wealth and property have been completely redistributed—are completely indistinguishable from just about every kind of socialism that's popular in the West today.

SOMETHING TO THINK ABOUT

IN OUR MODERN FREE-MARKET SYSTEM, PEOPLE ARE VOLUNTARILY CHOOSING TO SHARE GOODS AND SERVICES WITHOUT MANDATES FROM GOVERNMENT.

THROUGH SERVICES LIKE UBER AND LYFT, WE SHARE CARS.

THROUGH SERVICES LIKE AIRBNB, WE SHARE VACATION HOMES.

THROUGH SERVICES LIKE RENT THE RUNWAY, WE SHARE HIGH-END CLOTHES.

PRIVATE PROPERTY OWNERSHIP CAN ALSO BE COLLECTIVE!

So, it's not fair to say all socialists are communists—even though many are, and they don't even know it—but, in practice, all communists are also socialists.

There's a really easy test you can take to determine whether you're a communist. It only consists of one question and there is no "wrong" answer. (Sounds like my kind of test.) Are you ready for it?

Rashida Resistance @AOC_2024_Squad4Life
Yes, I'm ready, @glennbeck.

💬 1   ⟲   ♡

Ok, here we go: Do you think that it would be great if we could someday transform America into a country where everyone, including all businesses, shares all their wealth collectively and peacefully? It doesn't have to happen tomorrow, next week, or even this century. It could take hundreds of years to achieve, but in your *perfect* world, is that ultimately what you'd like to see happen?

Rashida Resistance @AOC_2024_Squad4Life
Yes, in a perfect world, we'd all share our wealth.

💬 1   ⟲   ♡

Ding, ding, ding. Congratulations! You're officially a communist. What have we got for our commie contestant, Bob? What's that? A slightly used Che Guevara T-shirt and a "get out of bread line free" pass. Wow! Soon, you'll be the talk of the commune with that beautiful used shirt. But don't forget, it doesn't belong to you. This shirt belongs to the community now, along with all your other stuff.

GHOST OF KARL MARX

"OH, WOW. CAN I PLAY, GLENN? I WANT TO PLAY. I REALLY THINK I COULD WIN THIS ONE."

Sorry, Ghost Karl. No cheating. We already know how you'd do on our little game show. You'll just have to wait in the bread line along with all the other comrades.

Rashida Resistance @AOC_2024_Squad4Life
Ok, @glennbeck. Very funny. But let's get back to the real issues here. You say socialism and communism are dangerous, but none of what I'm hearing sounds very dangerous to me. What's so wrong with societies collectively sharing wealth?

💬 1   🔁   ♡

Look, if you and a bunch of your socialist friends want to go start a soybean commune in upstate New York, go right ahead. I like soybeans just as much as the next guy—which is to say, I *hate* them and loathe their very existence—but if that's what floats your boat, then by all means, float away. All I'm asking is that you leave me and the other 7 billion people in the world alone. We don't want to farm soybeans with you. If you and your pals would stop trying to take all of *our* hard-earned wealth and property away from us, all would be well.

The biggest problem with socialism and communism isn't that it's impossible for some small group of people to voluntarily live together collectively, it's that socialists and communists want to use government to force people like me to live by *your* rules. You want to take my freedom away from me—and billions of others too—so that you can build *your* perfect socialist society. That's where everything falls apart. Socialism and communism are inherently authoritarian systems and completely incompatible with having a nation of free people, because in a nation of free people, most will always choose not to engage in socialism voluntarily. The only way to take their property and wealth, then, is to forcefully seize it from them, just as Marx suggested in *Communist Manifesto*. To enact socialism on a large scale, you must have force and control.

Rashida Resistance @AOC_2024_Squad4Life
Well, that's just not true, @glennbeck. I don't favor any form of authoritarianism. I am a democratic socialist. I would never back a system that has one ruthless dictator at the top of society making all societal decisions. I know that's what right-wing radio and television personalities like you think all socialists believe, but it's just not true. I only support democratic socialism, and democracy is obviously never authoritarian.

♡ 1   ↩   ♡

I've been listening to socialists speak and reading socialist literature for years now, and I have no doubt that nearly all the socialist groups in America and Europe believe that they are committed to democracy. The Socialist Party USA's "Statement of Principles," which we already discussed a little earlier, clearly indicates that organization's socialist model includes democratic principles. According to SPUSA,

"In a socialist system the people own and control the means of production and distribution through democratically controlled public agencies, cooperatives, or other collective groups."

The Communist Party USA declares on its website that it actively promotes "unity, equality, [and] democracy."[49]

The United States' largest socialist organization—boasting a membership list that includes U.S. Reps. Alexandria Ocasio-Cortez, D-N.Y., and Rashida Tlaib, D-Mich.— even included "democracy" in its organization's name: the *Democratic* Socialists of America.

Of course, history has shown that many socialist societies, including some of those that had the most horrific, violent, authoritarian regimes ever to walk the Earth, started as democracies and then transformed—some more quickly than others— into dictatorships. But we'll get to that later. For now, let's pretend it's possible to have a socialist society that maintains its commitment to democracy. That doesn't mean those people are "free" in any meaningful sense. On its own, democracy can be just as tyrannical as any other form of government.

Rashida Resistance @AOC_2024_Squad4Life
Of course it can't, @glennbeck. Democracy is, by its very nature, supportive of freedom.

💬 1   ↻   ♡

Oh, really? I wonder if those Japanese Americans who were forced during World War II into concentration camps by the U.S. government—solely because of their race— would agree that democracy is always supportive of freedom.

LiBERTY vs. DEMOCRACY

Author, political theorist, and one of the founders of the American libertarian movement, Rose Wilder Lane explains the shortcomings of pure democracy in an essay titled "Democracy." The following is an excerpt:

As Madison says, some common passion or interest will sway a majority. And because a majority supports the ruler whom a majority chooses, nothing checks his use of force against the minority. So the ruler of a democracy quickly becomes a tyrant. And that is the swift and violent death of the democracy.

This always occurs, invariably. It is as certain as death and taxes. It occurred in Athens twenty-five centuries ago. It occurred in France in 1804, when an overwhelming majority elected the Emperor Napoleon. It occurred in Germany in 1932, when a majority of Germans—swayed by a common passion for food and social order—elected Hitler.

Madison stated the historic fact: in democracy there is nothing to check the inducements to sacrifice the weaker party. There is no protection for liberty. Hence it is, that democracies always destroy personal security (the Gestapo, the concentration camps) and the rights of property (what rights of property ownership are there in Europe, now?) and are as short in their lives as they are violent in their deaths.[1]

And what would African Americans living in the South in the nineteenth century say if you asked them whether democracy guaranteed they would be free? Countless Jim Crow laws were imposed on African Americans throughout the southern states by *democratically elected* state and local governments. Jim Crow laws severely restricted job opportunities for blacks, forced African American children to attend different schools and play in different parks than their white peers, and required black Americans to be treated as second-class citizens in virtually every aspect of life. In New Orleans, officials even segregated prostitution.

And here's a fun fact for you: Jim Crow laws were used by the Nazis as a model for their own racist policies. In 1935, the Nazis passed the Law for the Protection of German Blood and German Honor and the Reich Citizenship Law, which are commonly known as the Nuremberg Laws.[50] These laws would become the foundation of the Holocaust. As recorded in an article for History.com, James Whitman, author of *Hitler's American Model*, noted, "America in the early 20th century was the leading racist jurisdiction in the world. Nazi lawyers, as a result, were interested in, looked very closely at, were ultimately influenced by American race law."

The Nazis were especially interested in those racist state laws that prohibited certain kinds of interracial marriage.

"America had, by a wide margin, the harshest law of this kind," Whitman said. "In particular, some of the state laws threatened severe criminal punishment for interracial marriage. That was something radical Nazis were very eager to do in Germany as well."

Racist laws aren't the only examples of democratically elected governments eliminating individual liberty. In 1838, Missouri's democratically elected government, led by Gov. Lilburn W. Boggs, issued an "extermination order" against Mormons in the state, allowing and even encouraging armed vigilantes to commit acts of violence against Mormons in an effort to drive them out of Missouri.[51]

In the late nineteenth century, U.S. Sen. James Blaine, who had previously served as the Speaker of the House of Representatives, unsuccessfully led a campaign to create a new constitutional amendment that would have banned government funding for private religious schools nationwide. Although this might sound as though the amendment was meant to be an anti-religion law, the proposed constitutional amendment was actually meant to target Roman Catholic schools.[52]

In the nineteenth century, most schools in America, including government-run school systems, were decidedly Protestant institutions and included certain activities Roman Catholic parents found objectionable. As a result, Catholics opened schools throughout the country and sought government funding to help keep the schools in operation. At the time, many states were composed of Protestant majorities, and they didn't like the idea of their tax dollars funding Catholic schools. Even though the federal constitutional amendment effort failed, dozens of states across the country passed state constitutional amendments that made it impossible for private schools to receive government funding.

Today, 37 states continue to have these so-called "Blaine Amendments" in place, although legislators and courts now use them to effectively block government funding for any kind of religious education. Ironically, many Protestant groups are now the leading proponents of repealing Blaine Amendments.

I could go on and on and on with more examples of how democracy is no guarantee of a free society, but I think you get the point. (Though I'm always nervous when making assumptions like this about socialists.)

Democratically elected governments have done all sorts of horrible things throughout the course of history, because an elected legislature can take your rights and freedoms away just as easily as a single tyrant or military dictatorship can. Just because a majority of people in society voted those officials into office doesn't make the actions of those governments any less tyrannical.

Rashida Resistance @AOC_2024_Squad4Life
Ok. So, let me get this straight: You don't like dictatorships or authoritarian governments. You don't like monarchies either, I'm sure. And now you're telling me democracy is no good either? What are you, then? An anarchist?

💬 1   ↺   ♡

Of course I'm not an anarchist. Government has an essential role to play in society, but that role is not to manage and control every aspect of our lives, it's primarily to protect the rights of every individual person—not just from foreign invaders, but from other citizens, too.

I know it might come as a surprise to you, but these conversations have been going on for centuries, even here in the United States. When America's Founding Fathers drafted our Constitution, they had already thought many of these concerns through, relying in large part on thousands of years of historical data. Our Founders knew that authoritarian governments created numerous problems, but they also knew that on its own, democracy could be just as dangerous. That's why when they created the United States, they enshrined numerous individual rights into the supreme law for our country, the Constitution. The entire purpose of the Bill of Rights was to guarantee that individuals would always have those protections, regardless of what the rest of society wants.

A.D.D. MOMENT

BUILDING THE NANNY STATE

One of the most important aspects of the U.S. Constitution is that it is a charter of "negative liberties," which means it's primarily concerned with preventing government from causing harm and damaging or destroying individual rights.

What many on the Left, including socialists, want is a constitution with "positive" rights, which would guarantee the government will provide certain goods and services-like "free" health care, "free" college," and "free" childcare services. Under such a system, most "rights" amount to nothing more than government entitlements; it puts government in charge of virtually every aspect of life. A far-reaching nanny state such as this would be almost impossible to implement under our current constitutional system. That's why socialists and progressives work so hard to put justices in America's courts who believe the Constitution is a "living document" that can be reinterpreted far beyond what America's Founders ever imagined.

Democratic republics are the best forms of government that have ever been created—but only when they exist alongside constitutional protections for individuals. Those protections are essential, because they put restraints on a society's majority, making it much more difficult to take away the rights of individuals.

Socialism, even democratic socialism, flips this entire way of thinking on its head. Instead of giving rights to individual people, it grants all of the power in society to the majority and the representatives they elect. Fundamentally, socialism is completely incapable of existing alongside individual freedoms.

Neal DiCaprio-Cortez @GreenNewNeal
.@glennbeck, many of the Founders were slave-owning racists. And you yourself have given numerous examples of how governments in the United States have abused their power to enact racist laws. Clearly, this whole "constitutional" system you love so much hasn't worked.

💬 1   ⟲   ♡

Many of the Founding Fathers were deeply flawed individuals, just like you and me. They weren't perfect, and many of them even openly recognized the hypocrisy of trying to create a free nation while also maintaining slavery in some parts of the United States. But can you find for me a "perfect" socialist or communist leader? Even those who aren't infamous for their numerous human rights violations led flawed lives.

History is full of imperfect people doing truly astounding things, and the Founding Fathers were no different. Although their constitutional republic hasn't been perfect or fully lived up to its foundational principle of liberty and justice for all people, it has, in many respects, advanced further toward that goal than any other society in human history. People in America have been freer, safer, and wealthier than just about anywhere on Earth, and that's because the Founders worked so hard to build their new world on eternal truths about individual rights and the prosperity that inevitably develops in free nations.

You and I can agree that America's past contains numerous instances in which people have unjustly suffered, but in nearly every instance, the primary reason that suffering occurred is that governments either refused to protect individuals' rights or actively worked to take those rights away. The best way to stop future abuses isn't to give more power and authority to the abusers.

 Neal DiCaprio-Cortez @GreenNewNeal
Marx's utopian socialism has never been achieved, and I admit that some socialist governments have made some tragic mistakes, but—

 1   ⟲   ♡

Yeah, "tragic mistakes" might be the understatement of the millennia.

 Neal DiCaprio-Cortez @GreenNewNeal
All right, but under capitalism, people have suffered too. The problem with socialism isn't that it can't work, it's that we just haven't had enough opportunities to fine-tune it. That's what the modern socialist movement is all about.

 1   ⟲   ♡

Only in a society in which individuals' rights are protected can people be truly free and prosperous, and capitalism is an essential part of that society. If people don't have the ability to freely own and transfer property and wealth, then they aren't really free; they are, to one degree or another, slaves of the state. And as slaves, who can they call when the state fails them, violates their rights, or obliterates prosperity? Who will right those wrongs?

HISTORY IS FULL OF EXAMPLES OF SOCIALISM'S FAILURES—

CATASTROPHIC

TERRIFYING

BLOODY

FAILURES...

GLENN
14.40.3 | 7.2 | 129

The truth is, as hard as it might be for you to admit it, socialism has been tried *repeatedly* over the past century, and every single time a new socialist movement featuring new socialist leaders emerges, they promise that "this time we'll get it right." As University of Massachusetts economist and socialist apologist Richard D. Wolff said in a 2019 debate hosted by the Soho Forum, twenty-first century socialism is "a new and a different socialism" that "has learned from its own earlier experiences and experiments."[53]

"And just like with capitalism," Wolff added, socialists "learn from [their] experiments how to make it better next time, how to correct the mistakes [they have] made, in the project that has animated socialists from the beginning: We can do better than capitalism."

But here's the truth: Socialists never do better "next time," because it doesn't matter who is in charge of the next great "glorious" socialist revolution. The problem runs much deeper than that. But you don't need to take my word for it. History is full of examples of socialism's failures—catastrophic, terrifying, bloody failures . . .

CHAPTER #3
FINAL PAGE
LAYOUT
COMPLETE

SOCIALIST "UTOPIAS" & THEIR BLOODY HISTORY OF FAILURE

MORE IDEAS
ON THIS...
-GB

"THE INHERENT VICE
OF CAPITALISM IS
THE UNEQUAL SHARING
OF BLESSINGS. THE
INHERENT VIRTUE
OF SOCIALISM IS
THE EQUAL SHARING
OF MISERIES."[1]

— WINSTON CHURCHILL

J uly 1, 1620: More than 102 men, women, and children were in the final stages of preparing for what would be the most harrowing journey of their lives, and one of the most important for the history of the world. The adventurers spent much of what wealth they had remaining in the final weeks of their time in Europe purchasing beer, dried beef, salt pork, oats, bacon, cider, butter, and wheat, among other foods, as well as canvas sheets for bedding, shoes, farming equipment, frying pans, skillets, soap, and other household items. Anticipation, excitement, and fear were in the air.

Approval
GLENN
Up
No. 14.40.3 Fix
No. 7.2 Page
Number
134

The trip couldn't come soon enough. For years, these so-called "Puritans"—the largest contingency of the adventurers—had faced persecution in England for their commitment to Protestant reforms of the Church of England, which had, in the minds of many Puritans, maintained far too many of the traditions and ideals of the Roman Catholic Church in the years that followed the Church of England's separation from communion with the papacy. The Puritans desperately wanted to worship God according to their own consciences, not the archbishop of Canterbury.

The persecution in England against some Puritans had grown so extreme in the early seventeenth century that many fled to Leiden, Holland, where they practiced their particular brand of Calvinism in relative peace for more than a decade. But the Puritans knew that they couldn't stay in Leiden forever. They needed a home of their own, and as fate—or God—would have it, an opportunity to build such a home in a distant, largely unsettled land far away from the monarchs and churches of Europe had fortuitously presented itself.

Investors in the Plymouth Company, which had been established by King James I in 1606, agreed to finance a new settlement of Puritans and other "adventurers" in America in exchange for having their expenses repaid, plus a share of the profits earned by the settlers. Under the terms established by James I, the company, like the endeavor in Jamestown, Virginia, would have the power to govern itself, a provision that presented the Puritans with an excellent opportunity to establish their new, free religious community.

But just weeks before the journey, the Plymouth Company's investors threw a wrench into the Pilgrims' plans. They insisted on altering the terms of the agreement for the new settlement, and in a panic, the Leiden Puritans' representative agreed to the new, more unfavorable conditions.

The final agreement would grant to everyone stock in the company, but those who agreed to provide additional provisions or funding would receive a double share, which was important because under the new terms—as recorded by William Bradford, the second governor of the Plymouth Colony—at the end of the initial seven-year period "the capital and profits, viz., the houses, lands, goods and chattels, shall be equally divided among the adventurers and planters."[2]

Further, under the agreement, during the initial period "all profits and benefits go by trade, traffic, trucking, working, fishing, or any other means, by any persons or person, shall remain in the common stock until the division," and "all such persons as are of this colony, are to have their food, drink, clothing, and all provisions, out of the common stock and goods of the said colony."

In the Puritans' New World, the whole society would share everything—including food, clothing, and, most importantly for many, the planters' houses and gardens—and then at the end of the period, all that the company had produced would be equally divided, with some of the wealthier settlers with more stock receiving a double share. Although Plymouth didn't exactly align with Karl Marx's *Communist Manifesto*, it certainly came close.

GHOST OF
KARL MARX

"OH, I LIKE WHERE THIS IS GOING!"

After long delays and a brutal 66-day journey on the *Mayflower*, the Pilgrims arrived in Massachusetts in November 1620—far north of their intended target, the Hudson River in modern-day New York—and eventually settled in Plymouth, which, quite astoundingly, shared a common name with the port from which the *Mayflower* initially left. Contrary to popular belief, Plymouth, Massachusetts was not named by the passengers of the *Mayflower*, but rather by explorer John Smith in an earlier voyage.[3]

The Pilgrims' first winter was catastrophic. Without any knowledge of the land, the Pilgrims struggled to find a steady source of food in New England, and disease decimated the group. As Bradford recorded in his journal, "In two or three months' time half of their company died, partly owing to the severity of the winter, especially during January and February, and the want of houses and other comforts; partly to scurvy and other diseases, which their long voyage and their incommodious quarters had brought upon them. Of all the hundred odd persons, scarcely fifty remained, and sometimes two or three persons died in a day."[4]

Aided by local Native Americans and the arrival of the ship *Fortune*, the Pilgrims were able to survive the winters of 1620–1621 and 1621–1622, but their community remained in a disastrous state relative to what the settlers had originally expected. However, 1623 would bring much better fortunes—thanks in large part to capitalist principles.

In an effort to repair their poorly functioning society, Bradford noted "they began to think how they might raise as much corn as they could, and obtain a better crop than they had done, that they might not still thus languish in misery. At length, after much debate of things, the Governor (with the advice of the chiefest amongst them) gave way that they should set corn every man for his own particular, and in that regard trust to themselves; in all other things to go on in the general way as before. And so assigned to every family a parcel of land, according to the proportion of their number, for that end, only for present use (but made no division for inheritance) and ranged all boys and youth under some family."[5]

Under the original terms of the Plymouth agreement, all crops would be shared equally and deposited to a common store, but this created numerous problems inherent to all socialist systems, as Bradford himself explained nearly 400 years ago:

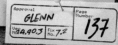

FOR THIS COMMUNITY (SO FAR AS IT WAS) WAS FOUND TO BREED MUCH CONFUSION AND DISCONTENT AND RETARD MUCH EMPLOYMENT THAT WOULD HAVE BEEN TO THEIR BENEFIT AND COMFORT. FOR THE YOUNG MEN, THAT WERE MOST ABLE AND FIT FOR LABOUR AND SERVICE, DID REPINE THAT THEY SHOULD SPEND THEIR TIME AND STRENGTH TO WORK FOR OTHER MEN'S WIVES AND CHILDREN WITHOUT ANY RECOMPENSE. THE STRONG, OR MAN OF PARTS, HAD NO MORE IN DIVISION OF VICTUALS AND CLOTHES THAN HE THAT WAS WEAK AND NOT ABLE TO DO A QUARTER THE OTHER COULD; THIS WAS THOUGHT INJUSTICE. . . . AND FOR MEN'S WIVES TO BE COMMANDED TO DO SERVICE FOR OTHER MEN, AS DRESSING THEIR MEAT, WASHING THEIR CLOTHES, ETC., THEY DEEMED IT A KIND OF SLAVERY, NEITHER COULD MANY HUSBANDS WELL BROOK [PUT UP WITH] IT.[6]

The decision to give each family its own parcel of land and to permit the private ownership of crops completely transformed the community.

"PROBABLY TRANSFORMED INTO A CAPITALIST NIGHTMARE, WHERE THE LEAST ABLE ARE PREYED UPON BY THE BOURGEOISIE!"

All right, Ghost Karl, stop interrupting. This chapter is going to be a horror show for your ideology, so if I were you, I'd take a long walk. Now, where was I . . .

According to Bradford, the private ownership model produced "very good success," because private property "made all hands very industrious, so as much more corn was planted than otherwise would have been by any means the Governor or any other could use, and saved him a great deal of trouble, and gave far better content."

Under the previous system, many of Plymouth's women "allege[d] weakness and inability" to avoid doing work, but after the reforms, "The women now went willingly into the field, and took their little ones with them to set corn."

From this point forward, the trials and tribulations of the Plymouth Colony's first few years would never again be repeated. And for Gov. Bradford, the entire experience with collective ownership and management of property, which they had tried for more than two years, had revealed beyond any doubt "the vanity of that conceit of Plato's and other ancients applauded by some of later times; that the taking away of property and bringing in community into a commonwealth would make them happy and flourishing; as if they were wiser than God."

AUTHOR'S NOTE

I HAVE ALSO OFTEN "ALLEGED WEAKNESS AND INABILITY" TO AVOID DOING WORK.

If socialism works, it should have worked in Plymouth. Plymouth was a small community that faced desperate times, shared a common heritage and ideals, and many of its citizens were devout believers in a religion that encourages unity and charity. And yet, many of the same inefficiencies and problems we've seen in dozens of socialist societies since Plymouth also plagued the Pilgrims. Why? Because regardless of the time, place, religion, or culture, socialism always fails—and often magnificently. It has arguably the worst track record of any political, social, or economic philosophy in the history of human civilization. There isn't a single example of socialism working when adopted on a large scale anywhere in the history of the world. (But, other than that, it's doing fine.)

GHOST OF

KARL MARX

"HARRUMPH..."

So, why would you, or anyone else, for that matter, support an idea with such a remarkably bad track record?

Neal DiCaprio-Cortez @GreenNewNeal
That's just not true, @glennbeck. There are the Scandinavian socialist nations of Sweden, Norway, and Denmark.

 1   ♡

Okay, before we go any further, let's agree to disagree for now about what you're calling "Scandinavian socialism." The evidence shows overwhelmingly that Sweden, Norway, and Denmark are not socialist nations—they're market economies with a few big socialist programs, very similar to what's happening in the United States now. Further, the data show Scandinavians are not better off than Americans, so the idea that we should adopt their model makes no sense on its face. But for now, let's hold off on dealing with the whole Scandinavian socialism myth until the next chapter. (See Chapter 5.)

What other examples do you have?

 Professor Tweed @checkurprivilegeplz
Well, there's also the Paris Commune of the nineteenth century. No one denies that this is an example of socialism.

💬 1   🔁   ♡

Ah, yes. I forgot about the Commune of Paris—a success story so famous almost no one has ever heard of it. I mean, how many people walking down the street not named "Bernie Sanders" would know what the heck the Paris Commune was? Oh, and how long did that "successful" commune last, again?

 Professor Tweed @checkurprivilegeplz
72 days.

💬 1   🔁   ♡

A whole 72 days, really? I've waited in lines at the DMV for longer than that. (Okay, not really, but you get the point.) The socialist government that ruled Paris in 1871 following the collapse of France's Second Empire was accompanied by bloodshed and a time of tremendous political and social upheaval. Not long after the commune was established, there was a war between the socialist revolutionaries in Paris and the French government, resulting in the deaths of 20,000 socialist revolutionaries (compared to only 750 government soldiers).[7] This is hardly a success story worth bragging about.

The fact that you're turning to the 72-day-long failed Paris Commune as a prime example of socialism working is proof that socialism doesn't work. If that's the best you've got, then, wow, socialism's track record must be just as bad as I think it is.

 Professor Tweed @checkurprivilegeplz
It's not the only example!

💬 1   🔁   ♡

I am sure you could point to a dozen or so really small communities that adopted socialism for a while without experiencing the usual death squads and famines, but when has it ever worked for a sustained period involving a group of people larger than one that can fit inside a movie theater? I'll save us both the time and answer for you: It hasn't. It has never worked on a large scale, and whenever it has been tried, it has ended with blood in the streets.

Socialist revolutions nearly always follow the same pattern, regardless of culture, race, religion, or history, and I'll prove it shortly with a list of examples of socialism's failures. But before we get to socialism's incredible history of failure, here's a brief and totally scientific outline of how socialist revolutions work:

COMMUNE OF PARIS

In March of 1871, shortly after France's defeat in the Franco-German war, a collection of communists, workers, and anarchists seized Paris and began constructing a commune. Within weeks, members elected a "Communal Council."

The commune worked on encouraging trade unions and worker's cooperatives. People constructed bakeries, nurseries, and other services needed by the people.

Seventy-two days into the experiment, the commune came to a violent end. In its haste to create a working society, the Council failed to adequately plan for outside threats. The German army, with help from the French army, marched in and destroyed the fledgling commune.[a]

HOW SOCIALIST REVOLUTIONS WORK

PHASE ONE: At least one group of people, usually those in society with relatively little wealth, are convinced by a handful of charismatic leaders that life would be oh so much better if they were in charge, rather than whoever has most of the political power at that time.

PHASE TWO: Those disenfranchised people seize power, often by winning democratically held elections, and then they appoint their charismatic leaders to the highest positions of power.

PHASE THREE: The shiny new socialist government steals wealth and property away from everyone who has it. "Pay your fair share, Grandma!"

PHASE FOUR: Those who have had their property and wealth taken from them get very angry, because, you know, they've been totally screwed in the name of "fairness."

PHASE FIVE: Opposition against the new socialist regime grows.

PHASE SIX: Socialist regime decides to silence its critics, often labeling them "saboteurs" and scapegoating them for all of the country's problems. The regime typically deals with these troublemakers by expelling them from their country or throwing them in jail. The socialist regime also eliminates all gun rights.

PHASE SEVEN: In resistance to the growing wave of tyranny and violence on the part of the new socialist regime, people take to the streets and protest. Many people who once supported the socialist regime realize that yeah, they probably made a big mistake.

PHASE EIGHT: Socialist regime grows fearful of revolution, so it starts to imprison and kill even more people.

PHASE NINE: Lots of people are murdered, imprisoned, exiled, beaten, tortured—and that's just the fate of those who stand in opposition to the regime in power. Just about everyone else is subjected to abject poverty, bread lines, endless bureaucracy, and economic chaos.

PHASE TEN: Tyranny lasts for years or even decades, until another revolution finally overthrows the socialist regime (think fall of the Berlin Wall).

EVOLUTION OF POLITICAL CORRECTNESS

1. SUGGEST
2. SHOUT
3. SHOVE
4. SHOOT

Professor Tweed @checkurprivilegeplz
I admit that this has occurred, but it's rare. Only in a few occasions will you find really tragic examples of socialist revolutions following this pattern.

◯ 1   ⟲   ♡

Really? Just a "few," huh? Let's go over some of the many examples of the failure and violence that stems from socialist revolutions. When we're finished, I have a feeling you're going to regret saying socialism has only failed on "a few occasions."

ANGOLA

In 1977, the socialist Popular Movement for the Liberation of Angola (MPLA) reportedly murdered "tens of thousands" of people when it seized power. Left-wing writer Lara Pawson, who was in Angola at the time of these killings, provides some disturbing details:

> "I BEGAN TO DISCOVER THAT THE IDEA OF A 1970S MPLA HEYDAY WAS JUST AS MISGUIDED. AN ANGOLAN COLLEAGUE TOLD ME ABOUT 27 MAY 1977, THE DAY AN MPLA FACTION ROSE UP AGAINST THE LEADERSHIP, AND THE HONEYMOON OF REVOLUTION CRASHED TO A HALT. SOME CALLED IT AN ATTEMPTED COUP, BUT MY COLLEAGUE INSISTED IT WAS A DEMONSTRATION THAT WAS MET WITH A BRUTAL OVERREACTION.

> "WHICHEVER STORY YOU BELIEVE," PAWSON ADDED, "SIX SENIOR MEMBERS OF THE MPLA WERE KILLED THAT DAY BY SUPPORTERS OF THE UPRISING. IN RESPONSE, PRESIDENT NETO, THE POLITBURO AND THE STATE MEDIA MADE MANY HIGHLY INFLAMMATORY STATEMENTS THAT INCITED EXTRAORDINARY REVENGE. IN THE WEEKS AND MONTHS THAT FOLLOWED, THOUSANDS OF PEOPLE— POSSIBLY TENS OF THOUSANDS—WERE KILLED. SOME OF THE EXECUTIONS WERE OVERSEEN BY CUBAN TROOPS SENT TO ANGOLA BY FIDEL CASTRO TO REPEL A SOUTH AFRICAN INVASION."[8]

Some socialists have denied that the MPLA was a truly Marxist organization, but the historical record shows it undoubtedly was. In fact, in the same year of the MPLA atrocities mentioned above, it went out of its way to brand itself as a Marxist-Leninist organization at a meeting of its national congress.[9]

A.D.D. MOMENT

MPLA literature featured a great example of Phase Six of the aforementioned socialism cycle. On the back of an MPLA pamphlet read the following message: "We will apply the Democratic Revolutionary Dictatorship to finally finish with saboteurs, with parasites, and with opportunists."

THE FAILURE OF A SOCIALIST SYSTEM MUST ALWAYS BE BLAMED ON SOMEONE ELSE.

CAMBODIA

In 1975, the Communist Party of Kampuchea, often called the Khmer Rouge, emerged as the victor of the seven-year-long Cambodian Civil War. The Khmer Rouge was composed of avid Marxists who attempted to impose their radical ideas using brutal force.

Under the Khmer Rouge's ruthless leader Pol Pot, all previous loyalties were abolished and strictly forbidden. Cambodians were banned from keeping their religious and family ties. All civil liberties were taken away. Every Cambodian was instead required to make the good of the collective his or her primary focus. To indoctrinate all children with a Marxist ideology, every child aged eight or older was separated from their parents in 1977 and required to join labor camps, where they were trained to treat the state as their parent.[10]

As the Holocaust Memorial Day Trust notes, the "Khmer Rouge ideology stated that the only acceptable lifestyle was that of poor agricultural workers," so they forced millions of people from their homes in the city to work as farmers. "Factories, hospitals, schools and universities were shut down. Lawyers, doctors, teachers, engineers and qualified professionals in all fields were thought to be a threat to the new regime. . . . Money was abolished and all aspects of life were subject to regulation. People were not allowed to choose their own marriage partners. They could not leave their given place of work or even select the clothes that they would wear."[11]

Millions of people across Cambodia were effectively forced into slavery—all in the name of building Marx's utopian society. Anyone daring to speak out against the regime was imprisoned or murdered. Hundreds of thousands of others died from starvation or disease. During the Khmer Rouge's four-year reign, an estimated 2 million people perished as a direct result of the Communist Party's policies.[12]

A.D.D. MOMENT

FOR THE GREATER GOOD

In 2008, two surviving senior leaders of the regime, Nuon Chea and Khieu Samphan, were found guilty of genocide for their participation in the actions in Cambodia by a United Nations-backed tribunal.

Nuon Chea, a Khmer Rouge leader and brother-in-law of Pol Pot, gave insight into the justification of the actions during the trial. "The CPK's policy and plan were solely designed to one purpose only," said Chea, "to liberate the country from the colonization, imperialism, exploitation, extreme poverty and invasion from neighboring countries."

"The CPK's policy was clear and specific: it wanted to create an equal society where people were the master of the country . . . The CPK's movement was not designed to kill people or destroy the country," said Chea.[b]

CHINA

It's impossible to briefly and accurately capture the horrors caused by the socialist policies imposed by China throughout much of the twentieth century. The amount of death, destruction, and misery experienced in China is on a scale never before seen in the history of the world.

Although estimates vary, the *Black Book of Communism*, widely considered to be the leading authority on socialism- and communism-related deaths, estimates 65 million Chinese died because of the reforms imposed by Mao Zedong's reforms, a figure that is supported by academics like Lee Edwards, Ph.D., the Heritage Foundation's distinguished fellow in conservative thought.[13,14]

Many of those who died under the leadership of communist Mao Zedong starved because of the government's complete mismanagement of the country's agricultural system. Edwards noted, "Deaths from hunger reached more than 50 percent in some Chinese villages. The total number of dead from 1959 to 1961 was between 30 million and 40 million—the population of California."[15]

Vaclav Smil, the Distinguished Professor Emeritus at the University of Manitoba and a fellow at the Royal Society of Canada, says the famine was largely the result of Mao's "Great Leap Forward":

A.D.D. MOMENT

STORIES FROM THE VICTIMS OF SOCIALISM

[During the famine] "People died in the family and they didn't bury the person because they could still collect their food rations; they kept the bodies in bed and covered them up and the corpses were eaten by mice. People ate corpses and fought for the bodies. In Gansu they killed outsiders; people told me strangers passed through and they killed and ate them. And they ate their own children. Terrible. Too terrible."[c] Yang Jisheng

> "THIS MASS MOBILISATION OF THE COUNTRY'S HUGE POPULATION WAS TO ACHIEVE IN JUST A FEW YEARS ECONOMIC ADVANCES THAT TOOK OTHER NATIONS MANY DECADES TO ACCOMPLISH," SMIL WROTE. "MAO, BEHOLDEN TO STALINIST IDEOLOGY THAT STRESSED THE KEY ROLE OF HEAVY INDUSTRY, MADE STEEL PRODUCTION THE CENTERPIECE OF THIS DELUDED EFFORT. INSTEAD OF WORKING IN THE FIELDS, TENS OF MILLIONS OF PEASANTS WERE ORDERED TO MINE LOCAL DEPOSITS OF IRON ORE AND LIMESTONE, TO CUT TREES FOR CHARCOAL, TO BUILD SIMPLE CLAY FURNACES, AND TO SMELT METAL. THIS FRENZIED ENTERPRISE DID NOT PRODUCE STEEL BUT MOSTLY LUMPS OF BRITTLE CAST IRON UNFIT FOR EVEN SIMPLE TOOLS. PEASANTS WERE FORCED TO ABANDON ALL PRIVATE FOOD PRODUCTION, AND NEWLY FORMED AGRICULTURAL COMMUNES PLANTED LESS LAND TO GRAIN, WHICH AT THAT TIME WAS THE SOURCE OF MORE THAN 80% OF CHINA'S FOOD ENERGY."[16]

When Chinese weren't being murdered, removed from their homes, or starving to death, they were being forced into more than 1,000 government-run labor camps. Edwards, citing work by Harry Wu, who once spent 19 years in Chinese labor camps, estimates 50 million Chinese were imprisoned in these labor camps over a three-decade period running from the 1950s to 1980s. Twenty million didn't survive.[17]

All told, the total number of Chinese believed to have been killed, exiled, imprisoned, or starved at the hands of the country's Communist Party in the twentieth century is nearly 100 million—a little less than one-third of the entire current U.S. population.

CUBA

For nearly three years, from 1956 to 1959, Cuba's 26th of July Movement—led by socialist Fidel Alejandro Castro Ruz, whose father was a wealthy sugarcane farmer— promised the people of Cuba that when this communist revolution was complete, Cuba would enter a new era of unprecedented equality and prosperity for all people. However, as has been the case with so many other socialist movements, once Castro gained power, he used his position to suppress individual freedom and control the island nation's economy with an iron fist, all to his own benefit.[18]

After defeating military forces loyal to former Cuban president Fulgencio Batista in 1959, Castro became Cuba's dictator, a position he would hold for 57 years. Castro's regime—which quickly found a strong ally in the Soviet Union—provided Cubans with "free" health care, education, and government-guaranteed jobs, but his harsh reforms effectively ended many private industries and abolished civil liberties like free speech and political liberty. Cubans were no longer permitted to protest or speak out against the Castro administration without risking imprisonment or potentially even death.

According to various estimates, Castro's regime was responsible for killing more than 140,000 people.[19] Hundreds of thousands more fled Cuba, often for the United States. During a five-month period in 1980 alone, more than 125,000 Cubans defected from their homeland to become Americans. In 1994, tens of thousands attempted to sail from Cuba to the United States on makeshift rafts. About 35,000 ended up settling in Dade County, Florida.[20] In many cases, the Cubans swimming, flying, and boating away from Cuba did so to escape truly horrifying living conditions. Things got so bad in the 1990s that some even resorted to eating cats and dogs.[21]

Cuba's history of failure hasn't seemed to affect many progressives and socialists in America, though. When Castro died in 2016, some hailed him as a hero of Cuba.

FOOD RATIONING IN 2019

The days of food rationing are not over in Cuba. Grappling with economic crisis, the Cuban government in June 2019 launched a program to ration basic goods, including chicken, eggs, rice, beans, and soap.[d]

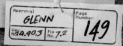

APPALLING POLITICAL VIOLENCE STILL COMMON-PLACE IN CUBA

Sirley Ávila León was elected as a delegate to the Municipal Assembly in Cuba in June 2005.

Her desire to alleviate the hardships suffered by her constituents and her continued advocation for family and community rights put her on the regime's radar.

In 2015, an attempt on her life was made by a machete-wielding attacker. Ávila survived the assassination attempt, but suffered major injuries. She spent several months recovering in a hospital in the United States.

After recovering, Ávila boarded a plane to return home to Cuba. She was never seen again.[e]

ABC's Jim Avila even called him the "George Washington of his country."[22]

NAZI GERMANY

The Nazis are the twentieth century's most infamous murderers—and justifiably so. According to a study published in 2013 by the Holocaust Memorial Museum, 15–20 million people were killed in 42,400 Nazi camps and ghettos in Europe in the 1930s and 1940s.[23]

However, despite these tragic figures, dozens of Hollywood movies, and the hundreds of books written about the Nazis, most Americans don't know that the Nazis were, indeed, national *socialists*. In fact, the term "Nazi" is simply an abbreviation for the party's full name: the National Socialist German Workers' Party.

Now, if you do a simple Google search, you'll find all sorts of people claiming the Nazis weren't *really* socialists. They'll say the Nazis just stole the name "socialist" for political reasons, and as proof, they'll offer historical evidence showing the Nazis did leave many businesses in the hands of private citizens. They didn't officially nationalize all industries, which, according to these folks, means Nazis couldn't possibly be considered socialists.

In a 2005 article for the Mises Institute, George Reisman, Ph.D., a professor emeritus at Pepperdine University, does a nice job—drawing on the work of Ludwig von Mises—explaining why the Nazis should unquestionably be considered "socialists."

"The basis of the claim that Nazi Germany was capitalist was the fact that most industries in Nazi Germany appeared to be left in private hands," Reisman wrote.[24]

"What Mises identified was that private ownership of the means of production existed in name only under the Nazis and that the actual substance of ownership of the means of production resided in *the German government*," Reisman explained further. "For it was the German government and not the nominal private owners that exercised all of the *substantive powers of ownership*: it, not the nominal private owners, decided what was to be produced, in what quantity, by what methods, and to whom it was to be distributed, as well as what prices would be charged and what wages would be paid, and what dividends or other income the nominal private owners would be permitted to receive."

As Reisman masterfully explained, the Nazis didn't have to officially "own" the nation's property to be socialists. By having total control over every aspect of property, individuals owned property in name only. The property might have belonged to a well-connected German on paper, but in practice, the property belonged to the Nazis.

Reisman added, "*De facto* government ownership of the means of production, as Mises termed it, was logically implied by such fundamental collectivist principles embraced by the Nazis as that the common good comes before the private good and the individual exists as a means to the ends of the State. If the individual is a means to the ends of the State, so too, of course, is his property. Just as he is owned by the State, his property is also owned by the State."[25]

Adolf Hitler and other leading Nazis did oppose the universal, globalist nature of many Marxist movements. Hitler and the Nazis weren't concerned about creating a global workers' paradise, but rather a fascist-socialist empire. But as George Watson noted for the *Independent* (U.K.), "His [Hitler's] differences with the communists, he [Hitler] explained, were less ideological than tactical. German communists he had

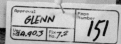

known before he took power, he told [Hermann] Rauschning, thought politics meant talking and writing. They were mere pamphleteers, whereas 'I have put into practice what these peddlers and pen pushers have timidly begun,' adding revealingly that 'the whole of National Socialism' was based on Marx."[26]

From these sources (and many more, too), it's clear the Nazis were exactly what they said they were: socialists. Anyone who tells you otherwise is deliberately misleading you or hasn't spent much time reading the history of Nazism.

EVER WONDER WHY THE NAZI FLAG IS RED?

The color red has long been used by socialist and communist parties as a way to show solidarity to their collectivist ideals. In *Mein Kampf*, Hitler noted what each of the Nazi colors represented, clearly highlighting that "red" was chosen to illustrate the Nazis' commitment to the "social idea of the movement": "In red we see the social idea of the movement, in white the nationalistic idea, in the swastika the mission of the struggle for the victory of the Aryan man, and, by the same token, the victory of the idea of creative work, which as such always has been and always will be anti-Semitic."[f]

NORTH KOREA

No one knows how many people have been killed, tortured, or imprisoned in North Korea at the hands of that country's communist dictatorship. However, estimates suggest the figure could be 3.5 million or more.[27]

The Committee for Human Rights in North Korea estimates there are about 120,000 people currently serving in various North Korean prison camps.[28] And life for many North Koreans outside of the country's prisons is far from ideal. Every economic and societal decision is made by the ruling government to ensure all resources are property managed and "fairly" distributed, as Human Rights Watch noted in a 2018 report: "The government uses forced labor from ordinary citizens, including children, to control its people and sustain its economy. A significant majority of North Koreans must perform unpaid labor at some point in their lives."

"ORDINARY NORTH KOREAN WORKERS ARE NOT FREE TO CHOOSE THEIR OWN JOB," THE REPORT'S AUTHORS ADDED. "THE GOVERNMENT ASSIGNS JOBS TO BOTH MEN AND UNMARRIED WOMEN FROM CITIES AND RURAL AREAS. IN MANY CASES, THESE ENTERPRISES DO NOT COMPENSATE THEM, FORCING THEM TO FIND OTHER JOBS TO SURVIVE AND PAY BRIBES TO BE ABSENT AT THEIR ASSIGNED WORKPLACE. FAILING TO SHOW UP FOR WORK WITHOUT PERMISSION IS A CRIME PUNISHABLE BY THREE TO SIX MONTHS IN FORCED LABOR TRAINING CAMPS."[29]

"Ji Seong-ho is a North Korean defector who grew up during the country's grueling famine in the 1990s. In order to survive, Ji would exchange stolen coal for food on the black market. While taking coal from a train car in 1996, a malnourished Ji lost consciousness and fell onto the tracks, losing his left hand and foot when a train ran over him. After a grueling amputation surgery, Ji was left to fend for himself. In 2006, he escaped to South Korea, where he is now a law student at Dongguk University. Ji is also the president of Now Action and Unity for Human Rights, where he helps broadcast information into North Korea and facilitates the resettlement of defectors in South Korea."[8]

JI SEONG-HO WAS THE NK DEFECTOR WHO ATTENDED TRUMP'S STATE OF THE UNION

> HUMAN RIGHTS WATCH ALSO NOTES THAT NORTH KOREAN STUDENTS HAVE REPORTED THAT GOVERNMENT OFFICIALS HAVE FORCED THEM TO WORK, WITHOUT PAY, IN THE COUNTRY'S FARMS. IN SOME CASES, STUDENTS HAVE BEEN REQUIRED TO WORK BETWEEN 10-16 HOURS PER DAY. THE STUDENTS SAY THAT THEY'VE BEEN TOLD ONE OF THE PRIMARY REASONS THEY NEED TO WORK ON FARMS IS TO HELP PAY THE SALARIES OF SCHOOL STAFF.

In order to keep strict control over the populace, North Korea's government has severely restricted travel and basic civil liberties. The only way for most North Koreans to have access to news and information is through state-run media and news outlets, which regularly broadcast socialist propaganda and perpetuate mythologies meant to reinforce the power of dictator Kim Jong-un and his military leaders.

In 2012, North Korea's state news agency, unimaginatively called "Central News Agency," reported that "archaeologists"—and I use that word in the loosest way possible—from the Academy of Social Sciences at North Korea's History Institute had discovered a "unicorn lair." Yes, that's right—a unicorn lair. *The Guardian* (U.K.) reported in 2012 that the Central News Agency said "that they [the fake archaeologists] have 'recently reconfirmed' the lair of one of the unicorns ridden by the ancient Korean King Tongmyong, founder of a kingdom which ruled parts of China and the Korean peninsula from the the 3rd century BC to 7th century AD. The KCNA goes on to state that the location happens to be 200 metres from a temple in the North Korean capital, adding: 'A rectangular rock carved with words 'Unicorn Lair' stands in front of the lair.'"[30]

Many of those who have spoken out against the government in North Korea have ended up being tortured or killed, often in incredibly gruesome ways. The Transitional Justice Working Group, a South Korean non-government organization, reports there are more than 300 "execution sites" across North Korea. In some cases, people have been executed publicly for "crimes" as small as viewing media from South Korea.[31] It's no wonder then that no one is willing to question the authenticity of those magical "unicorn lairs."

SOVIET UNION

We've already spent some time talking about the Soviet Union, and we're going to spend a lot more time discussing it throughout the remaining chapters of this book, but it's important to mention here that although sources vary, it's likely 40–70 million people were killed, imprisoned, or exiled by the Communist Party in the Soviet Union in the twentieth century. In fact, some of the worst human rights violations in human history occurred as part of the Russian communists' efforts to create a socialist utopia. For example, about 1 million people were executed by Communists during the "Great Terror" in 1937–38.[32]

In one of the most tragic episodes of Soviet history—which is really saying something, by the way, because this is a country absolutely overflowing with horror stories—as many as 5 million people were killed by a government-created famine in 1932–1933, with much of the death occurring in Ukraine, Siberia, and Kazakhstan. The famine was a direct result of policies implemented by Soviet leader Joseph Stalin, who sought to punish peasants throughout the Soviet Union who refused to go along with the Soviet's plan to collectivize farmland.[33]

Stalin dispatched special agents throughout Ukraine, Kazakhstan, and elsewhere to raid homes and businesses suspected of not turning over their food to government officials. Whole villages were effectively banned from having access to enough food

"STALIN'S SECRET GENOCIDE"

SOMETIMES REFERRED TO AS "HOLOMODOR," OR "STALIN'S SECRET GENOCIDE," THIS GOVERNMENT-CREATED FAMINE CHANGED THE FACE OF UKRAINE FOREVER.

BECAUSE OF ITS GRAIN PRODUCTION, UKRAINE WAS CALLED THE "BREADBASKET OF EUROPE." THIS MADE CONTROL OVER UKRAINE CRITICAL FOR THE SURVIVAL OF THE USSR. "WITHOUT UKRAINE, THERE IS NO USSR," SAID ANNE APPLEBAUM, PULITZER PRIZE-WINNING AUTHOR.

THE PEOPLE OF UKRAINE WERE LARGELY OPPOSED TO THE CONCEPTS OF COLLECTIVIST FARMING AND FREQUENTLY PUSHED FOR SOVEREIGNTY.

WITH THE GOAL OF EXACTING COMPLETE CONTROL OVER UKRAINE, STALIN ENACTED POLICIES TO CRUSH THE COUNTRY INTO SUBMISSION.

STALIN SENT PAVEL POSTYSHEV AND AN ARMY OF SECRET POLICE TO DESTROY THE POLITICAL LEADERS OF UKRAINE AND TAKE OVER THE COUNTRY.

AFTER TAKING COMPLETE CONTROL, THE STATIONED SOVIET ARMY GUARDED THE GRAIN AND KEPT IT FROM THE UKRAINIAN PEOPLE—THE GRAIN WAS NOW STATE PROPERTY.

THE STRATEGY WAS TO STARVE THE POPULATION INTO SUBMISSION, AND REPLACE THE FARMERS WITH LOYAL SOVIETS. "IN MANY OF THE PLACES WHERE THE FAMINE WAS MOST DEVASTATING," SAID APPLEBAUM, "RUSSIANS WERE BROUGHT IN TO REPLACE UKRAINIAN VILLAGERS. IN OTHER WORDS, THE NATURE OF THE COUNTRY CHANGED AFTER THE FAMINE."

THIS IDEA OF FOREVER CHANGING THE CULTURAL LANDSCAPE WAS TAKEN EVER FURTHER. AS ANDREA GRAZIOSI, PROFESSOR OF HISTORY AT THE UNIVERSITY OF NAPLES FEDERICO II, EXPLAINS HOW IN SCHOOLS "ALL THE DICTIONARIES WERE REMOVED AND CHANGED SO THAT THE LANGUAGE BECAME CLOSER TO RUSSIAN."

THE "HOLOMODOR" WAS LARGELY HIDDEN FROM THE WORLD. IN FACT, THE FIRST ACADEMIC ACCOUNT OF THIS HORRIFIC EVENT WAS PUBLISHED 53 YEARS LATER, IN 1986: *THE HARVEST OF SORROW*, BY ROBERT CONQUEST.[h]

to survive, and anyone caught secretly hiding food was killed. Peasants who resorted to stealing wheat from state-controlled storehouses were sent before firing squads. Even as the Soviet Union was exporting a million tons of grain in 1933, it continued to starve the people of Ukraine and Kazakhstan.

Petro Matulla grew up in a village 75 miles from Kiev, Ukraine. In a 2009 report by NPR, a reporter asked Matulla if he remembered anything about the tragedies of the 1932–1933 famine. Although Matulla was only four years old at the time, he recalled Soviet agents coming to his home and taking whatever food they could find, and he remembered vividly the reason for the raids: "So you wouldn't eat. So you'd die."[34]

Matulla also recalled seeing a "dead mother was laying on the street, and the baby was sucking on her breast." Matulla's family was only able to survive because his grandfather had secretly hid a sack of grain beneath the family's barn. Others in the village weren't so lucky. Many of them starved to death.[35]

The Soviets didn't merely stop Ukrainians and others from eating food, either. They also prevented people from fleeing the country as well. Soviet soldiers blockaded villages, and those who did manage to escape were forced to return home to starve.[36]

It's hard to put these incredible tragedies in context, especially because the death tolls involved are so large, but to give you some sense of the scale of the death and destruction caused by the Soviet Union, if a government were to kill, exile, imprison, or starve someone every minute of every single day, it would take more than 75 years before matching the horror of the low end of the 40–70 million estimate previously discussed.

Americans have never experienced anything like what occurred in the Soviet Union in much of the twentieth century, and God willing, they never will.

Los Angeles Times

AN ARTICLE PUBLISHED IN
THE L.A. TIMES IN MARCH
1990 CHRONICLES STORIES
FROM ROMANIANS

"Not even if we had a war would it look like this," said Gheorghe Cristea, who described roads lined with skeletons.

Constantin Surescu, a farmer, told how police and town officials showed up at his door: "They ordered us to destroy our own houses. Many people said, 'don't want to do this.' If you said 'No,' they came in the night and got you and beat you up."

After his house was destroyed, Surescu was moved to a government-provided shelter. "They gave me an apartment but I didn't want to stay," said Surescu. "I felt like I was in a hospital. It was cold. There was water on the walls. It was like being in a grave."[i]

ROMANIA

In the wake of World War II, the Soviet Union seized control of many Eastern European countries, including Romania. Although the communists in Romania were relatively unpopular at the end of the war, Soviet officials and agents suppressed all resistance to their efforts to create a socialist state. In 1946, a Soviet sympathizer was "democratically elected" in Romania, winning 80 percent of the vote.[37]

Over the following three decades, Romanian central planners botched one public project after another, creating significant economic turmoil. The nation's debt became so extreme by 1982 that the socialist government resorted to demanding exports of most of the country's production, including in industry and agriculture, creating deadly shortages of essential products like food and medicine.

Government officials frantically tried to enact one socialist reform after another to stabilize the country, but none were successful. One particularly remarkable—in the worst possible way—example of central planning gone wrong involved Romanian officials bulldozing thousands of towns and villages across the country. Residents were then forced to move to "agrotechnical centers," where they worked in government-approved jobs.

Prior to being ousted in 1989, Nicolae Ceaușescu, Romania's dictator and the general secretary of the Romanian Communist Party, transformed the country into a virtual "police state." As one report by *The Guardian* (U.K.) notes, archival documents show the Ceaușescu regime even employed a vast network of children to spy on their parents, teachers, and others in their communities: "The secret police of Romanian dictator Nicolae Ceaușescu recruited thousands of children to spy on schoolfriends, parents and teachers, according to communist-era archives. They show that the Securitate blackmailed children across Romania into becoming informers in the late 1980s, as the whiff of liberalization in the Soviet bloc prompted Ceaușescu to tighten his grip on the country."[38]

Anyone caught by the Communist Party's spies engaging in behavior deemed to be harmful to the ruling regime or the collective was imprisoned, exiled, or killed. From 1947 to 1989, it is believed that 435,000 people died because of policies enacted by the left-wing government in the Socialist Republic of Romania.[39]

VENEZUELA

I've already talked in detail about Venezuela's economic chaos, but you can't talk about socialism's bloody and disastrous history without at least mentioning this prime example of why collectivism never works.

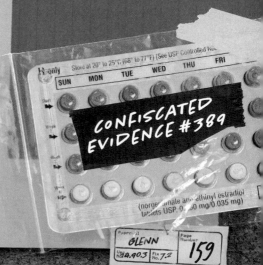

CONFISCATED EVIDENCE #389

As bad as things have become in Venezuela—riots, starvation, political instability, hyperinflation—it's very likely the worst has yet to come for Venezuelans, who continue to watch helplessly as the self-described socialist leaders of that nation destroy the country's economy and impose countless totalitarian policies. The economic destruction created by the costly socialist programs, irresponsible spending practices, and government regulations and price controls imposed by President Nicolas Maduro and former president Hugo Chavez grew so dire that even before the current political chaos, child malnutrition became widespread. *The New York Times* reported in late 2017 there had been 2,800 cases of child malnutrition reported during the previous 12 months. Four hundred children died as a result of poor nutrition during the same period.[40] Later in December 2017, *The Wall Street Journal* reported nearly 8,300 people had been killed in the Venezuelan government's "brutal crime crackdown."[41]

Throughout 2019, hundreds of Venezuelans were killed, injured, or detained by government agents.[42] More than 4 million people have fled the country to escape the economic devastation and turmoil created by the socialists running the country.[43] And, unfortunately, it looks like things could get significantly worse in the coming years.

VIETNAM

Determining precisely how many people were killed by the communists in Vietnam is extremely difficult because of the numerous long-lasting wars that occurred in the country throughout much of the twentieth century. However, the widely cited scholar R.J. Rummel estimated in 1994 the communist government in Vietnam had killed more than 1.6 million people in the twentieth century, including many innocent civilians who were butchered following the departure of the United States from the country toward the end of the Vietnam War.[44]

In addition to the many atrocities committed by the communist government in Vietnam, many of those killed died as a direct result of socialist policies and poor central planning. Food rationing was particularly problematic. From the 1960s to the 1980s, it was standard practice for non-farming Vietnamese to receive most of their food directly from the socialist government.[45] It wasn't uncommon for Vietnamese to receive just 28 pounds of food per month, mostly items like rice and dried tapioca. The rationing continued well after the Vietnam War ended because of socialist bureaucrats' failure to manage food supplies. In an interview with German state-owned publication *Deutsche Welle*, Gerhard Will, an academic at the German Institute for International and Security Affairs, noted, "In the 1980s, the supply of food items was even worse than during war times."

ZIMBABWE

Socialist Robert Mugabe, the former president of Zimbabwe, was responsible for the murder, torture, or imprisonment of tens of thousands of people. Some estimates say his government killed nearly 50,000 Zimbabweans.[46]

"From January 1983, a campaign of terror was waged against the Ndebele people in Matabeleland in western Zimbabwe," Stuart Doran noted in a report for *The Guardian* (U.K.).[47] "The so-called Gukurahundi massacres remain the darkest period in the country's post-independence history, when more than 20,000 civilians were killed by Robert Mugabe's feared Fifth Brigade."

Doran further reported that although "[n]o one has accepted the blame for the violence . . . the recent release of historical documents has shed new light on those responsible. In a conversation with Cephas Msipa, one of the few remaining Zapu ministers of what had been a government of national unity, Sekeramayi reportedly

Ian Kay, a farmer in Zimbabwe, and his family were routinely threatened by the Mugabe regime. Mugabe's men raided his home, burnt down his huts, and maimed his horse.

When threats failed to provide the desired results, Kay was beaten by a crowd wielding sticks wrapped with barbed wire and left for dead. His son was tortured and mutilated.

Kay said, "They eventually broke the door down and I went out. And they beat me further in the school ground. . . . they tied my arms together and took me up the road. They said they were going to take me to my house to see how many guns I had and to move into the house."

This was not a personal attack on Kay, but rather part of a "land reform" effort to address "unequal" farmland distribution in the country.[k]

said that 'not only was Mugabe fully aware of what was going on' but the Fifth Brigade was operating 'under Mugabe's explicit orders.'"

Even in his final years in office, despite being more than 90 years old, Mugabe remained committed to radical, racist, Marxist policies. In 2017, Mugabe announced his government would not prosecute people who had murdered innocent white farmers years earlier.[48]

In its report on the announcement, *Newsweek*'s Conor Gaffey noted, "Zimbabwe implemented a controversial land reform program in 2000 that saw squatters invade and seize hundreds of white-owned farms around the country. The violent seizures resulted in the murder of several white farmers, with many more displaced, and close associates of Mugabe given large chunks of land."[49]

On the other hand, Mugabe was honored as a "leader for tourism" by the United Nations' World Tourism Organisation in 2012. And, while it's true that he allowed the inflation rate to reach 89,700,000,000,000,000,000,000%, he was able to hold it under 90,000,000,000,000,000,000,000%. So, it wasn't all bad news.

We've already discussed how without strong protections for individuals, democracies can be just as dangerous as dictatorships and other forms of government. (See Chapter 3.) In the United States, Japanese Americans, African Americans, Mormons, Catholics, Chinese, and numerous other groups have at one point or another been

Neal DiCaprio-Cortez @GreenNewNeal
.@glennbeck, these are all examples of authoritarian
socialism, not democratic socialism.

💬 1   ⟲   ♡

the victims of democratically elected governments that ignored the constitutional protections for individual liberty promised to those groups. Democracy guarantees only one thing: If tyranny exists in a democratically elected government, it's likely a majority of people agree with it—or at least that they did at some point in the past.

It's also really important to keep in mind that in many of the examples of socialism's failure mentioned above, as well as countless other historical examples unrelated to socialism, authoritarian governments were at first democratically elected. For example, in 1791, France held its first democratic election. Just two years later, in 1793, the French Revolution's "Reign of Terror" was instituted by the revolutionary government's ironically named Committee of Public Safety, leading to the execution of 1,400 people.[50] Similarly, the Nazis rose to power after winning a huge share of parliamentary seats in Germany's 1932 elections.[51] And for many decades, socialist politicians were democratically elected in Venezuela. (Even though some of the most recent elections in Venezuela have been deemed by much of the global community to be illegitimate, many previous elections were considered fair.[52])

SOCIALISM IN DALLAS, TEXAS?!

When most people think of socialism, they typically don't think of Texas. But perhaps they should. Dallas was once home to one of the most notable socialist experiments in American history.

In 1855, Victor Prosper Considerant, one of France's most influential democratic socialists, emigrated to Dallas with 200 socialist colonists in the hopes of creating a collectivist utopia in the United States, which he called La Réunion.

Considerant had spent the better part of the previous two years promoting his grand vision of establishing a network of socialist colonies throughout the Southwest through his French writings, especially *Au Texas* (1854). He also published his socialist dreams in English in *The Great West* (1854).

At its height, in 1856, about 350 residents had settled in La Réunion. But like all experiments in socialism, La Réunion soon collapsed. Facing difficult weather conditions and a lack of skilled workers, the leaders of La Réunion disbanded the colony in January 1857, less than two years after it started.[1]

SOCIALIST FUN FACT!

Even though most socialists find him to be as evil as all of the dictators in this chapter combined, Donald Trump was also democratically elected. [And yes, I hear you whining about the electoral college. Maybe I'll destroy those arguments in the next book.]

To say democracy is a guarantee that people's individual rights will be protected is completely contradicted by hundreds of years of historical examples of democracy devolving into tyranny. This is why it's so important for democracy to be coupled with protections for individual liberty (in the United States, the Bill of Rights and Constitution), something that simply cannot exist in a socialist society.

To blame free markets for societal problems like hunger is just plain dumb. At its foundation, free-market capitalism is simply a system in which people have the ability to freely own property and freely exchange it. That's it. To say capitalism is to blame for societal problems is like saying freedom is to blame.

If people are suffering, I do believe it's important for communities and neighbors to help each other. But it must be voluntary, not forced, coerced, or mandated—and that's what socialism is.

Rita Resistance @AOC_2024_Squad4Life
Well, lots of people die from capitalism, too. People starve every single day because of capitalism.

♡ 1   ⇄   ♡

In a free society, no matter how productive an economy is, there will always be people who are poorer than others, but there is nothing stopping people in a free society from freely helping other people. So, to say free-market capitalism is somehow morally deficient as a system just isn't true. It's the people in the system who have failed the poor. They're the ones that need to change, by being more compassionate, loving, kind, and generous.

The "invisible hand" of free markets works for all of us in that it always improves efficiency and helps people achieve their goals. The question is, what do we want? What are our goals?

However, if you're saying *crony* capitalism and corruption are responsible for creating unfairness, slowing economic growth, and unjustly picking "winners" and "losers," then I couldn't agree more. But crony capitalism, as we already discussed in Chapter 2, only exists when government has too much power. Take that power away from government—through federal and state reforms and potentially new constitutional amendments—and cronyism will disappear along with it.

Perhaps most importantly, although it's true that there are still people suffering in America and in other countries with market-based economies, the historical record shows overwhelmingly that these nations provide people with the best possible chance at obtaining prosperity. People in market-based economies are wealthier, healthier, and happier than people in economies in which most decisions are made by a centralized power, a fact well documented in recent years by the many societies that have chosen to abandon their socialist economies or policies in exchange for more economic freedom.

India is one of the best examples of the power of capitalism. In the 1990s, India transitioned away from many of its socialist programs and opened its market to foreign investment. It also refused to enact strict regulatory schemes in emerging tech-heavy industries, a mistake the country's socialists had made in many other industries earlier in the century. The results of India's move toward freer markets has been nothing short of a miracle. In 1993, more than 430 million Indians were living below the international poverty line, but by 2011, the country's tremendous economic growth had pulled more than 164 million people out of poverty.[53] In 2017, Arthur Brooks, president of the American Enterprise Institute, estimated the number of Indians who had escaped poverty was 200 million.[54] (See Chapter 9 for more.)

CAN YOU SHOW ME ONE PLACE THAT HAS HAD A SIMILAR RECORD OF SUCCESS BY RELYING ON SOCIALISM

If you want to reduce poverty and improve living standards, capitalism has been proven to be the best way to do it. Socialism, on the other hand, leads to misery and death. Sounds like a pretty easy choice to me.

Professor Tweed @checkurprivilegeplz
The only reason capitalism has been even moderately successful is because of socialist programs, regulations, etc. If government had more power, things would be much better.

  💬 1   🔁   ♡

The tired, old promise that giving more power to government will solve all of society's ills has been repeated ad nauseam by socialists and progressives for more than a century, despite overwhelming evidence showing that no matter how much money and authority Americans give to government, societal problems persist. Presidents Woodrow Wilson, Franklin Roosevelt, Lyndon Johnson, Jimmy Carter, Barack Obama, and others pledged that their reforms would finally put an end to poverty, crime, drugs, suffering, and dozens of other problems, and none of those promises were kept. For example, after a half-century of Johnson's "Great Society" welfare programs, which have cost trillions of dollars, the national poverty rate remains roughly the same as it was in the 1960s.[55] And despite countless promises by President Obama that his policies would make health coverage and college more affordable,[56] health insurance costs and college expenses[57] are significantly higher than they were when Obama implemented his reforms.

There's also absolutely no connection between sustained economic growth and socialist or progressive policies. In fact, one of America's most successful periods— the "roaring" 1920s—included much fewer social programs and regulations. During the 1920s, unemployment rarely rose above 4 percent, and the total U.S. economy grew by a whopping 42 percent.[58] America's total wealth doubled.[59] If giant national government programs are so important to the success of the U.S. economy, why did America experience so much growth in the 1920s?

This important period in history also offers another vital economics lesson. During the Great Depression, progressives insisted that the best way to deal with economic crises is to give government greater control over the economy and to have government pump money into the marketplace as a way of "boosting" growth. This idea, popularized by British economist John Maynard Keynes,[60] has since become standard practice among socialists and progressives in both the Democratic and Republican parties and is partially responsible for the current $22 trillion national debt.[61] However, data from the 1920s shows that this isn't the best way to deal with economic downturns. In fact, the data reveal when government gets out of the way, the economy is more likely to recover quickly.

Before the 1920s "roared," it experienced a significant recession. The federal government faced significant debts remaining from World War I, and consumer price inflation had increased by more than 20 percent.[62] The country entered a major recession in 1920, and by 1921, unemployment hit 11.7 percent.[63] But instead of slashing interest rates and increasing government spending, the Republican-led Congress cut spending and rolled back government's involvement in the market, and the Federal Reserve increased interest rates to 7 percent, a record high at the time.

Robert Murphy, the senior economist at the Independent Energy Institute and a professor at the Free Market Institute at Texas Tech University, notes that from fiscal year "1919 to 1920, federal spending was slashed from $18.5 billion to $6.4 billion—a 65 percent reduction in one year. The budget was pushed down the next two years as well, to $3.3 billion in FY 1922."[64]

According to those who advocate for government's involvement in the marketplace, the recession of 1920–1921 should have been substantially worse than it turned out to be. Spurred by free-market policies, the economy rapidly recovered. By 1922, unemployment had dropped from 11.7 percent to 6.7 percent. By 1923, unemployment hit 2.4 percent.[65] The recession ended with breakneck speed. In fact, it was perhaps the quickest economic turnaround in the United States in the past century.

By contrast, the economic recovery during the Great Depression was agonizingly slow, despite massive new government programs and persistently low interest rates. During the first full year of the Great Depression, 1930, unemployment hit 8.7 percent.[66] In 1932, unemployment soared to 23.6 percent, and it remained above 20 percent through 1935. By 1938, a full eight years after the recession started, unemployment was still extremely high, at about 19 percent, and it wasn't until defense spending tripled in 1942 because of World War II that America finally recovered from the economic downturn.[67]

As Murphy notes, "The conclusion seems obvious to anyone whose mind is not firmly locked into the Keynesian or monetarist framework: The free market works. Even in the face of massive shocks requiring large structural adjustments, the best thing the government can do is cut its own budget and return more resources to the private sector."[68]

This lesson from the 1920s and 1930s perfectly illustrates why centralizing decision-making is literally the worst thing that can be done. The more power you put in the hands of a relatively small group of bureaucrats, the worse things get. The best way to improve economic growth and increase prosperity for all people, not just the wealthy, is to get government out of the way and let individuals—inventors, innovators, entrepreneurs—make their own economic choices.

Socialism doesn't allow for that kind of freedom in the marketplace. By design, it centralizes economic decision-making and eliminates market-based incentives. That's why it always results in lower productivity and often economic chaos. And because the only way socialists believe they can fix economic problems is by increasing their power over an economy, rather than provide market incentives, socialism inevitably devolves into tyranny and often violence. After all, the cheapest way for governments to get people to work harder is to put a gun to the back of their heads, right?

Neal DiCaprio-Cortez @GreenNewNeal
Just because socialism hasn't worked well in some countries doesn't mean it has
flopped everywhere. You've been intentionally ignoring the places where socialism has
worked, nations like Denmark, Norway, and Sweden.

💬 1   ⟲   ♡

Socialism hasn't worked well in "some" countries? *Some* countries? No, socialism
hasn't worked *anywhere*, despite dozens of attempts in nations large and small. And
by "hasn't worked," I mean it's led to unprecedented destruction and mayhem. It's
literally one of the most dangerous philosophical ideas ever conceived, causing the
death, exile, or imprisonment of well over 160 million people—and that's just in the
countries mentioned earlier in this chapter. From Asia to Africa to Europe, socialism
has terrorized the world for more than a century, and no amount of tweaking
socialism will ever be able to fix it. Socialism is rotten to the core.

I'm glad you brought up so-called Scandinavian socialism, though. Perhaps more
than anything else, the myth that countries like Denmark, Norway, and Sweden are
perfect little socialist paradises has fooled people into believing socialism can work.
The truth, however, tells a very different story . . .

END OF CHAPTER #4

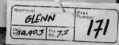

5
SWEDISH-STYLE SOCIALISM

FINAL
APPROVED
-GB

DEBUNKING SCANDINAVIAN SOCIALISM MYTHS

"WHEN I TALK ABOUT DEMOCRATIC SOCIALIST, I'M
NOT LOOKING AT VENEZUELA. I'M NOT LOOKING AT
CUBA. I'M LOOKING AT COUNTRIES LIKE DENMARK
AND SWEDEN."[1]

— BERNIE SANDERS

For millions of Americans, nothing screams "utopia" quite like Sweden—happy, smiling faces, delicious meatballs, and cheap furniture as far as the eye can see. What a country! But not a week goes by without some socialist snake-oil salesman proudly exclaiming Sweden and other Scandinavian countries offer the rest of the world a blueprint to a bright, beautiful, collectivist future.

For example, America's king of peddling socialist poison, comrade Bernie Sanders, often points to Scandinavia as his primary proof of socialism's grand potential. In the run-up to the 2016 presidential election, ABC's George Stephanopoulos asked Sanders whether he thought a self-described "democratic socialist" could get elected in a traditionally capitalism-loving country like America. In response, Sanders said, "Well, so long as we know what democratic socialism is. And if we know that in countries, in Scandinavia, like Denmark, Norway, Sweden, they are very democratic countries, obviously."[2]

Yes, it's true Scandinavians love their *democracy*, but socialism—eh, that's a completely different story. Although Nordic Europeans have at times in the past embraced and adopted some socialist policies and programs—just like Americans have—they have largely maintained their market economies. Scandinavian "socialism" is really just free-market economics with social safety nets underneath, virtually the same as what we have in the United States. In fact, when it comes

to regulations, certain educational reforms, government spending, and other policies, Scandinavians are freer than many Americans.

I know, I know—this probably all sounds like a crazy right-wing conspiracy, but it's true. Scandinavians aren't socialists, at least not in any meaningful sense of the term. But don't take my word for it. Listen to what Danish Prime Minister Lars Lokke Rasmussen has to say. He is, after all, just a *little* more Scandinavian than Brooklyn-born Bernie Sanders.

In 2015, during a speech at Harvard's Kennedy School of Government, Rasmussen noted, "Some people in the U.S. associate the Nordic model with some sort of socialism. Therefore, I would like to make one thing clear: Denmark is far from a socialist planned economy. Denmark is a market economy."[3]

For those of you who aren't fluent with Danish political-speak, allow me to translate: "Hey Bernie, stop calling us socialists."

Since Rasmussen shut down any notion of Denmark as a "socialist" country, Sanders and numerous other American socialists have repeatedly claimed the opposite is true, including during the 2020 presidential campaign. Now, I know Bernie Sanders looks like a crazy old man who should be feeding pigeons at the park—not the guy in charge of the nuclear launch codes—but even he should know by now that Scandinavians aren't socialists. So why are he and other socialists like Alexandria Ocasio-Cortez spending so much time raving about the alleged "successes" of Nordic socialism?

American socialists don't just desperately *want* Scandinavians to be a shining example of socialism, they *need* it to be true. The history of socialism is soaked in blood, racism, and economic chaos. Almost everywhere it has ever been tried, people have had their rights stolen away. In many cases, they have been enslaved and

butchered. In light of the horrifying, bloody history of socialism and communism, socialists need something, anything that they can point to as a success story. So, they're betting on you being gullible enough not to fact-check them when they swear that Sweden is a socialist Magic Kingdom.

So, what's a good socialist to do when he or she finds out the Scandinavian socialism fairy tale that's been endlessly told to a whole generation of wide-eyed socialists isn't true? Continue telling the lie, of course. In the minds of many socialists, it's better to have your facts wrong but your heart in the right place than it is to be a truth-telling capitalist pig. (The ends *always* justify the means, remember?)

But let's spend a few seconds to drink the Bernie Kool-Aid—which, let me warn you, may seem sweet at first, but eventually starts tasting like my grandfather's prune juice mixed with Metamucil. Even if Nordic nations really were the bastions of collectivism so many attendees at Democratic Socialists of America conventions argue they are, what makes socialists think you can impose a system working in a tiny, highly homogeneous part of the world on one of the largest, freest, most diverse nations in the history of humanity? *Arrogance.*

Denmark has a population of less than 6 million. Norway also has less than 6 million citizens. Combined, these two countries have a population that's only a little larger than the Chicago Metropolitan Area and half the size of New York City's metro. In fact, America has at least 20 states with populations comparable to or larger than Denmark or Sweden.

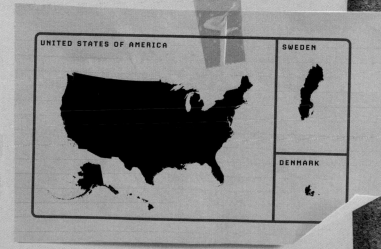

Have you ever tried making dinner plans with six friends? You might have some difficulties, sure. Maybe someone has a gluten allergy or something but usually, most people can agree on a single restaurant without bloodshed. But can you imagine making dinner plans with 327 strangers? What a nightmare. Most people are flexible, but undoubtedly, you'll have to work around a number of people's unique needs. Pete can't go to the nearby seafood place because of a shellfish allergy. Maria is banned from Applebee's for having one too many drinks at her company's most recent Christmas party. Eight more people are vegan, seven are on a paleo diet—whatever the heck that is—and four are pescatarian. And don't forget about Steve. He has an irrational fear of kangaroos, so Outback Steakhouse would trigger him. I guess that's out too. The more people involved, the more diverse the group and the more difficult it is to design a night (or economy) that pleases everyone. (And God help the waiter who has to split the check.)

And that's just population. There are also significant differences related to culture, racial diversity, religion, immigration, and diet. (Good luck finding a Twinkie in Sweden!)

So, not only are Scandinavian countries decidedly not socialist utopias, they also make for extremely bad comparisons. But, I doubt our socialist friend will listen to me (or the Scandinavians themselves), at least not first without saying something like ...

Professor Tweed @checkurprivilegeplz
Oh, come on, @glennbeck! Everyone knows Scandinavians are socialists—and successful ones at that.

💬 1   ↺   ♡

So, you're saying Danish prime minister Rasmussen was confused, lying, or just plain wrong when he said, "I would like to make one thing clear: Denmark is far from a socialist planned economy"?

Let's take a careful look at the facts.

In the Heritage Foundation's *2019 Index of Economic Freedom*, Heritage researchers ranked Iceland 11th in economic freedom, followed by Denmark at 14th, Sweden at 19th, and Finland at 20th.[4] The United States ranked 12th in 2019 and 18th in 2018.

Yes, you read that correctly. Over the past two years, the conservative Heritage Foundation says people in Iceland, Denmark, Sweden, and Finland have a comparable amount or more economic freedom than Americans do.

Additionally, Denmark, Iceland, Finland, Norway, and Sweden all scored higher than the United States in Heritage's "Business Freedom," "Fiscal Health," and "Government Integrity" rankings,[5] and every Scandinavian country scored higher than the United States in Heritage's "Property Rights" category, too.

Does this sound like socialism to you? A high level of business freedom, responsible government spending practices, a low level of corruption, and strong property rights protections? Wait, don't answer that question. I've got more.

Perhaps most telling of all, prior to the passage of the Tax Cuts and Jobs Act in 2017, the corporate tax rates in Scandinavia were considerably lower than the U.S. corporate rate. Have you *ever* met a socialist who didn't want to dramatically increase taxes on corporations? Looking at you, Liz Warren. And even after slashing its corporate rate from 35 percent to 21 percent in 2017, the United States still has a higher corporate tax rate than the one enjoyed by corporations in two Scandinavian countries—Finland (20 percent) and Iceland (20 percent)— and a rate that's only slightly lower than most of the other Scandinavian nations.[6]

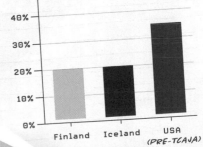

CORPORATE INCOME TAX[a]

GLOBAL RANKINGS[b]

HERITAGE FREEDOM INDEX 2019

ICELAND: 11TH   SWEDEN: 19TH

USA: 12TH   FINLAND: 20TH

DENMARK: 14TH

HERITAGE FREEDOM INDEX 2018

ICELAND: 11TH   USA: 18TH

DENMARK: 12TH   FINLAND: 26TH

SWEDEN: 15TH

[HERITAGE FREEDOM INDEX]

"BUSINESS FREEDOM" 2019

DENMARK: 7TH   ICELAND: 10TH

FINLAND: 8TH   SWEDEN: 12TH

NORWAY: 9TH   USA: 15TH

[HERITAGE FREEDOM INDEX]

"FISCAL HEALTH"
2019

NORWAY: 15TH   SWEDEN: 23RD

DENMARK: 20TH   FINLAND: 63RD

ICELAND: 21ST   USA: 131ST

[HERITAGE FREEDOM INDEX]

"GOVERNMENT INTEGRITY"
2019

FINLAND: 3RD   DENMARK: 8TH

NORWAY: 4TH   ICELAND: 12TH

SWEDEN: 6TH   USA: 21ST

[HERITAGE FREEDOM INDEX]

"PROPERTY RIGHTS"
2019

FINLAND: 5TH   DENMARK: 10TH

SWEDEN: 6TH   NORWAY: 11TH

ICELAND: 8TH   USA: 26TH

And how do you think these Scandinavians managed to amass their current wealth in the first place? By embracing free-market capitalism, not rejecting it. Countries like Denmark and Sweden became wealthy in the mid-twentieth century by adopting relatively low tax rates and other free-market principles. It was only later that they started to embrace left-wing ideals.[7]

Professor Tweed @checkurprivilegeplz
Denmark, Norway, and Sweden haven't totally adopted socialism yet, but they are clearly headed in that direction.

◯ 1   ⟲   ♡

You are exactly right—well, in a world where what you just said means the opposite. After decades of low economic growth, financial crises, and failing welfare programs, many Scandinavian countries have rejected the socialism of their grandparents and traded it in for market-based, capitalistic policy reforms.

Take Sweden, for example. In an article for *Reason*, John Stossel and Tanvir Toy recount an interview Stossel conducted with Swedish historian Johan Norberg. During the interview, Norberg, who is currently a senior fellow at the Cato Institute, explained that one reason Sweden has a reputation of being "socialist" is that during the 1970s and 1980s, the country adopted some radical left-wing policies.[8] But as Norberg notes, those policies didn't last forever.

"Our economy was in crisis, inflation reached 10 percent, and for a brief period interest rates soared to 500 percent," Norberg said. "At that point, the Swedish population just said, 'Enough. We can't do this.'"

What, exactly, caused these massive economic problems? Many of the same policies supported by comrade Bernie and other leading American socialists today. Some socialists never learn.

One of the most disastrous programs of the period was one of Europe's most socialistic: wage earners' funds. In the 1970s, progressive labor unions bullied Swedish politicians into enacting laws that forced private companies to contribute a certain percentage of their profits into worker-owned funds that would be used to buy shares in those companies. Over time, the funds would essentially force businesses to transfer ownership from lawful individuals to workers, effectively socializing whole industries.

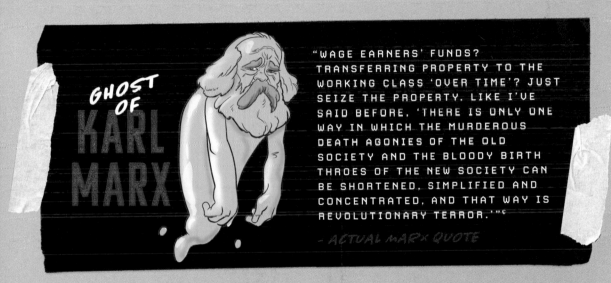

GHOST OF KARL MARX

"WAGE EARNERS' FUNDS? TRANSFERRING PROPERTY TO THE WORKING CLASS 'OVER TIME'? JUST SEIZE THE PROPERTY. LIKE I'VE SAID BEFORE, 'THERE IS ONLY ONE WAY IN WHICH THE MURDEROUS DEATH AGONIES OF THE OLD SOCIETY AND THE BLOODY BIRTH THROES OF THE NEW SOCIETY CAN BE SHORTENED, SIMPLIFIED AND CONCENTRATED, AND THAT WAY IS REVOLUTIONARY TERROR.'"⁶

– ACTUAL MARX QUOTE

Yeah, thanks for the crazy interruption, Karl. What was I saying? Oh yeah, the wage earners' fund program was an unmitigated failure. It turns out that when you take property away from business owners, it doesn't exactly inspire them to invest more time, money, and resources into growing their business. Who could have ever guessed that?

Klaus Eklund, a former Swedish economic adviser to the nation's prime minister, recalled that the socialist wage earners' funds led to significant civil and economic unrest. During this period, "a large part of the population, including small entrepreneurs, small shop owners and so on, became extremely agitated and angry, because they felt the unions were going to take their companies away from them," Eklund said.[9] Hmm . . . shocking development, I know.

Tens of thousands took to the streets on October 4, 1983, to protest the wage earners' funds, and by the end of the march, it's estimated that nearly 100,000 people filled the streets. "People came by buses, by air, and by cars from all over Sweden. And then during the march through Stockholm, people from the streets started to march with us," said one of the participants.

Keep in mind that Sweden's population in the 1980s was only 8 million. A similar-sized protest in the United States today would require more than 4 million people.

Wage earners' funds are perhaps the nicest, kindest way to use an authoritarian government to steal other people's businesses, and even they proved to be too much to stomach. Despite Sweden's disastrous history with wage earners' funds, which the country eventually abandoned altogether, they are still backed by some American socialists in groups like the Democratic Socialists of America.

After years of developing costly and unsustainable new welfare programs and enacting socialist mandates like wage earners' funds, in the 1970s, "The international oil crisis forced the Swedish government into pure Keynesianism and the currency, consequently, was devalued frequently and extensively over about a decade," the Mises Institute reports. "The following 'happy 1980s' offered no solution to the bankrupt nation state, which financially imploded in the early 1990s as the international markets sobered up after a real-estate boom."[10]

The economic destruction caused by Sweden's socialist policies was so dramatic that researchers found there was virtually no job growth in the country from 1950 to 2005.[11]

Zip. Zilch. None.

The oppressive taxes levied on the citizenry led to the loss of national treasures like film actor and director Ingmar Bergman and even Swedish icon IKEA. Bergman wrote about his decision to leave Sweden in his autobiography, in which he explained that he felt targeted and humiliated by "a collection of prestige-seeking poker players" in the State Tax Authority.[12]

Why is it that we never hear *that* part of Scandinavia's history from America's progressive and socialist politicians? Selective amnesia.

The economic chaos didn't last forever. Beginning in the 1990s, the country started to implement important free-market policies, including spending cuts and reforms to its vast welfare system. As a result of these changes, Sweden's economy boomed, benefiting everyone.

"Sweden went from having half of the economic growth that developed countries experienced in the 1970s and 1980s to having 50 percent growth above the average developed country," notes the Atlas Network, citing work by Norberg. "Family incomes increased four-fold in that same timeframe."[13]

Other Scandinavian nations and regions in Europe experienced similar free-market renaissances in the wake of the collapse of the Soviet Union and the fall of the Berlin Wall.

IKEA, A COMPANY THAT DERIVES HALF OF ITS NAME FROM SWEDISH HERITAGE (E = ELMTARYD, A FARM WHERE THE FOUNDER WAS RAISED. A = AGUNNARYD, THE FOUNDER'S HOMETOWN). A COMPANY WHOSE PRIMARY COLORS WERE DETERMINED BY THE SWEDISH FLAG. IKEA, A COMPANY STEEPED IN NATIONAL PRIDE, LEFT THE COUNTRY IN THE 1970S DURING THE HEIGHT OF SWEDEN'S EXPERIMENTATION WITH SOCIALISM IN LARGE PART DUE TO HIGH INCOME AND CORPORATE TAXES.[d]

A.D.D. MOMENT

ASTRID LINDGREN, 1924

PIPPI'S REVOLT!

"Astrid Lindgren is the eighteenth most translated author in the world, and one of the most well-known Swedish authors (most known for her stories about Pippi Longstocking). She became an author relatively late in life, and an influential voice on everyday issues even later. Because of her popularity, people listened to what Lindgren had to say.

"At the age of 68 she submitted an opinion piece to the Swedish daily *Expressen* on the subject of a loophole in the Swedish tax system, which meant that she, as a self-employed writer, had to pay 102 per cent tax on her income. Lindgren wrote the piece in the style of a fairytale, and it had an immediate impact. 'Pomperipossa in Monismania,' published in 1976, became front-page news and led not only to a change in the tax law, but eventually to the fall of the social democratic government that had been in power for 44 years."[c]

Unlike in the United States, which has steadily expanded many of its welfare programs over the past several decades, Scandinavian countries have moved in the opposite direction. They still have numerous social welfare "safety nets," sure, but they have largely reversed course on many of the socialist policies they once had in place—policies American progressives and socialists claim would make our country better than ever, despite a mountain of evidence to the contrary.

Professor Tweed @checkurprivilegeplz
Maybe Scandinavian countries do have some market-based features, but what about all their big welfare programs, like universal health care? Those programs clearly show Scandinavians are socialists.

♡ 1   ⟲   ♡

Having *some* socialized industries in place doesn't mean an entire economy can fairly be labeled "socialist." Imagine for a moment a conservative's paradise, a true bastion of individual freedom. (Just the thought of people having control over their own money and property is likely making our friend Professor Pete nauseated, but let's spend a few minutes to think this through.)

In a conservative's utopia, government's only function is to protect the rights of individual people and keep communities safe. There are no government-run social safety nets, because charities composed of church groups, philanthropists, and concerned, compassionate citizens take care of those in need. (Contrary to socialists' beliefs, it actually happens a lot.)

Without massive, multi-trillion-dollar welfare programs, there's no need for many forms of taxation, including federal income taxes. There's also no reason to have Social Security, because the elderly, in the absence of huge income taxes, have been able to keep and invest their own money for their entire lives, and families are encouraged to take care of people when they grow old or fall on hard times.

The elimination of most federal regulatory burdens and some unnecessary state and local regulations has allowed for enhanced economic growth and job opportunities. People are wealthier and freer than ever, and in most cases, they have the money to pay for their own children's education, both at the K–12 and college levels.

Without most taxes, welfare programs, or government regulations, our conservative utopia is about as free as any nation has ever been. But what if our fictional utopia were to retain public, collectively owned roadways? Does that mean that our perfect conservative world would really be just another example of *socialism*? Of course not. And I doubt there's a single economist in the entire world—on the right or left—who would disagree.

The truth is, every country on Earth has some government-provided services, and yet no one would say every country has a "socialist" economy. Yes, many Scandinavian nations still have big social safety nets in place and some socialized services— including a few big ones—but they are still worlds away from being what Bernie Sanders, Ocasio-Cortez, and others have been calling for. And Karl Marx—the most influential socialist in world history—would totally reject that Scandinavian countries have systems that come even remotely close to his own vision of what a socialist society should look like—although he would probably approve of their hipster beards.

 Professor Tweed @checkurprivilegeplz
Fine, whatever it is you want to call the prevailing ideology in Scandinavia, that's what I want, and that's what I mean by "democratic socialism."

💬 1   🔁   ♡

Any socialist who claims he or she wants America to be more like Scandinavia either doesn't understand what's really going on in Nordic nations, is lying, or isn't really a socialist.

INCOME TAXES

Let's take a brief look at taxes, for example. Socialists say they are all about forcing businesses and wealthy individuals to "pay their fair share"—whatever that means.

They want to dramatically increase tax rates on some middle-income and all wealthy individuals and businesses, so that they can redistribute the wealth to lower-income people.

This isn't just a policy proposal socialists *like*, it's a cornerstone of their whole ideology, one that dates all the way back to Karl Marx. (You know, the whole "from each according to his abilities, to each according to his needs" thing.)

Socialists believe that if you have more wealth at your disposal, you should be forced to give it up, because they've determined the only reason some people have so much more money than others isn't because they are more talented or intelligent or innovative or hardworking or anything like that, and it isn't because they earned it by providing society with a desired good or service. Rather, they say people with wealth—including many in the middle class—should give it up because the only way they got it in the first place is, in part, by exploiting others.

This is exactly why all of the progressive and socialist presidential candidates running in 2020 have said they would fund their numerous proposed trillion-dollar government programs by imposing huge tax increases on the wealthy.

THE LEFT'S DEFINITION OF "FAIR SHARE"

"FAIR SHARE" => CURRENT TAX RATE

A.D.D. MOMENT

THE 1% IN THE EYES OF SOCIALISTS

Approval
GLEN
List
$34.90.3
Film
No. 7.2
Page Number
189

Sen. Elizabeth Warren's "wealth tax" proposal would create a 2 percent levy on those with $50 million or more in assets and a 3 percent tax on those with assets worth $1 billion or more.[14]

Bernie Sanders's tax reform plan would create a new progressive wealth tax structure that would confiscate as much as 8 percent of a family's net worth.[15]

Sen. Kamala Harris and Joe Biden said they want to repeal the 2017 Tax Cuts and Jobs Act because, in Harris's words, it "benefited the top 1 percent and the biggest corporations in this country."

Indiana mayor Pete Buttigieg said he wants to increase tax rates for the top income brackets only, while also imposing a wealth tax and financial transactions tax.[17]

If Scandinavians are socialists—or even just progressives—we should expect their tax codes to be in line with many of these proposals, but—brace yourself—they undeniably are not.

It's true that, generally speaking, Scandinavian countries have very high taxes. But unlike the proposals offered by the leading Democratic Party presidential candidates and socialists, the tax systems in places like Denmark, Norway, and Sweden impose high tax burdens on *everyone*. Yes, the wealthier in these countries pay higher tax rates than lower-income people, but, in the end, *everyone* pays a hefty price.

Kyle Pomerleau, the Tax Foundation's chief economist and vice president of economic analysis, notes, "Scandinavian income taxes raise a lot of revenue because they are actually rather flat. In other words, they tax most people at these high rates, not just high-income taxpayers. The top marginal tax rate of 60 percent in Denmark applies to all income over 1.2 times the average income in Denmark. From the American perspective, this means that all income over $60,000 (1.2 times the average income

of about $50,000 in the United States) would be taxed at 60 percent. Sweden and Norway have similarly flat income tax systems."[18]

A.D.D. MOMENT

SIDE NOTE

So, let's play this out. If America were to adopt a Danish income tax model and you earn $60,000 per year annually, you would only end up keeping roughly $24,000 of your own money over the course of the year, or about $480 of your weekly paycheck of $1,200.

DOES THAT SOUND "FAIR" TO YOU?

"Compare this to the United States," Pomerleau said. "The top marginal tax rate of 46.8 percent (state average and federal combined rates) kicks in at 8.5 times the average U.S. income (around $400,000). Comparatively, few taxpayers in the United States face the top marginal rate."

Put simply: In Scandinavia, middle-class earners are expected to pay much more than they do in the United States. In fact, although socialists and progressives are seemingly always ranting about how supposedly "unfair" the current U.S. tax system is because the wealthy don't pay enough of the tax burden, the top 17 percent of earners in America already pay three-fourths of all income tax revenue, despite the fact they use relatively few government services. This is a far more progressive, socialistic system than what they have now in many parts of Scandinavia.

EVERYONE PAYS

And that's just income taxes. Many Scandinavians are also required to pay a large value-added tax (VAT). In Denmark, for example, all Danes are forced to pay a 25 percent VAT on goods and services, in addition to numerous other fees and taxes on products. This makes the price of virtually everything more expensive, harming lower-income consumers more than any other group.

So, if Americans were to adopt the Danish income tax model, they would, on top of forfeiting 60 percent of their paychecks to the government right from the start, also be forced to pay 25 percent more on nearly everything they buy. Admit it, you're starting to feel "taxed enough already," aren't you?

Unsurprisingly, most American socialists and progressives *hate* value-added taxes like these, because they do absolutely nothing to redistribute wealth. Not a single leading Democrat is proposing one as a primary way to raise funds for their big, shiny, new welfare programs.

SWEDEN'S SCHOOL CHOICE

Taxes aren't the only area in which Scandinavians differ from American socialists. Consider school choice programs. In Sweden, all parents are eligible to receive a voucher that allows them to enroll their child in any school in the country, whether they are public or private, and the program has proven to be successful for those who take advantage of it.

According to a report by public policy organization EdChoice, "The most vigorous study on the Swedish school voucher system by Stockholm University researchers Anders Böhlmark and Mikael Lindahl concludes that students in non-public (or Independent schools as they are called in Sweden) perform better than their public school peers both in the short term, with increased test results and grades, and the long term, with higher grades in secondary school and at university. Both for-profit and nonprofit private schools showed this positive effect. Furthermore, a recent national survey in Sweden showed that parents who had children enrolled in Independent (private) schools were 10 percent more likely to be satisfied than those with children in municipal schools."[19]

In the United States, not a single leading progressive or socialist politician supports creating a universal school choice program. In fact, they have been ruthlessly fighting against school choice for decades. Comrade Bernie isn't even in favor of charter schools, one of the most moderate forms of school choice. Socialists disdain choice in basically every arena—you know, except abortion.

On Sanders's 2020 campaign website, Bernie claims "few charter schools have lived up to their promise. . . . Charter schools are led by unaccountable, private bodies, and their growth has drained funding from the public-school system."[20]

Sanders then lamented that "the proliferation of charter schools has dispropor-tionately affected communities of color—17 percent of charter schools are 99 per-cent minority, compared to 4 percent of traditional public schools. This has led the NAACP, the NEA [National Education Association], AFT [American Federation of Teachers] and others to criticize the charter movement for intensifying racial segre-gation. The damage to communities caused by unregulated charter school growth must be stopped and reversed."

At best, this is a wildly misleading, albeit common, claim spread by socialists like Sanders. There's no question that racial minorities are "disproportionately affected" by charter schools, but that's because they disproportionately benefit from them. Countless academic studies show that when individuals have more education freedom, education quality improves—just as it does in virtually every industry. Because government-run schools in many inner-city communities are so terrible, it's more likely for school choice programs to develop in those communities, and thus more likely that the people living there will use them.

A 2016 analysis by EdChoice examined 100 empirical studies of school choice programs, and the results were nothing short of remarkable.[21] In the vast majority of papers analyzed, researchers determined school choice programs improve educational outcomes and/or lower costs.

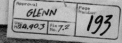

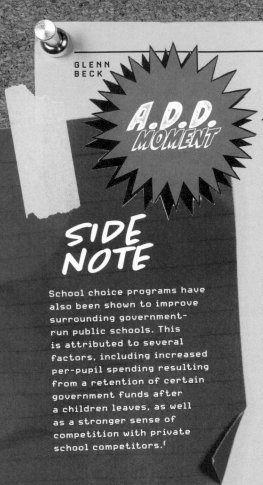

A.D.D. MOMENT

SIDE NOTE

School choice programs have also been shown to improve surrounding government-run public schools. This is attributed to several factors, including increased per-pupil spending resulting from a retention of certain government funds after a children leaves, as well as a stronger sense of competition with private school competitors.[f]

The benefits of school choice experienced by countless parents across the country are the primary reason why the idea of expanding school choice is widely supported by numerous minority groups, including African Americans. A January 2019 survey found 67 percent of Americans likely to vote in the 2020 election were in favor of school choice policies similar to the program in Sweden—including 67 percent of African Americans, 73 percent of Hispanics, and 56 percent of Democrats. Yes, even Democratic voters support school choice.[22]

Swedes clearly see the value in school choice, too, so why doesn't comrade Bernie—the same guy who is constantly raving about how wonderful Sweden is? Let me answer that for you. It's because it would be an admission that competition and choice are proven to deliver better results than government's best intentions. But remember, when empirical evidence shatters their socialist fairy tale, they have no choice but to repeat the lie.

NORWAY'S ADDICTION TO OIL

One of the most remarkable differences between American socialists and some Scandinavians is on the issue of energy. While democratic socialists in United States like Alexandria Ocasio-Cortez fight tirelessly to try to rid the world of our most affordable energy sources, like natural gas and oil, the Scandinavian nation of Norway has been getting wealthy pumping oil out of the ground—and a ton of it, too.

The Norwegian Ministry of Petroleum and Energy reports, "In the 50 years since Norwegian petroleum activities began, about 47 per cent of the estimated total recoverable resources on the continental shelf have been produced and sold. Thus, there are large remaining resources, and it is expected that the level of activity on the Norwegian shelf will continue to be high for the next 50 years as well."[23]

Again, a good translation of this Scandinavian political-speak is, "We've been producing a ton of oil for decades, and we aren't going to be stopping anytime soon."

Norway is one of the largest oil exporters in the world. In fact, Norway, which only has a population of less than 6 million, has been so successful at earning mountains of cash selling the very same oil products routinely demonized by American socialists that it now has a sovereign wealth fund totaling $1 trillion.[24]

In 2019, reports also surfaced showing that Norway is working with Chinese companies and the government of China—the world's largest emitter of carbon-dioxide emissions—to expand its oil exports in Asian markets and to cooperate with Chinese oil producers on oil and gas exploration.[25] Can you imagine anyone in the Democratic Party today supporting such efforts?

These new relationships between Norway and China followed several years of reduced trade and business activities resulting from a decision by the Norway-based Nobel Committee to award a Chinese dissident with the Nobel Prize in 2010. China only agreed to thaw its relationship with Norway after the government agreed not to "support actions that undermine" the Chinese government's interests.[26]

 Professor Tweed @checkurprivilegeplz
.@glennbeck, Norway and other Scandinavian countries have spent a fortune investing in renewable energies like wind and solar.

💬 1   ⟲   ♡

Yeah, but they are using the fortune they have amassed from fossil-fuel production to do it. And there's no sign they plan to stop anytime soon. Norway projects it will within the next decade match or exceed its record for petroleum production, all while we're being warned by American socialists that the world is on the verge of a climate change catastrophe because of man-caused global warming.

You say you want the United States to be just like Scandinavia, but do you *really* mean it? You want a culture that's extremely homogeneous? You want fewer business and financial regulations? You want lower- and middle-income people to pay a greater tax burden? You want school choice? You want balanced budgets (or close to it)? You want the United States to continue growing its fossil fuel production? These policies are "democratic socialism" to you?

Professor Tweed @checkurprivilegeplz
I don't know if I want all those policies to be adopted here in the United States, but I do want the United States to adopt the socialist aspects of their economies, because Scandinavians are much better off than we are. Clearly their big socialistic welfare programs have made life much better for Scandinavians than what we're stuck with in America.

💬 1   🔁   ♡

Ah, yes, the whole "everything is better in Scandinavia" myth. That's one of my favorites!

First of all, let's remember that in order to be like Scandinavians, we would need to flatten our tax system and reduce regulations and government spending. Is that really what you want to do?

Second, although there's no doubt—none at all—that nations like Denmark and Sweden have a lot to offer and certainly are not comparable to socialist hellholes like Venezuela, there's absolutely no evidence to suggest the people there are much better off than most folks in America.

For starters, middle-income Scandinavians have to pay outrageously high taxes. As I noted earlier, if the United States were to have a comparable tax structure as the one in place in Denmark, Americans would have to pay a whopping 60 percent of all income earned over $60,000 to the government. Although that would be Comrade Sanders's dream come true, it would be a nightmare to most Americans.

In Sweden, 44 percent of all total domestic income is paid in taxes, while in the United States, the tax burden amounts to just 26 percent of total income. That's a big reason why Americans' average disposable income—which includes what people pay in taxes—is higher than in any of the Scandinavian countries, and even in the entire world.[27]

This translates to bigger houses, bigger cars, and even bigger appliances. If you ever make a habit out of watching television marathons of shows like *House Hunters International*, you'll start to notice terms like "American fridge" or "American-style." That's because having a large fridge or even an in-home washing machine or dryer is not nearly as common in other countries as it is in America.

And Americans like it that way, too. According to a 2018 Gallup survey, about 45 percent of U.S. adults say they want more disposable income and that their taxes are too high[28]—a fact made even more stunning when you consider it's estimated just 44 percent of Americans pay federal income taxes.[29] Do you really think if these Americans had their tax burdens nearly doubled, in line with what citizens pay in Scandinavia, they would think they are better off?

Americans in many parts of the country also have access to lower housing prices and bigger homes than in most of Scandinavia, and Americans pay substantially less for important goods and services, like motor-vehicle fuel[30] and many foods.

Rashida Resitance @AOC_2024_Squad4Life
Ok, but what about single-payer health care? That's clearly a "socialist" idea adopted by Scandinavians, and wherever it has been tried, people are much better off.

💬 1   ⇄   ♡

And there it is. As soon as you brought up the Scandinavian socialism myth, I knew we would eventually end up discussing single-payer health care, the pot of gold at the end of every American socialist's rainbow.

Whenever people like Bernie Sanders endlessly praise the "achievements" of Scandinavia, they aren't referring to the relatively free markets of Denmark, school choice programs of Sweden, or the energy policies of Norway. They are nearly always attempting to convince Americans to support government programs similar to Scandinavians' socialized health care systems.

Look, no one hates the bureaucratic nonsense, paperwork, and absurd rules of the modern health insurance system more than I do. (Just *try* reading those ridiculous health insurance contracts without having your head explode.) But putting government bureaucrats in charge of the health insurance industry won't fix our very flawed system. It will only make it worse. Much worse. Much, much worse.

Single-payer health care models are appealing to many because they offer health coverage to everyone, making them far less complex than the current system. Patients don't need to worry about navigating the health insurance system. Doctors don't need to worry about hiring staff to comply with impossible-to-understand insurance arrangements. (Although they do have to worry about plenty of additional government regulations.) And people are covered regardless of whether they work, so there is no preexisting conditions problem that must be dealt with.

On the surface, it seems to many like a better, easier to understand system. But for every one advantage single-payer programs provide, there are countless other unavoidable and serious flaws.

GOVERNMENT WASTE

One such flaw is that government-run programs almost never spend money efficiently. This is precisely why Amtrak, the Postal Service, and numerous government agencies are constantly operating above their budgets and routinely fail to provide services that match the quality of their privately-owned competitors. I mean, seriously, is anyone still willing to make an argument in favor of the Postal Service? It lost $3.9 billion in fiscal year 2018.[31]

EXTRA Nº 07   **Breaking News**   REPORT JUST IN!

POSTAL SERVICE REPORTS
$3.9 BILLION
IN LOSSES FOR FISCAL YEAR 2018

When it comes to government waste, one of the biggest culprits is Medicaid—which, remember, is a government health care program. In 2017, government officials acknowledged that the improper payment rate for Medicaid is very likely higher than the official 10 percent estimate, and in 2015, the Government Accountability Office reported improper payments totaled at least $137 billion.[32] Can you imagine how many *trillions* of dollars would be wasted if the same federal government that wastes more than $100 billion per year were to be put in charge of the entire health care system?

You might think federal officials would be embarrassed by this poor record, but they aren't. The national government has a long track record of wasting taxpayers' money on truly outrageous government projects. Just one of the hundreds of examples a simple internet search will reveal is the government's decision to spend $518,000 "to study how cocaine affects the sexual behavior of Japanese quails."[33] (By the way, are birds really snorting cocaine now? How did I miss this news story? Although, it would explain a lot about Woody Woodpecker.)

As ridiculous as it is to study the sexual proclivities of coked-up Asian quails, there are other even more egregious examples of waste. For instance, the federal government spends an estimated $1.7 billion per year servicing *empty* government-owned buildings.[34] (Of course, maybe that's a good thing. Better to pay for an empty government building than one full of bureaucrats hell-bent on finding ways to waste even more money.)

And these are just the tip of the iceberg. Citizens Against Government Waste has identified more than 600 recommendations to reduce government waste in its *Prime Cuts* report. According to CAGW, if the government were to make its recommended cuts, it would save a whopping $429.8 billion in the first year, and more than $3 trillion in just five years.[35] There's your infrastructure-improvement fund.

Given this tremendous amount of waste, it's clear that government is completely unequipped to operate the United States' gigantic and extremely complex health care system. At the very least, shouldn't the government be expected to cut its current level of waste before taking on massive new projects?

EXPENSIVE. LIKE ... *REALLY EXPENSIVE*

A second problem is single-payer health care systems are hugely expensive for taxpayers. An analysis of Sanders's "Medicare for All" plan by Charles Blahous at the Mercatus Center at George Mason University determined Sanders's proposal would cost, at minimum, a stunning $32 trillion in additional federal spending over just 10 years.[36]

And that's likely an extremely conservative estimate, too. Many of the existing Medicare for All plans, including Sanders's plan, include provisions that would

mandate the federal government only pay the same reimbursement rates given to doctors and hospitals in the current Medicare system. But there's just one problem: Applying Medicare reimbursement rates across the country would very likely bankrupt most of America's hospitals. On average, Medicare only reimburses hospitals 87 cents for every dollar spent.[37] How do hospitals stay in business? By charging people with private health insurance significantly more for health care services to make up the difference.

But even if we assume that Medicare for All will only cost the lower-end $32 trillion estimate, Blahous notes "doubling all currently projected federal individual and corporate income tax collections would be insufficient to finance the added federal costs of the plan."

Many socialists and progressives say they could pay for Medicare for All by raising taxes on the richest Americans, but this is a lie, plain and simple. The Tax Foundation calculated how much money would be raised by increasing the top marginal tax rate to 70 percent for the wealthiest earners, and it found it would only increase revenues by $300 billion annually.[38] That's less than 1 percent of the 10-year cost of the lower-end estimate for Medicare for All. *Less than 1 percent.*

Even worse, you could confiscate every dollar from every single person on *Forbes'* list of the 400 richest Americans—including Amazon's Jeff Bezos, Microsoft's Bill Gates, Berkshire Hathaway's Warren Buffett, and Facebook's Mark Zuckerberg—and it would only amount to $2.9 trillion—less than 10 percent of Medicare for All's 10-year cost.[39] Nice try, Comrade Sanders. Your math sucks.

You can't expect to tax the wealthy and pay for gigantic government programs like Medicare for All. The middle class will also have to pay much more in taxes, too, just as they do in Scandinavia. The Heartland Institute, a free-market think tank,

A.D.D. MOMENT

FORBES 400 RICHEST AMERICANS[g]

1. JEFF BEZOS
$160 BILLION

2. BILL GATES
$97 BILLION

3. WARREN BUFFETT
$88.3 BILLION

4. MARK ZUCKERBERG
$61 BILLION

5. LARRY ELLISON
$58.4 BILLION

estimates the passage of single-payer health care would mean "millions of middle-class individuals and families would need to pay thousands of dollars more every year for health coverage than they do now."[40]

Heartland's analysis shows if Medicare for All becomes law, households earning $50,000–$75,000 would see their federal income tax bills in 2022 increase by an average of $7,773 to $9,171. Households earning $75,000–$100,000 would pay $12,612 to $14,880 more in new taxes. That increase in tax burden would leave your average American family asking important questions like, "Can we go another year or two without buying a new car?," and "What flavor ramen do you want to microwave for dinner today?"

RATIONING

A third problem is health care rationing. Because large tax increases such as these often cause so much damage to an economy, in many cases governments choose to combine tax increases with health care rationing, creating harmful and sometimes dangerous increases in the amount of time patients are required to wait before being seen by a doctor.

Although long wait times exist in virtually every single-payer health care system, some of the most detailed reports on wait times come from Canada, whose system is routinely praised by Bernie Sanders and other socialists.

The Canada-based Fraser Institute reports each year the average time Canadians must wait to receive medically necessary elective treatment, from the time a patient is first referred to a specialist by a general practitioner to the moment he or she receives the needed care. The Fraser Institute's analysis shows Canadians often must wait for months for important treatments and even some forms of medical testing.[41]

The average wait for Canadian patients needing cardiovascular surgery is nearly 10 weeks. Patients seeking general surgeries must wait for more than three months. Gynecological treatments take on average more than 20 weeks. Orthopedic surgical patients must wait more than nine months. Need brain or spine surgery with a neurosurgeon? You should expect to wait on average more than 26 weeks.

Now, I'm not a doctor—that's a shocking admission, I know—but I'm pretty sure that people suffering with tumors *in their brains* shouldn't wait for six months before receiving treatment. And yet, that's exactly what's happening in Canada.

For many specialties, wait times in Canada are significantly longer than in the United States. For example, U.S. patients needing orthopedic surgery wait only an average of 11 days from the moment of referral to the first appointment with an orthopedic surgeon.[42] In Canada, the average wait for a similar appointment is longer than 14 weeks. That's the kind of math even a socialist can understand. Maybe.

APPOINTMENT REMINDER

Date: **11/2/2025**

Time: **3PM**

2020 SOCIAL ST.
COMMUNIST HILLS, CALIFORNIA

1-800-GOOD-LUCK
HEALTHCARE.GOV

EDITOR'S FACT CHECK

GLENN IS ACTUALLY A DOCTOR. HE RECEIVED AN HONORARY DOCTORATE IN HUMANITIES FROM LIBERTY UNIVERSITY AND IS NOW WORKING ON OPENING HIS OWN EAR, NOSE, AND THROAT CLINIC IN IDAHO.

Things aren't much better in England, another country with a single-payer health care system. Rationing has become such a terrible problem there that government health care administrators recommended in 2018 that patients should start meeting with their primary care doctors in groups as large as 15.[43] You know, the group therapy approach to *all* kinds of health care treatments. Sounds great!

"It is billed as an attempt to alleviate strain on family doctors, many of whom complain of being overworked," *The Telegraph* reported in October 2018.

"Group appointments of between 10–15 people with the same condition have been piloted in Slough in Berkshire, London, Birmingham, Manchester, Sheffield, Newcastle and Northumberland. Doctors at the Royal College of GPs' annual conference . . . said the groups were a 'fun and efficient' way to carry out consultations with patients who shared the same conditions."

Yeah, nothing says "fun and efficient" like telling 14 of your neighbors about that weird thing growing on the back of your neck, or how that anti-fungal cream

A.D.D. MOMENT

SIDE NOTE

Regional Clinical Commissioning Groups (CCG) across the UK are initiating rationing restrictions to cope with budget short-falls. Some CCGs are delaying procedures for smokers and the obese. Others are suspending services, including in vitro fertilization.[h]

you've been prescribed just doesn't seem to be working as well as you'd like. And who doesn't like discussing hemorrhoids with complete strangers?

Additionally, let's not forget the U.S. federal government already operates a single-payer health care system—the Veterans Health Administration—and it's a complete disaster. Not only are VA hospitals often outdated and poorly funded and managed, they also suffer from numerous service problems, including long wait times. According to a 2019 report by *USA Today*, "At roughly 70 percent of VA hospitals, the median time between arrival in the emergency room and admission was longer than at other hospitals, in some cases by hours, according to a USA TODAY analysis of the department's data. That included Loma Linda, where the median wait is more than 7½ hours."[44]

IF THIS IS HOW THEY TREAT AMERICA'S HEROES, HOW WELL DO YOU THINK THEY WILL TREAT YOU?

Is it any wonder then that patient satisfaction at VA hospitals is much lower than in non-VA hospitals? *USA Today* reported VA scorecards of patients' satisfaction with their treatment, "Nearly every VA facility—141 out of 146—scored below other facilities on a majority of questions surveyed."

 Professor Tweed @checkurprivilegeplz
Well, maybe it's true that many other single-payer health care systems are flawed, but Scandinavians have proven that government can effectively provide high-quality health care to everyone.

 1

Actually, no, they haven't. Many of the same problems plaguing the health care systems of government-managed systems around the world are also rampant in Scandinavia.

Nowhere has this been more obvious than in Finland. In 2019, Finland's coalition government, including Prime Minister Juha Sipila, resigned after failing to push through reforms that would have restructured the country's collapsing single-payer health care system.[45]

The primary problems in Finland are skyrocketing costs and demographic changes. Like the United States—and most of the Western world—Finland's population is aging, pushing the country's already outrageously high tax burden on a shrinking group of working-age Finns. By 2030, more than one-quarter of the country is expected to be 65 years old or older.[46]

In order to keep Finland's health care model afloat, policymakers need to raise taxes even higher, ration care and cut costs, and/or make substantial changes to the way the system is organized. Sipila's proposed reforms would have cut health care funding by billions of dollars by 2029. "We need reforms, there is no other way for Finland to succeed," Sipila said.

When Sipila failed to garner enough political support to make the necessary reforms, much of the administration resigned.

As one Reuters report noted, Finland isn't the only Scandinavian country struggling to keep its single-payer system from falling apart: "Other Nordic countries have also grappled with the need to cut costs. . . . Denmark will gradually increase the retirement age to 73—the highest in the world—while cutting taxes and unemployment benefits to encourage people to work more."[47]

In Sweden, not only are policymakers raising the retirement age to force citizens to work later into their lives so that they'll keep contributing tax revenues, they have also done the unthinkable: They have "opened up parts of the healthcare system to the private sector in a bid to boost efficiency."

Wait a second. Let's read that again. Swedes are turning to the private sector "to boost efficiency." Huh. It turns out there's nothing magical about Scandinavians' government-managed health care systems after all.

Rashida Resistance @AOC_2024_Squad4Life
If what you're saying is true, why do Scandinavians live so much longer than the average American?

 1   ⟲   ♡

It's easy to understand why you might think life expectancy is a good indicator of how well a health care system is functioning, but the more you look at health care data, the more obvious it is that life expectancy isn't a good way to judge a country's quality of life or the quality of available health care services.

The reported life expectancies of Chile, Greece, and Slovenia are also better than the United States' life expectancy, but you don't see Americans rushing to move to Greece or raving about the high living standards in Slovenia.

In fact, the Organisation for Economic Co-operation and Development's *Better Life Index* ranked the United States seventh in its "Health" category in 2019, higher than every Scandinavian country and dozens of others with single-payer health care systems.[48]

"SOCIALIST" NORDIC COUNTRIES ARE ACTUALLY MOVING TOWARD PRIVATE HEALTH CARE

"The problem for their argument is that, despite these extremely generous programs, some of these countries are seeing a steady growth of private health insurance. . . .

"Between 2006 and 2016, the portion of the population covered by private insurance increased by 4% in Sweden, 7% in Norway, and 22% in Denmark. . . .

"This growing European interest in private health insurance typically stems from dissatisfaction with the state-run systems, which often provide poor or incomplete coverage and long wait times.

"By contrast, private plans offer wider coverage, shorter wait times, access to private facilities, and more flexibility in patient choice.

"For instance, in a 2009 survey, nearly half of Danes felt waiting times were unreasonable while only about a third disagreed."[i]

You might be wondering why the United States has a lower life expectancy if it's not directly related to differences in the quality of health care systems. The answer is complex, but here's the CliffsNotes version: Americans are too fat and love to drive cars.

ONE NATION UNDER FAT

Due largely to cultural differences, Americans are considerably fatter than people in many other countries around the world—and much heavier than Scandinavians. (Trust me, I know. I've got a donut hanging out of my mouth as I write this.) Diet plays a critical role in determining life expectancy because many of the deadliest diseases in Europe and North America are directly or indirectly related to diet, especially heart disease, the United States' number-one killer.[49]

In fact, despite having less than 5 percent of the world's total population, the United States is home to about one-quarter of the world's severely obese men.[50] Ladies, you're not off the hook, either. There are more severely obese women in America than anywhere else on Earth.

The situation in Scandinavia is *very* different. Many Scandinavian countries have much healthier diets and lower BMIs. For instance, Denmark's average BMI is among the lowest one-quarter and one of the lowest in Europe.[51]

Some have argued that access to health care is the primary reason for these differences, but

Scandinavians have long had better diets and lower BMIs compared to many parts of the United States,[52] dating back well before the development of modern health care.

If we want our fellow Americans to live longer lives, we don't need a bureaucratic takeover of the health care industry, we need to replace our love for donuts, Twinkies, and Big Macs with fruits and—eh, those green things everyone is always talking about.

AMERICA'S LOVE AFFAIR WITH CARS

Since the early twentieth century, Americans have been absolutely in love with the automobile. By as early as 1913, 80 percent of the world's cars were being produced in the United States.

There's nothing better—or more quintessentially American—than getting the family together and hitting the open road. The feeling of freedom, the wide expansive roadways that stretch for thousands of miles, the sense of adventure, the screaming children in the backseat—okay, I could do without the screaming, but you get my point.

Americans love cars, but their constant driving comes with a much higher risk of motor-vehicle fatalities. The World Health Organization reports the likelihood of dying from a road traffic accident is significantly higher in the United States than in Scandinavia. In 2016, Americans were more than three times as likely to die from a traffic accident as Danes and more than four times as likely as Norwegians or Swedes.[53]

When you take traffic-related and obesity-related deaths into account, the life expectancy differences between nations drop. These aren't the only factors, of course, but they are important ones that often get ignored by those who think, based on no hard evidence, that increased government involvement can fix the U.S. health care system.

Rashida Resistance @AOC_2024_Squad4Life
Well, even if you're right, it's also true that the United States spends much more on health care than any other country in the world. A socialized health care system could keep costs under control.

♡ 1   ⟲   ♡

America's health care system is far from perfect, and one of its biggest problems is that health care is much more expensive than it ought to be. But, as I already explained in Chapter 1, much of the problem is being driven by government's involvement in the industry.

The health insurance and health care systems are significantly flawed because the forces that normally exist in markets have been removed, blocked, or weakened by regulations and the tax code. Making health care more affordable would require unleashing innovators, entrepreneurs, and consumers from the shackles of the current government-manipulated marketplace.

But that's only part of the issue. Sometimes, it's true that you get what you pay for. And while Americans do end up paying *a lot* for health care, they also have access to the best health care facilities and doctors the world has ever seen. Many of the world's most talented physicians and medical researchers travel from across the globe to come to the United States, where they can worship (or not worship) God in the way they choose, own a home, speak freely, and enjoy equal treatment under the law—all while earning a heck of a lot more than they can elsewhere.

America is home to many of the most important and exciting medical innovations, in large part because of the promise that those who provide important, breakthrough medical technologies and innovations will be rewarded financially for their achievements and hard work. I know it's hard for socialists to acknowledge, but history, anthropology, and even biology clearly show people are generally motivated by self-preservation and personal (including family) enrichment.

There isn't a flood of medical doctors, researchers, and other professionals banging down Finland's door to join its failing health care system, but that's exactly what's been going on in the United States for decades.

Neil DiCaprio-Cortez @GreenNewNeal
If that's true, then why do I keep hearing about America's growing doctor shortage?

💬 1   🔁   ♡

Because there is a doctor shortage. But that's not because there aren't enough people wanting to become licensed U.S. physicians, it's because the current system has numerous bureaucratic controls that significantly limit the number of doctors licensed every year. Without those requirements, many of which are unnecessary, we'd have more than enough physicians.

Neil DiCaprio-Cortez @GreenNewNeal
Without government-provided health care, people truly be free. So, maybe government-managed health care isn't perfect, but at least people have the freedom to live their lives without fear of getting sick while living without access to the health care services they need.

💬 1   🔁   ♡

No one is suggesting that it's good for individuals or society that some Americans are still living without health insurance coverage. But the goal ought to be to create a system that makes health insurance and health care affordable for everyone—a goal that really can be achieved. It shouldn't be to put the same ridiculously irresponsible people in charge of health care who have run up a $22 trillion national debt.

I'm glad you referred to the importance of "freedom," though. Liberty has real value. In fact, it's the foundation of our society. Without freedom, everything else would collapse: the economy, our families, our faith—everything. But history has repeatedly shown that freedom and socialism are completely incompatible. They literally can't coexist, because at the heart of socialism is the belief that individual rights don't mean as much as accomplishing the goals of whoever is in charge of the government—you know, the people with all the guns and tanks.

Even in the most peaceful countries that have socialized health care systems, there is some degree of tyranny. There must be, because without it, there's no way to manage the system effectively.

Single-payer health care models only allow for one option—hence the "single" in "single-payer." Whatever the government decides, goes. And if that happens to conflict with the rights of individuals, well then, that's unfortunate, but at the end of the day, whatever is considered to be in the best interests of the collective must be the primary goal. And who decides that? The tiny minority of people at the top of society who claim they are representing the best interests of the collective—whether they actually are or not.

There are endless examples of how government has used its power to silence individuals or take away their rights, especially on the issue of health care. But let's turn to one both of us are old enough to remember—although I'm willing to bet only one of us will: Barack Obama's war on the religious rights of Catholic nuns.

Following the passage of the Affordable Care Act in 2010, the Obama administration's Department of Health and Human Services issued a regulation mandating many employers offer their employees health insurance coverage that included "free" contraceptives, including birth control—even if it violated the religious beliefs of the employer.

Following the mandate, several religious nonprofit organizations—including Little Sisters of the Poor, a Catholic order of nuns—refused to provide the contraception coverage and sued, alleging, among other things, that the mandate violated federal law and their religious liberties. The Obama administration imposed tens of millions of dollars in fines, and the case ended up in the U.S. Supreme Court.

In May 2016, the Supreme Court ruled against the Obama administration in *Zubik v. Burwell* on narrow grounds, blocking the fines and sending the cases back to lower courts. At the time of this writing, the nuns and other religious organizations involved in the lawsuit are *still* fighting in court, a decade after the Affordable Care Act first became law, despite efforts to resolve the issue by the Trump administration.

Regardless of what you think about abortion or contraception, at least two things are crystal clear from the nuns' saga: First, the Obama-era contraception mandate would force the members of these nonprofit organizations to violate their religious beliefs, and second, the Obama administration knew it was trying to impose its views on these religious groups, but thought that its goal of providing affordable birth control pills was more important.

Although Obamacare isn't a single-payer system, these problems only become more frequent and more extreme when government has total or near-total control over health care. And it also serves as an important illustration of how socialists and many progressives view individual rights. Do socialists and progressives care about religious freedom? Some do, sure, but only if that freedom doesn't get in the way of some other, more important goal of those in charge, like making nuns pay for birth control.

In single-payer health care systems, religious liberty—and indeed, many other kinds of personal freedom—never survives. It can't survive. Its mere existence means those in charge don't have absolute power, and even though they rarely admit it, obtaining power is nearly always one of the chief goals of government officials operating socialist programs.

Consider, for example, the heart-wrenching case of Alfie Evans in the United Kingdom—a country in which the health care system has been completely socialized. In 2018, Alfie, a 23-month-old boy from Liverpool, was suffering with a deadly degenerative neurological condition. Alfie's parents, Tom and Kate, did what any parent would do in a similarly tragic situation: absolutely everything they could to save their son's life.[54]

Unfortunately, the health care professionals at Alfie's hospital, the government-managed Alder Hey Children's Hospital in Liverpool, England, determined they should withdraw care and allow Alfie to die, despite pleas from the parents for care to continue. The parents then requested to move Alfie out of Alder Hey Hospital, potentially to another country, but the staff at Alder Hey refused.

Alfie's parents sued, hoping to obtain permission from a U.K. court to send Alfie to Italy, where officials even went so far as to offer Alfie citizenship in a last-ditch attempt to have the boy sent to a children's hospital in Rome. But the courts refused

and instead allowed Alfie's life-support to be removed.[55] Alfie died soon thereafter. Or, put more bluntly and accurately, the government-run hospital in England *killed* Alfie by withholding care.

In its final ruling on the Evans case, the United Kingdom's Supreme Court issued a truly stunning and horrifying decision about the rights of parents that will hopefully serve as a warning to all who desire to put government in charge of the health care industry in the United States.

"[P]arental rights are not absolute. . . . [existing laws] make it clear that when any question of the upbringing of a child comes before the courts, the child's welfare is the paramount consideration," the judges wrote, adding that "the best interests of the child are the 'gold standard' which is not only adopted by our law but also reflects the international standards to which this country is committed."

And who, exactly, decides what's in the best interests of Alfie Evans? According to the United Kingdom, it's not the parents, who don't know enough to make that decision. It's hospitals, doctors, other medical professionals, and, of course, the courts.

"It is therefore clear law that the parents do not have the right to use the writ of habeas corpus to acquire the custody of their child if this will not be in his best interests," the justices continued. "The decisions of the trial Judge clearly amount to decisions that the parents have no right to direct Alfie's future medical treatment. This is not a criticism of them. How could it be? It simply means that they cannot take Alfie away from Alder Hey for the purpose of transporting him at some risk to other hospitals which can do him no good."

And as if that weren't enough, the judges also wrote, "It has been conclusively determined that it is not in Alfie's best interests, not only to stay in Alder Hey Hospital being treated as he currently is, but also to detain him . . . for that purpose. The release to which he is entitled, therefore, is release from the imposition of treatment which is not in his best interests."

Put more bluntly, because the doctors and courts think Alfie should die, that's in his best interests. Keeping this baby alive is nothing more than an "imposition."

What can we learn from this tragedy? Maybe the doctors at Alder Hey and the judges and lawyers involved in the ensuing legal battle really did have the best interests of Alfie and his parents in mind when they determined Alfie's life wasn't worth living. It's true that it's unlikely Alfie would have survived had he ended up in Italy, or anywhere else for that matter. Yes, miracles do happen, but the chances of survival were slim, and the chances of Alfie living a normal life were virtually nonexistent.

But this case isn't about whether it was time for Alfie's life to end, and I hope that's not what you take away from the story. It's about who has the right to make that decision, and upon what basis does that right exist. We're not talking about your run-of-the-mill bickering over regulations, gas taxes, or bans on saturated fat. This is about life and death, and who has the power to make those choices.

In the United Kingdom, just like in many Scandinavian countries and most of the rest of the world, the answer couldn't be clearer: Government has the ultimate authority to decide what happens to you. Government has the ultimate power to determine what's in your "best interests"—even if it that means death.

> "YOU MUST ALL KNOW A HALF-
> DOZEN PEOPLE AT LEAST WHO
> ARE NO USE IN THIS WORLD,
> WHO ARE MORE TROUBLE THAN
> THEY ARE WORTH. JUST PUT
> THEM THERE AND SAY, 'SIR OR
> MADAM, NOW WILL YOU BE KIND
> ENOUGH TO JUSTIFY YOUR
> EXISTENCE?'"
>
> GEORGE
> - BERNARD
> SHAW

Do you think your life is worth living? Do you think your child's life is worth living? Or even just worth trying to save? In socialistic systems of every kind—even if a system's policymakers are democratically elected and relatively peaceful—it doesn't matter what *you* as an individual think or feel or believe. Your "rights" are nothing more than permission slips granted to you by the only higher power that really matters to socialists: government.

Neil DiCaprio-Cortez @GreenNewNeal
.@glennbeck, you say you care about rights, and maybe on some level you do. But health care is a right—one that capitalists have been denying people for centuries. By standing against laws that would provide all people with access to free health care, you're not only leaving people without care they want and need, you're depriving them of basic human rights that we're all entitled to.

 1

SHOULDN'T YOU HAVE THE RIGHT TO DEFEND YOURSELF AND MAKE YOUR OWN HEALTH CARE DECISIONS?

Every single American should have access to affordable health care services—and they could, too, if government were to just get the heck out of the way of health care innovators and entrepreneurs. I support ideas that will increase access to health care, and I even support allowing states to create safety nets for those who truly can't take care of themselves.

But on the issue of whether health care is a "right" that *must* be provided to everyone, I couldn't possibly disagree more. If everyone really is entitled to health care services, then that means others have lost their fundamental rights to work for a wage they believe to be fair, control their own lives and property, and to make health care decisions for themselves.

Or, to put it into terms even Alexandria Ocasio-Cortez can understand: The only way to make health care a right is to take away other people's rights, and any "right" that requires the destruction of others is really no right at all. ← *THAT'S SOCIALISM IN A NUTSHELL*

I know it's popular for socialists and progressives to claim people are entitled to various goods and services. Virtually every one of the *gazillion* 2020 Democratic presidential candidates insisted health care must be provided to everyone because, as Elizabeth Warren said during one of the presidential primary debates, "Health care is a basic human right. We fight for basic human rights, and that's why I'm fighting for Medicare for All."

I know this sounds appealing at first, but the more you think about it—I mean, really think about it—the less it makes sense.

If health care must be provided to all people, then that means some person—who also has rights—must provide it and pay for it, right? (At least until the robot uprisings.) This means doctors, physician assistants, nurses, and others in the health care industry must give care to those in need, but certainly no one would argue they would have to provide it for free. That would make them slaves. But if health care providers aren't to be forced into slavery, then they must be paid a wage. How much should they get paid?

In a free society, compensation is determined by free exchange: You have money. I have something you want to buy. We agree on a price, and then we trade. That can't exist in a socialized medical system—or any socialized system, for that matter—because if health care providers are only required to work under conditions they freely agree to, then it's possible that their compensation will be higher than what the socialized medical system can afford to pay, or even just lower than what the system is willing to pay. So, doctors and other providers in a socialist system don't

have any power to negotiate prices. They get paid whatever the people in society say they deserve—even if it's much lower than they would receive in a free-market model.

Imagine how absurd this would be if applied to almost any other industry. For example, let's say Americans get together and demand socialized fast-food joints. Everyone has the right to a juicy burger. In a socialized system, burgers would be paid for through tax revenues. Everyone who wants a burger would be free to have one, whenever he or she (or xe) desires.

In such a scheme, how much do burger-flippers get paid? Well, whatever we, as a society, choose to pay them. So, to keep our taxes low, let's say we choose to pay burger flippers almost nothing, maybe just a few dollars an hour. Even if the burger-flippers think the wage is "unfair," because they think their time or talents are worth more than what they are being paid, it wouldn't matter. All that would matter is that we, the people, demand burgers, and since we have a "right" to as many juicy burgers as we want, they would have to make them for whatever we decide to pay. If this isn't a form of exploitation, I don't know what is.

And as silly as it might seem on the surface to compare universal access to health care to universal access to burgers, remember that in socialism, "rights" are whatever the majority of people say they are. So, what's to stop the collective from deciding there really is a "right" to free burgers or free cars or free internet or free housing or anything else?

Professor Tweed @checkurprivilegeplz
Wait, @glennbeck, This is nothing more than a strawman argument. We're not talking about paying doctors less than a living wage. We can pay them fairly and still guarantee health care as a right.

 1

No, you can't. Because deciding what is "fair" requires freedom on the part of the worker. If health care workers have absolutely no ability to negotiate their wages, then they don't have "freedom" in any meaningful sense. They are forced to either find a new profession or work for whatever society—represented by the government— decides to pay, whether it's a "good" wage or not. In socialized medicine, health care workers have virtually no rights. All the power rests with the collective.

 Professor Tweed @checkurprivilegeplz
If taking away some of the rights of health care providers is what it's going to take to ensure all people have access to free health care, then that's a price worth paying.

♡ 1   ⇄   ♡

You might think so, sure. It's easy to take away the rights of others. But think carefully about what you're calling for here. You want to give nearly endless power over health care to the very same government socialists say is constantly engaging in crony deals with large corporations and special interests. The same government many socialists claim is "racist" and "sexist." If you don't trust the way the system works now, why would you want to give those in power even more power?

Once you put a socialist system in place, you're at the mercy of the rest of society. Now, maybe today you're not worried about that. You think the tides have turned in your direction and that most people will generally support your positions. (That seems a little delusional, by the way—since, you know, Donald freaking Trump was recently elected president and Republicans have had control of at least one chamber of Congress in all but four years since 1995.) But even if you think the socialism wave is going to last for a few more years, surely you can't be so crazy to think it will last *forever*.

Even if socialists sweep the next few elections, someday, people will once again control Washington who hold views you find reprehensible, and they could use their

power to force you to live in ways that violate your personal beliefs. Socialism is dangerous because unbridled power is dangerous—not just for people like me, but for everyone, *including you*.

We've already seen governments in countries with single-payer health care try to control personal behavior or even punish people because they have been deemed by the bureaucrats in charge to be less than ideal, for one reason or another. For example, *The Guardian* reports, "Couples are being turned down for NHS [National Health Service] fertility treatment in some areas of England because the man is too old or too fat, despite neither criteria forming part of national guidelines or being proven to affect the success of IVF [in vitro fertilization]."[56]

England's National Institute of Health and Care Excellence—which goes by the insanely creepy Orwellian acronym "NICE"—also produced a report estimating the cost-effectiveness of in vitro fertilization and concluded providing obese women with IVF resources is probably not a good investment of the government's limited money and time.[57] If translated into official policy, wouldn't this reform be the very definition of oppression? Because a woman is deemed "too fat," the health care system won't help her have a child? Sounds an awful lot like eugenics to me.

Government-managed systems have also been caught rationing care for people based on age. For instance, the London-based *Times* reported in April 2019, "Tens of thousands of elderly people are left struggling to see because of an NHS [National Health Service] cost-cutting drive that relies on them dying before they can qualify for cataract surgery, senior doctors say."[58] *Death* as a health care policy seems a little counterproductive.

So, the supposedly compassionate, bleeding hearts running England's health care system are now *allowing people to go blind* so that they can prioritize health care spending elsewhere. Is this what advocates of government-run health care mean when they promise Americans they will all have "quality" health care? Blindness?

And eyesight isn't the only thing Americans should be worried about losing under a single-payer plan. Rationing could be implemented for almost anything based on age. Under a single-payer health care system, if grandma is "too old" to warrant a costly hip replacement, well, that could be too bad for grandma—and you, too, if you're stuck taking care of her.

The same could be true for brain tumors. Maybe it's not worth spending limited government resources to keep an older person's cancer from spreading when there are younger people waiting for a similar procedure.

Professor Tweed @checkurprivilegeplz
But socialists aren't talking about rationing care. Bernie Sanders, Elizabeth Warren, and others who support single-payer plans guarantee that everyone will have access to the care they need. They have never said they are going to ration people's care.

◯ 1   ⇄   ♡

Of course, many of those who want to ram single-payer health care down Americans' throats aren't admitting that there will be significant rationing. Why would they? Admitting that rationing could be a problem would undermine their efforts to create a single-payer system and obliterate the notion that we have reached a post-scarcity world.

Recent history has shown socialists and progressives routinely make health care promises they can't deliver—and many they never had any intention of delivering in the first place. When Barack Obama was peddling Obamacare to a very concerned American public, he promised, "If you like your health care plan, you can keep it," despite countless warnings from health care experts that the provisions of the bill would almost certainly require numerous individuals and families to purchase new, much more expensive health insurance policies.

After the Affordable Care Act became law, *millions* of people lost the health insurance coverage they liked, as well as access to their doctors. Even PolitiFact, which is hardly sympathetic to free-market causes, acknowledged Obama misled the public, naming Obama's promise its "lie of the year" for 2013.[59] (Why can't we get awards shows for things like this? I'd watch the Fibbie Awards.)

Allowing people to keep their health insurance wasn't the only broken promise Obama made, either. He also repeatedly pledged that his health care legislation would "cut the cost of a typical family's premium by up to $2,500 a year."[60] Instead of having their health insurance bills cut, premiums and deductibles increased dramatically, in many cases more than doubling.

And when the Obama administration wasn't busy writing—along with a bunch of far-left special-interest groups—one of the worst pieces of health care legislation ever devised, it was scheming up ways to lie to the American people so that it could get it passed.

One of the architects of the Affordable Care Act, Jonathan Gruber—an economics professor at the Massachusetts Institute of Technology who was paid hundreds of thousands of dollars to help write the legislation—admitted during an October 2013 event that the Affordable Care Act was deliberately crafted to mislead Americans, who he said suffer from "stupidity."

"In terms of risk-rated subsidies, if you had a law which said healthy people are going to pay in—it made explicit that healthy people pay in, sick people get money—it would not have passed," Gruber said. "Lack of transparency is a huge political advantage. And, basically, call it the stupidity of the American voter or whatever, but, basically, that was really, really critical for the thing [the Affordable Care Act] to pass."[61] Isn't it comforting to know how much your government believes in your "stupidity"?

Professor Tweed @checkurprivilegeplz
Just because some politicians lied in the past about Obamacare and didn't make accurate predictions about its effects doesn't mean socialists and progressives promoting single-payer health care are lying now, or that they will get it wrong this time around.

💬 1   🔁   ♡

Yeah but Obamacare wasn't the first time health care promises have been broken. Both political parties have been making and breaking health care promises for decades. And many of the same politicians who supported Obamacare and repeated the false promises made by President Obama are now making similar wildly unrealistic commitments and predictions about Medicare for All. If they misled you before, what makes you think you can trust them now?

This is always how progressives and socialists behave. They promise you the world, and when they fail, they blame it on someone else—usually the opposing political party or some unlucky group of scapegoats they can pin their failures on. Then they make even more promises they know they can't keep: "Just give us a little more money. Just sacrifice a little more of your freedom. In the end, it will all be worth it. Trust us."

They're not worthy of your trust. Remember, these are the same people who spent half a million dollars to study the effects of cocaine on the sexual behavior of Japanese quails.[62]

And we don't need to speculate about the possibility of government-led rationing. In recent years, some politicians have openly called for it. For example, in an effort to shore up the state's skyrocketing Medicaid budget—which, by the way, is largely the result of Medicaid expansion policies put into place by the Affordable Care Act—Massachusetts submitted a proposal to the federal government to reform its Medicaid

program so that it could cut drug coverage options. (The Trump administration eventually rejected the plan.)

Writing for the *Washington Examiner*, Hadley Heath Manning, a senior policy analyst and director of policy at the Independent Women's Forum, explained the "Massachusetts' proposal includes . . . a 'closed formulary' for Medicaid beneficiaries. This means the program may offer only one drug per class (a class is something like antidepressants or anticonvulsants used to prevent seizures). For patients, this means the government will essentially dictate to physicians how to treat patients, interfering between patients and doctors."[63]

For patients who rely on pharmaceuticals, this concept could lead to serious health care problems. People often respond very differently to multiple drugs in the same "class." It is not uncommon for patients to try out a number of drugs to determine which one fits best with their body's biochemistry. Effectively forcing patients to take drugs that might not work well for them would have a profound impact on people's health and well-being. And yet, that's exactly what Massachusetts attempted to do—all in the name of cutting costs, also called "rationing."

Professor Tweed @checkurprivilegeplz
Why wouldn't we want well-qualified experts making decisions? We could hire the best and brightest minds to set health care prices and determine appropriate courses of treatment. Doctors and other health care professionals would be the ones to make these choices. We could have councils filled with the world's best doctors making national health care choices. What would be wrong with that?

◯ 1   ⇄   ♡

A whole lot, actually. For starters, any good doctor—or even an honest crappy doctor—would tell you that the best kind of health care decision-making occurs when doctors and patients work directly together. The human body is incredibly complex;

it's not like an old tractor or something. "Just plug in that new heart, Jeb. Should work just fine."

The best treatment is deeply personal and occurs when doctors have a complete understanding of their patients. In many cases, hundreds or even thousands of variables are taken into account. Sometimes, it takes *years* for patients to find the right treatment. You can't have a high-quality medical system and a system in which health care decisions are made by a board of doctors who have never met a patient and don't know the intricate nuances of that person's medical history.

THE GOVERNMENT DOES NOTHING MORE EFFICIENTLY OR EFFECTIVELY THAN THE PRIVATE SECTOR—OTHER THAN OPERATE THE MILITARY, WHICH MEANS THE ONLY THING GOVERNMENT DOES REALLY WELL IS DESTROY.

And this all assumes, of course, that federal and state health care agencies would be composed mostly of real health care experts. In reality, this rarely occurs. Throughout the world, health care decisions are being made by government bureaucrats with no actual medical expertise. In some cases, they are appointees chosen purely for political reasons or even as a favor. This system is notoriously prone to corruption, inefficiencies, and downright stupidity.

Government-run health care systems also incentivize government agencies to further restrict personal freedoms and implement policies that try to change people's behaviors. If government is paying for your health care, why would it allow you to

smoke tobacco cigarettes or eat burgers every night for dinner? Government doesn't necessarily need to restrict these freedoms, of course, but it could, and there are good reasons to believe the U.S. government would do exactly that under any kind of a government-run health care scheme. Is a government with an Anti-Burger Bureau really the kind of America you want for your children?

Progressive and socialist lawmakers in some of the largest cities in America have already imposed taxes on sugary drinks like soda, including in Boulder, Colorado, Philadelphia, San Francisco, Seattle, and Berkeley, California.[64] Hefty cigarette taxes have been imposed in more than two dozen states, and in some of the most liberal states—Connecticut, New York, and Rhode Island—cigarette excise taxes top $4 per pack, even though numerous studies show these taxes disproportionately affect the poor.[65]

The People's Republic of San Francisco has not only banned candy and soda from its schools, it also imposed a ban on chocolate milk.[66] "Sorry Tommy, chocolate milk is just too dangerous for kids to drink."

 Professor Tweed @checkurprivilegeplz
Ok, maybe the more government gets involved in health care, the more rationing there is. But at least these people aren't dying in the streets. If it were up to you, anyone who isn't working full time would lose access to health care, even if they are sick. Isn't it better to have to deal with some health care inefficiencies and rationing than to have people without access to health care? That's what makes socialism a better system. Things might get worse for some people, but at least everyone has what they absolutely need.

   💬 1   🔁   ♡

If the only "solution" to the problems facing our current health care system you can come up with requires significantly worsening health care and/or reducing access to services for more than 100 million Americans, then that's not much of a "solution" at all.

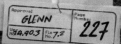

Our health care industry is dysfunctional, slow-moving, and full of inefficiencies, but the way to fix the system isn't to give more power to the same dysfunctional, slow-moving, and inefficient people who broke the system in the first place, or to force some people to suffer so others' lives can be improved. Helping people at the expense of hurting many others is never a good option, and it's not the way people behave in a truly free nation.

That doesn't mean we should just throw our hands up in the air and give up, either. There are really smart, tested health care policy solutions that can significantly lower costs and provide people with access to affordable health care without restricting choice or putting government in charge of our burger consumption. (After all, what's the point of living without burgers?)

One great option that has been shown to lower costs and improve access is permitting physicians to offer direct primary care (DPC) agreements. Direct primary care agreements allow primary care doctors to contract directly with their patients. Under a direct primary care agreement, patients pay a monthly fee, often less than $100, in exchange for a long list of primary care services, like check-ups, physical exams, and blood tests. These agreements can save thousands of dollars per year in health care and health insurance costs, because contracting directly with doctors cuts out health insurance middlemen and overhead for providers. It also frees up physicians to spend more time with patients and less time dealing with paperwork. That's not a small benefit, by the way. About half of a doctor's time is spent dealing with administrative activities.[67]

DPC practices can reduce a health care practice's overhead by as much as 40 percent, according to the Docs4PatientCare Foundation, and some research shows patients enrolled in direct primary care agreements are significantly less likely to need hospital services.[68,69]

This might sound like a radical change, but it's not. It's common sense. Health insurance should only be used to cover expensive health care costs, like broken arms and heart surgery, not vaccinations and physicals. Using health insurance to pay for relatively inexpensive health services is like using your car insurance to pay for oil changes and tire rotations. There's a reason almost no one buys car insurance that covers routine car maintenance—it's really, really expensive. So, why do we use our health insurance to pay for routine health care?

A second, potentially game-changing policy reform that could completely change the way the health insurance system works is to allow people to band together to buy health insurance as a group, commonly called "association health plans" (AHPs).

Under the current system, most people either get their health coverage from an employer or the government, through Medicaid or Medicare. This puts those who don't qualify for Medicaid or Medicare and don't receive health insurance from their employers left to buy insurance as individuals, which is really unfortunate, because the Obamacare health insurance plans they are stuck purchasing are extremely expensive.

There are a lot of reasons why individual health insurance plans are so costly, but one of the biggest is that individuals have almost no consumer power when they buy insurance plans. They are often forced to buy plans loaded with coverage they might not need or want, and because they are only buying coverage for themselves and their immediate family members, they can't negotiate prices the same way a large employer or unions can.

If private groups of individuals could get together and buy health insurance, they could negotiate much better prices, and the bigger the association, the better the prices. Just imagine the deal groups like the National Rifle Association or AARP,

both of which have millions of members, could negotiate with health insurers. And because associations with members in multiple states could purchase health insurance across state lines, people would have more options than ever. Further, health coverage wouldn't be tied to an employer. That means if Bill loses his job, Bill and his family wouldn't automatically lose their health insurance.

Association health plans have tremendous potential for helping lower-income people as well. Charitable organizations, churches, and other groups could form associations that provide health insurance at reduced rates, or even for free, to lower-income families. People with more money in their pockets might pay extra for these health insurance plans than they otherwise would, but they would do so voluntarily, knowing that they are helping another family at their church, business, or someone who is committed to a shared cause.

Instead of being reliant on a massive government bureaucracy that spends more money than Joe Biden on teeth whitener or Bernie Sanders on adult diapers—yeah, that's a lot of cash, I know—people would instead benefit from the generosity of their neighbors. Communities would once again be empowered to take care of each other, and to do it without massive tax hikes and threats from the IRS.

Charity, not coercion and manipulation, can help America's uninsured population, but only if the American people are given the ability to do so. Current laws make all these ideas unworkable or even impossible. Again, it's clear government is often the biggest roadblock to improving people's lives—not some greedy corporation or middle-income families who don't want to pay more than half their income in taxes, like they do in Scandinavia.

END OF CHAPTER 5

NO UNEMPLOYMENT

NO CRIME

HEALTHCARE FOR ALL

FREE BIRTH CONTROL

BUILDING A 21ST CENTURY SOCIALIST PARADISE NIGHTMARE

FINAL
APPROVED
-GB

Approval
GLENN
Usage No. 14.40.3 Fix No. 7.2

Page Number
233

HOW TECHNOLOGY & MODERN MONETARY THEORY MAKE SOCIALISM MORE DANGEROUS THAN EVER

"THE PARTY SEEKS
POWER ENTIRELY FOR
ITS OWN SAKE. WE ARE
NOT INTERESTED IN
THE GOOD OF OTHERS;
WE ARE INTERESTED
SOLELY IN POWER,
PURE POWER. WHAT
PURE POWER MEANS
YOU WILL UNDERSTAND PRESENTLY. WE ARE
DIFFERENT FROM THE OLIGARCHIES OF THE PAST
IN THAT WE KNOW WHAT WE ARE DOING."[1]

— 1984,
GEORGE ORWELL

We're living in remarkable times. New economic and philosophical theories and technological achievements that were once totally unthinkable have become mainstream. "Smart" homes featuring voice-controlled appliances and services allow people to control the temperature on their oven, dim lights, water their lawn, and order a product made on the other side of the world—all without ever leaving the couch. More than 20 million homes now even feature small robots that clean floors and vacuum rugs.[2]

Today, people of every economic class walk around with smartphone supercomputers in their pockets that allow them to communicate with friends and family, watch television, listen to podcasts and radio shows, find information on virtually any topic imaginable, and even order from peer-to-peer car services like Uber, which will pick up and drop off riders in nearly every city in America, all at a moment's notice.

Medical innovations are helping people live longer than ever. For the first time in human history, people residing in even some of the poorest countries are expected to live to at least 60 years of age. According to Jane Barratt, Ph.D., the secretary general of the International Federation on Aging, "Worldwide, 901 million people are over the age of 60 today. That number is projected to reach 1.4 billion by 2030 and nearly 2.1 billion by 2050."[3] (By the way, these projections don't bode well for the British cataract surgery crisis I told you about in Chapter 5.)

Innovation and the proliferation of knowledge are dramatically improving many aspects of our lives, and change is only going to ramp up in the coming decades. We're already seeing a doubling of technological innovation every decade, and noted scientist and futurist Ray Kurzweil—the same guy who anticipated the emergence of the internet years before most people had ever heard of it—predicts that over the next half-century, the world will experience 32 times more progress than humanity enjoyed in the twentieth century.[4]

While much of this innovation will improve human life, it will also force the world to deal with some complex ethical issues and economic disruptions. For example, in China, artificial intelligence has already displaced countless workers. As June Javelosa reported for Futurism.com, in 2017 "a Chinese factory replaced 90 percent of its human workforce with automated machines, resulting in a 250 percent increase in productivity and 80 percent drop in defects. Foxconn, an Apple supplier, also cut 60,000 jobs and replaced them with robots."[5] Javelosa also reported "137 million workers across five Southeast Asian countries are in danger of being displaced by

automated systems in the next 20 years." China is working to become the world leader in AI technology. China expects that by 2030, its AI industry will be worth $148 billion, and AI-related industries will be worth more than $1 trillion.[6]

Today, socialists argue—as they have for more than a century, going all the way back to Marx himself—that these advancements will create a tremendous need for centralized economic planning and wealth redistribution. Because technology could force millions of people out of their jobs over the next few decades, socialists argue *someone* or *something* is going to have to take care of them, and who would be better equipped to do that than the federal government's vast army of supposedly benevolent bureaucrats? And who better to pay for all of the government's new social programs than the "greedy" capitalists who chose to rely on robots and AI, rather than humans, to make and distribute their goods and services?

Other socialists say we shouldn't allow companies to replace workers with AI in the first place, or that the federal government should offer a guaranteed job to anyone who has lost his or her job because of technological advancements—or because of any other cause, for that matter.

This thinking has been going on for centuries. In the early nineteenth century, in the midst of the Industrial Revolution, textile workers and weavers in England broke into factories to smash the machines that had made many of their jobs obsolete.[7] These "Luddites"—a name these anti-technology protesters gave themselves to honor another, likely mythological machine-smashing worker named Ned Ludd— argued that the jobs displaced by technology might never be replaced, and thus that they should be destroyed to protect their employment. (Either that or *Terminator*'s John Conner overshot by a hundred years or so when time traveling and decided to crush the cybernetic uprising in its crib.)

Approval
GLENN
Unit
84.403 | Fix No. 7.2
Page Number
237

Of course, the Luddites eventually found other jobs and stopped smashing machines. New markets opened, spurred by the immense wealth created by the Industrial Revolution—just as it had in previous eras and in the generations since the Luddite protests. When entrepreneurs and innovators are empowered to operate in a truly free market, technology creates opportunities for other economic developments. In free markets, it's natural for industries to develop and jobs to change, not disappear— and that's usually a good thing, too. Who do you know who would actually be willing to work in a nineteenth-century factory?

That doesn't mean we aren't heading for disruptive times, though. We absolutely are, and Americans need to start having some important conversations about the role technology and government will play in our future, rather than spending all of their time at each other's throats on Facebook and Twitter.

Even more important, though, than the economic disruptions that are sure to come over the next century because of technological advancements is how technology could be used—and, indeed, already is being used—by progressives and socialists to control, force, and manipulate societies. Socialists failed to implement peaceful, successful socialist systems in the past in large part because it became far too difficult to control people. All the indoctrination and reeducation camps in the world can't teach people to fundamentally alter their human natures—a lesson that took many socialist and communist regimes a century of failure and hundreds of millions of dead bodies to learn. But socialists have more tools than ever now to monitor, track, and control behavior, making it easier than ever to build their perfect little "utopias."

When coupled with protections for individual liberties, technological innovation can be very beneficial for human society. But without those protections—which, let's not forget, don't exist in collectivist countries—technology can be exceedingly dangerous.

Neal DiCaprio-Cortez @GreenNewNeal
No, new technology is going to make it easier than ever for socialist governments to provide for the least among us and to adequately redistribute wealth so that hundreds of millions of people aren't suffering and starving.

💬 1   ⇄   ♡

Market economies in places like India are already using technology to lift hundreds of millions of people from extreme poverty. (See Chapter 9.) Socialist governments, on the other hand, have a long history of using technology to control people and enhance their own power. The reason for this is that when socialist systems inevitably break down, as they have every single time they've ever been tried, socialist governments are left with two options: They can relent and institute free-market reforms—as Sweden and other Scandinavian countries have done (see Chapter 5)—or they can resort to force and coercion as a means to achieve their collectivist goals. As described in Chapter 4, this force and coercion routinely results in unimaginable horror and bloodshed.

We don't need to turn to history books to see how socialist and authoritarian governments use technology in truly *terrifying* ways, either. All we need to do is look around the world today, especially to what's going on in China. Exhibit 1: Xinjiang province.

XINJIANG

Xinjiang is the largest province-level division of China, constituting about 640,000 square miles of the northwestern portion of the country.[8] The subdivision is officially considered an autonomous region and is home to ethnically diverse populations. One of the largest populations is the Uighurs, a Turkic-speaking, mostly Muslim demographic.[9]

The region has a long history of government control involving various tyrannical rulers. Xinjiang officially became a part of China in 1949 after the Chinese Civil War. Numerous separatist conflicts followed. At one point, separatists declared independence of East Turkestan, the Uighur name for Xinjiang. This movement was short-lived, however. China established Xinjiang as an autonomous region in 1955.

When Xinjiang became a part of China in 1949, China began a campaign to integrate the region into the greater Chinese economy while largely leaving the population free to continue operating with its well-established cultures still in place. This arrangement, while never perfect, has since deteriorated.[10] Violence in the region has increased in recent years, including knife-wielding attacks and suicide bombings. These attacks are attributed to the region's large Uighur population. In response to these attacks, the Chinese government began to crack down on Uighurs, separatists, and other political dissidents in the area. In the name of pursuing greater safety and security in the region, the Chinese government substantially increased its growing surveillance state on everyone, not just those considered to be dangerous.

While surveillance by its most general definition has existed in China for decades, the technological age ushered in an era of surveillance in China that even the most prolific dystopian authors of the twentieth century could not imagine.

During a Congressional-Executive Commission on China hearing in 2018, the then U.S. ambassador to the United Nations Economic and Social Council, Kelley E. Currie, described the "highly intrusive" system established by China:

> CHINESE AUTHORITIES HAVE CONSTRUCTED A HIGHLY INTRUSIVE, HIGH-TECH SURVEILLANCE SYSTEM IN XINJIANG, WHICH MANY EXPERTS FEAR WILL BE EXTENDED THROUGHOUT CHINA. THIS SYSTEM INCLUDES THOUSANDS OF SURVEILLANCE CAMERAS, INCLUDING IN MOSQUES; FACIAL RECOGNITION SOFTWARE; OBLIGATORY CONTENT-MONITORING APPS ON SMARTPHONES AND GPS DEVICES ON CARS; WIDESPREAD NEW POLICE OUTPOSTS WITH

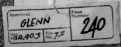

TENS OF THOUSANDS OF NEWLY-HIRED POLICE AND EVEN PARTY PERSONNEL EMBEDDED IN PEOPLE'S HOMES; AND COMPULSORY COLLECTION OF VAST BIOMETRIC DATASETS ON ETHNIC AND RELIGIOUS MINORITIES THROUGHOUT THE REGION, INCLUDING DNA AND BLOOD SAMPLES, 3-D PHOTOS, IRIS SCANS, AND VOICEPRINTS.[11]

In 2005, the Chinese government launched a program called "Skynet," a national security network composed in part of hundreds of millions of cameras across the country. (If you weren't scared enough already, "Skynet" is the same name given to the killer artificial intelligence system in the *Terminator* movies.) Building upon this, in 2015 China launched another surveillance program called "Sharp Eyes," which aims to obtain coverage of every inch of "key public areas" and "key industries" by the end of 2020.[12]

You've got to hand it to the Chinese, they don't bother coming up with cute names for their authoritarian surveillance systems with typical Orwellian doublespeak. "Let's name our massive, all-encompassing, AI-enhanced national surveillance program after the genocidal artificial intelligence system in the *Terminator* franchise. When our citizens hear about surveillance, we *want* them to think of murderous robots. What a great idea!" (But maybe I'm being too hard on the Chinese. I guess it's possible they're just big Arnold Schwarzenegger fans.)

A.D.D. MOMENT

HONG KONG PROTESTERS DESTROY LAMPPOSTS?

If you have seen any footage of the 2019 protests in Hong Kong, you'll notice many of the demonstrators are hiding their faces. They cover their faces with surgical masks, bandanas, and more. This is mainly because of the fear of the Chinese surveillance state and the potential for government retribution.

These protesters have also been filmed cutting down lampposts with saws due to the fear these posts contain cameras, audio surveillance systems, or even facial-recognition sensors.

Of course, government officials deny any such technology is being used to collect data on Hong Kong citizens. The protesters aren't so sure.[a]

If this type of monitoring sounds time- and resource-intensive, it's because it is. In just the Xinjiang region, there are more than 1 million officials in place to oversee this gargantuan surveillance system.[13] The plan is to further implement artificial intelligence to automate some of the work. AI would be used to look for patterns, track social media activity, and identify suspicious behavior.

Chinese technology firms are supplying the technology to go much further. iFlyteck Co., a Chinese firm that specializes in speech recognition software, is helping the government "build a national voice pattern database." Theoretically, this database would allow the Chinese Ministry of Public Security to be able to identify individuals as they speak over the phone.[14] CloudWalk, another Chinese technology firm, supplies facial recognition software that identifies specific individuals or groups of people.[15]

Additionally, Xinjiang citizens are required to install surveillance software onto their smartphones. This software sifts through a person's data and "flags" them for Chinese officials to investigate if certain patterns are found.[16] Citing a *New York Times* investigation, the U.S. Commission on International Religious Freedom noted in a 2019 report how Chinese officials are using these smartphone applications to potentially track millions of people, including travelers listening to "mainstream and nonviolent" religious recordings:

> "IN JULY 2019, A TEAM OF JOURNALISTS FROM THE NEW YORK TIMES AND OTHER MEDIA OUTLETS PUBLISHED A REPORT ABOUT AN APP CALLED FENGCAI—PRODUCED BY A SUBSIDIARY OF THE CHINESE TELECOMMUNICATIONS COMPANY FIBERHOME NETWORKS— THAT CHINESE BORDER AUTHORITIES ROUTINELY INSTALL ON SMARTPHONES BELONGING TO TRAVELERS ENTERING FROM CENTRAL ASIA," NOTED THE COMMISSION. "THE APP CHECKS CONTENT ON EACH PHONE AGAINST A LIST OF MORE THAN 73,000 DOCUMENTS, PICTURES, VIDEOS, AUDIO RECORDINGS, AND OTHER ITEMS. ALTHOUGH SOME OF THESE ITEMS ARE RELATED TO KNOWN TERRORIST GROUPS—SUCH AS ISLAMIC STATE OF IRAQ AND SYRIA (ISIS) TRAINING MATERIALS—THE LIST ALSO INCLUDES ITEMS RELATED TO MAINSTREAM AND NONVIOLENT RELIGIOUS PRACTICE,

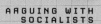

> SUCH AS AUDIO RECORDINGS OF QUR'AN VERSES RECITED BY
> PROMINENT CLERICS AND WRITINGS BY THE DALAI LAMA."[17]

Together, these vast surveillance systems allow the government to keep a close eye on everyone and everything going on in the Xinjiang region. With a click of a button, a person's personal data can be pulled up in an instant, including government records, information on education and family relations, and even where that person has traveled to in the past. The goal is for absolutely nothing to go unnoticed.[18]

REEDUCATION CENTERS

But what, you might be wondering, happens when something does go noticed. Well, that's when the real fun begins. The Chinese government uses its long list of surveillance tools to identify whomever they consider to be "dangerous" or "radical"— which is pretty much anyone who doesn't toe the Communist Party's line. But don't worry. If you're one of the millions or tens of millions—no one really knows—who have been "flagged" by China's surveillance systems, you're not dragged before firing squads like the communist regimes of old, you get to take a luxurious, all-inclusive trip to one of China's many stunning "reeducation" centers.[19] It's like commie summer camp for grown-ups, complete with sing-alongs and group bonding activities.

Those who enter China's reeducation centers have the privilege of being "deradicalized" by receiving a steady stream of communist propaganda.[20] Visitors are also given vocational training so they can, upon release, reenter society as productive members of the community. (I wonder if this is what Bernie Sanders has in mind when he talks about "free" higher education.)

United Nations estimates suggest there are at least 1 million people detained in these centers,[21] which human rights organizations have labeled "concentration camps."

> "CHINA'S REPRESSION OF RELIGION IS NOT NEW, BUT ITS ABILITY TO HARNESS THESE TECHNOLOGIES HAS EXPANDED THE SCALE AND SCOPE OF THE THREAT TO RELIGIOUS FREEDOM IN THE COUNTRY."
>
> *— TENZIN DORJEE*
> CIRF COMMISSIONER

U.S. Secretary of State Mike Pompeo referred to the mass detentions in China as "one of the worst human rights crises of our time" and the human rights "stain of the century."[22]

The power of the state is not solely directed at the Uighurs, either. According to a report compiled by the U.S. Commission on International Religious Freedom (CIRF), the Chinese government has used this intrusive surveillance state to oppress various religious minority groups. According to CIRF, China has:

> "SEIZED CONTROL OF KEY TIBETAN MONASTERIES AND EXPELLED THOUSANDS OF MONKS AND NUNS."

> "ARRESTED THOUSANDS OF CHRISTIANS AND CHURCH LEADERS WHO REFUSED TO JOIN THE STATE-SANCTIONED CHURCH."

> "INTENSIFIED A CAMPAIGN TO ERADICATE THE FALUN GONG AND REPRESS OTHER BANNED GROUPS, SUCH AS THE CHURCH OF ALMIGHTY GOD."

> "CLOSED OR DEMOLISHED DOZENS OF BUDDHIST AND TAOIST TEMPLES."[23]

SOCIAL CREDIT SCORES

China isn't only using its nationwide, all-seeing surveillance system to control the behavior of Uighurs and religious minorities, it's also in the early stages of rolling out a national points-based credit system that it's hoping will turn all the citizens of

China into good, subservient little boys and girls. I present to you, Exhibit 2, China's "social credit" system.

The purpose of the Social Credit System —which currently exists as a patchwork of regional systems across China—is to measure the trustworthiness and value of a citizen. Government officials apply points to each citizen based on his or behavior. Officials have chosen a variety of factors to take into account when assigning a social credit score, including one's financial history, legal infractions, driving habits, social media presence, what websites one visits, whether you spread "fake news," how critical one is of the government, how much time one spends playing video games or watching TV, and numerous other factors.

Citizens start out with an established number of points—in the city of Rongcheng, it's 1,000 points[24]—but as citizens engage in behaviors the state deems to be undesirable, points are taken away. As one report by *Foreign Policy* notes, "Get a traffic ticket; you lose five points. Earn a city-level award, such as for committing a heroic act, doing exemplary business, or helping your family in unusual tough circumstances, and your score gets boosted by 30 points. For a department-level award, you earn five points. You can also earn credit by donating to charity or volunteering in the city's program."

Based on his or her score, each citizen is assigned a letter grade, ranging from A+++ (yes, *three* pluses) down to D. Apparently, no one receives an F grade. That's too bad, though. I think it would be really useful to finally have an objective way to determine who is a "Failure" in life and who isn't.

The scores are then used to reward or punish citizens. "Some offenses can hurt the score pretty badly," *Foreign Policy* reported. "For drunk driving, for example, one's score plummets straight to a C. On the other hand, triple As are rewarded with perks such as being able to rent public bikes without paying a deposit (and riding them for free for an hour and a half), receiving a $50 heating discount every winter, and obtaining more advantageous terms on bank loans."

Those with low scores might be prevented from using public services, enrolling their child in a private school, or even restricted from purchasing train or airline tickets. The Associated Press reported that in 2018, 17.5 million air travel ticket purchases were blocked due to low social credit scores.[25]

Although the program is still in its infancy—dozens of pilot programs are in various stages of development[26]—the end goal is spelled out in a planning document released by the Chinese State Council in 2014:

> "ACCELERATING THE ESTABLISHMENT OF A SOCIAL CREDIT SYSTEM IS AN IMPORTANT FOUNDATION FOR COMPREHENSIVELY IMPLEMENTING THE SCIENTIFIC VIEWPOINT OF DEVELOPMENT AND BUILDING A HARMONIOUS SOCIALIST SOCIETY," THE COUNCIL WROTE, ADDING, "IT IS AN IMPORTANT METHOD FOR IMPROVING THE SOCIALIST MARKET ECONOMY SYSTEM, AND FOR ACCELERATING AND INNOVATING IN SOCIAL GOVERNANCE; AND IT HAS IMPORTANT SIGNIFICANCE FOR STRENGTHENING THE AWARENESS OF CREDITWORTHINESS AMONG MEMBERS OF SOCIETY, FORGING A POSITIVE CREDIT ENVIRONMENT, RAISING THE NATION'S OVERALL COMPETITIVENESS AND PROMOTING SOCIAL DEVELOPMENT AND THE IMPROVEMENT OF CIVILIZATION."[27]

The government wants to achieve the goals of "raising the nation's overall competitiveness" and improving civilization not by allowing free association and voluntary transactions, but by developing a massive system of government surveillance and coercion. The plan is to have a fully implemented system up and running by the end of 2020.[28]

As the Chinese State Council's planning document noted, the Social Credit System is perfectly in line with socialist principles. In the past, socialist regimes had to resort to authoritarian tactics merely to identify those who could be violating state laws

by doing things like engaging in unsanctioned economic activity or speaking out against the ruling government. But now, it's easier than ever for the Communist Party in China to identify and punish troublemakers and reward their most loyal comrades.

It should be apparent that China's surveillance state, reeducation camps, and social credit scores are extremely dangerous and open the door to a tremendous amount of abuse. They are already helping the Chinese government violate human rights on a daily basis—all in the name of benefiting the collective. This is how socialists often use technology—not to improve people's lives, but for control and manipulation.

Rashida Resistance @AOC_2024_Squad4Life
This is all very disturbing, @glennbeck, but this wouldn't happen in America. Our government would never abuse technology like this and spy on its citizens.

💬 1   🔁   ♡

If by "never" you mean hundreds of millions of times per year, at minimum, then we're in complete agreement.

Although it's true the U.S. government has not conducted a surveillance campaign comparable to the size and scope of China's "Skynet" or "Sharp Eyes" programs, it has engaged in numerous surveillance activities that violate civil liberties and could easily be expanded as part of a much larger surveillance system.

In 2013, former National Security Agency (NSA) contractor Edward Snowden revealed that federal officials had been secretly collecting billions of records of communications made by American citizens, all without obtaining a warrant.[29] Whatever you think of Snowden, this violation of Americans' privacy rights should shock you. Two of the most important and far-reaching of the Snowden-identified NSA spying programs, Prism and Upstream, were renewed in 2018, with support from members of both major political parties and President Trump.[30,31]

According to technology news website CNET, "The Prism and Upstream programs exist to collect online communications of foreigners outside the US. Prism takes the communications directly from internet services like email providers and video chat programs, and Upstream taps into the infrastructure of the internet to pull in the communications while they're in transit. The programs collect the communications of Americans 'incidentally,' such as when Americans communicate with targeted foreigners overseas. For technical reasons, the NSA also scoops up Americans' internet traffic that can't be separated from the bits and bytes that contain the communications of intended spy targets."[32]

Patrick Toomey, the senior staff attorney for the ACLU's National Security Project, noted that although federal officials say the Prism program is only meant to target foreigners, "that's only half the picture."[33]

"In reality," Toomey wrote in 2018, "it [federal government] uses PRISM as a backdoor into Americans' private communications, violating the Fourth Amendment on a massive scale. We don't know the total number of Americans affected, even today, because the government has refused to provide any estimate."

Members of Congress and federal officials who support the NSA's spying efforts say it's necessary to fight terrorism, but in the process of spying on foreign suspects, government is also amassing a gigantic trove of innocent Americans' communications. And in some cases, the government has been caught using that information in various other investigations of U.S. citizens.[34]

Toomey notes, "One of the most problematic elements of this surveillance is the government's use of 'backdoor searches' to investigate individual Americans. Although the government says PRISM is targeted at foreigners who lack Fourth Amendment privacy rights, it systematically combs through its PRISM databases for the emails and messages of Americans. Indeed, FBI agents around the

country routinely search for the communications of specific Americans using their names or email addresses—including at the earliest stages of domestic criminal investigations."

In 2017, the Electronic Frontier Foundation described one such example: "The case centered on Mohammed Mohamud, an American citizen who in 2012 was charged with plotting to bomb a Christmas tree lighting ceremony in Oregon. After he had already been convicted, Mohamud was told for the first time that information used in his prosecution was obtained using Section 702. Further disclosures clarified that the government used the surveillance program known as PRISM, which gives U.S. intelligence agencies access to communications in the possession of Internet service providers such as Google, Yahoo, or Facebook, to obtain the emails at issue in the case."[35]

Now, let's be clear: By all accounts, it appears Mohamud is truly a terrorist who deserves to rot in prison (and hell) for his attempted Christmas bombing. But this case isn't about Mohamud. It's about whether the federal government should have the power to use the billions of communications agents have "incidentally" collected of Americans to spy on people who have done absolutely nothing wrong. So far, courts have largely defended the federal government's power to use such surveillance data and communications collected through programs like Prism, as the Ninth Circuit Court of Appeals did in the case against Mohamud.[36]

For every terrorist caught using these mass surveillance programs, there are tens of millions of people whose privacy rights are violated—and private tech companies are helping federal officials do it. Because the NSA and other government agencies don't on their own have direct access to Americans' email and social media accounts, photos, and videos, they have pressured private companies into giving them access to Americans' personal data. In 2013, when Snowden first went public with information about the federal government's spying programs, several major tech companies had already started cooperating with federal officials, including Apple, Facebook, Google, and Microsoft.[37] Which means the feds basically have access to everything.

In 2016, Reuters reported, "Yahoo Inc last year secretly built a custom software program to search all of its customers' incoming emails for specific information provided by U.S. intelligence officials, according to people familiar with the matter. The company complied with a classified U.S. government demand, scanning hundreds of millions of Yahoo Mail accounts at the behest of the National Security Agency or FBI, said three former employees and a fourth person apprised of the events."[38] Wait, *people still use Yahoo*?

Reuters further reported that in 2017 alone, the NSA "collected 534 million records of phone calls and text messages of Americans . . . more than triple gathered in 2016."[39] No word yet on how many of those records were cat GIFs.

It's not hard to imagine how a socialist government, even in America, could use this information to advance collectivist goals. For example, how long will it be before government starts combing through its vast record of communications to identify potentially troublesome Americans who are guilty of "hate speech" or "religious zealotry" or spreading "fake news"? Perhaps government agents wouldn't be able to imprison Americans on the basis of finding someone engage in "hate speech"—that darn Constitution is always getting in the way of authoritarianism—but they could use that information for further investigations or perhaps as part of some future American social credit scoring system. We already have a vast credit score-tracking industry—how hard would it be to tack on the "social" part?

Other new technologies that have recently been rolled out by private companies could also be used to ensure people are being "good citizens" or "paying their fair share" or properly contributing to society. For example, business magazine *Fast Company* reports:

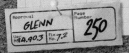

A COMPANY CALLED PATRONSCAN SELLS THREE PRODUCTS—KIOSK, DESKTOP, AND HANDHELD SYSTEMS—DESIGNED TO HELP BAR AND RESTAURANT OWNERS MANAGE CUSTOMERS. PATRONSCAN IS A SUBSIDIARY OF THE CANADIAN SOFTWARE COMPANY SERVALL BIOMETRICS, AND ITS PRODUCTS ARE NOW ON SALE IN THE UNITED STATES, CANADA, AUSTRALIA, AND THE UNITED KINGDOM.

PATRONSCAN HELPS SPOT FAKE IDS—AND TROUBLEMAKERS. WHEN CUSTOMERS ARRIVE AT A PATRONSCAN-USING BAR, THEIR ID IS SCANNED. THE COMPANY MAINTAINS A LIST OF OBJECTIONABLE CUSTOMERS DESIGNED TO PROTECT VENUES FROM PEOPLE PREVIOUSLY REMOVED FOR "FIGHTING, SEXUAL ASSAULT, DRUGS, THEFT, AND OTHER BAD BEHAVIOR," ACCORDING TO ITS WEBSITE. A "PUBLIC" LIST IS SHARED AMONG ALL PATRONSCAN CUSTOMERS. SO SOMEONE WHO'S BANNED BY ONE BAR IN THE U.S. IS POTENTIALLY BANNED BY ALL THE BARS IN THE U.S., THE U.K., AND CANADA THAT USE THE PATRONSCAN SYSTEM FOR UP TO A YEAR. (PATRONSCAN AUSTRALIA KEEPS A SEPARATE SYSTEM.)

JUDGMENT ABOUT WHAT KIND OF BEHAVIOR QUALIFIES FOR INCLUSION ON A PATRONSCAN LIST IS UP TO THE BAR OWNERS AND MANAGERS. INDIVIDUAL BAR OWNERS CAN IGNORE THE BAN, IF THEY LIKE.[49]

What would stop a socialist-led federal government from using machines like these to track people's behavior in restaurants, bars, and other public places across the country, punishing those deemed to be irresponsible with fines or tax increases? What would stop a government agency tasked with fighting against "hate speech" from assessing higher taxes on people deemed to be sexist or racist? Or perhaps the government could create a program that gives tax breaks to Americans who wear devices that track whether people are living a healthy lifestyle. People who run, lift weights, and eat green things—you know, crazy people—would get financial rewards, while the good ole' fashioned American steak and Twinkie eaters like me would be forced to pay more to cover our increased costs to society. If you think this is crazy, consider all the sugar and soda taxes that are imposed or being proposed in cities across the country. This scenario would likely seem particularly appealing with a

A.D.D. MOMENT

HARPA & RED FLAG LAWS

After the 2019 mass shootings in Dayton, Ohio, and El Paso, Texas, proposals for "red flag" laws were offered as potential solutions to American gun violence.

"Red flag" laws are intended to look for signs of potential violence in gun owners. If a "red flag" is raised, then authorities could remove firearms from a person without due process.

This concept was taken much further in a proposal to use HARPA—the Health Advanced Research Projects Agency—to help target potential violent actors. Under this proposal, HARPA, which was originally designed to coordinate health information, would use information from the government, academia, and the private sector to identify "neurobehavioral signs" of "someone headed toward a violent explosive act."

The proposal listed private-sector technologies that could be used to collect data, including "Apple Watches, Fitbits, Amazon Echo and Google Home." Can you image the government using data collected by your Amazon Echo to take away your firearms without any due process? The potential for abuse is terrifying.[b]

single-payer health care model in place. If government is paying your health care bills, why shouldn't you be required to live healthier or have a little less privacy?

And if you think social credit systems couldn't exist in the United States, then think again. Similar social scoring systems are becoming increasingly more common in various industries, including in those heavily tied to government, like higher education. In May 2019, College Board—the nonprofit organization that administers the SAT college entrance exams as well as Advanced Placement testing—announced it planned to include an "adversity" score as part of its future SAT testing.[41]

According to College Board, the "adversity" score was designed to allow college admissions officers "to view a student's academic accomplishment in the context of where they live and learn." The score "doesn't provide information about the student. It provides information about the student's environment."[42] I suppose "adversity score" sounds better than "excuses list."

Inside Higher Ed reported, "Among the factors that would go into the adversity index are some that are economic (proportion of students at a school who are eligible for free or reduced lunch), that reflect economic challenges (housing instability) and educational status (percentage of students who go on to college). A score would be on a scale up to 100."

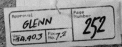

As *Inside Higher Ed* noted in its report, "The SAT has been criticized for years because wealthy students earn higher scores, on average, than do those who are middle class, who in turn earn higher scores, on average, than do those who are from low-income families." The "adversity" score is meant to right this perceived wrong by helping admissions departments give an advantage to students from more difficult socio-economic environments. It's not fair, they reasoned, that students who actually performed well on the SATs and in their classes be rewarded for their hard work because they go to good schools and live in good neighborhoods.

The backlash College Board experienced after rolling out its plan forced it to abandon its plan for an "adversity" score later in 2019,[43] but this example displays exactly the kind of social engineering socialists are hoping to achieve through the use of technology, testing, and centralized control that in previous generations has been difficult or impossible to fully implement.

Neal DiCaprio-Cortez @GreenNewNeal
Government social engineering and spying might make us all uncomfortable, but it's not like government would use technology to harm innocent people—just those who are doing things they shouldn't be. And government using technology to advance the greater good makes perfect sense to me. Why shouldn't government encourage people to act responsibly?

 1

Every authoritarian government that has ever existed makes the argument that government restrictions on freedom, especially mass surveillance, is only meant to target those who are breaking laws or engaging in "undesirable" behavior. The tyrants in China who have rounded up millions of religious minorities and "political dissidents" and forced them into "reeducation camps" are saying exactly that. And this "greater good" argument is precisely what President Franklin Roosevelt said during World War II, when he imprisoned 120,000 Japanese Americans merely for committing the crime of belonging to the wrong racial group. (See Chapter 3.)

Approval
GLENN
Use
No. 14.903 | Fix No. 7.2
Page Number
253

This presents a good illustration of why socialism is so dangerous: "Good," "bad," and "undesirable" are largely subjective ideas that can change with every new election. Surely you'll agree that what President Barack Obama thought was "good" for America was not the same as what President Donald Trump insists is "good" for the country today. By giving government the power to take away people's rights, privacy, property, and wealth in the name of the "public good," you're empowering the majority of people in society to have total control over the minority, which inevitably leads to abuse. You can't have a truly free nation *and* socialism, in large part because socialism concentrates too much power in the hands of government. The technological advancements made in recent decades would only make that problem significantly worse.

Professor Tweed @checkurprivilegeplz
.@glennbeck, I think you're cherry-picking your examples of how technology and new ways of managing society can be potentially dangerous. Many government controls of society have dramatically improved lives and the economy. For example, millions of people have been lifted from poverty and the severity of numerous recessions has been reduced because of government's takeover of the money supply and the elimination of the gold standard. That proves that government's control over the economy can produce positive results.

 1

Actually, since government abandoned the gold standard in 1973, the poverty rate has largely remained unchanged.[44] What has changed, however, is that the United States has run up a $23 trillion tab and indebted Americans to numerous foreign nations around the world, putting our economy, society, and national security in grave danger.[45]

Professor Tweed @checkurprivilegeplz
This is just more proof of your backwards thinking.
Now that government can print its own money without
needing to worry about gold or silver, it can spend as
much as it wants. Government doesn't need to worry
about debt because it can always just print more
money when it needs it. This is a perfect example
of how new ways of thinking about economics and
technological improvements are making socialism a
much more attractive option

　　　♡ 1　　　　　　⇅　　　　　　♡

*COINCIDENCE?
DOUBTFUL.
VERY DOUBTFUL.*

AT the end of 2019, the U.S.
national debt was $23
trillion, about the same amount
as the total spent on welfare
programs since the passage
of President Lyndon Johnson's
"Great Society" reforms.[c]

Well, we can agree on one thing: Without the gold standard,
government can spend as much money as it wants, and it
often does. That's why America is running a trillion-dollar
deficit with nearly full employment. But just because
government *can* spend a seemingly infinite amount of money doesn't mean that it
should, or that the effects of massive deficits won't be incredibly detrimental—and
potentially disastrous—in the years to come.

The growing wave of so-called "economists" claiming that government can print a
seemingly infinite amount of money without any negative economic consequences,
a view commonly called "Modern Monetary Theory," presents one of the most
significant threats to the long-term survival of the United States—and no, that's not
an exaggeration.

According to Modern Monetary Theory (MMT) proponents, policymakers have not
properly taken advantage of government's ability to print its own money. They think
lawmakers are spending far too much time worrying about "fiscal responsibility"
and balanced budgets. Instead, they say government should print the money it needs
to accomplish important public policy goals, regardless of how much debt is being
incurred. (Now that I think about it, MMT could also stand for "Monopoly Money
Technique.")

Modern Monetary Theory is rapidly gaining support with many well-connected economists and far-left politicians. Among the theory's most ardent supporters is L. Randall Wray, a professor of economics at Bard College who has in recent years been running around Washington, D.C., trying to convince lawmakers that debt doesn't matter. In fact, as recently as November 2019, Wray was invited to testify on behalf of MMT in front of the Democratic Party–led House Budget Committee.

MMT has also grabbed the attention of socialist Alexandria Ocasio Cortez, who stated in a 2019 interview the theory deserves to be "a larger part of our conversation."[46]

But perhaps the most vocal, and arguably the most influential, advocate of MMT is Stephanie Kelton. In recent years, Kelton, a professor of public policy and economics at Stony Brook University, has appeared on dozens of leading media outlets, where she regularly preaches the alleged benefits of Modern Monetary Theory. She has also served as the chief economist of the Democratic Party's staff on the U.S. Senate Budget Committee and as a senior economic adviser to Bernie Sanders' 2016 and 2020 presidential campaigns.[47]

In a 2019 interview with CNBC, Kelton explained why she believes deficits don't mean all that much:

> MMT STARTS WITH A REALLY SIMPLE OBSERVATION AND THAT IS THAT THE U.S. DOLLAR IS A SIMPLE PUBLIC MONOPOLY. IN OTHER WORDS, THE UNITED STATES CURRENCY COMES FROM THE UNITED STATES GOVERNMENT. IT CAN'T COME FROM ANYWHERE ELSE. AND THEREFORE, IT CAN NEVER RUN OUT OF MONEY. IT CANNOT FACE A SOLVENCY PROBLEM, BILLS COMING DUE THAT IT CAN'T AFFORD TO PAY. IT NEVER HAS TO WORRY ABOUT FINDING THE MONEY IN ORDER TO BE ABLE TO SPEND. IT DOESN'T NEED TO GO AND RAISE TAXES OR BORROW MONEY BEFORE IT IS ABLE TO SPEND.
>
> SO WHAT THAT MEANS IS THAT THE FEDERAL GOVERNMENT IS NOTHING LIKE A HOUSEHOLD. IN ORDER FOR HOUSEHOLDS OR

Approval
GLENN
Update
No. 14.90.3 Fix No. 7.2
Page Number
256

PRIVATE BUSINESSES TO BE ABLE TO SPEND, THEY'VE GOT TO COME UP WITH THE MONEY, RIGHT? AND THE FEDERAL GOVERNMENT DOESN'T HAVE TO BEHAVE LIKE A HOUSEHOLD. IN FACT, IT BECOMES REALLY DESTRUCTIVE FOR THE ECONOMY IF THE GOVERNMENT TRIES TO BEHAVE LIKE A HOUSEHOLD. YOU AND I ARE USING THE U.S. DOLLAR. STATES AND MUNICIPALITIES—THE STATE OF KANSAS OR DETROIT—THEY'RE ALSO USING THE U.S. DOLLAR. PRIVATE BUSINESSES ARE USING THE DOLLAR. THE FEDERAL GOVERNMENT OF THE UNITED STATES IS ISSUING OUR CURRENCY, AND SO WE HAVE A VERY DIFFERENT RELATIONSHIP TO THE CURRENCY. THAT MEANS THAT IN ORDER TO SPEND, THE GOVERNMENT DOESN'T HAVE TO DO WHAT A HOUSEHOLD OR A PRIVATE BUSINESS HAS TO DO: FIND THE MONEY. THE GOVERNMENT CAN SIMPLY SPEND THE MONEY INTO THE ECONOMY AND WHEN IT DOES, THE REST OF US END UP RECEIVING THAT SPENDING AS PART OF OUR INCOME.[48]

Sounds awfully convenient, right? U.S. politicians have long operated this way, that "government doesn't have to behave like a household." Now they just have a fancy-sounding academic theory to justify their behavior.

That doesn't mean MMT supporters like Kelton think debt and deficits are totally meaningless, however. According to Kelton, the deficit matters, "It's just that it matters in ways that we're not normally taught to understand." According to Kelton:

NORMALLY, I THINK PEOPLE TEND TO HEAR DEFICIT AND THINK IT'S SOMETHING THAT WE SHOULD STRIVE TO ELIMINATE, THAT WE SHOULDN'T BE RUNNING BUDGET DEFICITS. THAT THEY'RE EVIDENCE OF FISCAL IRRESPONSIBILITY. AND THE TRUTH IS THE DEFICIT CAN BE TOO BIG. EVIDENCE OF A DEFICIT THAT'S TOO BIG WOULD BE INFLATION.

BUT THE DEFICIT CAN ALSO BE TOO SMALL. IT CAN BE TOO SMALL TO SUPPORT DEMAND IN THE ECONOMY AND EVIDENCE OF A DEFICIT THAT IS TOO SMALL IS UNEMPLOYMENT. SO, DEFICITS CAN BE TOO BIG, BUT THEY CAN ALSO BE TOO SMALL. AND THE RIGHT LEVEL OF THE DEFICIT IS THE ONE THAT GETS YOU A BALANCED OVERALL ECONOMY. THE ONE THAT ALLOWS YOU TO ACHIEVE HIGH LEVELS OF EMPLOYMENT AND LOW INFLATION.[49]

Kelton's view is that as long as an economy isn't experiencing inflation, a government can continue to print as much money as it desires to pay for as many government programs at it wants. But as she stated in her CNBC interview, Kelton—as well as other MMT advocates—also says that one of their priorities is to keep interest rates low, because lower interest rates encourage lending, which in turn encourages economic activity.

This strategy presents a big problem, however, as anyone with even a shred of familiarity with economics knows. Printing money to increase the money supply eventually causes inflation, and the more money that's printed, the more inflation that inevitably results. The reason for this is simple: If you have more dollars in an economy but the same number of people, goods, and services, introducing more money decreases the value of all existing money, which means you've got to spend more cash to get the same goods and services.

When inflation does occur, central banks have historically raised interest rates—the amount charged to pay back loans—to reduce inflation by effectively taking money out of the money supply. So, it seems like Kelton wants to have her cake and eat it too. She wants the government to print money to pay for new social programs, but she doesn't want to raise interest rates to control the inflation that often comes when money is printed.

As we've already seen, Kelton does acknowledge that inflation creates a lot of economic problems, so how do she and other MMT supporters plan to prevent runaway inflation? When Kelton was asked a similar question, she responded, "I think the first question is to understand what the source of the inflationary pressure is and then to move forward with a policy tool that you think is going to help you get at that inflation. If you've got inflation resulting from energy price increases it's probably not going to do much to have the Fed raise interest rates or even to have Congress raise taxes. You've got to do something else that's going to work."[50]

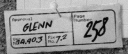

What, exactly, is that "something else"? For Kelton, inflation isn't typically driven by the money supply per se, but rather by specific inflationary drivers in certain sectors of the economy. Kelton's solution for preventing and managing runaway inflation isn't to increase interest rates to discourage lending and encourage savings, it's raising taxes, which MMT supporters would use to take money out of the economy, and expanding the authority of a centralized government to control markets through regulations, price controls, and other top-down measures. Or, as Matthew Klein wrote for *Barron's*:

> THE BEST WAY TO UNDERSTAND MMT IS TO THINK OF IT AS THE PEACETIME VERSION OF WARTIME ECONOMIC MANAGEMENT: GOVERNMENTS CAN DO WHATEVER IS NECESSARY TO SATISFY THE "PUBLIC PURPOSE" AS LONG AS THEY MAINTAIN THEIR AUTHORITY OVER THE POPULACE. THE U.S. GOVERNMENT WAS ABLE TO RUN BUDGET DEFICITS WORTH MORE THAN 20% OF GROSS DOMESTIC PRODUCT DURING WORLD WAR II WITHOUT RISKING EITHER INFLATION OR ITS OWN CREDITWORTHINESS—BUT IT NEEDED TO USE RATIONING, WAGE AND PRICE CONTROLS, AND FINANCIAL REPRESSION TO DO SO. . . .
>
> IN GENERAL, HOWEVER, THE MMT SOLUTION TO INFLATION IS TO INCREASE GOVERNMENT CONTROL OF ECONOMIC ACTIVITY. AS MMT THEORISTS SCOTT FULLWILER, ROHAN GREY, AND NATHAN TANKUS PUT IT, "THE MORE ACTIVELY WE REGULATE BIG BUSINESS FOR PUBLIC PURPOSE, THE TIGHTER THE FULL EMPLOYMENT WE CAN ACHIEVE." THEY ALSO ADVOCATE LIMITING CONSUMERS' ABILITY TO BORROW TO BUY SPECIFIC GOODS AND SERVICES IF THEIR PRICES ARE RISING TOO QUICKLY. PAVLINA TCHERNEVA OF BARD COLLEGE ADDS THAT "INCOMES POLICIES" AND "WAGE RULES" COULD ALSO HOLD DOWN INFLATION IF NEEDED.[51]

It's not hard to see why socialists would be attracted to an economic theory that advocates for an "increase [of] government control of economic activity," but any monetary scheme based on the idea that we should be greatly *expanding* our already large national debt to spur economic growth is completely devoid of reality, or even common sense.

Professor Tweed @checkurprivilegeplz
That's not true. Modern Monetary Theory supporters are right. If government had more power over the economy, it could manage the industries driving inflation and prevent hyperinflation from occurring. MMT has the power to dramatically increase economic growth.

💬 1   🔁   ♡

Oh, really? Let's a take a close look at some of the biggest reasons why the Modern Monetary Theory strategy would be absolutely disastrous—we're talking Howard Dean screaming at the Iowa caucuses disastrous.

1. FAKE GROWTH

First, any "growth" created by printing money isn't real economic expansion, but rather a gigantic illusion, a figment of the imagination—you know, like Beto O'Rourke's chances of becoming president or the idea that Hillary Clinton has an actual human heart. (Mark my words, someday, we're going to find out Hillary is mostly machine.)

By printing huge sums of money to twist and turn the economy in the way central planners see fit, they would be doing nothing more than creating big, fat market bubbles, just like they did with the housing market prior to the 2008 financial crisis. The reason for this isn't complicated: By printing cash and funneling it into industries that wouldn't otherwise be growing based on real market forces, people end up making *really* bad economic decisions. They overextend themselves and make investments they ordinarily would never make. This is what created the financial crisis in 2008. The entire housing market and much of the financial services industry were nothing more than a gigantic house of cards. Many of the key players involved—

investors, real estate agents, mortgage companies, banks—were acting irresponsibly because government created perverse incentives for them to do so. (See Chapter 2.) When their bad, risky decision-making caught up to them, the whole house of cards collapsed, dragging the world economy down with it.

Under Modern Monetary Theory, government would constantly be creating these bubbles, but it wouldn't merely incentivize people to make poor economic choices, it would essentially force people to act against natural market forces by pumping so much money into the industries the central planners want to prop up that they become the most affordable or attractive option.

2. WAIT, THESE ARE THE "GENIUSES" IN CHARGE?

Second, Modern Monetary Theory advocates say they could prevent these bubbles from developing in the first place, as well as inflation, by putting government agents in charge of the economy who would effectively manage the various industries so well that the dangers posed by printing too much money could be avoided entirely. "Just put the right people in charge and make the right decisions, and everything will be fine. Trust us."

When Kelton was asked about controlling inflation under MMT, she explained this concept in detail:

> SO THE BEST DEFENSE AGAINST INFLATION IS A GOOD OFFENSE, AND WHAT MMT DOES IS TO TRY TO BE I THINK KIND OF HYPERSENSITIVE TO THE RISKS OF INFLATION. . . . AND SO WHAT WE WOULD SAY IS: LOOK, IF YOU ARE CONGRESS AND IF YOU ARE CONSIDERING A NEW SPENDING BILL, INSTEAD OF THINKING ABOUT THE WAYS IN WHICH THAT NEW SPENDING WILL ADD TO THE DEFICIT OR ADD TO THE DEBT, YOU SHOULD BE THINKING ABOUT THE WAYS IN WHICH

> THAT NEW SPENDING HAS THE RISK OF ACCELERATING INFLATION.
> AND THEN AVOID DOING THAT.
>
> SO INSTEAD OF GOING TO THE CONGRESSIONAL BUDGET OFFICE
> AND SAYING, "WOULD YOU TAKE A LOOK AT THIS PIECE OF
> LEGISLATION AND GIVE US FEEDBACK? WE'D LIKE TO KNOW WHAT
> THIS BILL WILL DO TO THE DEBT AND THE DEFICIT OVER TIME."
> INSTEAD, GO TO THE CONGRESSIONAL BUDGET OFFICE OR OTHER
> GOVERNMENT AGENCIES AND SAY, "WE'RE CONSIDERING PASSING
> THIS TRILLION-DOLLAR INVESTMENT IN INFRASTRUCTURE. THIS
> IS OUR BILL. WOULD YOU LOOK AT IT? AND WE PLAN TO DO THIS
> SPENDING OVER THE COURSE OF THE NEXT FIVE YEARS. TELL
> US IF THAT WOULD CREATE PROBLEMS IN THE REAL ECONOMY.
> EVALUATE THE INFLATION RISK AND COME BACK TO US AND GIVE US
> SOME FEEDBACK."[52]

This might be the most delusional part of Modern Monetary Theory, which is really saying something. Kelton's grand plan to control inflation is for politicians to make really smart economic decisions—which they almost never do—and for agencies like the Congressional Budget Office to make *extremely accurate* predictions about costs and inflation years into the future—which it rarely does. Sounds like a great idea. Now, just add it to the socialism stew and let simmer. Smells wonderful.

When have government bureaucrats and central planners ever proven they can manage *anything* effectively, never mind the largest economy in the world? In fiscal year 2018, the U.S. Postal Service (USPS) lost $3.9 billion.[53] Amtrak, which is run by the government, had in 2018 its best year since 1973—and it still lost $168 million.[54] If the government can't deliver the mail or run a train system without losing billions of dollars every year, why would it be able to effectively manage nearly every important industry in the country?

3. WHEELBARROWS FULL OF CASH—
AND NOT IN A GOOD WAY

Third, if MMT supporters like Kelton were to print trillions upon trillions of dollars in additional cash and federal bureaucrats were to fail to effectively manage the economy, which history has shown would undoubtedly occur, then the country would inevitably enter a period of high inflation. Normally, well-functioning central banks would try to control inflation by imposing interest rate increases, which typically slow economic growth, but MMT supporters like Kelton deny this strategy. They say they could use government to solve inflationary problems by better managing the parts of the economy spurring inflation. So, for example, if higher energy prices are determined to be one of the causes of inflation, government could simply create energy-related regulations or price controls to slow the inflation.

Although this "theory" has been treated as something revolutionary, it's actually not much different than the monetary policies enacted by socialist governments throughout the past 100 years. For example, after Venezuelan socialist leader Hugo Chavez died in 2013, socialist Nicolas Maduro took over the South American country and continued many of the same expensive government programs Chavez enacted. Unfortunately for Maduro, the high oil prices Chavez's regime enjoyed for years crashed, forcing Maduro to decide between printing obscene amounts of money to keep those programs afloat or scaling back the national government's numerous socialist policies.[55] Maduro chose to print money, and the results were cataclysmic. The government's commitment to printing currency to pay for services it couldn't afford caused hyperinflation, with rates surpassing 100,000 percent in 2018 and 10 million percent in 2019.[56]

Chavez and Maduro had enacted numerous regulations, price controls, and other mandates to limit inflation, but none of them worked. Why? Well, Modern Monetary Theory apologists would say the problem is Venezuela borrowed some of its money in other currencies, so it couldn't manage all of its debt as easily as other countries might be able to.[57] But that's a very weak answer. Venezuela could have cut government spending, reduced the size of its numerous welfare programs, and then used the savings to make loan payments and cover essential services—all commonsense approaches—but it didn't. Why? Because the political motivations of those in charge outweighed their desire to make good economic choices. That's a problem that exists in every political system, not just in countries like Venezuela.

Government's failure to effectively control economies has led to hyperinflation throughout world history. During World War I, Germany's Weimar Republic printed trillions of marks and took on massive loan debt in an effort to help fund its effort to conquer Europe.[58] By 1923, things had become so bad that it took 200 billion marks to buy a single loaf of bread.[59] Germans had to use wheelbarrows full of cash to purchase basic goods. Money became so worthless, women made dresses out of marks, and some people even used money to wallpaper their homes.[60] (Using marks was actually cheaper than buying wallpaper.)

From 2007 to 2009, Zimbabwe also experienced tremendous hyperinflation due to economic mismanagement and socialist policies that included land confiscation. In 2008, inflation became so extreme—peaking at 500 billion percent—the country was forced to abolish its currency.[61] A decade later, in June 2019, Zimbabwe experienced another bout of high inflation, surpassing 175 percent.[62]

Although the United States has never experienced the kind of hyperinflation we've seen in other parts of the world, it has suffered through periods of relatively high inflation. Under the Jimmy Carter administration, Americans endured annual

inflation rates of 9 percent or higher from 1978 to 1980, with inflation reaching as high as 13.3 percent in 1979.[63] This crippled the economy in the late 1970s and early 1980s and forced the Federal Reserve to raise interest rates as high as 18 percent.

U.S. DOLLAR: THE WORLD RESERVE CURRENCY

The U.S. dollar became the world's dominant reserve currency during the 1944 Bretton Woods Agreement. This designation means the U.S. dollar is used by central banks across the world in transactions, investments, and for other monetary purposes. This system simplifies transactions carried out by central banks by not requiring them to constantly convert their currency.

This status provides the United States economic system with great stability. If countries around the world all use and accept the U.S. dollar, it creates a global appetite for U.S. treasuries.

This does not mean, however, that the dollar will always be the world's premier reserve currency. Many countries also use the euro and/or China's renminbi for reserve proposes.

The concept of using a basket of currencies has also been floated from time to time. Called "Special Drawing Rights (SDR)," this supplementary currency could replace the dollar if instability were to occur in the future.[d]

There's absolutely no reason to believe that we can't see the high inflation rates of the 1970s return to the United States, especially if the country pursues monetary policies in line with Modern Monetary Theory. In fact, if MMT theorists have it their way, Americans would be *lucky* to experience the kind of inflation that occurred in the 1970s.

Professor Tweed @checkurprivilegeplz
Whoa, @glennbeck, wait a second. What about Japan? It has been printing money for decades and doesn't have runaway inflation.

💬 1   🔁   ♡

Okay, but that's only part of the story. Japan is often held up by Modern Monetary supporters as the prime example of the validity of their whole "debt doesn't matter" theory. It's true that Japan has a much higher debt-to-GDP ratio—about 240 percent[64]—than we have in the United States. (Debt-to-GDP ratios are commonly used by non-MMT economists to determine how fiscally responsible a country is.) But although Japan has printed trillions of dollars without suffering from high inflation, that's not a guarantee that it won't face runaway inflation in the future. Eventually, the deflationary forces that have been at work in Japan will subside, and when they do, Japan will likely face crippling inflation rates.

"A CRASH IS GOING TO COME AT SOME POINT, AND THEN WE'LL SEE THAT M.M.T. DIDN'T HAVE ANY MERIT AFTER ALL."

– KOHEI OTSUKA
OPPOSITION MEMBER OF JAPAN'S
UPPER HOUSE FINANCE COMMITTEE

But I'll play along and assume that Japan will defy hundreds of years of history and everything we know about economics and continue to print trillions of dollars' worth of yen without suffering runaway inflation. Even if that were to occur, all that would do is guarantee the continuation of Japan's long, agonizing record of nonexistent economic growth. Despite spending trillions of dollars on government programs, "construction-related public investment," and other expenses over the past three decades, Japan's GDP (in current U.S. dollars)

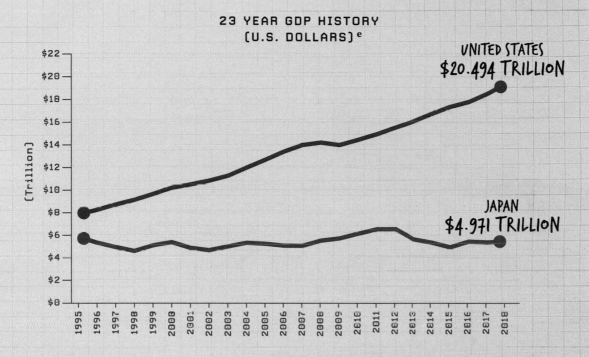

23 YEAR GDP HISTORY
(U.S. DOLLARS) e

UNITED STATES
$20.494 TRILLION

JAPAN
$4.971 TRILLION

[Trillion]

has barely increased. Even more stunning, from 1995 to 2018, Japan's GDP actually decreased by more than 8 percent. Over the same period, America's GDP *increased* by 168 percent.[65] This is a direct result of Japan's spending policies, which allow its government—which is just as incompetent as the central planners here in Washington, D.C.—to have too much power over the economy.

If Japan's floundering, nearly dead economy is the best example MMT theorists can come up with for why we should trust them to take over the entire U.S. economy, then that should tell you everything you need to know about Modern Monetary Theory.

Okay, let's get back to the list . . .

4. CONTROL AND CLASS WARFARE

The fourth reason Modern Monetary Theory should be avoided at all costs is the most important: At the end of the day, the primary purpose of the theory is to centralize economic control in the hands of a relatively small group of people, not to improve economic growth. MMT is nothing more than socialism with a shiny new coat of paint, as some of the biggest advocates of the theory have openly admitted.

In reaction to an article critical of Modern Monetary Theory, Pavlina R. Tcherneva, a program director and associate professor of economics at Bard College and a research associate at the Levy Economics Institute, wrote for the socialist publication *Jacobin* that one of the primary goals of MMT is to engage in "class struggle" by using Modern Monetary Theory to "render the wealthy obsolete." According to Tcherneva:

> HENWOOD [THE CRITIC OF MMT] DOES NOT ACKNOWLEDGE THAT ONE OF THE MOST EFFECTIVE WAYS OF ENGAGING IN THIS [CLASS] STRUGGLE IS TO RENDER THE WEALTHY OBSOLETE—AS IN, WE WILL STOP PRETENDING THAT WE NEED THEM TO PAY FOR THE GOOD SOCIETY. IN A WORLD WITH A SOVEREIGN CURRENCY AND MODERN MONETARY AND FISCAL INSTITUTIONS, WE NEVER REALLY DID, AND WE SURE DON'T NOW. AND THE PUBLIC NEEDS TO KNOW IT. THAT'S THE MMT MESSAGE.
>
> FOR THE RECORD MMT, AS HENWOOD ACKNOWLEDGES, HAS ALWAYS ARGUED FOR TAXING THE WEALTHY TO ADDRESS THE PROBLEMS OF INEQUALITY AND POLITICAL POWER, BUT WE ALSO OFFER A DIFFERENT KIND OF EMPOWERMENT—ONE THAT COMES WITH LIFTING THE VEIL OF MONEY.
>
> I WOULD SAY THAT HENWOOD (LIKE OTHER "TAX-THE-RICH-TO-PAY-FOR-PROGRESS" LEFTIES) IS TETHERED TO THE WEALTHY BY AN IMAGINARY UMBILICAL CORD THAT HOLDS HIS PROGRESSIVE AGENDA HOSTAGE TO HIS OPPRESSORS. TO ME, THIS IS THE DEFINITION OF A SELF-INDUCED PARALYSIS.

> TIME TO CUT THE CORD. MMT HAS A PROFOUND EMANCIPATORY
> POWER AND THE LEFT WOULD DO WELL TO AWAKEN TO
> ITS POTENTIAL.[66]

The more you listen to supporters of MMT, the more obvious it is that their real motivation isn't to improve the economy, but rather to punish the rich and use the government as a tool to redistribute wealth. This notion was probably expressed most bluntly by economist L. Randall Wray, another professor at Bard College. (What the heck are they putting in the water over there at Bard?) In reaction to the very same article criticized by Tcherneva, Wray wrote:

> FOR FAR TOO LONG LEFT-LEANING DEMOCRATS HAVE HAD A CLOSE
> SYMBIOTIC RELATIONSHIP WITH THE RICH. THEY'VE NEEDED THE
> "GOOD" RICH FOLK, LIKE GEORGE SOROS, BILL GATES, WARREN
> BUFFET [SIC], BOB RUBIN, TO FUND THEIR THINK TANKS AND
> POLITICAL CAMPAIGNS. THE CENTRIST CLINTON WING, HAS
> REPAID THE GENEROSITY OF WALL STREET'S NEOLIBERALS WITH
> DEREGULATION THAT ALLOWED THE CEOS TO SHOVEL MONEY TO
> THEMSELVES, VASTLY INCREASING INEQUALITY AND THEIR OWN
> POWER. AND THEY IN TURN REWARDED HILLARY-WHO BY HER OWN
> ACCOUNT ACCEPTED WHATEVER MONEY THEY WOULD THROW IN HER
> DIRECTION.
>
> TODAY'S PROGRESSIVES WON'T FALL INTO THAT TRAP. "HOW YA
> GONNA PAY FOR IT?" THROUGH A BUDGET AUTHORIZATION. UNCLE
> SAM CAN AFFORD IT WITHOUT THE HELP OF THE RICH.
>
> AND, BY THE WAY, THEY'RE GOING TO TAX YOU ANYWAY, BECAUSE
> YOU'VE GOT TOO MUCH-TOO MUCH INCOME, TOO MUCH WEALTH, TOO
> MUCH POWER. WHAT WILL WE DO WITH THE TAX REVENUE? BURN IT.
> UNCLE SAM DOESN'T NEED YOUR MONEY.[68]

For many of the leading MMT theorists, taxes aren't meant to raise revenues or even primarily to take money out of the economy; their primary purpose is to punish the wealthy and create a more "just" and "fair" society—assuming, of course, you believe that taking people's money away from them and burning it can ever be considered "fair."

WHEN GOVERNMENT IS EMPOWERED WITH THE ABILITY TO MANAGE VIRTUALLY EVERY ASPECT OF HUMAN LIFE...

MMT, at its core, is not primarily about spurring economic growth. Modern Monetary Theory is mostly designed to address class warfare by punishing the wealthy and coercing and manipulating society to bend to the whims of the elites pulling all the levers in Washington, D.C.—the same principles at the heart of socialism.

Advancements in technology and new economic theories can open the door to revolutionary societal changes, and we should welcome these changes when they are a product of *voluntary* interactions and free markets. But when government is empowered with the ability to manage virtually every aspect of human life, we should start to worry.

We are quickly approaching a time in history when governments are no longer going to be constrained by their inability to enact absolute control over their citizens. The technologies described in this chapter and the concept of Modern Monetary Theory blow the doors off long-standing limitations on government power and pave the way for a time when government will be able to enact and enforce any mandate it deems necessary.

When mixed with socialism, all this could make for a truly horrifying totalitarian cocktail.

CHAPTER #6
FINAL PAGE
LAYOUT

№ 07

SAINTS, SINNERS, & SOCIALISTS

FINAL APPROVED -GB

Approval GLENN

Ver. No. 4.90.3 Fix No. 7.2

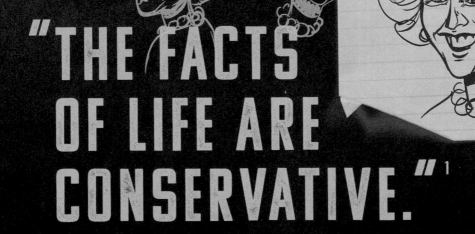

Socialism doesn't work. At the very least, its implementation creates catastrophic economic consequences, and more often than not, it also results in widespread death, suffering, and despair. On the other hand, they do build some nice statues of the dictators.

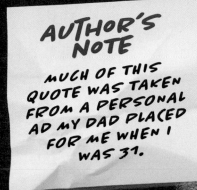
By this point in our conversation, I think socialism's history of unparalleled failure has been well established. But what we haven't spent much time doing is discussing *why* socialism has been so remarkably unsuccessful. And when it comes to socialism, the "why" matters. Some socialists—the honest ones—admit that their prized philosophy has a really bad track record, but they think it's possible to make socialism workable by putting the right people in power, building new safeguards, or having a better plan in place for the future.

These socialists are suffering from a terrible case of denial. They're like women who find themselves dating a real loser but keep the relationship alive anyway because they think the "loser" can change. They say their boyfriend "doesn't have a job, lives in his parents' basement, can't afford his own car, and seems to shower only on holidays. And, not like Flag Day either...only the big ones. But I can find a way to make this relationship work. I can 'fix' him." But here's the thing, ladies: sometimes, you can't "fix" him. Sometimes, you end up with a guy who is just a dirty, unkempt, unsuccessful *loser*, and the best thing you can do for yourself is to move on.

Socialism is the abusive loser boyfriend of political and economic ideologies. Sure, he's got some interesting things to say, nice smile, a bit subversive and rebellious, so you'll overlook his seemingly endless list of flaws and try to "fix" him. In the end, the relationship always ends the same way—with a box of his crap thrown out your bedroom window. Save yourself the heartache and get out of the doomed relationship now.

As much as you'd like to "fix" socialism, you can't. It literally never works and never lasts, because at its foundation, socialism is so rotten, so flawed, and so broken that no amount of planning or effort could ever make it successful. The best you can hope for is a little less death, destruction, and tyranny than usual.

The reason why socialism doesn't work is that humans are human. For it to have any chance of success, people would have to be fundamentally different creatures whose natures would have to be completely altered in line with socialist principles. Unsurprisingly, that has never happened, and it never will.

When the Founding Fathers were deciding how to structure America's new government, the primary question that needed to be tackled was how to create a government powerful enough to defend itself against foreign invaders and protect the rights of individuals while not making it so powerful that it would grow out of control and eventually transform into a tyrannical monster. Many of the Founders were avid students of history, and as such, they understood the pitfalls other societies had previously fallen into. They also knew that designing a well-functioning society depended on having a proper understanding of human nature.

For example, in a 1788 essay by James Madison published in the *Independent Journal* in New York—which would eventually become known as essay number 51 in the *Federalist Papers*—Madison wrote:

> BUT WHAT IS GOVERNMENT ITSELF, BUT THE GREATEST OF ALL REFLECTIONS ON HUMAN NATURE? IF MEN WERE ANGELS, NO GOVERNMENT WOULD BE NECESSARY. IF ANGELS WERE TO GOVERN MEN, NEITHER EXTERNAL NOR INTERNAL CONTROLS ON GOVERNMENT WOULD BE NECESSARY. IN FRAMING A GOVERNMENT WHICH IS TO BE ADMINISTERED BY MEN OVER MEN, THE GREAT DIFFICULTY LIES IN THIS: YOU MUST FIRST ENABLE THE GOVERNMENT TO CONTROL THE GOVERNED; AND IN THE NEXT PLACE OBLIGE IT TO CONTROL ITSELF. A DEPENDENCE ON THE PEOPLE IS, NO DOUBT, THE PRIMARY CONTROL ON THE GOVERNMENT; BUT EXPERIENCE HAS TAUGHT MANKIND THE NECESSITY OF AUXILIARY PRECAUTIONS.[2]

Madison was right; men are inherently flawed and ambitious, so government is needed to help protect the rights of individuals. However, to prevent government from becoming too powerful, the people must have the ability to act as the "primary control on the government." But even then, Madison notes that "auxiliary precautions" are necessary. Why? Because at any time the public could use government as a tool to take away the rights of individuals—one of the primary flaws of any socialist model.

"It is of great importance in a republic not only to guard the society against the oppression of its rulers, but to guard one part of the society against the injustice of the other part," Madison wrote. "Different interests necessarily exist in different classes of citizens. If a majority be united by a common interest, the rights of the minority will be insecure."

Madison's remedy for this problem was a federalist system in which there would be numerous states, communities, and "factions" holding each other accountable. If power is spread out across an entire nation, it becomes much more unlikely that a majority faction would develop and take away the rights of the minority.

Although many of the other Founders agreed with Madison's view, they were skeptical that such protections would be enough to guarantee the rights of

A SOVIET UNDERSTANDING OF "RIGHTS"

The Constitution of the Union of Soviet Socialist Republics guaranteed its citizens numerous "rights," including a right to "free" education and health care and a variety of personal liberties, such as the freedom to associate and free expression.

Why is it, then, that the Soviet Union was one of history's most egregious human rights violators? Well, the devil is in the details.

Although the Soviet Constitution did include various protections for individuals, they were all subject to one extremely important constitutional provision, one that must be present in all socialist societies. Article 39 reads, in part: "Enjoyment by citizens of their rights and freedoms must not be to the detriment of the interests of society or the state, or infringe the rights of other citizens."

Or, put more simply, your "rights" only exist if they don't get in the way of the "interests" of the collective. And who decides that? Well, the government, of course. Does that sound like a free society to you?

individuals and the states. For that reason, they demanded a "Bill of Rights" be added to the Constitution that would help to keep the federal government from becoming too powerful.

So, the Founders built two important checks on the power of government and the majority of society into their Constitution: federalism and constitutional guarantees for individual liberty. Both were meant, in part, to stop the very developments socialists now regularly call for: granting nearly all power either to a small minority in government or, in the case of democratic socialism, to the majority population.

30 SECOND GUIDE TO GOVERNMENT SPENDING

BUYING SOMETHING...	USING YOUR OWN MONEY	USING SOMEONE ELSE'S MONEY	
FOR YOURSELF	QUADRANT № 01 HIGH CONCERN FOR QUALITY & COST	QUADRANT № 02 HIGH CONCERN FOR QUALITY, LOW CONCERN FOR COST	INDIVIDUALS BUY IN QUADRANT NO. 01
FOR SOMEONE ELSE	QUADRANT № 03 LOW CONCERN FOR QUALITY, HIGH CONCERN FOR COST	QUADRANT № 04 LOW CONCERN FOR QUALITY, LOW CONCERN FOR COST	GOVERNMENTS BUY IN QUADRANT NO. 04

Socialism's primary purpose is to enhance the power of the collective by seizing power, wealth, property, and rights from individuals. This is an extremely dangerous way to structure society, as evidenced by the numerous socialism-related catastrophes mentioned throughout this conversation, because humans are terrible central planners who are much better at managing their own affairs than they are managing the affairs of others. People are also much more likely to work harder, more efficiently, and longer days when they are motivated by a reward for themselves or their families. When you take that incentive away and turn it into an abstract "do it for the motherland" slogan, people stop working efficiently, and economic chaos eventually ensues.

Rewards and competition haven't only been proven to be effective ways to increase efficiency and productivity in the workplace and classrooms, they are essential parts of every environment on Earth that have always been part of the human experience.[3] Children naturally compete for attention from their parents and race other children in school yards. Societies have developed massive, complex entertainment systems built around competition, like professional sports. In nature, animals of every kind compete with each other for scarce resources and mates. Reward systems can even be found in the lore and legends of ancient religions and mythologies, as well as throughout humans' long tradition of storytelling: After defeating the dragon, the noble knight always gets the hidden treasure. Similarly, Han Solo wins the heart of the princess after helping blow up the Death Star. (I told you I would work in an Original Trilogy reference.)

Competition and the rewards that flow from it are literally everywhere. By denying that reality, socialists work against fundamental laws of nature. It's no wonder then that they have been so unsuccessful.

There is no way to train people to genuinely desire to act against their own self-interests. (And yet, people still sign up for Twitter accounts.) That doesn't mean people are incapable of helping others without some kind of monetary reward; obviously, people engage in charitable activities all the time—and not just in the sense that they give money to charitable organizations. They also do simple things like walk an old lady across the street, help a neighbor bring in the groceries, stay behind church services to sweep floors, and a million other little things, too. But it's wrong to assume that these *voluntary* activities aren't tied to the self-interests of those who engage in them. Those who choose to help others do so for all sorts of reasons, but all of them come down to one thing: They truly believe that they would rather help another person than do some other activity.

However, socialism, even democratic socialism, destroys voluntary choice. It demands actions on the part of others, even if those people do not want to engage in them. It's a philosophy built on the idea that force and coercion can be used to accomplish good things—and by "good things," I mean whatever the collective decides it wants at the time. This is the least-inspiring way to get humans to help others, because people are often required to engage in actions they really, really don't want to do.

Free, capitalistic societies do the opposite: They allow everyone to pursue their own personal hopes, dreams, and ambitions. They don't tell people how or where to live or work, they provide an environment in which millions upon millions of people choose to make those decisions for themselves. The end result isn't a world in which everyone has everything they want—but socialism doesn't produce such a world either, even in its most utopian form. What capitalism—real capitalism, not crony capitalism—does do, however, is provide people with the freedom to pursue the lives they desire most.

Clay Guevara @coffeeshopcommie
Many people are greedy and self-centered, and that greed is the root of most of our problems. If you allow people to have total control over their wealth and property, they will greedily keep it for themselves while others suffer.

♡ 1   ⟲   ♡

Greed does create problems, but no government mandate or law is going to change people's hearts. There are, of course, problems in every free society, but it's not because there's something wrong with free markets or individual liberty; it's because people are not perfect. To build a better world, we don't need to take rights away from individuals, we need people to *voluntarily* change and *choose* to act in ways that will help others who are truly in need. It must be a free choice, not something that is imposed on them, and it can only happen in a world in which people have the liberty required to make those decisions. Socialism doesn't provide that opportunity.

Clay Guevara @coffeeshopcommie
We can just enforce benevolence.

💬 1   ⟲   ♡

If you're forcing and mandating people to act in a certain way, then it's not really "benevolence" or "charity"; it's effectively nothing more than tyranny, and tyranny never produces a well-functioning, happy society.

Neal DiCaprio-Cortez @GreenNewNeal
How can it be considered tyranny if the collective is simply making people act in a way that benefits everyone?

💬 1   ⟲   ♡

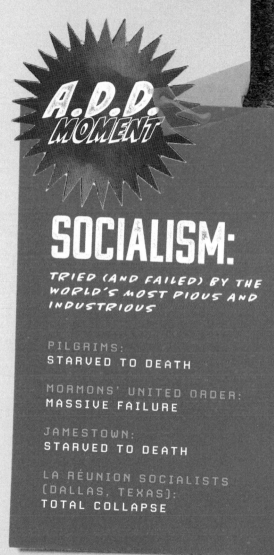

A.D.D. MOMENT

SOCIALISM:

TRIED (AND FAILED) BY THE WORLD'S MOST PIOUS AND INDUSTRIOUS

PILGRIMS:
STARVED TO DEATH

MORMONS' UNITED ORDER:
MASSIVE FAILURE

JAMESTOWN:
STARVED TO DEATH

LA RÉUNION SOCIALISTS (DALLAS, TEXAS):
TOTAL COLLAPSE

Every dictator, king, emperor, and tyrannical government that has ever existed has insisted that its mandates, government programs, and taxes are for the betterment of mankind—regardless of whether that was actually true. And the essence of tyranny isn't that a centralized power is making inefficient decisions, but rather that it's making decisions on behalf of everyone else. In other words, tyranny is the absence of freedom. And every socialist system, even a theoretical one that manages an economy efficiently (something that never existed), requires a reduction of freedom. It's an essential part of collective property ownership and management—whether it's in just a single industry or throughout an entire economy.

It's also important to remember that there's absolutely no evidence at all that collective property ownership and management or raising taxes improve prosperity. Some of the states with the highest tax rates and largest welfare programs also have huge impoverished communities. For example, progressive Democrats in Rhode Island have had continuous control of both the state's House of Representatives and Senate since 1959—more than 60 consecutive years—and yet the state has traditionally had the worst poverty rate in New England. Further, many of the U.S. cities with the highest rates of extreme poverty have been for decades controlled by progressives and/or socialists, including Buffalo, Detroit, New York City, and Philadelphia, among many others.[4] Similarly, many of the cities with the highest drug and crime rates have also been controlled by progressives and socialists for many decades, like Baltimore, Detroit, and St. Louis.[5]

If it were possible to fix America's poverty problem by giving power to government and creating welfare programs, it would have happened long ago.

Professor Tweed @checkurprivilegeplz
Humans are advancing toward a better, more collectivist future. The problems associated with progressive policies and socialism in the past won't exist in the twenty-first century because people are improving and evolving.

💬 1   🔁   ♡

Remember the whole "I can fix him" analogy from earlier? Yeah, you're doing it again—just like socialists have been doing for more than a century. And while you and others like you work to try to change socialism, you should know many socialists are working to change you.

In 1924, Leon Trotsky, one of the leading figures of the Russian Revolution and an original member of the Soviet Politburo, wrote a series of essays called *Literature in Revolution*. In one of his essays, Trotsky described a truly remarkable (and delusional) "transformation" of mankind that would soon come in the workers' paradise the Russians believed they were building.

According to Trotsky, under utopian socialism, "The human species, the coagulated *Homo sapiens*, will once more enter into a state of radical transformation, and, in his own hands, will become an object of the most complicated methods of artificial selection and psycho-physical training."[6]

Trotsky believed that this transformation would effectively improve humanity, and that this was "entirely in accord with evolution."

CODIFYING RACISM

It's common to hear socialists and progressives laud Charles Darwin's most famous work, *On the Origin of Species*, but what you almost never hear them mention is the full title of the work: *ORIGIN OF SPECIES BY MEANS OF NATURAL SELECTION OR THE PRESERVATION OF FAVOURED RACES IN THE STRUGGLE FOR LIFE*.

Prior to Darwin's writings on evolution, many people saw Africans as "savages," a view held as a result of ignorance, fear, or greed. But Darwin's work codified the view and justified racism on allegedly scientific grounds.

In many respects, socialists and progressives still use evolution as a discriminatory tool, this time as an excuse to dismiss the opinions of their rivals. Those who disagree with them are often considered to be a more evolved, more intelligent part of humanity. Those who "cling to guns or religion," as Barack Obama once said, are treated as though they are not fully human.

Trotsky wrote, "Man first drove the dark elements out of industry and ideology, by displacing barbarian routine by scientific technique, and religion by science. Afterwards he drove the unconscious out of politics, by overthrowing monarchy and class with democracy and rationalist parliamentarianism and then with the clear and open Soviet dictatorship. The blind elements have settled most heavily in economic relations, but man is driving them out from there also, by means of the Socialist organization of economic life."

According to Trotsky, man's human nature, which "is hidden in the deepest and darkest corner of the unconscious, of the elemental, of the sub-soil," will also soon be replaced, and this change was inevitable and "self-evident." Trotsky insisted, "The human race will not have ceased to crawl on all fours before God, kings and capital, in order later to submit humbly before the dark laws of heredity and a blind sexual selection. Emancipated man will want to attain a greater equilibrium in the work of his organs and a more proportional developing and wearing out of his tissues, in order to reduce the fear of death to a rational reaction of the organism towards danger. There can be no doubt that man's extreme anatomical and physiological disharmony, that is, the extreme disproportion in the growth and wearing out of organs and tissues, give the life instinct the form of a pinched, morbid and hysterical fear of death, which darkens reason and which feeds the stupid and humiliating fantasies about life after death."

According to Trotsky, the socialist "new man" would become so powerful and rational that he would even cease to fear death: He "will make it his purpose to master his own feelings, to raise his instincts to the heights of consciousness, to make them transparent, to extend the wires of his will into hidden recesses, and thereby to raise himself to a new plane." Trotsky said this socialist revolution would even "create a higher social biologic type, or, if you please, a superman."

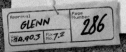

This wildly idealistic view of the transformation of mankind can be found, to varying degrees, throughout socialist and communist states, although none quite match Trotsky's enthusiasm. Why are such views so common among socialists? Because the earliest socialist and communist revolutionaries knew and openly discussed the reality that without a transformation of mankind, the whole "let's share all our property and wealth and sing kumbaya by the campfire every night" thing wasn't going to happen. People needed to be better, and they would be better, as Trotsky explained, because once they have been freed from the shackles imposed by capitalism, they would be free to "evolve" and see the errors of the old world.

Of course, these transformations never happened. Just two years after Trotsky promised a new socialist utopia, he was pushed out of his leadership role in the Politburo. A year later, he was removed from the Soviet Central Committee. Then he was exiled from the Soviet Union and forced to flee the continent of Europe. He spent the next dozen years or so living in Mexico City, until he was brutally murdered with an "ice axe" by an assassin sent by the Soviet government.[7] So, yeah, that whole new man, "superman" Soviet theory—let's just say it didn't work out the way Trotsky expected it to.

A.D.D. MOMENT

OTHER ATTEMPTS AT CRAFTING A MODEL SOCIALIST CITIZEN[a]

CAMBODIA: Pol Pot sought to create a Cambodian "master race" using social engineering

USSR: Stalin commissioned officials with the task of using psychological conditioning to create the "Soviet new man."

CHINA: Mao followed in Stalin's footsteps, believing Pavlovian conditioning could help craft desired actions.

NAZI GERMANY: The Nazis pursued policies and eugenics to achieve a "strong and pure" Aryan race.

AUTHOR'S NOTE

FOR A FORM OF GOVERNMENT THAT WAS SUPPOSED TO FREE PEOPLE FROM FIGURATIVE SHACKLES, THEY SURE PUT A LOT OF PEOPLE IN LITERAL SHACKLES.

SOCIALIST ASSASSINATION TIP

When murdering your rivals, don't bother to haul an ice axe in your luggage all the way from Moscow. Just swing by a Home Depot and pick up a regular axe. Your bag will be lighter and your target will be dead just the same. Plus, you'll lower emissions on the plane flight!

Human nature fundamentally doesn't change, and the best proof of that is the very fact that no matter how many times socialists have tried to create a "new man," they've failed. No matter how many times they've tried to conquer foundational truths about man's self-interests, they've failed. No matter how many times they've promised a glorious revolution that would lead to the birth of a new "superman" human race, they've failed—and spectacularly.

The very fact that we're having this conversation is proof that people cannot overcome their fundamental natures simply by learning from history, *especially* when it comes socialism. I know it's been a while since we talked about the horror show that socialism has been over the past 100 years, so let's do a very brief refresher: Socialist Soviet leader Joseph Stalin is estimated to have killed 20–30 million people during his reign in the first half of the twentieth century.[8] From 1975 to 1979, more than 2 million people were slaughtered in the "killing fields" of socialist Cambodia.[9] More than 100,000 were killed by Fidel Castro's socialist regime in Cuba.[10] More than 3 million have been killed by North Korea's authoritarian socialist regime, and hundreds of thousands more have been imprisoned in the country's labor camps. Venezuelans are enduring years of economic, social, and political chaos because of decades of socialist policies.

If the socialists in North Korea didn't learn from the mistakes of the socialists in the Soviet Union, and the socialists in Cambodia didn't learn from the socialists in North Korea and the Soviet Union, and if the socialists in Venezuela didn't learn from the socialists in Cambodia, Cuba, North Korea, and the Soviet Union—along with dozens of other examples—what makes you think that American socialists know something that socialists in Asia, the Caribbean, Europe, and South America did not? (And before you answer, remember that your response could be used against you as proof of racism in a future Kangaroo Court of Public Opinion. They have a lot of those these days.)

Technology and our understanding of the universe unquestionably change over time, and humans can learn from the past to improve the future. But, fundamentally, human nature doesn't change, and the primary reasons socialism continues to fail throughout the world is that one thing all people have in common, on every continent and in every era, is that they are human and share certain foundational characteristics that can't be legislated out of existence by well-meaning socialists.

HUMAN CARNAGE SCOREBOARD[b]

Country Name:	Deaths:
CHINA	65,000,000 +
USSR	20,000,000 – 30,000,000
NAZI GERMANY	15,000,000 – 20,000,000
NORTH KOREA	1,000,000 – 3,000,000
CAMBODIA	2,000,000
VIETNAM	1,600,000 +
ROMANIA	435,000 +
CUBA	100,000 +
ZIMBABWE	50,000
ANGOLA	10,000 – 20,000 +
VENEZUELA	10,000 +

Professor Tweed @checkurprivilegeplz
Ok, @glennbeck. But you admit that humans have flaws, right?

💬 1   🔁   ♡

Yes. Right now, you're talking to a big, walking, talking example of a flawed human being.

Professor Tweed @checkurprivilegeplz
Well, we have to deal with those flaws somehow, right? Collective economic decision-making is the best way to do that, because well-educated, highly trained administrative experts can direct and order society and distribute wealth equitably in ways that flawed individuals cannot."

💬 1   🔁   ♡

Since the birth of progressivism and the writings of Prussian radical Georg Wilhelm Friedrich Hegel in the nineteenth century, the free people of the world have repeatedly been told that if only they were willing to give their liberty and property rights away to the state, an army of well-trained administrators could pull all the levers and twist all the knobs of society in such a way that everyone would be better off. They are "experts," after all. Who the hell are you?

But as I've noted throughout this conversation, the more authority and economic control is centralized in the hands of a select few—however "qualified" they might seem—the worse things get. There are two important reasons why this is the case.

First, the primary reason societal problems exist is that humans aren't perfect. Why would you think a handful of imperfect people could manage the

SIDE NOTE

IF THE AVERAGE PERSON CANNOT BE TRUSTED, ISN'T QUALIFIED TO MANAGE HIS OR HER OWN AFFAIRS, AND NOT EDUCATED ENOUGH TO MAKE HIS OR HER OWN DECISIONS, THEN WHY DO SOCIALISTS BELIEVE THAT PERSON IS CAPABLE OF CHOOSING THE MOST QUALIFIED "EXPERTS" TO MANAGE SOCIETY?

countless billions of economic decisions made throughout a free-market economy by hundreds of millions of individuals? Why would imperfect people far removed from individuals' unique circumstances be better equipped to manage those individuals' lives? The more you centralize authority, the easier it is for a system to become inefficient, broken, and corrupt.

Second, as I mentioned earlier, people are primarily motivated by their own self-interest. When you take that away, you leave them with no reason to work harder, work longer hours, or to be careful with others' money and resources.

For example, imagine you have a socialized farm in a mostly socialized society. Every farm worker at our fictional workplace—let's call it "Mao's Broccoli Plantation"—receives the same pay, regardless of how talented he or she is or how much effort the worker contributes to the farm's output. Under this system, the worst worker on the farm earns the exact same pay as the most productive, innovative worker. Under this model, it doesn't take long for Broccoli Plantation workers to realize that they don't need to work as hard as they did before to earn the same wealth, so they don't.

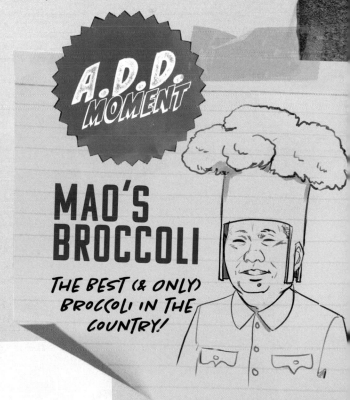

broccoli *noun*

[broc·co·li | \ ˈbrä-kə-lē \]

Green thing that wives buy to taunt you. Deadly in most cases.

All they must do is work as hard as the worst-performing worker. They can't fire everyone, right? *Someone* needs to produce the broccoli being shoved down American kids' throats at government-run schools. And even if they do fire every worker, who cares? It's a socialist society after all, so the collective has promised to take care of the workers either way. It's a true slacker's paradise. Your co-worker who comes in late, does the bare minimum, and leaves at 4:54 p.m. everyday will feel right at home. This socialist model inevitably leads to a "race to the bottom," one that once it's applied across an entire nation typically results in a gigantic economic collapse.

Of course, we don't have to speculate about how all this works out. In addition to the dozens of examples presented earlier in our little talk, consider the following examples of failed central planning:

MAO'S "GREAT LEAP" BACKWARDS

After socialist Mao Zedong seized control of China, he implemented one of his most substantial (and disastrous) reform programs, the "Great Leap Forward." Among the Great Leap's many failures was the collapse of agricultural production—which, you know, is a pretty big deal for the country with the world's largest population.

As the White House's Council of Economic Advisers noted in a 2018 report on the failures of socialism, "Mao's government implemented the so-called Great Leap Forward for China from 1958 to 1962, including a policy of mass collectivization of agriculture that provided 'no wages or cash rewards for effort' on farms. The per capita output of grain fell 21 percent from 1957 to 1962; for aquatic products, the drop was 31 percent; and for cotton, edible oil, and meat, it was about 55 percent."[11]

IF THE "EXPERTS" ARE SO SMART AND CAPABLE OF MANAGING SOCIETY, WHY ARE THEY WRONG ABOUT SO MANY THINGS ON SO MANY DIFFERENT OCCASIONS?

In the 1970s, many Chinese farmers secretly privatized their land, causing grain production in 1979 to increase by six times compared to 1978.[12]

CALIFORNIA'S BULLET TRAIN TO ... BAKERSFIELD?

In an effort to increase "green" transportation options and limit traffic, California voters approved in 2008 a high-speed rail project that would have connected Los Angeles and San Francisco, two of the state's largest cities. A decade later, the rail project became the poster child for government projects gone wrong.

By mid-2018, the high-speed rail line was running more than a decade behind schedule and its final cost projection had jumped to as high as $100 billion, $67 billion more than the original projection of $33 billion.[13,14] Things got so bad that California officials gave up on trying to connect the line from Los Angeles to San Francisco. Even worse, because the geniuses who planned the rail line's construction chose to start the project in California's Central Valley, the line will not reach either Los Angeles or San Francisco. Instead, it's now only projected to operate from *Merced* to *Bakersfield*. Yes, Merced to Bakersfield—which, by the way, are only less than 170 miles away from each other by car. And that assumes the state chooses to operate the

HIGH-SPEED RAIL DERAILED BY POLITICS

What's a government program without a little political consideration? When the California high-speed rail project was greenlit, bureaucrats all over the area tried to wet their beaks.

Compromises and backroom deals altered the original path of the train line. Instead of taking the most direct path, the train line was moved so that it would journey though the Central Valley to stop at various population centers. The route was also planned to detour to Palmdale and travel directly to San Jose, both stops that were not part of the original plan.

All these changes were made to satisfy public officials who could now parade their political "achievements" in front of their constituents.

But although these deviations made politicians happy, they also significantly slowed down the production of the rail line and its costs. Ah, politics, isn't it just ... terrible?

rail line at all. Some analysts have predicted the state might never actually use the line, because the costs wouldn't be worth the relatively few economic benefits.

If California, the largest state in the country and one of the states most committed to building "green" transportation systems, can't manage to build a high-speed rail line between its two most important cities, what makes anyone think government can effectively manage everyone's health care—or anything else, for that matter?

MINIMUM WAGE MADNESS

One of the signature issues for American progressives and socialists is increasing the federal minimum wage to at least $15 per hour. The idea seems simple enough to socialists: If greedy companies are forced to pay their workers more, then workers would be better off. But here's the thing, huge amounts of data show boosting the minimum wage often results in negative economic consequences, especially for lower-income workers, the very people minimum wage laws are meant to help.

For example, after Seattle increased its minimum wage to $13, lower-wage employees reported working 9 percent fewer hours and earned $125 less per month on average, according to researchers at the University of Washington.[15] Similar results have been experienced in other cities across the country as well, and the Congressional Budget Office estimated in 2019 that increasing the federal minimum wage to $15 per hour would result in as many as 3.7 million fewer jobs and a $9 billion decrease in real income in 2025—and that assumes a slower rollout of the $15 minimum wage than what many Democrats are now calling for.[16,17]

If collective economic decision-making really does work, then why are there so many examples—literally thousands in America alone—of it failing?

"The minimum wage law very cleverly is misnamed. The real minimum wage is zero. That is what many inexperienced and low skilled people receive as a result of legislation that makes it illegal to pay them what they are currently worth to an employer."[c]

-Thomas Sowell

Professor Tweed @checkurprivilegeplz
Socialist governments learn from their inefficiencies and then adjust their systems so that they operate much more effectively.

💬 1   🔁   ♡

SOCIALIST CHEAT SHEET

THE MORE YOU TRY TO RAISE THE GOVERNMENT MINIMUM WAGE, THE MORE PEOPLE EARN THE REAL MINIMUM WAGE, WHICH IS ZERO.

Actually, they usually just start shooting people in the streets. You see, in a socialist society, you can't motivate people using profits—at least, not if you want to be consistent. And in most cases, socialist governments can't afford to pay workers more money anyway, because the efficiency of the entire marketplace usually ends up in the gutter. So, if you can't motivate workers by paying them more money, which is how capitalism operates, then what are you left with? You put a gun to the back of their heads—sometimes literally—and demand that people work harder. Anyone who complains ends up dead, exiled, in a prison labor camp, or, if they are really lucky, they end up escaping with as much wealth as they can to countries like the United States, further exacerbating the socialist country's economic problems.

Clay Guevara @coffeeshopcommie
Well, socialists shouldn't let wealthy people take their wealth to some other country.

💬 1   ⇄   ♡

Wow. That sounds very authoritarian of you, Mr. Guevara. What would you like them to do, then? Lock them away in prison after seizing all of their wealth and property?

Clay Guevara @coffeeshopcommie
No, but we could force them to pay a tax if they are going to leave the country with wealth that could be used to help pay for important goods and services here.

💬 1   ⇄   ♡

Whenever such "exit taxes" are discussed, most of those with substantial amounts of wealth move their resources out of the country before their property can be taken from them, so threats of wealth taxes typically end up causing much more harm than good. But this provides a good opportunity to point out that for socialism to "work" at all—and I'm using "work" here very liberally—it must be in place throughout the entire world.

One of the biggest reasons isolated socialist states fail so quickly is that as soon as they start to dramatically increase taxes and seize property, everyone with wealth and property gets the hell out of Dodge.

GHOST OF
KARL MARX
"MAY I?"

Sure, Karl, you've been good for a while. Shoot!

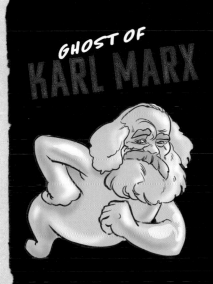

GHOST OF
KARL MARX

AS I WROTE IN *THE COMMUNIST MANIFESTO*, "THE
COMMUNISTS ARE FURTHER REPROACHED WITH
DESIRING TO ABOLISH COUNTRIES AND NATIONALITY.
THE WORKING MEN HAVE NO COUNTRY. WE CANNOT
TAKE FROM THEM WHAT THEY HAVE NOT GOT. ...
NATIONAL DIFFERENCES AND ANTAGONISMS BETWEEN
PEOPLES ARE DAILY MORE AND MORE VANISHING,
OWING TO THE DEVELOPMENT OF THE BOURGEOISIE,
TO FREEDOM OF COMMERCE, TO THE WORLD-MARKET,
TO UNIFORMITY IN THE MODE OF PRODUCTION AND IN
THE CONDITIONS OF LIFE CORRESPONDING THERETO.

THE SUPREMACY OF THE PROLETARIAT WILL CAUSE
THEM TO VANISH STILL FASTER. UNITED ACTION,
OF THE LEADING CIVILISED COUNTRIES AT LEAST,
IS ONE OF THE FIRST CONDITIONS FOR THE
EMANCIPATION OF THE PROLETARIAT."

Translation: If socialists want to do away with capitalism, "one of the first conditions"
is "united action" among the world's nations—or, more realistically, some kind of
global government.

There are good reasons why many, although not all, socialists and communists have
called for some form of global government. How can any good socialist say he or she
supports true economic equality on the one hand, often calling it a moral imperative,
while on the other allowing billions of people in other nations to live in poverty? The
only philosophically consistent brand of socialism is one in which all of the *world's*
resources are shared—not just the resources of a single country.

Approval
GLENN
14.90.3 | Fix
No. 7.2
Page
Number
297

SOCIALIST FUN FACT!

The difference between Nazis and Soviets was the difference between *national* socialism and *international* socialism. Also, the Soviets killed more people.

Of course, if we were to spread around all the world's wealth, it would create huge problems for those of us in North America and Europe, who have become accustomed to modern luxuries like grocery stores, clean running water, and heat. Spreading the wealth of the West equally around the rest of the world wouldn't make anyone wealthy, but it would make a whole lot of people much poorer.

More importantly, societies and cultures around the world are different—not necessarily inferior, just different. And in many cases, what works for one group of people won't work for another. People have naturally grouped together based on shared characteristics for a reason; it's an inherent part of who we are, and we've all experienced it. It's why some places feel like "home" and others don't. Global government, which is practically essential if the entire world is going to adopt socialist principles, defies this foundational concept and tries to force people to abide by the same philosophies, rules, and ideas, even though they don't want to.

Professor Tweed @checkurprivilegeplz
Even with these problems, socialism is still a better system, because under capitalism, the rich end up hoarding their wealth when that money could be put to good use by government, which is much better at managing wealth.

💬 1   🔁   ♡

True. In fact, I personally have a room filled with gold coins. I spend hours doing backstrokes through the various piles of doubloons and pirate booty.

⚠ **WARNING**

Diving into a giant room of gold coins like Scrooge McDuck may cause injury and even death. Gold is a metal and does not share physical qualities with liquid.

Okay, now take a moment to imagine just how ridiculous an idea that is. In reality, this myth of wealth closets full of cash is simply not true. Business owners don't typically "hoard" their wealth. They often use their money to invest in new business ventures or to expand existing ones. And even when they don't, many business owners use their wealth as collateral to obtain loans that can be used for those purposes.

That doesn't mean businesses are always spending or investing every penny they have. Obviously, many business owners and shareholders choose not to spend their resources. But does that mean the money is being wasted, or that they are simply being good stewards of their wealth? And unless those wealthy people you referred to as "hoarders" are putting their cash underneath their mattresses at night, much of their wealth stored in bank and financial accounts is being used to spur investment indirectly. The more money banks have, the more they can loan money out.

For more than a century, wealthy business owners have also played a key role in establishing and maintaining important educational, cultural, and charitable organizations. The modern-day "Robber Barons" of our time, people like Bill Gates and Jeff Bezos, have used the profits generated by their successful businesses—which, let's remember, provide products and services people love—to fund numerous important philanthropic programs.

For example, the Bill and Melinda Gates Foundation, one of the world's largest charities, spent more than $1.8 billion on global development efforts in 2018 alone, including on programs to address nutrition, vaccine delivery, and reduce polio. The Gates Foundation also spent more than $1.3 billion on global health issues like malaria, HIV, and children's health in developing nations.[18] Since its inception, the Gates Foundation has made more than $50 billion in grant payments, much of which have been used to help some of the world's poorest communities. Without capitalism,

WASTE REPORTS[d]

Attempted to increase trust between Tunisian political parties and citizens (State) - $2,000,000

Converted an abandoned mental hospital into DHS HQ (GSA and DHS) - $2,120,040,355.35

Supported "Green Growth" in Peru (USAID) - $10,000,000

Fixed vehicles New York City falsely claimed Superstorm Sandy damaged (FEMA) - $5,303,624

Increased the capacity of the Pakistani film industry (State) - $100,000

Paid out billions from Medicare in improper payments (CMS) - $48,000,000,000

Taught English and IT skills at Madrassas (State) - $150,000

Studied frog mating calls in Panama (NSF) - $466,991

Paid for Google Scholar searches in Hawaii (NSF, NOAA, USFS, DOI, NASA) - $51,722,107

Paid for property confiscated in Afghanistan by the ANDSF (USACE) - $325,485

none of this would have been possible. Of course, capitalism also produced the Microsoft Zune. They can't all be winners.

Money in the hands of private individuals is almost always spent more wisely than when it's in the hands of government agents, because, again, humans are naturally more inclined to be better stewards of their own resources than they are of others' wealth and property or collectively owned resources. Government bureaucrats are notorious money-wasters.

Sen. Rand Paul's, R-Ky., "Waste Reports" have revealed more than $1.8 billion in government waste.[19] Even more stunning, government watchdog Citizens Against Government Waste outlined more than 600 recommendations to reduce government waste in its most recent *Prime Cuts* report. According to CAGW, if the government were to make its recommended cuts, it would save an astounding $429.8 billion in the first year, and more than $3 trillion in just five years.[20]

The reason government bureaucrats are so wasteful isn't because they are inherently bad or even irresponsible people, it's because they have no reason to be cautious when spending other people's money. In many cases, they are just doing what their boss told them to do, and that boss is just doing what his or her boss commanded, and on and on it goes. And let's be honest: A few extra hundred thousand dollars wasted here or there isn't going to raise any red flags in a multi-trillion-dollar, endlessly complex government bureaucracy.

To a limited extent, these problems exist whenever you have a large bureaucracy, including in private industry, but the biggest difference is that private companies do have an incentive to try to eliminate as much waste as possible: profit. The more money that's saved, the more money business owners, shareholders, and others get to keep in their own pockets. Businesses can't *force* their customers to pay higher prices, and if they raise prices too high, they run the risk of losing their customers altogether.

In the private marketplace, competition between businesses keeps costs down. But when it comes to government, competition is rarely ever a concern. In fact, in many cases, government agencies are encouraged to spend more money than they need to ensure that their agencies receive similar funding amounts in the future. Agencies that spend less than what has been budgeted run the risk of having future budgets slashed, creating an incentive to spend money irresponsibly.

Clay Guevara @coffeeshopcommie
Ok. Let's say government doesn't spend money efficiently. It doesn't matter. All that money eventually ends up in the hands of regular people, and that's a good thing. It's better that government give money to people for doing nothing or for working jobs that aren't needed than for wealthy people to have lots of cash sitting in their bank accounts.

 1

Mr. Guevara, this is a really warped, albeit increasingly common, view of how economics works. Waste and destruction of property doesn't lead to economic growth, it ruins it. This idea is best illustrated by what economists call the "broken-window fallacy"—which was first described by Claude-Frederic Bastiat, a noted nineteenth-century French economist.

The broken-window fallacy goes a little something like this: Imagine a medium-sized, mostly middle-class community in Pennsylvania. In town, there are numerous small businesses, including a glazier who sells windows to most of the town's residents and other businesses. So, one day, the town's village idiot—let's call him Sal Gore—decides that in order to save the planet from an impending global warming catastrophe, every single homeowner and business owner should replace their conventional windows with more insulated, "green" windows.

Gore runs around town screaming at residents and businesses to swap their windows, but he's not having much luck. Most people's windows are in good shape and they don't want to spend money on new windows in order to try to stop global warming 80 years into the future. Frustrated, Sal Gore gathers his closest friends together—let's call them Bernie Spanders and Alexander Ocasio-Cortezio—and they come up with what they think is a brilliant plan: Instead of convincing people to buy new windows, they decide they will just run around town destroying them. Not only will this force people to have "greener" homes, they reason, it will also increase economic growth, because the local glazier will now have to replace a whole town's worth of windows.

So, around midnight on the second Tuesday of November, they run—well, in the case of Bernie Spanders, ride on an old Hoveround scooter—around town destroying everyone's windows. The next day, orders for new "green" windows flood the local glazier, who is now doing more business than ever thanks to the latest window crime spree.

According to socialists' logic, the damage caused by Sal Gore, Bernie Spanders, and Alexander Ocasio-Cortezio led to increased economic growth. Prior to all that window-smashing, demand for windows was relatively low, but now, demand couldn't be higher. The plan worked so well, in fact, the three renegades are planning to light everyone's gasoline-powered cars on fire next—you know, to help boost local electric car sales.

Sounds like a great plan, right? But before smashing all your neighbors' windows around town, let's think this one through. The new windows will unquestionably create more demand, and thus more business, for the local glazier, but the money spent on new windows that otherwise wouldn't have been necessary has now been diverted away from other important economic uses. Instead of having enough money to hire a new worker, the local coffee shop has to delay the hiring so it can pay for its new windows. Instead of having more money to take the family out to a nice restaurant, a local worker must spend that cash on a new window. Instead of spending the day with a prospective client, a local business owner spends the next two days installing a new window.

"If we discovered that space aliens were planning to attack, and we needed a massive build-up to counter the space alien threat, and inflation and budget deficits took secondary place to that, this slump would be over in 18 months."[e]

- PAUL KRUGMAN

NOBEL PRIZE-WINNING ECONOMIST, PERSON YOU WOULDN'T WANT TO HANG OUT WITH

You see, money and time are scarce, which means there is a limited amount of it, and if people have to spend their money and time fixing broken windows, it means they are spending less time and money on other endeavors that would help to grow the economy. This is why it matters when government wastes time and money, because those resources could have been used more efficiently in the private marketplace, increasing economic growth for everyone.

SIDE NOTE

Keynesian economic plans, illustrated by the broken window fallacy, work in a similar fashion as tariffs. Both schemes operate as incredibly inefficient attempts to redistribute wealth. One government-chosen industry receives the windfall, while everyone else just falls flat on their faces.

The bottom line is, economies work best when people have the ability to spend their own money and time on those things they believe will be most valuable, because they know better than some disinterested government bureaucrat hundreds or even thousands of miles away what would most improve their own lives. Remember, humans are terrible central planners and completely incapable of properly managing the lives of other people.

Clay Guevara @coffeeshopcommie
Ok, but when most of the wealth is concentrated in the hands of a relatively small group of people, they become power-hungry, greedy, and they end up controlling society, and that's exactly what has happened in capitalist countries. We need to take that wealth away from them to spread power around.

💬 1   🔁   ♡

If wealth really does equal power, then the federal government is already controlling society. The U.S. government has and spends more money than all of the wealthiest businesses and people in America—and it's not even close.

The three most valuable brands in the world today are Amazon, Apple, and Google. Amazon is currently listed as the most valuable brand, at about $315.5 billion. Apple is worth about $309.5 billion, and Google barely trails behind Apple, at $309 billion.[21] Combined, these three behemoths are worth less than $1 trillion—not even enough to match the national government's expected budget deficit for the 2019 fiscal year.

Even more incredibly, *Forbes* reported in 2018 that the 400 richest Americans—including Bill Gates, Warren Buffett, and Jeff Bezos—have a total net worth of $2.9 trillion.[22] To put that in perspective, the U.S. government spends more than $4 trillion every year. That means even if the federal government were to confiscate every penny from everyone on the

SIDE NOTE

Are federal bureaucrats really the "experts," or just people who take wealth and power from others because they couldn't find a way to make fortunes of their own?

Forbes 400 list, plus confiscate Amazon, Apple, and Google and then sell those businesses, it couldn't come up with enough funding to pay for just one year's worth of spending at the federal level alone—never mind state and local spending.

STOP & THINK: HAVE MICROSOFT, AMAZON, AND APPLE MADE YOUR LIFE AND THE LIVES AROUND YOU BETTER OR WORSE?

It always amazes me that socialists like yourself seem obsessed with taking wealth away from those who have it because you believe they have too much power over society, all while demanding we give even more power to government. Bernie Sanders and others have even gone so far as to insist that wealthy Americans have created an "oligarchy" that rules over the country's economy—a claim that simply isn't supported by the data.

If your goal is to decentralize power by decentralizing wealth, then the last thing you should want is to concentrate more wealth in the hands of the federal government, a relatively small group of people that controls much of the nation's lands, wealth, natural resources, and laws. Congress, which is supposed to serve as the people's representatives, is only composed of 535 people. So, 535 people, plus the president and nine Supreme Court justices, have control over most of the United States, a nation of more than 330 million and the most powerful country in the history of the world? Boy, that sounds an awful lot like an "oligarchy" to me.

And socialists can talk about the alleged "danger" of having much of the wealth in the United States controlled by a relatively small group of private Americans, but let's not forget that it's the federal government that owns the tanks, guns, and nuclear bombs—not Jeff Bezos and Bill Gates. What's the worst Jeff Bezos can do to you, anyway? Cancel your Amazon Prime subscription?

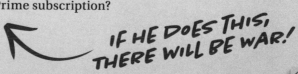

IF HE DOES THIS, THERE WILL BE WAR!

This is why a discussion of human nature is so important. If humans really do abuse their power—and socialism is built on that idea—then why would we expect the human beings running the government to be any better? In the pursuit of trying to fix socialists' perceived "power" problem, they make it much, much worse.

Neal DiCaprio-Cortez @GreenNewNeal
You're such a hypocrite, @glennbeck. I've heard you talk about the 'dangers' of Facebook, Google, and YouTube, and how you're worried they're working to silence voices on the right. Those are private companies. I guess you only care about out-of-control capitalism when it's bad for conservatives.

🗩 1   ⇄   ♡

No, I stand by my concerns about Facebook, Google, YouTube, Twitter, and other tech giants. They represent one of the greatest dangers facing individual liberty and the dissemination of free speech in the history of the United States. But I think you misunderstand some of the biggest reasons why these companies have become so powerful and potentially dangerous.

To say tech giants like YouTube are some of the most powerful organizations in the world is a gigantic understatement. Together, Facebook, Google, and YouTube control most of what Americans watch, learn, and see on the internet, and much of the world as well.

YouTube has more than 2 billion monthly users, who watched a combined 250 million hours of content *every single day* in 2019, a 39 percent increase compared to the previous year.[23]

Sixty-eight percent of all Americans say they use Facebook, and the number is even higher among Millennials and those who are slightly older and younger than Millennials. Eighty percent of Americans aged 18–49 say they use Facebook, according to a survey by the Pew Research Center.[24]

Although Google is notoriously secret about the number of users it has, it confirmed in 2016 that its users conduct at least 2 *trillion* searches per year, or about 5.5 billion per day.[25]

AUTHOR'S NOTE

AskJeeves.com butlers as many as 12 searches per month.

In our current Information Age, Google, Facebook, and YouTube are kings, and like all kings, they've started to use their power to target the people they consider to be their "enemies"—supporters of free-market policies and individual liberty.

The worst kept secret in Silicon Valley is that most of America's tech giants are controlled by people who align closely with progressive or even socialist values, and that many of those who don't agree with those beliefs are forced to either conform or get out. According to one survey conducted in 2018, two-thirds of Silicon Valley employees who consider themselves to be conservative, very conservative, or libertarian say they don't feel comfortable discussing their ideological views with the people they work with.[26]

In 2017, the problem allegedly got so bad at Google that employees were fired for criticizing the company's leadership team, which the employees said had created a culture of bias against conservatives. One of the ex-employees, James Damore, had written an internal memo while he worked at Google alleging, among other things, that "Google's left bias has created a politically correct monoculture that maintains its hold by shaming dissenters into silence."[27,28]

It's bad enough that tech companies like Google are creating work environments that "shame" conservatives—and anyone else who is "dissenting" against the politics of Google's leadership team—but what's much more dangerous is how Google, Facebook, YouTube, and others have used their power to quietly favor certain kinds of political speech over others, making it difficult for anyone who doesn't toe the socialist-progressive line to reach new and existing audiences.

For example, in 2018, the *Daily Signal*, a publication of the Heritage Foundation, had one of its videos pulled from Facebook that shows a physician warning the public about the dangers of "puberty blockers." These drugs have been disgustingly used by some parents and physicians to stop children from experiencing puberty because, as Planned Parenthood notes on its website, "If you're transgender, intersex, or nonbinary, puberty may feel especially hard. Sometimes during puberty the changes going on in your body might not line up with your gender identity."[29]

These drugs are, unsurprisingly, extremely dangerous to give children unless they have some other medical condition that might require them. For example, Lupron, a drug approved by FDA to treat prostate cancer, can cause significant health problems, including joint pain, osteoporosis, and severe depression. More than 20,000 complaints of adverse reactions to Lupron have been filed with the FDA. Half have been determined to be serious health issues.[30]

What, exactly, is wrong with a video telling parents that it's dangerous to give drugs to their children to block puberty? Well, apparently it doesn't align with the disturbing views of some at Facebook. They blocked the video after it received 70 million views, and Facebook's ad team only agreed to restore the video after immense pressure from the *Daily Signal* and other conservatives.

Dennis Prager's PragerU, which has hundreds of videos posted on YouTube addressing economic, political, and social issues from a free-market perspective, has had many of its videos banned or restricted over the past few years, including one video about the Ten Commandments, which YouTube labeled "inappropriate" content for "sensitive" audiences.[31]

I've seen this bias firsthand. Not only have numerous videos posted of *The Glenn Beck Program* experienced biased treatment, but also many of Blaze Media's most influential voices have had their work removed or labeled as "inappropriate" by tech companies like Facebook and YouTube. For example, conservative commentator and comedian Steven Crowder, whose videos have been viewed more than 800 million times on YouTube alone, had his YouTube account demonetized after a writer for the left-wing publication *Vox* organized a campaign to have Crowder banned from the platform for making "homophobic" jokes. This occurred even after YouTube announced Crowder's channel did not violate the platform's community standards.[32,33]

There are dozens of other examples I could point to. There's absolutely no doubt that many of the biggest tech companies in the United States are working to silence conservative voices, and that represents a significant threat, not just to conservatism, but to free speech in general—regardless of what side of the aisle you're on. If Google, Facebook, and others can silence conservative political speech they don't like, then they could come for you next. That's how opponents of free speech *always* operate. The power companies like Google and Facebook have over the internet—and thus over public speech—is only likely to grow in the coming years.

Now, does this mean I think government should do something to stop these private companies from becoming too powerful? Yes, they should stop *protecting* them. I'm not asking for more rules and regulations, I'm simply calling for the existing rules and regulations to be applied equally.

Many people on the Left think I'm being a hypocrite for sounding the alarm about big tech companies and their power over free speech, but that's because they don't understand how government has created this problem in the first place, and how it continues to allow it to exist by not acting.

AN ALGORITHM MISTAKE
OR ELECTION MEDDLING?

After the first Democratic presidential primary debate for 2020, Congresswoman Tulsi Gabbard made headlines for being the most Googled candidate. Her staunch anti-war message resonated with potential voters. In an attempt to capitalize on this flood of interest, the Gabbard campaign began promoting Tulsi with online advertisements.

In these crucial hours of public interest, the Gabbard campaign's Google ad account was disabled. After the campaign appealed the decision to disable the account, a Google spokesperson chalked this up to a mistake in the algorithm. By the time the account was reinstated, the damage was already done.

The Gabbard campaign filed a complaint in a U.S. District Court alleging Google censored her campaign, violating her free speech and harming her chances at becoming the nominee.[f]

Section 230 of the U.S. Communications Decency Act allows open platforms to escape liability for the posts of their users.[34] For example, if in a fit of rage, a degenerate coworker—let's call him Stu—decides to post dozens of totally false claims about his saintly boss in a series of Facebook posts, Facebook can't be held legally liable for Stu's defamatory statements. If, however, Stu were to quit his job and become a writer for the *New York Times* and publish defamatory statements at the *Times*, the newspaper would share in the liability.

The idea here is that social media outlets like Facebook and search engines like Google are not "publishers," they are platforms that provide a forum for people to communicate with one another, and thus shouldn't be responsible for what their users say and do. Publishers, however, should be liable for their false statements, because if they aren't, then there would be nothing stopping them from constantly defaming people they don't like.

Section 230 is a really important law. Without it, many social media platforms couldn't exist, because they would constantly be sued for the terrible things some of their users say and do. But here's the thing, that protection is only supposed to belong to companies and organizations that are truly acting as "platforms." Once you start to ban certain kinds of political speech because you only want your platform to share a specific set of views you like, then it's no longer an open platform—you've now crossed over into "publisher" territory.

Social media companies like Facebook and Twitter would have to radically change their business models or close down if they were subject to the same legal standards that publishers like Blaze Media and the *New York Times* are held to every single day. So, they continue to deny that they are treating certain kinds of political speech differently than others, even though anyone who has been involved in this business for half a second—or someone who just regularly reads the news—knows this isn't the case.

Do I want YouTube, Facebook, and Google to close because they don't like conservatives? Not at all. I want them to play by the same rules as everyone else: either they should become publishers and take responsibility for the content on their platforms and in their search results, or they should get out of the way and let conservatives speak freely through their platforms. This doesn't mean they have to let people threaten or harass others, by the way. They can and should have some community standards. But platforms and search engines shouldn't punish political voices they don't like while benefitting from special legal protections, and that's exactly what they are doing now.

What's happening today with tech giants like YouTube, Facebook, Google, Twitter, and others isn't proof that we need socialism because corporations are out of control, it's proof that the centralization of power is dangerous and that when government becomes powerful, it can and often does make crony deals with private industry. Your solution—if you were even concerned enough about the problem to suggest one—would be to give government even more power over the internet. So, instead of having to worry about left-wing executives at Google and YouTube silencing speech, I'd have to worry about left-wing government officials doing the same thing. And under a Republican administration, perhaps you'd be worried about someone like the proto-fascist caricature you imagine President Donald Trump to be doing it to *you*.

Socialism doesn't work in large part because people are motivated by competition and rewards, but also because when human beings are given massive amounts of power over others, history has shown that they, acting in accordance with their nature, typically abuse that power—and there are millions of dead bodies around the world that prove it. I know you've heard this a million times, but get ready for a million and one: "Power tends to corrupt, and absolute power corrupts absolutely."

END OF CHAPTER 7

ECO-SOCIALISM & CLIMATE CHANGE

FINAL
APPROVED
-GB

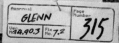

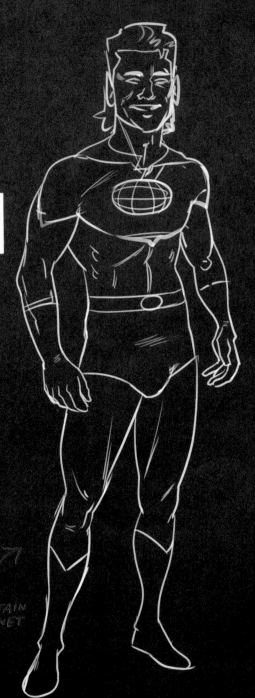

GLENN
BECK

HOW SOCIALISM DESTROYS WEALTH & THE PLANET

CAPTAIN PLANET

"[W]E HAVE REACHED WHAT SOME ACTIVISTS HAVE STARTED CALLING 'DECADE ZERO' OF THE CLIMATE CRISIS: WE EITHER CHANGE NOW OR WE LOSE OUR CHANCE. ALL THIS MEANS THAT THE USUAL FREE MARKET ASSURANCES—A TECHNO-FIX IS AROUND THE CORNER! DIRTY DEVELOPMENT IS JUST A PHASE ON THE WAY TO A CLEAN ENVIRONMENT, LOOK AT NINETEENTH-CENTURY LONDON!—SIMPLY DON'T ADD UP. . . . BECAUSE OF OUR LOST DECADES, IT IS TIME TO TURN THIS AROUND NOW. IS IT POSSIBLE? ABSOLUTELY. IS IT POSSIBLE WITHOUT CHALLENGING THE FUNDAMENTAL LOGIC OF DEREGULATED CAPITALISM? NOT A CHANCE."[1]

— NAOMI KLEIN

A global warming crisis is upon us. Rising tides will soon swallow whole cities. The sun will scorch the earth, destroying our crops and food supplies. Hundreds of millions of people will be forced to join mass migrations to flee wars and famine. Tornados, hurricanes, and extreme heat will kill tens of thousands. And worst of all, we only have about a decade left before it will be too late. The world is ending, and capitalism is to blame.

THIS MAY REMIND YOU OF THE FOLLOWING QUOTE FROM ONE OF AMERICA'S MOST IMPORTANT DOCUMENTARY FILMS, *GHOSTBUSTERS...*

PETER VENKMAN: ...or you could accept the fact that this city is headed for a disaster of biblical proportions.

MAYOR LENNY: What do you mean, "biblical"?

RAY STANTZ: What he means is Old Testament, Mr. Mayor. Real Wrath-of-God type stuff!

PETER VENKMAN: Exactly.

RAY STANTZ: Fire and brimstone coming down from the skies! Rivers and seas boiling!

EGON SPENGLER: 40 years of darkness! Earthquakes, volcanoes!

WINSTON ZEDDEMORE: The dead rising from the grave!

PETER VENKMAN: Human sacrifice, dogs and cats living together, mass hysteria!

------------------------------ END SCENE ------------------------------

YOU MAY NOT REMEMBER

The villain that lets all the ghosts out and almost destroys the world is from the Environmental Protection Agency. Environmentalists really do make great movie villains!

At least, that's what Americans have been told now for the past half-century by "climate justice warriors" on the Left like Naomi Klein, a *New York Times* best-selling author and one of the most influential climate activists in Canada and the United States. Unlike many other progressives and socialists, Klein doesn't necessarily hate all aspects of capitalism; she admits that it's good at boosting economic productivity, for example. But Klein says that whatever benefits capitalism might provide are far outweighed by the environmental havoc free markets are supposedly imposing on the planet.

In her best-selling book *This Changes Everything*, Klein does spend some time making the usual Marxist arguments about wealth redistribution—she even quotes Marx directly[2] at one point—but most of her focus is on convincing the reader that an impending climate crisis demands action and "radical" changes to the way we think about society and economics:

"The challenge, then," Klein wrote, "is not simply that we need to spend a lot of money and change a lot of policies; it's that we need to think differently, radically differently, for those changes to be remotely possible. Right now, the triumph of market logic, with its ethos of domination and fierce competition, is paralyzing almost all serious efforts to respond to climate change. Cutthroat competition between nations has deadlocked U.N. climate negotiations for decades: rich countries dig in their heels and declare that they won't cut emissions and risk losing their vaulted position in the global hierarchy; poorer countries declare that they won't give up their right to pollute as much as rich countries did on their way to wealth, even if that means deepening a disaster that hurts the poor most of all. For any of this to change, a worldview will need to rise to the fore that sees nature, other nations, and our own neighbors not as adversaries, but rather as partners in a grand project of mutual reinvention."[3]

Klein's work has become increasingly popular among many left-wing groups, politicians, and socialists. For example, Klein was one of the key figures behind Canada's popular "Leap Manifesto," a precursor to the Green New Deal.[4] (By the way, am I the only one really creeped out by the Leap Manifesto's title? It sounds *awfully similar* to Mao Zedong's murderous "Great Leap Forward" campaign, right? So much so, in fact, that the "Frequently Asked Questions" section of the Leap Manifesto's official website includes a short section that attempts to distance itself from the "Great Leap Forward.")[5]

Klein's work has been hailed by just about every leading figure in the climate crisis movement, from Washington, D.C., to New York and Hollywood. For example, actors John Cusack and Tim Robbins both endorsed Klein's 2007 anti-capitalism book *The Shock Doctrine*,[6] and Rachel McAdams and Donald Sutherland were among the many signers of the Leap Manifesto.[7] One of Klein's close allies and an endorser of Klein's *This Changes Everything*,[8] Bill McKibben, was named to the Democratic Party's 2016 Platform Committee by Senator Bernie Sanders.[9]

Although it's not often expressly stated, the reason Klein's whole "capitalism must go to save the planet" schtick is so popular among those on the Left—especially so-called "eco-socialists"—is that it serves as the perfect last-ditch argument for those who can't win the socialism-versus-capitalism debate by talking about economics. If the world is ending from a capitalism-caused climate crisis, then it doesn't really matter whether capitalism has lifted hundreds of millions of people from poverty over the past two decades. According to the eco-left, they'll all be refugees or dead soon because of climate change.

There are two massive, totally unavoidable problems with this position. First, it assumes people actually want to enact the climate change policies proposed by progressives and socialists but that there are capitalist forces preventing them from doing so. But that's simply not true. Anyone who wants to spend more to build "green" housing, start a compost, or even live completely electricity-free can do so. Just ask the Amish. By opting not to go green, people are freely *choosing* to prioritize more affordable energy over reducing carbon dioxide (CO_2) emissions. A free-market economy would create a CO_2-free society if that's what people truly wanted. But they don't—at least, not enough to reduce U.S. CO_2 emissions down to zero. A November 2018 survey of American adults found only 23 percent are willing to pay at least $40 extra per month to battle climate change. Forty-three percent wouldn't even pay $1 extra per month.[10] Similarly, a 2019 survey found 68 percent of Americans wouldn't agree to pay $10 per month or more in higher electric bills to help stop climate change.[11]

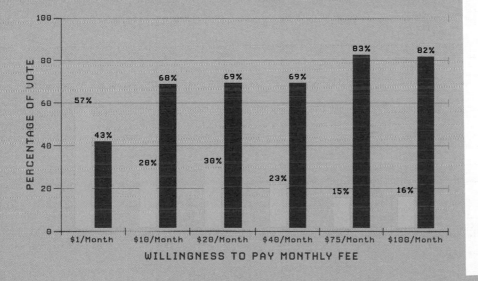

Suppose a proposal was on the ballot next year to add a fee to consumers' monthly electrical bill to combat climate change. If this proposal passes, it would cost your household $___ every month. Would you vote in favor of this monthly fee to combat climage change, or would you vote against this monthly fee?[a]

IN FAVOR
OPPOSED

Many on the Left like to pretend that capitalism imposes products and services on people that they don't want—like oil, natural gas, and other conventional energy sources, for example—but generally speaking, the opposite is true. The options available in a free marketplace are nothing more than a reflection of the desires of the consumers and businesses operating within that market. (That's not to say our current energy marketplace is totally "free"; it most certainly isn't. The energy industry is already heavily regulated, and already forces many consumers to purchase renewable energy options they don't want.)

When socialists say we need to end capitalism to save the planet, what they really mean is that we must end all freedom in the marketplace to save the planet. According to socialists, only once the bureaucratic masterminds in Washington, D.C., have complete control over our economy will the world be able to avoid total catastrophe. How convenient. It turns out that the very thing the Left wanted all along—control over society—is now supposedly necessary to save the planet from what Senator Elizabeth Warren says is an "existential crisis."[12]

This brings us to the second big problem with Klein's theory: It's not likely the planet is actually facing the dire end-of-the-world scenario the Left insists it is.

Neal Ocasio-Cortrez @GreenNewNeal
Wow. I knew you were crazy, @glennbeck, but I didn't take you for a climate change denier. We're headed for a climate catastrophe. Even if capitalism is better at providing people with goods and services, capitalism is completely incapable of stopping catastrophic climate change.

💬 1   ⇄   ♡

Let's be clear here, because there's so much confusion and misunderstanding on both sides of this issue: Earth's climate *is* warming. The evidence shows Earth's climate has been warming for more than a century. The issues are who or what are causing most of the recent warming, how much damage will that warming cause, do the benefits of that warming outweigh the potential problems, and what can be done to stop it, if anything. Those issues are serious and worthy of consideration, especially in light of what socialists are asking us to give up in order to stop global warming: our freedom—and, more importantly, hamburgers. (We'll get to that later.)

Neal Ocasio-Cortrez @GreenNewNeal
All these issues have already been decided. 97% of scientists agree that climate change is caused by human carbon dioxide emissions and that it's going to be catastrophic if we don't act immediately.

💬 1   ⇄   ♡

The popular "97 percent" claim is nothing more than a big, fat myth—and I'm talking really fat, like a Michael Moore-sized myth.

The claim that 97 percent of climate scientists agree about global warming mostly stems from several extremely shoddy studies conducted over the past two decades that attempted to determine whether there was an overwhelming consensus on the causes and consequences of climate change. The first study—which was actually not a study but rather an opinion article—was conducted by far-Left Harvard professor Naomi Oreskes.

Oreskes claimed to examine 928 abstracts of articles published by academic journals from 1993 to 2003.[13] She found 75 percent supported the position humans are responsible for most of the warming occurring over the past 50 years (25 percent didn't address the issue), but Oreskes chose not to examine whether those scientists thought the warming was dangerous, and she also left out papers that directly contradicted that view by noted climate scientists who had published in peer-reviewed journals over the studied period.[14]

A second "study" often cited to prove the "97 percent consensus" myth is an article published in 2009 by a University of Illinois student and her master's thesis adviser. It consisted of a survey containing only two primary questions, one that asked whether mean global temperatures have "generally risen, fallen, or remained

A.D.D. MOMENT

THE RELIGION OF CLIMATE ALARMISM[b]

REFERRING TO GLOBAL WARMING ALARMISTS AS BELONGING TO A CLIMATE CULT HAS BEEN AN ACCUSATION FOR DECADES. IT'S NOT AN ACCUSATION I THROW AROUND TOO OFTEN, BUT I MUST ADMIT, THEY ARE REALLY STARTING TO MAKE IT EASY. HERE ARE JUST A FEW EXAMPLES:

1. Mayor Pete Buttigieg, during the seven hour CNN climate townhall event, equated nonaction on climate to sinning. "This is less and less about the planet as an abstract thing and more about specific people suffering specific harm because of what we're doing right now. At least one way of talking about this is that it's a kind of sin," said Buttigeig.

2. NBC created a website dedicated to people sharing their "climate confession." Say two Hail Marys and watch *An Inconvenient Truth* and you'll be absolved of your sins, I'm sure.

3. "Comedian" Sarah Silverman compared media darling Greta Thunburg to Jesus. "You think you will recognize Jesus when he comes back? I see him all around. He is this girl. And y'all don't even see it," Silverman tweeted.

relatively constant" compared with "pre-1800s levels," and whether human activity is a "significant contributing factor" to changing temperatures.[15] Of the 3,146 scientists who completed the survey, 90 percent said global temperatures have warmed, and 82 percent said humans were a "significant contributing factor"—not 97 percent.

Importantly, only 5 percent of the respondents were identified as "climate scientists." Most were earth scientists, and only a small fraction (less than 10 percent) said more than 50 percent of their peer-reviewed papers published in the five years prior to the survey were on the subject of climate change.[16] These scientists were not asked whether they thought climate change would be catastrophic or whether humans could do anything to stop it, but even if they had been, it wouldn't have meant much, since so few of those surveyed were actually climate scientists.

In 2013, one of the most widely cited "consensus" studies was conducted by a team led by John Cook, who is now a professor at George Mason University. Cook found 97 percent of those peer-reviewed papers he reviewed implicitly or explicitly claimed human activity is responsible for at least some of the recent warming experienced.[17] However, Cook's study was thoroughly rejected by numerous climate scientists, including David Legates, Ph.D., a professor at the University of Delaware, who reconstructed Cook's study and found "only 41 papers—0.3 percent of all 11,944 abstracts or 1.0 percent of the 4,014 expressing an opinion, and not 97.1 percent" had supported the position that humans are causing most of the current warming.[18]

Other studies have been conducted attempting to show a 97 percent consensus, but generally, they employ similarly flawed methods as those mentioned above. There simply has yet to be a comprehensive study conducted of most climate scientists that shows whether they believe human-caused warming will be catastrophic. There have been some surveys, however, that point in the opposite direction.

A 2016 survey conducted by George Mason University's Center for Climate Change Communication and the American Meteorological Society (AMS) found that only 29 percent of AMS members think the climate change that has occurred over the past 50 years is "largely or entirely due to human activity."[19] And although 67 percent of those surveyed said they think more than half of the recent warming has been caused by human activities, only 47 percent of those AMS members who said the climate in their local area will change over the next half-century think the changes will be "primarily harmful." Nearly 50 percent said they don't know what the changes will be or that they think the changes will be mixed between beneficial and harmful effects. Twenty-two percent of all respondents indicated that they didn't think their local climate will change at all over the next 50 years or that they didn't know if it would.

As Steven Koonin, former undersecretary for science in the Obama administration, noted in an influential article published in the *Wall Street Journal* in 2014—titled "Climate Science Is Not Settled"—the immense number of variables that affect the climate leaves the most important questions regarding humans' impact unanswered.

"We often hear that there is a 'scientific consensus' about climate change," Koonin wrote. "But as far as the computer models go, there isn't a useful consensus at the level of detail relevant to assessing human influences."[20]

There are also dozens of other prominent scientists and meteorologists who actively reject the view that humans are causing a climate catastrophe, including Legates, a professor of climatology at the University of Delaware and former visiting research scientist at the National Climate Data Center;[21] Willie Soon, a physicist at the Harvard-Smithsonian Center for Astrophysics and the Mount Wilson Observatory;[22] Will Happer, Ph.D., the Cyrus Fogg Bracket Professor of Physics emeritus at Princeton University and the former senior director of the White House National Security

Council;[23,24] John Christy, Ph.D., the Distinguished Professor of Atmospheric Science and director of the Earth System Science Center at the University of Alabama in Huntsville;[25] and Roy Spencer, Ph.D., the Principal Research Scientist at the University of Alabama in Huntsville and former senior scientist in climate studies at NASA's Marshall Space Flight Center.[26]

These highly prestigious scientists—and many more, too—have for years been challenging the view that human-caused climate change will be catastrophic. These aren't bloggers, talking heads, or, worst of all, radio talk show hosts. They're scientists with long and impressive careers of excellence in their fields. Christy and Spencer even won NASA's "Exceptional Scientific Achievement Medal" for their temperature monitoring work. Of course, that doesn't mean we should automatically believe everything they say about climate change, but it does call into question the idea that there is an insurmountable scientific consensus on whether climate change will be catastrophic.

So, let's briefly reconsider the most important facts on the question of consensus: (1) The research often cited as ironclad proof that there's a "97 percent consensus" is embarrassingly bad and easy to dismiss. (2) There are surveys like the one conducted by AMS and George Mason University that show there are large parts of the scientific community that don't think climate change is going to be catastrophic. (3) There are prestigious, award-winning scientists who have been arguing for decades that climate change isn't going to be catastrophic. Many of them even think the benefits of a warming world—assuming warming continues—will far outweigh the costs.

I'm not a climate scientist—surprise statement of the year, I know—and I admit that it's *possible* human activities are driving climate change now and will continue to cause warming in the future. I also believe that regardless of how many or few problems climate change causes that people should *choose*—not be forced—to do what they can to be responsible stewards of the planet. But does the evidence show

there is a 97 percent scientific consensus insisting that we're heading for a hellish global warming nightmare if we don't hand over the entire economy to socialist bureaucrats in Washington, D.C.? The answer is a hard "no."

Neal Ocasio-Cortrez @GreenNewNeal
Ok, maybe there isn't a 97 percent consensus among scientists, but most environmental organizations and many climate scientists and government agencies in the United Nations and U.S. federal government say climate change is human-caused and will be catastrophic in the decades to come.

 1

That's true, but just because environmentalists predict something is going to happen doesn't mean it actually will. They don't exactly have a stellar track record of predicting catastrophe, to say the least.

Environmental organizations, climate scientists, and government agencies have been making inaccurate environment and climate predictions for a half-century, and the reason is really simple: It's incredibly difficult to predict what's going to happen with global climate—or really any global problem—decades into the future. There are just far too many factors that need to be taken into account. This shouldn't be a controversial point, but it has become one because the climate change disaster debate has become so politicized.

There are many examples of climate scientists, activists, and government officials making wildly inaccurate climate change predictions. For example, Dr. John Christy and climate scientist Richard McNider, Ph.D., tested the accuracy of 102 climate models in a 2017 analysis and found that 37 years of climate show the real-life temperature increases were only one-third of what had been predicted.[27] Christy and McNider have also found that the effect CO_2 has on global temperature is much smaller than what the United Nations' Intergovernmental Panel on Climate Change has predicted.[28] In other words, according to research by Christy and McNider and

others, many climate modelers have been horribly wrong about the temperature record over the past four decades.

Scott Armstrong, professor at the Wharton School at the University of Pennsylvania, and his colleague Kesten Green decided to audit the most highly publicized forecasts of future temperature based on how closely they were following the principles of good forecasting. Predicting the future is difficult, and if you stray from a methodical and proven approach, your results can turn into a mess no less disastrous than Hillary Clinton's Wisconsin strategy. Of the 89 principles of forecasting Armstrong and Green tested, the United Nations predictions failed on 72 of them.[29]

Look, we've seen the "we're all going to die" doomsday predictions from socialists and others on the Left before, and they are just as outlandish today as they were 60 years ago. In 1967, Stanford scientist Paul Ehrlich predicted the "time of famines" would soon be upon us, and that by 1975 it would be at its worst. Ehrlich also said that the predictions made by "experts" at the time that the world food supply would need

to be doubled by 2000 to feed the global population "may be possible theoretically, but it is clear that it is totally impossible in practice."[30]

Two years later, in 1969, Ehrlich—who once said, "Giving society cheap, abundant energy would be the equivalent of giving an idiot child a machine gun"[31]—made another doomsday prediction, insisting that "unless we are extremely lucky, everybody will disappear in a cloud of blue steam [pollution] in 20 years."[32]

My memory isn't as good as it used to be, but I don't recall the killer "blue steam" cloud of 1989 wiping out everyone I knew or the global famine crisis of 1975. And here we are now, 20 years beyond the 2000 prediction, and hunger has actually been in decline throughout much of the world.[33]

In 1971, the *Washington Post* reported Dr. S. I. Rasool, a scientist with NASA and Columbia University, prognosticated that within 50 years, "the fine dust man constantly puts into the atmosphere by fossil fuel-burning could screen out so much sunlight that the average temperature could drop by six degrees," creating a new "Ice Age."[34]

In 1974, a headline in *The Guardian* (U.K.) newspaper warned, "Space satellites show new Ice Age coming fast."[35]

A.D.D. MOMENT

WE NEVER DID GET AN ATTACK BY THE "BLUE STEAM," HOWEVER OUR SOCIETY HAS BEEN INFECTED WITH THE SLIGHTLY MORE TERRIFYING "BLUE MAN GROUP."

Time magazine also breathlessly warned of a global ice age, reporting in 1974, "when meteorologists take an average of temperatures around the globe they find that the atmosphere has been growing gradually cooler for the past three decades." The cooling trend "shows no indication of reversing," *Time* also reported, adding that "telltale signs are everywhere" and that "Climatological Cassandras are becoming increasingly apprehensive, for the weather aberrations they are studying may be the harbinger of another ice age."[36]

In 1978, the *New York Times* reported that an "international team of specialists" predicted that there is "no end in sight" to the global cooling trend of the 1970s.[37]

Then, suddenly, in the late 1970s and early 1980s, when Earth's climate started to warm, many in the scientific and environmental communities suddenly shifted their focus. Instead of blaming human activity or nature for creating an impending ice age, they started to warn of a looming man-made global warming catastrophe. In 1979, the *New York Times* reported, "There is a real possibility that some people now in their infancy will live to a time when the ice at the North Pole will have melted, a change that would cause swift and perhaps catastrophic changes in climate."[38]

Later in 1979, the *New York Times* reported a panel of experts formed by the National Academy of Sciences issued a report to the White House indicating that "within a half-century such combustion could double the amount of carbon dioxide in the atmosphere and thereby warm it an average of about 6 degrees Fahrenheit—enough to cause major climate changes that conceivably could turn farmland to desert or make deserts fertile"[39]—a prediction not even the most staunch global warming alarmist would agree with today.

In 1982, the National Research Council said a doubling of the amount of CO_2 could occur by 2050, causing temperatures to rise by 2.7 degrees to 8.1 degrees Fahrenheit,[40] roughly the same as the current predictions for 2100.[41] That means the National

Research Council's 1982 warning was off by 50 years—and that assumes the current predictions will actually take place.

In 1988, NASA scientist James Hansen warned that temperatures in 2050 will be "6 to 7 degrees higher than they are today [in 1988]," causing the number of days in Washington, D.C., with temperatures topping 90 degrees Fahrenheit to increase from 35 per year to 85 days, nearly three months.[42] But since Hansen made his forecasts, the average number of hot days in Washington has actually decreased.[43]

By 1989, United Nations officials were predicting that "entire nations could be wiped off the face of the Earth" if global warming isn't stopped by 2000.[44]

The 1990s and early 2000s featured a seemingly endless array of false global warming predictions. For example, in 2000, Dr. David Viner, a research scientist at the climatic research unit of the University of East Anglia, said that within just a few years, snowfall in Britain would become "a very rare and exciting event," adding, "Children just aren't going to know what snow is."[45]

Former Vice President and Climate-Alarmist-in-Chief Al Gore made dozens of false or misleading claims and predictions in numerous speeches and in his 2006 Oscar-award-winning documentary, *An Inconvenient Truth*. Gore told a United Nations climate conference in 2009 that climate scientists had told him there is a "75 percent chance the entire polar ice cap will melt in summer within the next five to seven years."[46] That never happened. Gore lamented the collapse of polar bear populations because of climate change, but new evidence shows polar bear populations have likely quadrupled over the past 50 years.[47] Gore predicted in 2006 that "Within the decade, there will be no more 'snows of Kilimanjaro," referring to Mount Kilimanjaro in Tanzania. But in March 2018, Doug Hardy at the Climate System Research Center at the University of Massachusetts reported Kilimanjaro experienced "the greatest snow accumulation on the glacier in years."[49]

According to climate change predictions made by scientists, government agencies, and activists over the past 60 years, temperatures should be much higher today than they are now or we should be in the midst of a new ice age, a cloud of "blue steam" should have killed off a large chunk of humanity, hundreds of millions of people—at minimum—should have starved to death, whole nations should have been consumed by rising sea levels, snowfall should have disappeared in the United Kingdom and on Mount Kilimanjaro, polar bear populations should have been wiped out, and the ice at the North Pole should have melted. And yet, none of these things have happened.

Based on its track record, I think it's fair to say a large portion of the scientific community has a tendency to overexaggerate the effects of climate change and make predictions that are not likely to come true.

Neal Ocasio-Cortrez @GreenNewNeal
Ok, perhaps climate scientists don't have a perfect record when it comes to making climate change predictions. But come on @glennbeck, get your head out of the sand! Of course global warming will eventually be catastrophic. We're already seeing more wildfires, heatwaves, and hurricanes because of climate change. We're also experiencing rising seas and lower crop production, putting human health and welfare at great risk. If things are already getting much worse, can you imagine how bad it will be in 80 years?

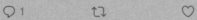

Based on the intense media coverage of all these natural disasters, I can't blame you for thinking that extreme weather events are getting significantly worse due to climate change. But in every single area you mentioned, the data show dangerous weather events aren't becoming more common.

WILDFIRES

According to the National Interagency Fire Center, which has tracked wildfires for nearly a century, the number of wildland fires has *decreased* over the past three decades. In 1985, there were 82,591 wildland fires. In 2018, the number was 58,083, the lowest recorded figure since 2013. From 1998 to 2008, the average reported number of wildland fires was 80,021, significantly more than average reported from 2008 to 2018 (68,001). And although the number of acres burned since 1985 has risen dramatically, it has stayed relatively flat since 2004.[50]

You might also be surprised to learn that many scientists believe the federal government is mostly to blame for the increased acreage burned by fires. In 2019, nearly 300 scientists authored joint-letters to Congress requesting that the federal government change its "dangerous" procedures following wildfires. According to the scientists, the federal government's decision to clear away logs after wildfires is increasing wildfire intensity.[51]

HEATWAVES

No one is more concerned about the possibility of an increasing number of heatwaves. I live in Texas, which in the summer basically becomes as hot as the surface of the sun, so the thought of heatwaves becoming even more intense isn't something I'd take lightly. But I have good news, my fellow Texans: The average number of days exceeding 100 degrees Fahrenheit has not increased substantially over the past 100 years. In fact, the decade with the highest number of recorded days with 100-degree F temperatures was in the 1930s.[52]

It's also incredible that for all the talk from socialists and progressives about the dangers of increased heatwaves—which, again, isn't really happening—there's no mention of the possibility that moderate warming could be a net benefit for the world. It is a fact that extreme cold temperatures are associated with far more death and environmental destruction. Colder weather is actually 20 times more deadly than hot weather.[53]

HURRICANES

Despite near-constant fearmongering from Democratic presidential candidates who have said that the hurricanes we're seeing today are a direct result of climate change, the overwhelming evidence shows hurricane activity has not worsened as a result of climate change. In 2018, researchers examining hurricane activity in the United States "found no significant trends in landfalling hurricanes, major hurricanes, or normalized damage consistent with what has been found in previous studies."[54]

In fact, when Hurricane Harvey, a Category 4 storm, hit the United States in 2017, it broke a record of 142 straight months—for those who are math-challenged like me, that's almost 12 years—without a Category 3 or higher storm making landfall in America.[55] The previous record was 96 months, which occurred from September 1860 to August 1869.

RISING SEAS

Perhaps the most striking and terrifying images related to global warming are those that simulate entire cities being swallowed up by rising seas. For example, in 2016 the *Washingtonian* published a series of maps showing huge swaths of Washington,

D.C., underwater from global sea level rise, including much of the National Mall, Smithsonian, and the U.S. Capitol building.[56] In 2017, *Newsweek* dedicated an entire article to answering the question: "How Long Before All of Florida Is Underwater?"[57] *Business Insider* and *24/7 Wall St.* published an article in 2018 identifying the "30 cities that could be underwater by 2060."[58]

All these predictions are largely based on estimates by the United Nations' Intergovernmental Panel on Climate Change (IPCC). Although IPCC acknowledges sea levels have been rising for thousands of years—a natural process in the wake of the last Ice Age—it says it's "very likely" sea-level rise is accelerating.[59]

But before you decide to throw in the towel and buy that big beautiful new houseboat to avoid the coming apocalypse, you should know that much of the sea-level data has been heavily affected by land subsidence, the "gradual settling or sudden sinking of the Earth's surface."[60] When high-quality tide gauges are evaluated, there is little or no evidence of sea-level acceleration.[61]

In 2017, researchers Albert Parker and Clifford Ollier examined six large tide gauge datasets, including 199 stations in the National Oceanic and Atmospheric Administration's database. They determined "all consistently show a small sea-level rate of rise and a negligible acceleration."[62]

Judith Curry, Ph.D., a climatologist and former chair of the School of Earth and Atmospheric Sciences at the Georgia Institute of Technology, researched the tide gauge record and found, "Tide gauges show that sea levels began to rise during the 19th century, after several centuries associated with cooling and sea level decline. Tide gauges also show that rates of global mean sea level rise between 1920 and 1950 were comparable to recent rates. Recent research has concluded that there is no consistent or compelling evidence that recent rates of sea level rise are abnormal in the context of the historical records back to the 19th century that are available across Europe."[63]

Oh, and there are other good, completely unscientific reasons to question the claim that sea levels are rising at dangerous rates. For example, if everyone living anywhere near America's coasts is going to end up underwater, why the heck are so many of the leading climate change "warriors" buying up beachfront property?

In 2019, Barack and Michelle Obama purchased a $14 million mansion on the absurdly overpriced and posh island Martha's Vineyard in Massachusetts.[64] (Apparently, public "service" has been very, very good for the Obama family.) While president, Barack Obama made it very clear he believed global warming is causing higher sea levels. For instance, during his 2015 State of the Union address, Obama warned that the "best scientists in the world" say that climate change will cause, among other things, "rising oceans, longer, hotter heat waves, dangerous droughts and floods."[65] Why, then, would Obama choose to spend a fortune on a mansion that's located on land that some climate alarmist researchers, including researchers who received funding from the Obama administration, say could one day be submerged beneath the ocean?[66]

Similarly, in 2005 Hollywood star and climate change alarmist champion of the world Leonardo DiCaprio purchased a 104-acre island in Belize and will soon open a luxury "eco-resort" on the property.[67] DiCaprio's purchase seems more than a little odd since he's the same guy who has been running around the world—well, more like flying in private jets around the world—over the past decade warning us about the coming climate apocalypse. He even made a documentary about climate change in 2016 called *Before the Flood*.[68] Call me crazy, but investing in an *island* resort doesn't sound like a good idea if you think islands all over the planet are about to be swallowed up by the oceans.

In 2010, Al and Tipper Gore bought an $8.8 million home in Montecito, California, one of the wealthiest communities in America.[69] (Gore is another guy who has found a way to make a killing on public "service." Hmm, I'm sensing a pattern here.) Gore's

ocean-view home—which includes a wine cellar, nine bathrooms, and six fireplaces (yes, six fireplaces)—isn't located right on the beach, but spending a fortune to live in a town that's famous for its beaches again seems like a strange choice if you think much of the place could get wiped off the map "in the near future" by a 20-foot rise in sea level.[70]

LOWER CROP PRODUCTION

It's common for many climate change doomsayers to say we're facing climate-related food shortages or that we soon will. But reports clearly indicate global crop production in many of the most important areas has been steadily increasing over the past decade. Data from the U.N. Food and Agriculture Organization show food production and crop yields for cereals, wheat, corn, and rice are all experiencing record highs or near-record highs.[71]

You might also be surprised to hear that higher levels of atmospheric carbon dioxide have been linked to increased greening of the Earth. In 2016, NASA reported that an "international team of 32 authors from 24 institutions in eight countries" found "a quarter to half of Earth's vegetated lands has shown significant greening over the last 35 years largely due to rising levels of atmospheric carbon dioxide."[72] The researchers found only 4 percent of the globe experienced browning.

Additionally, in 2019, a NASA study found human activity in China and India had significantly contributed to Earth's greening. It also determined that greening across the entire Earth had increased during the two decades prior to the studied period.[73]

As all these data show, we're not experiencing the Mad Max global warming hell that socialists and progressives are always telling us about. In fact, some researchers say the risk of dying from climate-related disasters like floods, droughts, storms, etc., has fallen by 99 percent since the 1920s.[74]

Rashida Resistance @AOC_2024_Squad4Life
Maybe these climate natural disasters haven't started yet, but you can't predict the future, @glennbeck. Many scientists believe we're headed for a climate catastrophe, and even if they've been wrong in the past, it's not a risk we can take. This is why we need a Green New Deal to stop a future climate crisis.

💬 1   🔁   ♡

Ah, yes, the Green New Deal, the most expensive, radical, extreme, socialist policy proposal offered since—well, ever. If I were looking for the quintessential terrible American socialist plan, "the green dream or whatever they call it"[75] would be my choice. (I promise, that will be the *only* time I quote Nancy Pelosi in this book.)

Although there have been a few different "Green New Deal" plans proposed by Democratic presidential candidates and Green Party nutjobs, the most influential, far-reaching plan is Alexandria Ocasio-Cortez's totally insane proposal, which she first rolled out in late 2018 before releasing a more comprehensive (and even more totally insane) version in February 2019.

The Green New Deal nonbinding congressional resolution Ocasio-Cortez released with Sen. Ed Markey, D-Mass., was co-sponsored by more than 90 members in the House of Representatives[76] and 12 members of the U.S. Senate, including Democratic presidential candidates Cory Booker, D-N.J., Kirsten Gillibrand, D-N.Y., Kamala Harris, D-Calif., Amy Klobuchar, D-Minn., Bernie Sanders, I-Vt., and the honorable Chief Elizabeth Warren from the tribe of ImaFraudapoke.[77]

The heart of the Green New Deal proposal is to eliminate nearly all fossil-fuel use in the United States in just 10 years.[78] That means every coal and natural gas plant would close, along with every coal mine and hydraulic fracturing ("fracking") site.

There wouldn't be any more oil drilling either, neither onshore nor offshore. Every gas station, frac sand mine, oil refinery, and most motor vehicle manufacturers would need to close or completely change their operations.

We're talking about *millions* of jobs lost—not thousands, tens of thousands, or even hundreds of thousands, but *millions* of jobs. The U.S. Department of Energy estimates there are more than 2 million Americans employed in traditional energy sectors and low-CO_2 nuclear and natural gas.[79] Another 2 million work in the gasoline-powered "Motor Vehicles and Component Parts" industry, not including auto dealerships.[80] Many of those working in these 4 million jobs would likely find themselves out of work or at risk of losing their employment if the Green New Deal were to become law. And who knows how many millions of additional jobs would be destroyed by imposing significantly higher energy costs on the entire economy.

And that's just the beginning. The Green New Deal would also require sucking trillions of dollars out of the economy to replace all of that lost electricity generation with wind and solar energy sources, which are much more expensive to operate. Americans would have to build thousands of new windmills and solar facilities and thousands of miles of new transmission lines—all merely to provide exactly the same amount of energy generation that we do now.

The American Enterprise Institute's Benjamin Zycher estimates the net annual cost of replacing fossil fuels with wind and solar energy sources would be $357 billion *per year*, or nearly $2,800 per household *per year*.[81] In reality, the burden would likely fall much harder on those who pay income taxes, middle-class and wealthy households.

The Green New Deal would also require spending trillions more to enact all sorts of truly off-the-charts crazy reforms. For example, Ocasio-Cortez's Green New Deal "Frequently Asked Questions" sheet—which she had to pull from her office's website shortly after posting it because of the incredible backlash it produced—said her proposal would involve building "highspeed rail at a scale where air travel stops becoming necessary."[82] Say goodbye to air travel, America, and say hello to being trapped in a metal tube with hundreds of other pissed-off people stuck traveling for days on train trips that would have only taken a few hours to complete on a plane. Sure, air travel is also sitting in a metal tube with hundreds of pissed-off people, but at least it's comparatively short.

THE VACANT LAND MYTH

ROBERT BRYCE, A SENIOR FELLOW AT THE MANHATTAN INSTITUTE, WRITES ABOUT "VACANT LAND MYTH"—THE IDEA THAT THERE ARE WIDE-OPEN AREAS THROUGHOUT THE COUNTRY JUST WAITING TO BE DEVELOPED INTO WIND AND SOLAR FARMS. TURNS OUT, THIS IS NOT THE CASE.

IN FACT, IN AREAS THAT MANY ASSUME HAVE THE MOST ENTHUSIASM FOR BUILDING MASSIVE WIND AND SOLAR FACILITIES, YOU FIND STAUNCH RESISTANCE FROM LOCALS. THIS INCLUDES PLACES LIKE UPSTATE NEW YORK, HOME STATE OF NEW YORK GOV. ANDREW CUOMO; MASSACHUSETTS, HOME TO SEN. ELIZABETH WARREN; AND EVEN VERMONT, HOME TO SEN. BERNIE SANDERS.

BUT THE MOST TELLING PIECE OF EVIDENCE FOR THIS CONCEPT COMES FROM THE BASTION OF AMERICAN LIBERALISM, CALIFORNIA. IN SAN BERNARDINO COUNTY, AMERICA'S LARGEST COUNTY, THE COUNTY'S BOARD APPROVED A MEASURE TO BAN LARGE-SCALE RENEWABLE ENERGY FARMS.

IF THIS TYPE OF RESISTANCE CAN BE FOUND IN THE LARGEST COUNTY IN THE BLUEST STATE, IMAGINE HOW DIFFICULT IT WOULD BE TO TAKE OVER AND DEVELOP THE HUNDREDS OF THOUSANDS OF SQUARE MILES OF LAND NECESSARY TO CONSTRUCT ALL THE WIND AND SOLAR FARMS, TRANSMISSION LINES, AND EVERYTHING ELSE REQUIRED UNDER THE GREEN NEW DEAL![c]

The FAQ and resolution also promised to provide every American with "safe, affordable, adequate housing" that's green-energy compliant. Yeah, the thought of having federal officials come to my house to make it more "safe," "adequate," and "green" doesn't sound horrifying at all. "Come on in, Mr. Bureaucrat, and please be sure to tell me everything that's not 'safe' about my home. Oh, you want to see the gun safe? Uh, no guns here, Mr. Bureaucrat. Let's go outside so I can show you my new green-energy-compliant compost in the backyard instead."

In another section of the FAQ, Ocasio-Cortez answers a "frequently asked question" about why the Green New Deal allows for a very limited amount of CO_2 to be emitted, rather than just banning all CO_2 emissions outright. Among the reasons given in her answer is, "We set a goal to get to net-zero, rather than zero emissions, in 10 years because we aren't sure that we'll be able to fully get rid of farting cows and airplanes that fast, but we think we can ramp up renewable manufacturing and power production, retrofit every building in America, build the smart grid, overhaul transportation and agriculture, plant lots of trees and restore our ecosystem to get to net-zero."[83]

I bet when you see cows peacefully grazing in a picturesque little pasture, you probably think something like, "Wow, those sure are some big cows." Or maybe, "Hey, it's a cow. Suddenly, I have a craving for milk." Or maybe just, "Steak, it's what's for dinner." Okay, I don't know what you say when you see a cow, but I do know this: Whatever you see, it's not what Alexandria Ocasio-Cortez sees—big, fat, Earth-destroying, rising-seas-causing, planet-endangering fart machines. That's right, fart machines. You see, cow farts produce methane, methane contributes to global warming, and global warming is going to kill us all. So, if we put on our Sherlock Holmes thinking caps, we'll realize, just like Comrade Ocasio-Cortez, that logic dictates we kill all the cows. It's elementary, dear Watson.

Now, as you know, Ms. Resistance, the stated purpose for causing all this economic mayhem is to stop global warming. Or, as the Ocasio-Cortez resolution puts it, the Green New Deal is "a new national, social, industrial, and economic mobilization on a scale not seen since World War II and the New Deal era" that's necessary to halt "climate change . . . a direct threat to the national security of the United States."[84] Maybe you think all the job-destroying, airplane-obliterating, and cow-killing is worth the trouble because climate change is, as you've already said, potentially "catastrophic." But here's perhaps the biggest problem with the energy provisions of the Green New Deal: It's trying to stop a problem we can't solve, no matter what the cause is.

Even if I accept the position that human beings' CO_2 emissions are the primary driver of climate change—which is entirely possible—and even if I accept that climate change will be catastrophic—a view I think is much less likely to be true, but okay, I'll go along for now—cutting U.S. carbon dioxide emissions down to zero would do absolutely nothing to stop a future climate change disaster. Nothing. Zip. Nada.

You see, as hard as it might be to accept what I'm about to tell you, it's a well-established fact, not an opinion, that U.S. CO_2 emissions do not drive global climate change. You don't have to take my word for it. Please, please, please—do your own homework. If you do, you'll find that U.S. carbon dioxide emissions only make up less than 15 percent of global CO_2 emissions,[85] and that countries such as China and India are rapidly increasing their annual CO_2 emissions as they continue to industrialize. In 2018, China—the world's largest emitter—increased its CO_2 emissions by 4.7 percent.[86] India increased emissions by 6.3 percent. Excluding China, the European Union, India, and the United States, emissions produced by the remainder of the world rose by 1.8 percent.

At this pace, even if the United States were to completely eliminate all carbon dioxide emissions and kill every single one of its farting cows, the increased CO_2 emissions

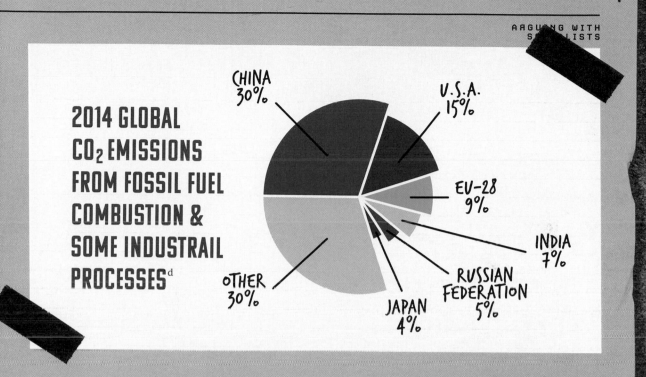

2014 GLOBAL CO$_2$ EMISSIONS FROM FOSSIL FUEL COMBUSTION & SOME INDUSTRAIL PROCESSES[d]

CHINA 30%

U.S.A. 15%

EU-28 9%

INDIA 7%

RUSSIAN FEDERATION 5%

JAPAN 4%

OTHER 30%

produced by the rest of the world would more than offset any U.S. reductions. Using the United Nations' own estimates, the future temperature impacts that would be avoided by eliminating all U.S. emissions would be less than two-tenths of a single degree by 2100, barely enough to measure accurately.[87]

Now, some have suggested that the United States can convince China, India, and dozens of other countries to commit economic suicide and switch to renewable energy sources, but that ain't happening. As Reuters reported in September 2019, "China's total planned coal-fired power projects now stand at 226.2 gigawatts (GW), the highest in the world. . . . The new China projects would be more than Germany's existing installed power capacity of around 200 GW by the end of 2018."[88] Additionally, the left-of-center Brookings Institution says "coal is king in India—and will likely remain so" through "2030 and beyond."[89]

Barring some incredible new technological energy innovation, the increased CO$_2$ emissions occurring in China, India, and throughout much of the rest of the world

will continue in the coming decades, regardless of what the United States does, because those countries desperately need access to affordable energy. They simply aren't concerned about the potential effects of climate change decades into the future, and if you were in charge of a country with hundreds of millions of people living beneath the international poverty line of $1.90 per day like the leaders in India are, you'd probably be more concerned with economic growth than polar bear populations too.[90] (And don't forget, there's no reason to worry about polar bears. They're doing just fine.) That means, regardless of whether we're headed for a CO_2-driven climate nightmare or not, the Green New Deal—and nothing else we do here in the United States—can stop it.

Rashida Resistance @AOC_2024_Squad4Life
The Green New Deal might not be a perfect solution, but at least @AOC, @BernieSanders, @ewarren, and others are trying to prevent this environmental disaster with policy plans like the Green New Deal.

💬 1   🔁   ♡

The Green New Deal actually has very little to do with protecting the environment and everything to do with trying to impose socialism on unsuspecting Americans—all under the guise of "saving the planet." The Green New Deal is nothing more than a big socialist Trojan horse.

Now, I know that many regular folks in the Democratic Party and members of environmental groups like the Sierra Club truly believe that the Green New Deal is all about saving the planet. So, when I say the proposal was designed to be a "socialist Trojan horse," I'm not suggesting this was planned by your run-of-the-mill progressive or even your local Joe Communist who religiously attends his monthly Democratic Socialists of America meeting at the local Starbucks. I'm referring to Alexandria Ocasio-Cortez, Bernie Sanders, Elizabeth Warren, Ilhan Omar, and

many of the other leaders of the progressive and socialist wings of the Democratic Party.

 Neal Ocasio-Cortrez @GreenNewNeal .@glennbeck, stop with the crazy conspiracy theory stuff. The Green New Deal is about saving the planet from global warming, that's all.

 1   ⟲   ♡

No conspiracy theories here. There's absolutely no question the Green New Deal is primarily about pushing the country toward socialism, not climate change. And here's how I *know* that's the case: Although the proposal calls for trillions of dollars in new spending to battle climate change, it also demands tens of trillions of additional dollars to pay for new government programs meant to advance socialist goals, including many programs that have nothing to do with climate change or the environment.

Among the Green New Deal's many socialist and/or progressive provisions are:

1. THE CREATION OF A FEDERAL JOBS GUARANTEE PROGRAM THAT WOULD PROMISE THE GOVERNMENT WILL PROVIDE "A FAMILY-SUSTAINING WAGE, ADEQUATE FAMILY AND MEDICAL LEAVE, PAID VACATIONS, AND RETIREMENT SECURITY TO ALL PEOPLE OF THE UNITED STATES,"[91] INCLUDING THOSE WHO ARE "UNWILLING TO WORK."[92]

2. THE ESTABLISHMENT OF A UNIVERSAL COLLEGE PROGRAM, PRESUMABLY PROVIDING MILLIONS MORE WITH A COLLEGE EDUCATION TUITION-FREE.[93]

3. THE CREATION OF A GOVERNMENT-RUN SINGLE-PAYER HEALTH CARE SYSTEM.[94]

A *REAL* INCONVENIENT TRUTH

According to a report by the Associated Press, when doing research for his upcoming documentary, *Planet of the Humans* director Jeff Gibbs had a shocking revelation. Gibbs, a long-time associate of filmmaker Michael Moore, said, "It turned out the wakeup call was about our own side. It was kind of crushing to discover that the things I believed in weren't real, first of all, and then to discover not only are the solar panels and wind turbines not going to save us . . . but (also) that there is this whole dark side of the corporate money . . . it dawned on me that these technologies were just another profit center."[e]

4. THE ESTABLISHMENT OF A NATIONAL "HEALTHY AND AFFORDABLE
    FOODS" GUARANTEE, AS WELL AS A GUARANTEE TO HAVE "ACCESS
    TO NATURE"—WHATEVER THE HECK THAT MEANS.[95]

5. PROVIDING ALL PEOPLE WITH "ECONOMIC SECURITY."[96]

6. A PROMISE TO ENSURE "A COMMERCIAL ENVIRONMENT WHERE
    EVERY BUSINESSPERSON IS FREE FROM UNFAIR COMPETITION AND
    DOMINATION BY DOMESTIC OR INTERNATIONAL MONOPOLIES."[97]

7. LAWS FOCUSED ON "STRENGTHENING AND PROTECTING THE RIGHT OF
    ALL WORKERS TO ORGANIZE, UNIONIZE, AND COLLECTIVELY BARGAIN
    FREE OF COERCION, INTIMIDATION, AND HARASSMENT."[98]

8. THE CREATION OF A SYSTEM OF NEW PUBLICLY OWNED BANKS.[99]

The American Action Forum projects the total cost of all the Green New Deal provisions—including the socialist programs mentioned above—is as high as $94.4 trillion, more than four times the current national debt, over just a 10-year period.[100] Of that potential $94.4 trillion cost, the energy and climate-related provisions would only amount to about 13 percent of the total spent. The single-payer health care estimate alone is $36 trillion over just 10 years.

Now, ask yourself this important question: If we really are on the verge of a climate catastrophe—oceans covering whole cities, millions of "climate refugees," killer heatwaves and hurricanes, and more—and if climate change really does pose an "existential threat" to humanity, then why would anyone who believes this want to spend a single penny on "free college," a government-guaranteed job, or single-payer health care? Why wouldn't we instead focus every resource we have on stopping the world from ending? Answer: Because this isn't about saving the environment, it's about advancing socialism. But, hey, don't take my word for it. Ocasio-Cortez's own chief of staff (now, her former chief of staff), Saikat Chakrabarti, said it better than I ever could.

In May 2019, a *Washington Post* reporter attended a little-publicized meeting between Chakrabarti and Sam Ricketts, the former climate director for Washington governor Jay Inslee's now failed presidential campaign. According to the reporter, Chakrabarti said, "The interesting thing about the Green New Deal, is it wasn't originally a climate thing at all."[101]

The reporter noted that "Ricketts greeted this startling notion with an attentive poker face," but, incredibly, Chakrabarti went even further: "Do you guys think of it as a climate thing? Because we really think of it as a how-do-you-change-the-entire-economy thing."

Even for a candidate as candid as Ocasio-Cortez, this was a stunning admission to make. I would praise Chakrabarti for his honesty, but it turns out his penchant for truth-telling only applies when he's talking about climate change. Chakrabarti resigned from Ocasio-Cortez's office in August 2019, right around the same time federal agents started investigating him for potentially violating campaign finance law.[102]

 Neal Ocasio-Cortrez @GreenNewNeal
Well, capitalism sure as heck isn't going to fix the environment. Only socialism, in some form, can do that, by forcing the market to accept renewable energy sources like wind and solar. Maybe those won't stop climate change, but at least they will help to improve other environmental problems.

 1

You've got it all backwards, Neal. Historically, socialism has been terrible for the environment. Throughout human history, environmentalism has largely been a luxury concern that people are only able to prioritize when they're not in the middle of an economic crisis. When there are severe economic problems to deal with—which is nearly always the case in socialist societies—people stop caring about protecting the environment. And can you blame them? If you had to spend much of your time worried about finding the best bread line in town, you probably wouldn't be too concerned about making sure the greater prairie chicken ends up on the Endangered Species List.

THE KUZNETS CURVE

Environmentalists and socialists alike will accuse free markets of destroying the environment in the name of profit. If capitalism is allowed to run amuck, they say, we will soon be living in a smog-filled, trash-clogged, urban nightmare. History shows this isn't true, however.

It is generally the case that when a country is developing, environmental concerns come second to economic expansion. However, this trend plateaus and then reverses when per-capita income provides citizens with a certain level of economic security.

It is only when people are wealthy enough that they no longer have to worry about survival that they start to pay attention to their environment. At this point in a country's development, more value is placed on reducing pollution and preserving nature.[f]

We've seen this play out dozens of times throughout history. Shawn Regan, a research fellow at the Property and Environment Research Center, notes that the historical record shows "the socialist economies of Eastern Europe and the former Soviet Union were not

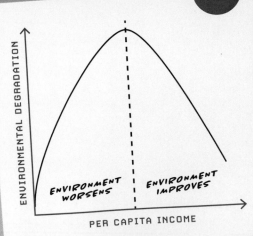

just economic failures; they were also environmental catastrophes."[103] Regan added that, "By one estimate, in the late 1980s, particulate air pollution was 13 times higher per unit of GDP in Central and Eastern Europe than in Western Europe. Levels of gaseous air pollution were twice as high as this. Wastewater pollution was three times higher."

Similar problems have occurred in other socialist nations as well. Many of Cuba's rivers and coastal areas are full of trash, oil, and even sewage.[104] In one report by the *Miami Herald*, a Cuban resident told a reporter that "he's heard talk about the dangers of the contaminated bay waters, but people 'don't care about that. You can see plastics, garbage, dead animals and debris everywhere. There's a shortage of garbage disposal places, so people throw it directly into the ocean. It's something very sad.'"[105]

Regan reports environmental disasters also plague Venezuela. According to Regan, reports show "socialist policies have contaminated the nation's drinking-water supplies, fueled rampant deforestation and unrestrained mining activity, and caused frequent oil spills attributed to neglect and mismanagement by the state-owned energy company."[106]

 Rashida Resistance @AOC_2024_Squad4Life
The only reason America's environment isn't a total disaster is because of protections put in place by socialists and progressives at the state and federal levels.

 1

Really? Have you been to Los Angeles, San Francisco, or Newark, New Jersey? They are some of the most disgusting, polluted cities in the nation, despite being run by progressives and socialists for decades. Much of San Francisco is about as sanitary as a toilet bowl. And not just any toilet bowl, I'm talking about a toilet bowl you would find in a porta-potty at an abandoned amusement park. Think I'm exaggerating?

In 2018, there were more than 28,000 reports of humans defecating in the streets of the city, more than five times the number reported in 2011.[107]

Additionally, of the American Lung Association's 10 worst cities for air quality (based on ozone), seven are in far-left California and number 10 on the list is the Democrat-dominated Newark–New York City metropolitan area.[108] And reports indicate many of the states with some of the cleanest environments are also some of the most conservative, like South Dakota, Wyoming, and Idaho.[109]

It's also worth noting that the Environmental Protection Agency—before it became the out-of-control behemoth it is now—was founded in 1970 by a Republican president, Richard Nixon, in reaction to growing environmental concerns about air quality and other pollutants.[110] Today, the market-based United States has one of the lowest concentrations of fine particulate matter—an important measure when determining air quality—in the entire world, beating many countries in Europe, like France, Germany, and the United Kingdom, and far surpassing socialist Cuba and Venezuela.[111]

Look, supporting individual freedom, property rights, and free markets doesn't mean you don't care about protecting the environment. I care deeply about being a good steward of the Earth. In fact, my ranch is completely powered by wind, solar, and natural gas. I'm one of those lunatics that bought solar panel technology back when it was half as good and three times more expensive. Why? Because I genuinely care about preserving nature and doing what I can (most people do!).

And I know a lot of other people who are committed to limiting the size and power of government and promoting economic liberty that share my love for nature. But the idea that the only way to protect the environment is to put government in charge is demonstrably untrue. History has shown the best way to promote environmentalism is to create prosperity. Environmentalism is a luxury created by capitalism, not

socialism. Without the wealth that has flowed from private property ownership rights granted to all people, we would have fewer environmental protections today than we do now, and even if we did have them, most people would ignore those regulations, just as they do throughout much of the world.

THE DECOUPLING OF ECONOMIC GROWTH & RESOURCE CONSUMPTION

SURVEYS CONDUCTED BY THE U.S. GEOLOGICAL SURVEY HAVE FOUND THAT IN RECENT DECADES, REAL GDP HAS GROWN WHILE THE USE OF NATURAL RESOURCES AND MINERALS HAVE PLATEAUED. THIS FINDING DISPELS THE IDEA THAT GREATER RESOURCE CONSUMPTION IS NEEDED FOR A DEVELOPED COUNTRY TO SUSTAIN ECONOMIC GROWTH, A SIGNIFICANT FINDING FOR THOSE CONCERNED ABOUT THE ENVIRONMENT AND BAD NEWS FOR THOSE ATTEMPTING TO USE ENVIRONMENTAL VIRTUE SIGNALING AS A MEANS TO PUSH AN ANTI-FREE-MARKET AGENDA.[5]

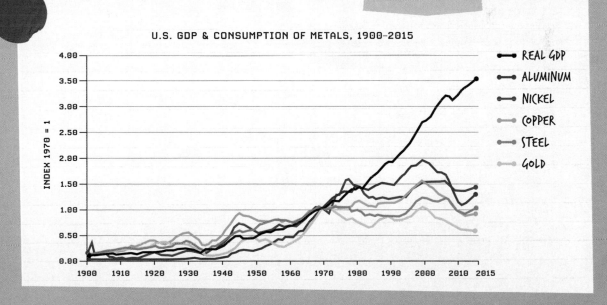

U.S. GDP & CONSUMPTION OF METALS, 1900–2015

Rashida Resistance @AOC_2024_Squad4Life
Ok, @glennbeck, Let's move on. I see there is no way I can—

💬 1   ↻   ♡

Wait, I'm not done yet. We can't move off the topic of climate alarmism without addressing a few more things. The fact is, politicians and bureaucrats are using climate change as an excuse to control every aspect of your life. I've already covered how they are using this supposed environmental crisis to pass legislation to create a ton of non-environmental-related programs. Well, it doesn't end there.

What happens when "fixing the climate" means controlling what appears on your dinner plate? A number of the Democratic presidential candidates had a lot to say about Americans' red meat consumption during CNN's September 2019 "Climate Crisis Town Hall." Presidential hopeful Andrew Yang talked about creating "economic incentives" to help "shape our system" when responding to a question about curbing red meat intake in America.[112]

Sen. Kamala Harris, after apologizing for enjoying a cheeseburger "from time to time," talked about "creating incentives" and promoting moderation in America's diet. Harris then said she would favor changing the food pyramid and dietary guidelines to reflect calls to reduce meat consumption. Just think about that for a moment—a mainstream former presidential candidate is actually advocating a change to America's dietary guidelines, not based on science or health, but on the basis of climate alarmism.[113]

If limiting red meat doesn't concern you, how about the concept of population control? Yes, I know there are a lot of kooky ideas out there being proposed by fringe wackos on both sides of the aisle, but I'm not talking about those people; I'm talking about America's "favorite" socialist, Bernie Sanders.

During the CNN town hall, when asked about whether he would pursue a policy agenda based on "educating everyone on the need to curb population growth," Sanders said, "the answer is 'yes.'"[114] And Sanders isn't alone. A number of people on the Left have expressed their support for limiting population growth, including Al Gore and Bill Maher, while others have said that their fears about environmental concerns have led them to rethink having children.[115]

In February 2019, Ocasio-Cortez went so far as to suggest that bringing children into the world could be immoral. "There's scientific consensus that the lives of children are going to be very difficult," she said. "And it does lead young people to have a legitimate question: is it okay to still have children?"[116]

We know at least one person agrees with Ocasio-Cortez. Writer Wes Siler, writing for online publication *Outside*, agreed to have a vasectomy "because of climate change." Claiming "there are simply too many humans on this planet," Siler says he chose to forgo having children for the rest of his life because, "Two people deciding to make fewer humans eliminates the entire cycle of consumption that would fuel that kid's life."[117]

Siler and Ocasio-Cortez aren't alone. Population control language was used in a climate change letter signed by thousands of scientists in November 2019. The letter—which incited dire headlines such as, "Climate Crisis: 11,000 Scientists Warn of 'Untold Suffering'"—referred to human population growth as a "profoundly troubling sign."[118] Labeling economic and population growth as "important drivers of increases in CO_2 emissions," the letter goes on to state that "the world population must be stabilized—and, ideally, gradually reduced."[119]

A recommendation like this raises the question: How do we go about reducing the world's population? Don't worry, the "experts" have some "solutions."

IT'S INCREDIBLE HOW OFTEN NEW FEARS ABOUT THE ENVIRONMENT WORK OH-SO-PERFECTLY WITH THE LEFTIST IDEAS OF THE PAST.

The letter suggests reducing worldwide fertility rates by simply expanding "family-planning services," and achieving "full gender equity" for women. Or, put more bluntly: We need more abortions to save the planet.

In 2016, academics at Georgetown University and Johns Hopkins University more thoroughly explored the idea of population control in a paper titled "Population Engineering and the Fight against Climate Change." In the paper, environmentalists Colin Hickey, Jake Earl, and Travis Rieder outlined several population-control policies that they said are "pragmatically and morally justified" and necessary to save the planet. The authors evaluate each option using a "coercion spectrum."[120]

The least-coercive side of the spectrum contained policies similar to that of the letter signed by 11,000 scientists previously referenced. (Hickey, Earl, and Rieder label expanding access to abortion as "choice enhancement.")

Further down the coercion spectrum is "preference adjustment," which aims to change cultural norms and encourage people to have fewer children through the use of propaganda. The authors envision the use of mass media, radio, TV, billboards, information campaigns, "assemblies in public schools," celebrity endorsements, and more to convince people to stop having kids.

The researchers also recommended policymakers consider "incentivization." Under this category, the government would use the tax code to "incentivize" people into having fewer children—effectively punishing families for having kids and awarding people for remaining childless.

In a free society, these moral questions are left to individuals, who can choose whether to have children based on any criteria they want—including crazy environmental

fears and doomsday scenarios. But under a socialist system, such decisions are inevitably put in the hands of the collective and the people they put in positions of power. Given all the insane things the Left has said in recent years about population control efforts, this shouldn't just concern you; *it should terrify you*. If it doesn't, it's time to get your head examined.

CHAPTER 8
FINAL PAGE
LAYOUT
COMPLETE

A BETTER WAY

FINAL
APPROVED
-GB

GLENN
BECK
FREE
MARKETS
=
FREE
PEOPLE
+
PROSPERITY
Approval
GLENN
Page Number
360
Fix No. 7.2

"THE MOMENT THE IDEA IS ADMITTED INTO
SOCIETY, THAT PROPERTY IS NOT AS SACRED AS
THE LAWS OF GOD, AND THAT THERE IS NOT A
FORCE OF LAW AND PUBLIC JUSTICE TO PROTECT
IT, ANARCHY AND TYRANNY COMMENCE. IF 'THOU
SHALT NOT COVET,' AND 'THOU SHALT NOT
STEAL,' WERE NOT COMMANDMENTS OF HEAVEN,
THEY MUST BE MADE INVIOLABLE PRECEPTS IN
EVERY SOCIETY, BEFORE IT CAN BE CIVILIZED
OR MADE FREE."[1]

— JOHN ADAMS

When was the last time you went to the grocery store and stood in awe at just how truly amazing these modern marvels are? Meats, breads, fruits, cheeses, and green things—eh, I mean vegetables— as far as the eye can see. And the Twinkies—oh, the Twinkies. You can buy dozens of them for less than 10 bucks. Grocery stores really are *remarkable* places.

Okay, you're probably thinking I've lost it, but don't close the book just yet. Really think about it. One hundred years ago, many homes still didn't have electricity or cars or refrigerators. If you wanted to store food, you needed to pay an "ice man" to come to your home to literally chip off a block of ice that could keep a small batch of produce cool. Televisions didn't exist, and neither did computers. It was common for people to die at birth, and many died from diseases that essentially no longer exist in the United States. Something as simple as the flu could wipe out millions in a single year. The Spanish flu of 1918 infected half-a-billion people worldwide, and it killed more than 675,000 Americans.[2]

INFECTIOUS DISEASE IS THE ONE THING THAT CAN COMPETE WITH THE DEATH COUNT OF SOCIALISM. BUT, GIVE THE SOCIALISTS A LITTLE TIME. THIS RACE ISN'T OVER YET!

YOU DON'T NECESSARILY NEED A CHOICE OF 23 UNDERARM SPRAY DEODORANTS OR OF 18 DIFFERENT PAIRS OF SNEAKERS...[a]

- BERNIE SANDERS

Today, people are healthier, wealthier, happier, and safer than they have ever been before. Americans generally live long lives, even those without much wealth, and high-quality, affordable food is available in every town in the country.

Man went from the farm and fire, to supermarkets and space travel in less than 200 years. Why? What happened?

At almost any other time in human history, going back for thousands of years, a store comparable to your run-of-the-mill modern

grocery store would have been considered a wonder of the world. Sure, markets existed in ancient times, and in some important cities, you could buy products from hundreds of miles away, but they were nothing like our modern grocery stores, where you can buy in a single trip apples from Washington State, oranges from Brazil, prosciutto from Italy, chocolate from Belgium, cheese from Wisconsin, cereal from Mexico, coffee from Colombia, and milk from a nearby dairy— now some believe this is a bad thing due to carbon emissions etc., but before we throw the baby out with the bathwater, let's realize what it means to the health and welfare of the entire world to destroy the very system that man has never seen before and has saved the lives of hundreds of millions of people.

And when you shop, you probably do so wearing clothes made from all over the world, too—a baseball cap from Bangladesh, a shirt produced in Indonesia, and jeans made in Turkey. As you walk through the grocery store, you'll see signs crafted by artists in New York City, televisions designed in Japan, and you'll always be able to shop in comfort, thanks to modern air-conditioning and heating systems. When you purchase items, you'll be able to pay for your entire order using a single plastic card, which will transmit financial data near-instantaneously and automatically to your bank, so that you'll know down to the penny how much money you have available to spend.

Many of us then drive home in a car that may also have been made on the other side of the world and listen the whole ride home to an audiobook purchased while waiting in the checkout line with a supercomputer smartphone. (Maybe you're even listening to the audio version of this book on the way home from the store now.)

For thousands of years, people couldn't even begin to fathom something as remarkable as a modern trip to the grocery store. But today, these wonders are ubiquitous. Americans don't stand in awe at grocery stores anymore. In fact, they often treat going to them as though it were a tedious chore. Many of us—myself included—don't take nearly enough time in our daily lives to stop and realize just how incredible our world is, nor do we take the time to think about how we got here. How is it that it took thousands of years for humans to produce these luxuries? Why is it that we develop more technological innovations in just one month in modern times than we did in whole centuries in the past? Were humans in the ancient world just plain stupid?

Although humans' technological achievements progressively increased over many millennia, the pace of that development has rapidly risen over the past 500 years, and especially in the past two centuries. And there's one thing that occurred during that period that sets it apart from every other period in human history: individual freedom. Once people were free to own their own property, open new businesses in relatively free markets, and speak, write, associate, and worship freely, the world began to dramatically progress in ways that it never had before.

This isn't a coincidence. Prior to the Enlightenment and creation of the New World, economies were often centrally planned and subject to the whims of a monarch, emperor, or military despot. People generally lived and died within a single, relatively small geographic area, often where they were born. Cultures, ideas, and innovations were typically slow to travel as a result. People had little reason or resources to leave their homes, and ruling classes kept lower classes from becoming too wealthy or powerful. People didn't bother innovating, except in their own personal lives, because the rewards for doing so were often confiscated by someone else. And when people weren't dying from disease or the elements, they were often fighting in some king's war or battling foreign invaders.

The development of personal liberty, the rule of law, and property rights created unprecedented opportunities. For the first time, people could pursue their passions and compete with others in relatively open marketplaces. The best ideas flourished, and the worst were quickly swept away. Only those who continuously innovated and

were willing to work hard thrived, weeding out many outdated ideas.

With the birth of America, humans enjoyed even greater individual liberties and property rights, and talented people from around the world flocked to its shores—from China, Ireland, Italy, Germany, and many other nations—to enjoy the economic and personal freedoms generations before them could have only dreamed of. Freedom built our marvelous modern world by rewarding innovators and allowing people to live without fear of being punished for their religious views or political philosophies, among other things.

That's not to say there weren't mistakes made along the way, including some incredibly tragic errors. It would take more than a half-century after the birth of America for slavery to be completely abolished, and many decades more before African Americans, women, and other groups would enjoy the full range of liberties others previously had benefited from. But once liberty was fully granted to all people, innovation and wealth in the United States increased even more quickly.

A FREER, RICHER WORLD

Throughout much of the Western world, those of us who believe in the power of free markets have been

THOUGHT EXPERIMENT...

Imagine being in the 1960s. Girls are screaming for the Beatles, TVs are still mostly black and white, and computers are the size of rooms. Now imagine the government deciding it wants to set upon a mission to create powerful supercomputers so small they can fit in your pocket, and they want enough for everyone. Also, they want to accomplish this within 50 years.

A politician would be laughed out of office, and rightfully so. Based on examples of government's failures presented earlier in this book, this hypothetical government mission would probably end up with the cell phone equivalent of the Trabant (if you don't know what a Trabant is, "google it" on your pocket-sized supercomputer).

But that impossible mission was accomplished by the free market.

Today, smartphones have more computing capabilities than the entirety of NASA did when it sent the first men to the moon in 1969. Modern smartphones are simultaneously supercomputers, high definition cameras, GPS devices, translators, TVs, and gaming systems, and provide countless other services. Oh, yeah, and they still make phone calls. And on top of all that, they are relatively cheap enough for most people to obtain without breaking the bank.

told for decades that our ideas were once meaningful but have since been replaced with better, more enlightened ideas about how to order society. We've been told that freedom is an outdated, quaint notion, one that's holding the world back from reaching its full potential. "If only you were willing to give away your freedom," we've been told, "to an army of well-educated, highly skilled bureaucrats, you'd have better lives and all of the world's ills could be cured."

But if history has taught us anything over the past century, it's this: More freedom equals wealthier, healthier, and safer communities, and the more centralized power becomes in society, the greater the tragedies that inevitably follow. This formula isn't merely based on the experience of one or two nations, but rather the entire world. And it isn't an idea that has only proven to be true in some distant period in history, but rather throughout all of history, including the modern age.

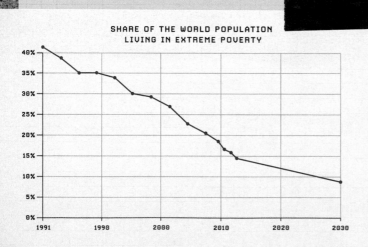

SHARE OF THE WORLD POPULATION LIVING IN EXTREME POVERTY

ACCORDING TO WORLD BANK DATA, THE % OF THE WORLD POPULATION LIVING IN EXTREME POVERTY FELL FROM 36% IN 1990 TO JUST 10% IN 2015.[b]

Almost nightly, at cocktail parties in cities like Los Angeles, New York, and San Francisco, socialists talk about how they're *so worldly* and how ignorant Americans are in the Heartland when it comes to the so-called achievements of the rest of the world. "If only those deplorables would spend more time reading *The New Yorker* and less time riding around on their tractors, they'd see how fabulously central planning works."

But if the "enlightened" Left spent more time looking at hard data and less time reading left-wing echo chambers like *The New Yorker*, they'd know that recent history has perhaps revealed the power of free-market economics better than any other time in history. While the Left has spent the past few decades trying to push America toward socialism, much of the rest of the world has been running in the opposite direction. And those that haven't—places like North Korea and Venezuela—have become, well, hellholes.

Take India, for example. As late as the 1980s, India was still trying (and failing) to find ways to make socialism work. Indian central planners knew they had access to tremendous natural resources and labor, but they couldn't find an effective strategy that would keep the nation's markets, wealth, and property tightly controlled while also spurring economic growth. India was rapidly falling behind the rest of the world.

As *Reason*'s Sam Staley notes, "India became the poster child for post–World War II socialism in the Third World. Steel, mining, machine tools, water, telecommunications, insurance, and electrical plants, among other industries, were effectively nationalized in the mid-1950s as the Indian government seized the commanding heights of the economy."[3]

The results were disastrous. "Manufacturing never took off," Staley explained, "and the economy meandered; India lagged behind all its trade-embracing contemporaries. Between 1950 and 1973, Japan's economy grew 10 times faster than India's. South Korea's economy grew five times faster. India's economy crawled along at 2 percent per year between 1973 and 1987, while China's growth leapt to 8 percent and

began matching rates for Hong Kong, Taiwan, and other Asian tigers. Even as that reality became clear as early as the late 1960s and early 1970s, India's policy makers refused to give up on economic planning."

As a result of this failure, by 1993 more than 430 million Indians were living below the international poverty line.[4] That's 100 million more people than the current population of the United States.

But then everything changed. In the early 1990s, India started to open its markets to foreign investment and stopped fixing its exchange rate. It chose not to impose the same burdensome regulations on the new and growing technology sector as it had in other industries. It eventually privatized some state-owned businesses and reduced regulations. With these additional freedoms came prosperity. India's gross domestic product grew (in current U.S. dollars) from $279 billion in 1993 to $2.72 trillion in 2018, an increase of 874 percent. Over the same period, Germany's GDP increased by just 94 percent.[5]

In his book *The Conservative Heart*, Arthur Brooks, the president of the American Enterprise Institute, explains that thanks to India's free-market reforms, India "is simply not the same country as it was in 1983," when socialist policies continued to hold the country back. Brooks notes, "In the past twenty years, poverty in India has been cut by more than half, as free enterprise has pulled some 200 million people out of poverty. Between 1965 and 1975, per capita income in India rose by just 0.3 percent annually. But from 2005 to 2013, that figure more than doubled, from $740 to $1,570. If India continues growing at these rates, it will cease to be a poor country in the next few decades."[6]

China has also experienced rapid economic growth since deciding a few decades ago to liberalize certain parts of its economy. This decision can be traced back to 1978, when Chinese officials traveled across the world to learn from the achievements

of other nations. Rainer Zitelmann, Ph.D., the author of *The Power of Capitalism*, notes, "Chinese delegations made over 20 trips to more than 50 countries including Japan, Thailand, Malaysia, Singapore, the United States, Canada, France, Germany and Switzerland," and what they found astounded them. After decades behind the "Bamboo Curtain," the Chinese saw the significant economic gains made by countries throughout the world, including many Asian nations long thought by the Chinese to be inferior. In particular, they were interested in the advancements made by Singapore.

At a meeting in 1978, former Singaporean prime minister Lee Kuan Yew told Chinese communist leader Deng Xiaoping that the success they were starting to experience in Singapore could be achieved throughout China, if the country were willing to open its markets and increase private property rights. According to the *South China Morning Post*, Lee reminded Deng "that the Singapore Chinese were descendants of illiterate landless peasants from Guangdong and Fujian,"[7] but now, those same Singaporeans were more successful and wealthy than many of those more educated families still living in China.

According to Lee's memoirs, Lee told Deng, "There was nothing that Singapore had done which China could not do, and do better." Lee then recalls that Deng "stayed silent," but over the next decade, Deng started to dramatically reform the country in line with some of the reforms suggested by Lee, and even "told the Chinese people to do better than Singapore." When that happened, Lee says he "knew [Deng] had taken up the challenge I quietly tossed to him that night 14 years earlier."

As I noted way back in Chapter 2, in the early 1980s, China responded to this challenge by decollectivizing its agricultural system and forming "Special Economic Areas" that allowed the Chinese to experiment with market-based reforms. As a result of the success of these experiments, the Chinese transitioned the country to its current model, one in which private property ownership is tolerated and markets are much freer than they have been since the Communist Party rose to power in the early twentieth century.

The effects of these reforms, as imperfect as they are, have been nothing short of astounding. From 1960 to 1990, China's GDP increased by about 500 percent ($300 billion), and from 1990 to 2018, China's GDP grew by $13.2 trillion, a 3,680 percent increase.[8]

That's not to say China and India have totally adopted free-market principles or that either nation has rid itself of poverty; they've done neither, in fact. As the Heritage Foundation wrote in a 2019 report, "China remains 'mostly unfree.' Nontransparent state-owned enterprises dominate the financial sector and many basic industries. The official ideology of 'Socialism with Chinese Characteristics' has chilled liberalization, heightened reliance on mercantilism, raised bureaucratic hurdles to trade and investment, weakened the rule of law, and strengthened resistance from vested interests that impede more dynamic economic development."[9]

HONG KONG AND CHINA'S "THIRD WAY"

Some have pointed to China's economic success as proof that there can be a "Third Way" to manage economies, a blend of limited private property ownership and socialist central planning and reduced individual freedom. But the Chinese need not look further than their own shores to find ironclad proof of why their top-down, heavily regulated, limited liberty model doesn't work nearly as well as those models that feature much freer markets.

Hong Kong—which had been under British control for 156 years—continues to have one of the freest and most successful economies in the world, thanks to a special agreement that has allowed it to operate with economic autonomy since rejoining China in 1997. According to reports by the Heritage Foundation, Cato Institute, and Fraser Institute, Hong Kong ranks first among all nations for its economic freedom.[10,11] Citizens of Hong Kong enjoy strong property rights protections, a very small regulatory burden, and many civil liberties protections. The income tax burden is also low, and the tax system is extremely efficient. Individuals only pay 15 percent of their income in taxes, and the top corporate rate is just 16.5 percent.[12]

Hong Kong's free-market policies have made its economy the envy of the world and have allowed it to far surpass the achievements gained in China. As I mentioned previously, since 1960, China has experienced remarkable economic growth. Its per-capita GDP has risen significantly, thanks in large part to the free-market reforms enacted in the 1990s and 2000s. But even with this growth and the huge demographic advantages China enjoys over Hong Kong, Hong Kong has substantially *expanded* its economic advantage over China. Since 1960, Hong Kong's per-capita GDP has risen from $429 to $48,717, an increase of 11,255 percent. Today, the per-capita GDP in Hong Kong is $38,947 more than it is in China. In 1960, the gap was just $340.[13]

Hong Kong's economic miracle hasn't been a mistake or a mere coincidence, and neither have similar economic booms experienced in places like Singapore. They are the direct result of free-market reforms, including increased property rights protections. And the growth experienced in nations formally dominated by strict socialist policies, like China and India, serves as a clear example of the power of economic freedom and individual choice. Even modest free-market reforms in those nations have liberated hundreds of millions of people from extreme poverty.

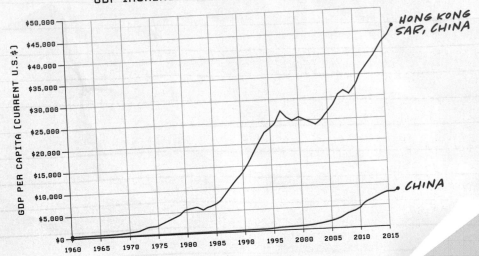

HONG KONG'S SKYROCKETING GDP

FROM 1960 TO 2018, HONG KONG PER-CAPITA GDP INCREASED FROM $429 TO $48,717[c]

CAPITALISM IS FOR DREAMERS

In the eighteenth century, few saw the potential of the United States. The kings, emperors, and aristocrats of Europe thought little of roughneck Americans on the other side of the world, and why would they? After all, Americans didn't have lavish palaces or a storied history—at least, not compared to the centuries-old monarchies of the Old World. Much of the United States was, as it is now, composed of immigrants or the children or grandchildren of immigrants. We had very different religious beliefs and, in many respects, cultures—and that was considered by many to be a weakness.

A nation that didn't share a uniform culture, religion, and governing structure was thought to be unsustainable and potentially vulnerable to foreign invasion.

But whatever disadvantages—real or imagined—the United States suffered from in its earliest days were more than made up for by Americans' devotion to the promise that "all men are created equal" and "endowed by their Creator with certain unalienable rights." Freedom in all aspects of life—personal, economic, and spiritual—drew millions of people, from every corner of the Earth, to the United States' "New World." And while they may not have had identical religious beliefs, personal ambitions, or a common ethnic heritage, they all shared in the same foundational idea that people freed from the shackles of an all-powerful, centralized ruling class could do amazing things, and that the world is a better place when people have the liberty to pursue their own unique passions, rather than have them imposed on them. For two centuries, America flourished because of liberty, not in spite it. And as a result, the United States is now the world's most powerful nation, even though it contains only a small fraction of the global population.

Free markets, coupled with constitutional rights and a representative republican government, are at the heart of America's success. Without free markets, the United States wouldn't be the economic juggernaut it is today. Its people wouldn't enjoy one of the highest living standards in the world, and they wouldn't have the highest disposable incomes, either.[14] They wouldn't have the world's most technologically advanced workforce or medical system. They wouldn't have been able to rid the country of countless diseases that have plagued mankind for centuries, and the United States wouldn't be the home to many of the world's most important and innovative businesses and scientists.

Without free markets, Americans wouldn't have been able to liberate Europe from Nazi Germany or save millions of people around the world from infectious diseases. They wouldn't have been able to win the Cold War and force the Soviets

FOR A GREAT RESOURCE OF ALL OF THE INCREDIBLE THINGS FREE MARKETS HAVE ACHIEVED, READ *ADDICTED TO OUTRAGE* BY GLENN BECK. THAT'S RIGHT, I'M SELLING YOU MY OWN BOOK INSIDE MY BOOK THAT YOU JUST BOUGHT. CAPITALISM AT WORK.

— GLENN :)

to withdraw from Eastern Europe, and they wouldn't have been able to serve as a home to countless refugees escaping tyranny from around the world. Without America's market economy, millions of additional people in countries in Africa, Asia, Europe, and South America would be living in poverty.

Without free enterprise, Americans wouldn't have been able to build the internet—the world's greatest example of the success of the free market. Virtually everyone—even socialists—agrees the internet is one of the modern world's most powerful marketplaces and sources of information, and the fact that it has largely been left alone by the world's army of regulators that have screwed up so many other parts of the global economy is a big reason why the internet remains so successful. Every day on the internet, countless thousands of businesses, news outlets, niche websites, and cooking blogs compete with one another, driving unprecedented innovation. The best ideas thrive, and the worst fade away. It's arguably the most efficient, freest marketplace in human history, and as a result, it's wildly successful. That's not a coincidence, it's free-market principles at work.

And when you are reflecting on the amazing innovations brought on by the internet and countless other game-changing inventions, think about what is in store for us in the next few decades. It is increasingly likely that the average person won't even have to travel to the grocery store. Packages containing any good you can image will be dropped off at your doorstep by automated drones, without you even having to physically order them. Within the next couple of decades, we'll have fleets of self-driving cars take us to any destination we desire at a level of comfort and safety far beyond what we experience today. And we cannot even fathom how artificial intelligence will revolutionize our entire world, especially the health care field. We are just now figuring out how to use AI to sift through unlimited amounts of medical data to develop diagnoses with better accuracy than the best medical experts ever could. With free markets driving innovation, the potential for human progress is quite literally unlimited.

A capitalist system that depends on truly free markets isn't merely one economic option out of several a free society could embrace, it is the *only* option for a liberated people. Any form of collective decision-making stifles diversity; it doesn't enhance it, because collective systems like socialism empower the majority to impose its will on minority groups of every kind. As Ayn Rand correctly recognized, "The smallest minority on Earth is the individual," and the individual is always deprived of its essential freedoms under a socialist model.

The image so many Americans now have of capitalism is one of corruption, backroom deals, and cronyism. But this isn't what I mean when I talk about the benefits of free markets. Crony capitalism is a funhouse-mirror distortion of capitalism, and it can only exist in a society in which government has been given far too much power. The last thing we should do to "fix" the problems pervasive in our current system is to give even more power to those who have worked so hard and so effectively to screw it up in the first place.

I understand why so many people find socialism to be an appealing option. They look around at the systems in place throughout the United States today and think, "This can't be the best we can do." They face ever-rising health care costs, send their kids to failing schools, pay outrageously high student loan bills, and watch as one promise after another made by politicians is broken. They know the economy isn't working for everyone, and they're right. Then they hear politicians, activists, academics, Hollywood celebrities, and even businesspeople who sound sincere say that free markets are the problem, that the existence of markets is the reason people are suffering. But there simply is no truth to these claims, as I've shown throughout this book.

Socialists also criticize free markets because they recognize that when people are free to make choices, some people make poor decisions. Some even suffer immensely because of them. In every free society on Earth, there are people struggling. Some are workaholics. Some are greedy. Some have substance abuse problems. Many are addicted to materialism. And it's not hard to find these problems in the United States, where consumerism has in many ways become a new religion.

No one understands these issues better than I do. When I was in my 30s, I had a highly successful and lucrative career—money, cars, and the latest and greatest television. And I spent most of my time chasing even more wealth and success, and boy, was I great at it. But here's the thing, I was miserable. On the surface, to many, my life looked near to perfection, but beneath the surface, my life was falling apart. In one sense, I was benefiting immensely from free markets. But in another sense, the materialism that had taken hold of my life was making it increasingly more difficult to do the things I knew in my heart were necessary to become a better person.

Free markets aren't good or bad. They don't cause problems. People, acting freely within those markets, create problems. Capitalism in a free society is merely a highly efficient vehicle for achieving whatever desires are in man's heart. Perhaps the internet is the best illustration of this. On the internet, you can find virtually anything you want. You can discover important truths from the past, develop a new breakthrough product or service, organize thousands or even millions of people to engage in a positive like-minded cause, or provide people with ideas or products that they simply can't get anywhere else.

But the internet can also be used to tear others down, gossip, harass, intimidate, lie, and steal. Some use the internet to feed their addiction to materialism or pornography. The internet can be used for any number of destructive, hateful, or even violent purposes.

So, is the internet good or bad? The truth is, it's neither. Like every market, the actions that occur within it are merely the reflections of the people in the market. If those within a free society are using their freedom to hurt others, it's not freedom that's the problem, it's the people. Socialists understand that people are flawed, but they think they can overcome those flaws by empowering the collective. Does this make sense? Why would 300 million flawed people be better equipped to manage the affairs of your own household, of people they know nothing about and have never met?

If you want to fix the many problems facing the world—and I have no doubt that if you've read this far into this book, you do—then the best thing you can do is to reform your own heart and be a force for good in the lives of those around you. If you think for even one moment that building yet another gigantic government social program is going to accomplish that, you're going to live the rest of your life in extreme disappointment.

Happiness comes from serving others, not serving yourself or forcing others to serve you. That's a lesson that took me many years to learn, but it's one that has allowed me to rebuild my life and fill those voids in my own heart that I tried foolishly for years to fill with material wealth and success.

When socialists encounter a problem, they simply ask, "How can I force people to act the way I think they should?" Entrepreneurs and small business owners, on the other hand, see the world as it is and ask, "How can I make a product or service so effective and inventive that others will desperately want to voluntarily buy it?" Socialism is an ideology of manipulation, control, and force. It can't function without coercion.

On the other hand, capitalism—a truly free-market system, not corrupt, crony capitalism—isn't, as so many socialists say, a system built on greed or hate or racism or corporatism. Free-market capitalism is for hard workers, entrepreneurs, planners, thinkers, freedom fighters, inventors, and, most importantly, *dreamers*.

Some Americans wrongly think that conservatives want to keep things as they are, but that's not what we're hoping to "conserve." We're not foolishly working to keep the world trapped in a time capsule, but rather to maintain and even enhance our freedoms so that we can radically change the world for the better. We're not opposed to progress. Quite the contrary, in fact; we're hopelessly obsessed with progress, which is why we're so opposed to government's tireless efforts to stop or slow innovation in the name of "social justice." There is nothing good for society that comes from stunting economic growth and nothing "just" about tyranny.

If you're a socialist, maybe you've read through this book and remain skeptical of the benefits of free markets and the dangers of socialism. Good. Question everything you've read here and everything you've heard elsewhere with *boldness*, and do your own homework. Don't take my word for it, or anyone else's for that matter. All that I ask is that you continue to pursue the truth in *all* things, but especially on the question of socialism. If you do, you'll find we have more in common than you might think—or want to admit.

GLENN BECK
ARGUING WITH SOCIALISTS

FOR MORE
INFO VISIT
GLENNBECK.COM

- END OF THE BOOK

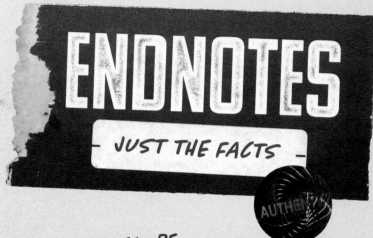

FACTS CAN BE
STUBBORN THINGS!

1. SETTING THE STAGE

1   See "Full Transcript: Donald Trump's Jobs Plan Speech," Politico, June 28, 2016, https://www
    .politico.com/story/2016/06/full-transcript-trump-job-plan-speech-224891

2   See Tara Golshan, "Read: Bernie Sanders Defines His Vision for Democratic Socialism in the
    United States," Vox, June 12, 2019, https://www.vox.com/2019/6/12/18663217/bernie-sanders
    -democratic-socialism-speech-transcript

3   Ted Cruz, Betsy DeVos, and Bradley Byrne, "America's Students Deserve Freedom to Choose
    Their Education Options: DeVos, Cruz, Byrne," USA Today, February 28, 2019, https://www
    .usatoday.com/story/opinion/2019/02/28/trump-school-choice-students-education-options
    -scholarships-tax-credits-column/3002868002

4   Elizabeth Warren, "Ending the Stranglehold of Health Care Costs on American Families,"
    Medium, November 1, 2019, https://medium.com/@teamwarren/ending-the-stranglehold-of
    -health-care-costs-on-american-families-bf8286b13086

5   "Socialism," Merriam-Webster's Dictionary, merriam-webster.com, accessed November 6, 2019,
    https://www.merriam-webster.com/dictionary/socialism

6   "Communism," Merriam-Webster's Dictionary, merriam-webster.com, accessed November 6, 2019,
    https://www.merriam-webster.com/dictionary/communism

7   "Capitalism," Merriam-Webster's Dictionary, merriam-webster.com, accessed November 6, 2019,
    https://www.merriam-webster.com/dictionary/capitalism

2. CAPITALISM: BABY OR BATHWATER?

GRAPHIC CALLOUTS

a   Susan Warren, "Ocasio-Cortez Blasts Capitalism as an 'Irredeemable' System," Bloomberg,
    March 9, 2019, https://www.bloomberg.com/news/articles/2019-03-10/ocasio-cortez-blasts
    -capitalism-as-an-irredeemable-system

b   Cardi B: Jenna Lemoncelli, "Cardi B Posted an Explosive Rant Demanding to Know What
    the Government is Doing with Her Tax Money: 'I Want Receipts,'" Business Insider,
    March 23, 2018, https://www.businessinsider.com/cardi-b-calls-out-government-tax
    -money-2018-3

c   Robber Barons: Thomas DiLorenzo, How Capitalism Saved America (New York, NY: Random House,
    2005).

d   Based on data from U.S. Food and Nutrition Service, "SNAP Data Tables," U.S. Department of
    Agriculture, accessed November 2019, https://www.fns.usda.gov/pd/supplemental-nutrition
    -assistance-program-snap

e   Tara O'Neill Hayes, "Medicaid Enrollment and Expenditure Projections: 2015-2024," American
    Action Forum, August 2, 2016, https://www.americanactionforum.org/weekly-checkup/medicaid
    -enrollment-expenditure-projections-2015-2024/

f   Jordan Peterson, "2017 Personality 13: Existentialism via Solzhenitsyn and the Gulag,"
    YouTube, March 11, 2017, https://www.youtube.com/watch?v=w84uRYq0Uc8

g   Encyclopaedia Britannica, "Special Economic Zone," accessed November 1, 2019, https://www
    .britannica.com/topic/special-economic-zone

h   Peter G. Peterson Foundation, "Student Debt Continues to Rise," July 18, 2018, https://www
    .pgpf.org/blog/2018/07/the-facts-about-student-debt

i   Matt Palumbo, "The High Cost of 'Free' College," bongino.com, November 25, 2018, https://
    bongino.com/the-high-cost-of-free-college

j   Mark J. Perry, "Chart of the Day. . . . or Century?," aei.org, American Enterprise Institute,
    January 11, 2019, https://www.aei.org/carpe-diem/chart-of-the-day-or-century. Data from U.S.
    Bureau of Labor Statistics.

----

1   Tristan Justice, "7 Staggering Quotes Made by Progressive Democrats' New Star," The Daily
    Signal, November 6, 2018, https://www.dailysignal.com/2018/11/06/7-staggering-quotes-made
    -from-progressive-democrats-new-star

2   Michael Burke, "Ocasio-Cortez: 'Capitalism is Irredeemable,'" The Hill, March 10, 2019, https://
    thehill.com/homenews/house/433394-ocasio-cortez-capitalism-is-irredeemable

3   Bernie Sanders, "Breaking Up the Oligarchy," speech at the CAP Ideas Conference in
    Washington, D.C., May 15, 2018, https://medium.com/@SenSanders/breaking-up-the-oligarchy-
    603bc0d47264

4   Justin Sink, "Congress Less Popular than Colonoscopies, Root Canals, Poll Finds," The Hill,
    January 8, 2013, https://thehill.com/blogs/blog-briefing-room/news/276121-poll-congress
    -less-popular-than-colonoscopies-root-canals-nickleback

5   See San Merica, "Trump Gets 2 Scoops of Ice Cream, Everyone Else Gets 1—and Other Top Lines
    from His Time Interview," CNN.com, updated May 11, 2017, https://www.cnn.com/2017/05/11
    /politics/trump-time-magazine-ice-cream/index.html

6   Federal Reserve Bank of St. Louis, "Who Owns Reserve Banks?," Making Sense of the Federal
    Reserve, accessed August 22, 2019, https://www.stlouisfed.org/in-plain-english/who-owns-the
    -federal-reserve-banks

7   Peter Schiff, from speech titled "Why the Meltdown Should Have Surprised No One," delivered
    at the Ludwig von Mises Institute's Austrian Scholars Conference, March 13, 2009, https://www
    .youtube.com/watch?v=EgMclXX5msc

8   Freddie Mac, "What We Do," freddiemac.com, accessed August 22, 2019, http://www.freddiemac
    .com/about/faqs.html

9   Peter Wallison, "Hey, Barney Frank: The Government Did Cause the Housing Crisis," The
    Atlantic, December 13, 2011, https://www.theatlantic.com/business/archive/2011/12/hey
    -barney-frank-the-government-did-cause-the-housing-crisis/249903

10 Charles W. Calomiris and Peter J. Wallison, "The Last Trillion-Dollar Commitment," aei.org,
    American Enterprise Institute, September 30, 2008, https://www.aei.org/publication/the-last
    -trillion-dollar-commitment

11 Peter Wallison, "The True Story of the Financial Crisis," The American Spectator, May 13, 2011,
    https://www.aei.org/publication/the-true-story-of-the-financial-crisis

12 Laura Woods, "10 Billionaires Like Oprah Winfrey Who Grew Up Poor," CNBC, September 11, 2017,
    https://www.cnbc.com/2017/09/11/10-billionaires-who-grew-up-dirt-poor.html

13 Branko Milanovic, Global Inequality: A New Approach for the Age of Globalization, Belknap
    Press: Cambridge, Massachusetts, April 11, 2016.

14 Gautam Nair, "Most Americans Vastly Underestimate How Rich They Are Compared with the
    Rest of the World. Does It Matter?," The Washington Post, August 23, 2018, https://www
    .washingtonpost.com/news/monkey-cage/wp/2018/08/23/most-americans-vastly-underestimate
    -how-rich-they-are-compared-with-the-rest-of-the-world-does-it-matter

15 Robert Rector, "The War on Poverty Has Been a Colossal Flop," The Daily Signal, September 16,
    2014, https://www.dailysignal.com/2014/09/16/war-poverty-colossal-flop

16 World Health Organization, "Household Air Pollution and Health," who.int, May 8, 2018, https://
    www.who.int/news-room/fact-sheets/detail/household-air-pollution-and-health

17 Chelsea Follett, "Middle Class Shrinking... As Households Become Richer," Cato at Liberty, Cato
    Institute, September 18, 2019, https://www.cato.org/blog/middle-class-shrinking-households
    -become-richer

18 U.S. Food and Nutrition Service, "Supplemental Nutrition Assistance Program Participation
    and Costs," U.S. Department of Agriculture, accessed August 22, 2019, https://www.fns.usda
    .gov/pd/supplemental-nutrition-assistance-program-snap

19 Samantha Artiga and Robin Rudowitz, "Medicaid Enrollment Under the Affordable Care Act:
    Understanding the Numbers," Kaiser Family Foundation, January 29, 2014, https://www.kff.org
    /health-reform/issue-brief/medicaid-enrollment-under-the-affordable-care-act
    -understanding-the-numbers

20 U.S. Centers for Medicare and Medicaid Services, "May 2019 Medicaid & CHIP Enrollment
    Data Highlights," medicaid.gov, accessed August 23, 2019, https://www.medicaid.gov
    /medicaid/program-information/medicaid-and-chip-enrollment-data/report-highlights
    /index.html

21 Federal Reserve Bank of Atlanta, "Wage Growth Tracker," frbatlanta.org, accessed August 23,
    2019, https://www.frbatlanta.org/chcs/wage-growth-tracker.aspx

22 U.S. Bureau of Labor Statistics, "Job Openings and Labor Turnover Summary," bls.gov, August 6,
    2019, https://www.bls.gov/news.release/jolts.nr0.htm

23 HealthPocket, "Average Market Premiums Decrease in 2019 For the First Time," healthpocket.com, November 28, 2018, https://www.healthpocket.com/healthcare-research/infostat/2019-average-market-premiums-decrease#.XWAR6HdFxPY

24 Edward Glaeser, "The War on Work—and How to End It," City Journal, 2017, accessed August 23, 2019, https://www.city-journal.org/html/war-work-and-how-end-it-15250.html

25 Federal Reserve Bank of St. Louis, "Civilian Labor Force Participation Rate: Men," FRED, fred.stlouisfed.org, accessed August 23, 2019, https://fred.stlouisfed.org/series/LNS11300001

26 Jonathan Ingram and Nicholas Horton, Work Requirements are Working in Arkansas: How Commonsense Welfare Reform is Improving Arkansans' Lives, Foundation for Government Accountability, January 9, 2019, https://thefga.org/research/work-requirements-arkansas

27 Lyndon Johnson, State of the Union Address before the 88th U.S. Congress, January 8, 1964, made available online by the National Archives and Miller Center at the University of Virginia, https://millercenter.org/the-presidency/presidential-speeches/january-8-1964-state-union

28 Robert Rector, supra note 15.

29 Samuel Stebbins, "The Cities Hit Hardest by Extreme Poverty," 24/7 Wall St., April 25, 2019, https://www.msn.com/en-us/money/realestate/the-cities-hit-hardest-by-extreme-poverty/ar-BBWg7PK

30 John York, "Firing a Bad Federal Employee May Get a Little Easier," The Heritage Foundation, July 19, 2018, https://www.heritage.org/government-regulation/commentary/firing-bad-federal-employee-may-get-little-easier

31 Ali Meyer, "Workers in Private Sector Are 3 Times More Likely to Get Fired Than Gov't Workers," Washington Free Beacon, August 11, 2016, https://freebeacon.com/issues/workers-private-sector-3-times-likely-get-fired-govt-workers

32 Ready, Willing & Able, "About: History," The Doe Fund, doe.org, accessed August 27, 2019, https://www.doe.org/about/history

33 Howard Husock, "Lesson For April 15: Why Government Can't Replace Charity," Forbes, April 10, 2014, https://www.forbes.com/sites/howardhusock/2014/04/10/lesson-for-april-15-why-government-cant-replace-charity/#79ddd86979e2

34 Cincinnati Works, 2018 Annual Report, accessed August 28, 2019, http://cincinnatiworks.org/wp-content/uploads/2019/04/2018-Annual-Report.pdf

35 Howard Husock, supra note 33.

36 Michael Tanner, "Five Myths about Economic Inequality in America," Policy Analysis, No. 797, Cato Institute, September 7, 2016, https://www.cato.org/publications/policy-analysis/five-myths-about-economic-inequality-america?gclid=CJ0KCQjwwIPrBRCJARIsAF1UT8_CC4EoaB2jFHmL-5RXX-LLDhG_ZOGpXtxQSYrxZZEaLsdLoNosoyMaAu3rEALw_wcB

37 Federal Reserve Bank of St. Louis, "Life Expectancy at Birth, Total for the United States," FRED database, accessed August 24, 2019, https://fred.stlouisfed.org/series/SPDYNLE00INUSA

38 Jayson Lusk, The Evolving Role of the USDA in the Food and Agricultural Economy, Mercatus Center, June 2016, https://www.mercatus.org/system/files/Lusk-USDA-v1.pdf

39 U.S. Census Bureau, "Computer and Internet Use in the United States: 2016," American Community Survey Reports, census.gov, August 2018, https://www.census.gov/content/dam/Census/library/publications/2018/acs/ACS-39.pdf

40 Michael Tanner, supra note 36.

41 Gene Fox, "The Government Takeover of Student Lending," Forbes, May 11, 2010, https://www.forbes.com/2010/05/10/student-loans-hcera-leadership-education-fox.html#448e28906edd

42 Ibid.

43 Ibid.

44 "Feds take over student loan program from banks," San Francisco Chronicle, March 10, 2010, https://www.sfgate.com/business/networth/article/Feds-take-over-student-loan-program-from-banks-3193888.php

45 See Justin Haskins, "Hey Bernie, I've Got $500,000 in Student Loan Debt—but You Can Keep Your Government Handout," FoxNews.com, June 27, 2019, https://www.foxnews.com/opinion/justin

-haskins-hey-bernie-ive-got-500000-in-student-loan-debt-but-you-can-keep-your
-government-handout, citing National Center for Education Statistics, "Average
undergraduate tuition and fees and room and board rates charged for full-time students in
degree-granting postsecondary institutions, by level and control of institution: Selected
years, 1963-64 through 2017-18," Table 330.10, Digest of Education Statistics, accessed
August 26, 2019, https://nces.ed.gov/programs/digest/d18/tables/dt18_330.10.asp

46   Susan Dynarski, "America Can Fix Its Student Loan Crisis. Just Ask Australia," The New York
     Times, July 9, 2019, https://www.nytimes.com/2016/07/10/upshot/america-can-fix-its-student
     -loan-crisis-just-ask-australia.html

47   OECD, "Population with Tertiary Education," OECD Data, accessed August 26, 2019, https://data
     .oecd.org/eduatt/population-with-tertiary-education.htm

48   OECD, "Statistical Insights: What does household debt say about financial resilience?,"
     oecd.org, accessed August 26, 2019, https://www.oecd.org/sdd/fin-stats/statisticalin
     sightswhatdoeshouseholddebtsayaboutfinancialresilience.htm

49   See, for example, edX, "HarvardX," edx.org, accessed December 3, 2019, https://www.edx.org
     /school/harvardx

50   Liberty University, "Liberty University Quick Facts," liberty.edu, accessed December 3, 2019,
     https://www.liberty.edu/aboutliberty/index.cfm?PID=6925

51   Dominic Rushe, "The US Spends More on Education than Other Countries. Why is It Falling
     Behind?," The Guardian (U.K.), September 7, 2018, https://www.theguardian.com/us-news/2018
     /sep/07/us-education-spending-finland-south-korea

52   Grace Lin, "States That Spend the Most and Least on Education," Yahoo! Finance, March 7, 2019,
     https://finance.yahoo.com/news/states-spend-most-least-education-090000945.html

53   Adam McCann, "2019's States with the Best & Worst School Systems," WalletHub, July 29, 2019,
     https://wallethub.com/edu/states-with-the-best-schools/5335

54   Greg Forster, A Win-Win Solution: The Empirical Evidence on School Choice (Fourth Edition),
     EdChoice, May 2016, http://www.edchoice.org/wp-content/uploads/2016/05/A-Win-Win-Solution
     -The-Empirical-Evidence-on-School-Choice.pdf

55   American Hospital Association and Manatt, Regulatory Overload: Assessing the Regulatory
     Burden on Health Systems, Hospitals and Post-acute Care Providers, October 2017, https://www
     .aha.org/sites/default/files/regulatory-overload-report.pdf

56   Aaron E. Carroll, "The Real Reason the U.S. Has Employer-Sponsored Health Insurance," The New
     York Times, September 5, 2017, https://www.nytimes.com/2017/09/05/upshot/the-real-reason
     -the-us-has-employer-sponsored-health-insurance.html

57   Ibid.

58   Edmund Haislmaier and Doug Badger, "How Obamacare Raised Premiums," Backgrounder, No. 3291,
     The Heritage Foundation, March 5, 2018, https://www.heritage.org/health-care-reform/report
     /how-obamacare-raised-premiums

59   HealthPocket, supra note 23.

60   Mark J. Perry, "If Cosmetic Surgery Has a Working Market, Why Can't Medical Care?," Foundation
     for Economic Education, fee.org, March 22, 2017, https://fee.org/articles/if-cosmetic-surgery
     -has-a-working-market-why-can-t-medical-care

61   Ibid.

62   Joseph A. DiMasi, Henry G. Grabowski, and Ronald W. Hansen, "Innovation in the Pharmaceutical
     Industry: New Estimates of R&D Costs," Journal of Health Economics, Vol. 47, May 2016,
     pp. 20-33, https://www.sciencedirect.com/science/article/abs/pii/S0167629616000291

63   U.S. Food and Drug Administration, "Frequently Asked Questions on Patents and Exclusivity,"
     fda.gov, accessed September 27, 2019, https://www.fda.gov/drugs/development-approval
     -process-drugs/frequently-asked-questions-patents-and-exclusivity

64   Bartley Madden, Free To Choose Medicine: Better Drugs Sooner at Lower Cost, Third Edition,
     (Arlington Heights, IL: The Heartland Institute, 2018), http://freetochoosemedicine.com

65   Kimberly Leonard, "Ted Cruz Bill Would Speed FDA Approval of Drugs OK'd in Other
     Countries," Washington Examiner, July 18, 2019, https://www.washingtonexaminer.com
     /policy/healthcare/ted-cruz-bill-would-speed-fda-approval-of-drugs-okd-in-other
     -countries

66   World Bank, "China: GDP (current US$)," data.worldbank.org, accessed September 12, 2019, https://data.worldbank.org/indicator/NY.GDP.MKTP.CD?locations=CN

3. IS SOCIALISM JUST "SHARING AND CARING"?

a   Mao Zedong, Quotations from Chairman Mao Tse-Tung: The Little Red Book. Initially published in 1964 by the People's Liberation Army's General Political Department.

b   From "Joseph Stalin: TIME Person of the Year 1942," Time Magazine, January 4, 1943.

c   Reuters, "Venezuela's New Plan to Beat Hunger: Breed Rabbits," reuters.com, September 14, 2017, https://www.reuters.com/article/us-venezuela-rabbits/venezuelas-new-plan-to-beat -hunger-breed-rabbits-idUSKCN1BP232; BBC News, "Venezuela's 'Plan Rabbit' Encounters 'Cultural Problem,'" bbcnews.com, September 14, 2017, https://www.bbc.com/news/world-latin -america-41265474

d   Encyclopaedia Britannica, "Hundred Flowers Campaign," accessed December 12, 2019, https:// www.britannica.com/event/Hundred-Flowers-Campaign

e   Charlie Parker, "Police Arresting Nine People a Day in Fight Against Web Trolls," The Times (U.K.), October 12, 2017, https://www.thetimes.co.uk/article/police-arresting-nine-people -a-day-in-fight-against-web-trolls-b8nkpgp2d; Brendan O'Neill, "Britain Turns Offensive Speech Into a Police Matter," Reason, September 15,2018, https://reason.com/2018/09/15 /britain-turns-offensive-speech-into-a-po; Sadie Levy Gale, "Arrests for Offensive Facebook and Twitter Posts Soar in London," Independent (U.K.), June 4, 2016, https://www .independent.co.uk/news/uk/arrests-for-offensive-facebook-and twitter-posts-soar-in -london-a7064246.html

f   Direct quote from Ryan McMaken, "Japanese Americans, Internment, Democracy, and the U.S. Government," Mises Institute, February 21, 2014,https://mises.org/blog/japanese-americans -internment-democracy-and-us-government

g   Lion Summerbell and Joshua Smith, "The Second Amendment is a Threat to Us All," Democratic Socialists of America, February 19, 2018, https://www.dsausa.org/democratic-left/the_second _amendment_is_a_threat_to_us_all

h   Friedrich A. Hayek, "Planning, Science, and Freedom," Nature, Issue No. 3759, November 15, 1941. Made available by the Mises Institute, https://mises.org/library/planning-science-and -freedom

i   See Rose Wilder Lane, "Democracy," in Mises Institute, "Liberty versus Democracy," July 4, 2007, https://mises.org/library/liberty-versus-democracy

----

1   See Mark Perry, "20 Quotes that Explain Why Capitalism is Better than Socialism," American Enterprise Institute, January 27, 2019, https://www.aei.org/carpe-diem/20-quotes-that -explain-why-capitalism-is-better-than-socialism, citing Ludwig von Mises, Bureaucracy (New Haven, CT: Yale University Press, 1944), https://mises-media.s3.amazonaws.com/Bureaucracy_3 .pdf

2   Frank Newport, "The Meaning of 'Socialism' to Americans Today," Gallup.com, October 4, 2018, https://news.gallup.com/opinion/polling-matters/243362/meaning-socialism-americans-today .aspx

3   E.J.E. Hobsbawm, "Karl Heinrich Marx," Oxford Dictionary for National Biography, updated May 28, 2015, https://www.oxforddnb.com/view/10.1093/ref:odnb/9780198614128.001.0001/odnb -9780198614128-e-39021

4   See Glenn Beck, Liars: How Progressives Exploit Our Fears for Power and Control (Threshold Editions: New York, NY, 2016).

5   See, for example, Joseph Schwartz and Jason Schulman, "Toward Freedom: Democratic Socialist Theory and Practice," December 21, 2012, dsausa.org, https://www.dsausa.org/strategy/toward _freedom

6   Karl Marx, The Communist Manifesto, Amazon Digital Services, Kindle Edition, n.d., pp. 13-14, ASIN: B00MJJ7YZE.

7   Socialist Party of Great Britain, "What Is Socialism?," worldsocialism.org, accessed May 25, 2018, https://www.worldsocialism.org/spgb/what-socialism

GRAPHIC CALLOUTS

8   Ibid.

9   Socialist Party USA, "Socialism as Radical Democracy: Statement of Principles of the Socialist Party USA," socialistpartyusa.net, accessed August 30, 2019, https://www.socialistpartyusa.net/principles-points-of-agreement

10 Karl Marx, supra note 6, p. 20.

11 Karl Marx, supra note 6.

12 Jeff Desjardins, "CHARTS: Venezuela's Economic Tragedy," Business Insider, September 6, 2017, https://www.businessinsider.com/charts-venezuelas-economic-tragedy-2017-9

13 Ibid.

14 Encyclopaedia Britannica, "Marcos Pérez Jiménez," britannica.com, last updated September 16, 2019, https://www.britannica.com/biography/Marcos-Perez-Jimenez

15 Jeff Desjardins, supra note 12.

16 Ibid.

17 Encyclopaedia Britannica, "The Hugo Chávez Presidency," britannica.com, accessed September 27, 2019, https://www.britannica.com/place/Venezuela/The-Hugo-Chavez-presidency

18 Caracas Newsroom, "Factbox: Venezuela's nationalizations under Chavez," Reuters, October 7, 2012, https://www.reuters.com/article/us-venezuela-election-nationalizations/factbox-venezuelas-nationalizations-under-chavez-idUSBRE89701X20121008

19 Ibid.

20 Ibid.

21 See Office of U.S. Sen. Bernie Sanders, "Must Reads," sanders.senate.gov, accessed September 1, 2019, https://www.sanders.senate.gov/newsroom/must-read/close-the-gaps-disparities-that-threaten-america

22 David Sirota, "Hugo Chavez's Economic Miracle," Salon, March 6, 2013, https://www.salon.com/2013/03/06/hugo_chavezs_economic_miracle

23 Washington Times Editorial Board, "Admiring Hugo Chavez," The Washington Times, March 7, 2013, https://www.washingtontimes.com/news/2013/mar/7/admiring-hugo-chavez

24 Ibid.

25 Steven John, "9 Mind-Blowing Facts About Venezuela's Economy," Market Insider, May 23, 2019, https://markets.businessinsider.com/news/stocks/venezuela-economy-facts-2019-5-1028225117#inflation-in-venezuela-may-hit-10-million-percent-this-year1

26 Ibid.

27 Valentina Sanchez, "Venezuela Hyperinflation Hits 10 million Percent. 'Shock Therapy' May Be Only Chance to Undo the Economic Damage," CNBC.com, August 3, 2019, https://www.cnbc.com/2019/08/02/venezuela-inflation-at-10-million-percent-its-time-for-shock-therapy.html

28 Sara Malm, "Starving Thieves Steal Animals from Venezuelan Zoo to EAT as the Country Struggles with Chronic Food Shortages," Daily Mail (U.K.), August 16, 2017, https://www.dailymail.co.uk/news/article-4797338/Police-believe-thieves-steal-Venezuela-zoo-animals-eat-them.html

29 Jonah ben Avraham, "Looking Closer at Free Speech," Socialist Worker, March 15, 2017, https://socialistworker.org/2017/03/15/looking-closer-at-free-speech

30 Ibid.

31 Constitution of the Union of Soviet Socialist Republics, Ninth Convocation, adopted on October 7, 1977, made available by Bucknell University, https://www.departments.bucknell.edu/russian/const/77cons02.html

32 California Alien Land Act of 1913, State of California, 1913, text made available by Moor Park College, accessed September 3, 2019, http://sunny.moorparkcollege.edu/~ccopsey/Hist14_Webdocs/CA1913AlienLandAct.pdf

33 See Glenn Beck, supra note 4.

34   Franklin Roosevelt Presidential Library and Museum, "Three Key Questions," accessed September 3, 2019, https://www.fdrlibrary.org/documents/356632/390886/Japanese+American+Internment+Three+Key+Questions.pdf/aa171cea-c4f0-4ab2-b674-5277d047331b

35   Robert Caro, Means of Ascent: The Years of Lyndon Johnson (Knopf: New York, NY, 1990).

36   W. Gardner Selby, "Lyndon Johnson Opposed Every Civil Rights Proposal Considered in His First 20 Years as Lawmaker," PolitiFact, April 14, 2014, https://www.politifact.com/texas/statements/2014/apr/14/barack-obama/lyndon-johnson-opposed-every-civil-rights-proposal

37   Ben Casselman, Matthew Conlen, and Reuben Fischer-Baum, "Gun Deaths in America," Five ThirtyEight, accessed September 3, 2019, https://fivethirtyeight.com/features/gun-deaths

38   Leah Libresco, "I Used to Think Gun Control Was the Answer. My Research Told Me Otherwise," The Washington Post, October 3, 2017, https://www.washingtonpost.com/opinions/i-used-to-think-gun-control-was-the-answer-my-research-told-me-otherwise/2017/10/03/d33edca6-a851-11e7-92d1-58c702d2d975_story.html

39   Michael Planty and Jennifer L. Truman, Firearm Violence, 1993-2011, NCJ 241730, Bureau of Justice Statistics, U.S. Department of Justice, May 2013, https://www.bjs.gov/content/pub/pdf/fv9311.pdf

40   Alan I. Leshner et al., eds., Priorities for Research to Reduce the Threat of Firearm-Related Violence (National Academies Press: Washington, D.C., 2013), https://www.nap.edu/read/18319/chapter/1

41   U.S. Census Bureau, "Homeownership Rate for the United States," retrieved from Federal Reserve Bank of St. Louis, accessed September 4, 2019, https://fred.stlouisfed.org/series/RHORUSQ156N

42   U.S. Small Business Administration, "2018 Small Business Profile," sba.gov, accessed September 4, 2019, https://www.sba.gov/sites/default/files/advocacy/2018-Small-Business-Profiles-US.pdf

43   Meagan Day, "The Electorate Is Already on Board with Socialism," Jacobin, August 30, 2019, https://www.jacobinmag.com/2019/08/page-kreisman-oregon-democratic-socialist

44   Adam Buick, "A Question of Definition: Socialism/Communism," Socialist Standard, Issue 886, June 1978, https://www.worldsocialism.org/spgb/socialist-standard/1970s/1978/no-886-june-1978/question-definition-4-socialismcommunism

45   Ibid.

46   Karl Marx and Frederick Engels, Manifesto of the Communist Party (Charles H. Kerr & Company: Chicago, IL, 1888), available online at https://en.wikisource.org/wiki/Manifesto_of_the_Communist_Party

47   "Capitalism," Merriam-Webster's Dictionary, merriam-webster.com, accessed November 6, 2019, https://www.merriam-webster.com/dictionary/capitalism

48   Socialist Party USA, "Socialism as Radical Democracy: Statement of Principles of the Socialist Party USA," socialistpartyusa.net, accessed September 6, 2019, https://www.socialistpartyusa.net/principles-points-of-agreement

49   Communist Party USA, "About CPUSA," cpusa.org, accessed September 7, 2019, https://www.cpusa.org/about-us

50   Becky Little, "How the Nazis Were Inspired by Jim Crow," History.com, updated May 20, 2019, https://www.history.com/news/how-the-nazis-were-inspired-by-jim-crow

51   Church of Jesus Christ of Latter-Day Saints, "Extermination Order," churchofjesuschrist.org, accessed September 7, 2019, https://www.churchofjesuschrist.org/study/history/topics/extermination-order?lang=eng

52   Dick Komer, Michael Bindas, and Tim Keller, "Answers to Frequently Asked Questions About Blaine Amendments," Institute for Justice, accessed September 7, 2019, https://ij.org/issues/school-choice/blaine-amendments/answers-frequently-asked-questions-blaine-amendments

53   Reason TV, "Capitalism vs. Socialism: A Soho Forum Debate," YouTube.com, posted November 14, 2019, https://www.youtube.com/watch?v=YJQSuUZdcV4&t=1553s

4. SOCIALIST "UTOPIAS" & THEIR BLOODY HISTORY OF FAILURE

a   See Encyclopaedia Britannica, "Commune of Paris," accessed December 12, 2019, https://www
    .britannica.com/event/Commune-of-Paris-1871

b   Steve George and Tim Hume, "Khmer Rouge Leaders Found Guilty of Genocide in Landmark
    Ruling," cnn.com, November 16, 2018, https://www.cnn.com/2018/11/16/asia/khmer-rouge
    -genocide-guilty-intl/index.html

c   Tania Branigan, "China's Great Famine: The True Story," The Guardian (U.K.), January 1, 2013,
    https://www.theguardian.com/world/2013/jan/01/china-great-famine-book-tombstone

d   Associated Press, "Cuba Starts Widespread Rationing of Food and Other Basics," May 10, 2019,
    https://www.cbc.ca/news/world/cuba-food-shortage-rationing-1.5132297

e   Andrew Egger, "One Woman's Struggle for Freedom in Castro's Cuba," The Daily Signal, July 26,
    2016, https://www.dailysignal.com/2016/07/26/one-womans-struggle-for-freedom-in-castros
    -cuba

f   National Museum of American History, "German 'Nazi' Swastika Flag," accessed November 1,
    2019, https://americanhistory.si.edu/collections/search/object/nmah_1357427

g   Human Rights Foundation, "Ji Seong-ho," accessed December 12, 2019, https://hrf.org/event
    _speakers_posts/ji-seong-ho

h   See Holodomor National Awareness Tour et al., "Holodomor: Stalin's Secret Genocide," YouTube,
    2016, https://www.youtube.com/watch?v=Sr5WkhEiqcY&t

i   Edith Lederer, "Villagers Lament Ceausescu's Razing of Homes: Romania: The Dictator Wanted
    to Eliminate Small Settlements so People Could Be Better Controlled. His Overthrow Saved
    Some Homes," Los Angeles Times and Associated Press, March 4, 1990, https://www.latimes.com
    /archives/la-xpm-1990-03-04-mn-2534-story.html

j   H. David, "Romania Ends Compulsory Childbearing," Entre Nous, 14-15, June 1990, https://www
    .ncbi.nlm.nih.gov/pubmed/12222213

k   Siobhan Heanue, "Zimbabwe's White Farmers Consider Returning Years After Brutal Land
    Seizures," ABC.net, Australian Broadcasting Corporation, August 29, 2018, https://www.abc.net
    .au/news/2018-08-30/zimbabwes-white-farmers-consider-return-after-land-seizures/10176760

l   Rondel Davidson, "La Reunion," Texas State Historical Association, accessed November 10, 2019,
    https://tshaonline.org/handbook/online/articles/uel01

---

1   Winston Churchill, speech before the U.K. House of Commons, October 22, 1945. Quote made
    available by the Churchill Project, Hillsdale College, accessed September 14, 2019, https://
    winstonchurchill.hillsdale.edu/socialism-is-the-philosophy-of-failure-winston-churchill

2   William Bradford, Of Plymouth Plantation, ed. Harold Paget (Portcullis Books, 2016), Amazon
    Kindle version, p. 49.

3   See, for example, History.com, "Plymouth Colony," updated August 20, 2019, https://www
    .history.com/topics/colonial-america/plymouth

4   William Bradford, supra note 2, p. 85.

5   William Bradford, Bradford's History of Plymouth Plantation: 1620-1647 (American Council of
    Learned Societies, 2011), Amazon Kindle edition.

6   Ibid.

7   Encyclopaedia Britannica, "Commune of Paris," accessed December 3, 2019, https://www
    .britannica.com/event/Commune-of-Paris-1871

8   Lara Pawson, "Angola's brutal history, and the MPLA's role in it, is a truth that we must tell,"
    The Guardian, May 5, 2014, https://www.theguardian.com/commentisfree/2014/may/05/angola
    -brutal-history-mpla-leftwing-discipline-betrayal

9   Encyclopaedia Britannica, "Popular Movement for the Liberation of Angola," accessed
    September 16, 2019, https://www.britannica.com/topic/Popular-Movement-for-the-Liberation
    -of-Angola

10 Holocaust Memorial Day Trust, "Khmer Rouge Ideology," hmd.org, accessed September 17, 2019,
    https://www.hmd.org.uk/learn-about-the-holocaust-and-genocides/cambodia/khmer-rouge
    -ideology/

GRAPHIC CALLOUTS

11   Ibid.

12   "Khmer Rouge: Cambodia's years of brutality," BBC News, November 16, 2018, https://www.bbc
     .com/news/world-asia-pacific 10604399

13   Jean-Louis Panne et al., The Black Book of Communism: Crimes, Terror, Repression (Cambridge,
     MA: Harvard University Press, 1999).

14   See Lee Edwards, "The Legacy of Mao Zedong is Mass Murder," The Heritage Foundation,
     February 2, 2010, https://www.heritage.org/asia/commentary/the-legacy-mao-zedong-mass
     -murder

15   Ibid.

16   Vaclav Smil, "China's Great Famine: 40 Years Later," BMJ, Issue 7225, pp. 1619-1621, https://www
     .ncbi.nlm.nih.gov/pmc/articles/PMC1127087

17   See Lee Edwards, supra note 14.

18   Erin Blakemore, "How the Castro Family Dominated Cuba for Nearly 60 Years," March 15, 2019,
     History.com, https://www.history.com/news/cuba-after-castro-miguel-diaz-canel

19   Investor's Business Daily, "The Fidel Castro Myth Debunked: The Death Of A Tyrant, Not A Hero,"
     Editorial Board, November 26, 2018, https://www.investors.com/politics/editorials/the-fidel
     -castro-myth-debunked-the-death-of-a-tyrant-not-a-hero, citing R.J. Rummel, Democide in
     Totalitarian States: Mortacracies and Megamurderers, in Israel Charny [Ed.], The Widening
     Circle of Genocide: Genocide: A critical Bibliographic Review, Volume 3 (Piscataway, NJ:
     Transaction Publishers, 1994), http://www.hawaii.edu/powerkills/CHARNY.CHAP.HTM

20   Fabiola Santiago, "History of the Cuban Revolution Marked by Tens of Thousands Fleeing the
     Island for the U.S.," Miami Herald, November 26, 2016, https://www.miamiherald.com/news
     /nation-world/world/americas/cuba/article117194848.html

21   Ibid.

22   "The Fidel Castro Myth Debunked: The Death of a Tyrant, Not a Hero," Editorial Board,
     Investor's Business Daily, November 26, 2018, https://www.investors.com/politics/editorials
     /the-fidel-castro-myth-debunked-the-death-of-a-tyrant-not-a-hero

23   See Matthew Day, "Nazis may have killed up to 20m, claims 'shocking' new Holocaust study,"
     The Telegraph, March 4, 2013, https://www.telegraph.co.uk/news/worldnews/europe/germany
     /9906771/Nazis-may-have-killed-up-to-20m-claims-shocking-new-Holocaust-study.html,
     citing data from the U.S. Holocaust Memorial Museum, https://www.ushmm.org

24   George Reisman, "Why Nazism Was Socialism and Why Socialism Is Totalitarian," Mises Institute,
     November 11, 2005, https://mises.org/library/why-nazism-was-socialism-and-why-socialism
     -totalitarian

25   Ibid.

26   George Watson, "Hitler and the Socialist Dream," Independent, November 22, 1998, https://www
     .independent.co.uk/arts-entertainment/hitler-and-the-socialist-dream-1186455.html

27   R.J. Rummel, "Democide in Totalitarian States: Mortacracies and Megamurderers," in Israel
     Charny [Ed.], The Widening Circle of Genocide: Genocide: A Critical Bibliographic Review, Vol. 3,
     Transaction Publishers, 1994. http://www.hawaii.edu/powerkills/CHARNY.CHAP.HTM

28   "North Korea: How many political prisoners are detained in prison?," BBC News, May 10, 2018,
     https://www.bbc.com/news/world-asia-44069749

29   Human Rights Watch, "North Korea: Events of 2018," hrw.org, accessed September 17, 2019,
     https://www.hrw.org/world-report/2019/country-chapters/north-korea

30   Ben Quinn, "Unicorn Lair 'Discovered' in North Korea," The Guardian (U.K.), November 30, 2012,
     https://www.theguardian.com/world/2012/nov/30/unicorn-lair-discovered-north-korea

31   Sarah Son and Markus Bell, "North Korea: How Public Execution Sites Are Being Mapped with
     Google Earth Satellite Images," The Conversation, August 28, 2019, http://theconversation
     .com/north-korea-how-public-execution-sites-are-being-mapped-with-google-earth-satellite
     -images-122246

32   See review by Palash Ghosh, "How Many People Did Joseph Stalin Kill?," International
     Business Times, May 3, 2013, https://www.ibtimes.com/how-many-people-did-joseph-stalin
     -kill-1111789

33 Encyclopaedia Britannica, "The Famine of 1932-33," accessed September 17, 2019, https://www
    .britannica.com/place/Ukraine/The-famine-of-1932-33

34 NPR Radio, "1930s Famine Still Mars Russia-Ukraine Relations," Morning Edition, aired July 21,
    2009, https://www.npr.org/templates/story/story.php?storyId=106835755

35 Ibid.

36 Ibid.

37 Encyclopaedia Britannica, "Communist Romania," accessed September 17, 2019, https://www
    .britannica.com/place/Romania/Communist-Romania

38 Daniel McLaughlin, "Ceausescu Regime Used Children as Police Spies," The Guardian (U.K.),
    July 21, 2006, https://www.theguardian.com/world/2006/jul/22/mainsection.international1

39 R.J. Rummel, Statistics of democide: genocide and mass murder since 1900, Transaction
    Publishers, 1997.

40 See Carolina Moreno, "Hundreds Of Children In Venezuela Are Starving To Death, Says New York
    Times Report," HuffPost, December 18, 2017, https://www.huffingtonpost.com/entry/hundreds
    -of-children-in-venezuela-are-starving-to-death-nytimes-reports_us_5a380d7fe4b0fc99
    878dd05d

41 Juan Forero and Maolis Castro, "Venezuela's Brutal Crime Crackdown: Executions, Machetes
    and 8,292 Dead," The Wall Street Journal, December 21, 2017, https://www.wsj.com/articles
    /venezuelas-brutal-crime-crackdown-executions-machetes-and-8-292-dead-1513792219

42 Vasco Cotovio and Emanuella Grinberg, "At Least 40 Venezuelans Have Been Killed in Recent
    Protests," CNN.com, January 29, 2019, https://www.cnn.com/2019/01/29/americas/venezuela
    -protests-deaths/index.html

43 Merrit Kennedy, "U.N. Says More Than 4 Million People Have Left Venezuela," NPR, June 7, 2019,
    https://www.npr.org/2019/06/07/730687807/u-n-says-more-than-4-million-people-have-left
    -venezuela

44 R.J. Rummel, supra note 27.

45 Rodion Ebbighausen, "Vietnam's fight Against Hunger–A Success Story," Deutsche Welle,
    dw.com, May 27, 2019, https://www.dw.com/en/vietnams-fight-against-hunger-a-success
    -story/a-18477927

46 See Kelvin Kudenga, "Mugabe should be jailed for his murderous crimes," The Zimbabwean,
    July 21, 2017, https://www.thezimbabwean.co/2017/07/mugabe-jailed-murderous-crimes

47 Stuart Doran, "New documents claim to prove Mugabe ordered Gukurahundi killings," The
    Guardian, May 19, 2015, https://www.theguardian.com/world/2015/may/19/mugabe-zimbabwe
    -gukurahundi-massacre-matabeleland

48 Conor Gaffey, "Zimbabwe President Robert Mugabe: 'We Will Not Prosecute Killers of White
    Farmers,'" Newsweek, August 16, 2017, https://www.newsweek.com/zimbabwe-president-robert
    -mugabe-white-farmers-651326

49 Ibid.

50 Encyclopaedia Britannica, "Reign of Terror," last updated August 29, 2019, https://www
    .britannica.com/event/Reign-of-Terror

51 Spencer Kimball, "Fact or Fiction: Adolf Hitler Won an Election in 1932," Deutsche Welle,
    dw.com, August 29, 2015, https://www.dw.com/en/fact-or-fiction-adolf-hitler-won-an
    -election-in-1932/a-18680673

52 Max Fisher, "Who Is Venezuela's Legitimate President? A Messy Dispute, Explained," New York
    Times, February 4, 2019, https://www.nytimes.com/2019/02/04/world/americas/venezuela
    -maduro-guaido-legitimate.html

53 World Bank, Poverty & Equity Data Portal, "India," accessed September 12, 2019, http://
    povertydata.worldbank.org/poverty/country/IND

54 Arthur C. Brooks, The Conservative Heart (New York, NY: Broadside Books, 2017), Kindle Edition,
    p. 112.

55 Robert Rector, "The War on Poverty Has Been a Colossal Flop," The Daily Signal, September 16,
    2014, https://www.dailysignal.com/2014/09/16/war-poverty-colossal-flop

56   Sally Pipes, "Good News About Obamacare Premiums Can't Hide Long-Term Pain Donald Trump is Trying
       to Fix," USA Today, October 8, 2018, https://www.usatoday.com/story/opinion/2018/10/08/obamacare
       -premiums-democrats-donald-trump-insurance-aca-coverage-mandate-column/1444804002

57   National Center for Education Statistics, "Average undergraduate tuition and fees and
       room and board rates charged for full-time students in degree-granting postsecondary
       institutions, by level and control of institution: Selected years, 1963-64 through 2017-18,"
       Table 330.10, Digest of Education Statistics, accessed August 26, 2019, https://nces.ed.gov
       /programs/digest/d18/tables/dt18_330.10.asp

58   Kimberly Amadeo, "What the Economy Was Like in the 1920s," The Balance, updated June 25,
       2019, https://www.thebalance.com/roaring-twenties-4060511

59   History.com, "The Roaring Twenties History," updated May 16, 2019, https://www.history.com
       /topics/roaring-twenties/roaring-twenties-history

60   Sarwat Jahan, Ahmed Saber Mahmud, and Chris Papageorgiou, "What Is Keynesian Economics?,"
       Finance & Development, Volume 51, No. 3, September 2014, https://www.imf.org/external/pubs
       /ft/fandd/2014/09/basics.htm

61   Mitchell Nemeth, "18 Facts on the US National Debt That Are Almost Too Hard to Believe,"
       Foundation for Economic Education, September 17, 2019, https://fee.org/articles/18-facts-on
       -the-us-national-debt-that-are-almost-too-hard-to-believe

62   Robert P. Murphy, "The Depression You've Never Heard Of: 1920-1921," Foundation for Economic
       Education, November 18, 2009, https://fee.org/articles/the-depression-youve-never-heard
       -of-1920-1921

63   Ibid.

64   Ibid.

65   Ibid.

66   Kimberly Amadeo, "Unemployment Rate by Year Since 1929 Compared to Inflation and GDP," The
       Balance, updated July 27, 2019, https://www.thebalance.com/unemployment-rate-by-year-3305506

67   Ibid.

68   Robert P. Murphy, supra note 62.

5. SWEDISH-STYLE SOCIALISM

a   The Heritage Foundation, 2018 Index of Economic Freedom, accessed November 29, 2018,
      https://www.heritage.org/index/ranking

b   The Heritage Foundation, 2019 Index of Economic Freedom, accessed December 12, 2019, https://
      www.heritage.org/index/ranking

c   See Samuel Gregg, "Remembering Karl Marx, Prophet of Violence and Terror," The Catholic
      World Report, May 4, 2018, https://www.catholicworldreport.com/2018/05/04/remembering
      -karl-marx-prophet-of-violence-and-terror

d   Inter IKEA Group, "Milestones in Our History," ikea.com, accessed December 12, 2019, https://
      inter.ikea.com/en/about-us/milestones

e   "Accidental Revolutionary," Nation of Sweden, sweden.se, accessed December 12, 2019, https://
      sweden.se/culture-traditions/astrid-lindgren-spoke-people-listened

f   EdChoice, "How Does School Choice Affect Public Schools?," edchoice.org, June 2017, https://
      www.edchoice.org/wp-content/uploads/2017/06/School-Choice-and-Public-Schools.pdf

g   Forbes, "Forbes Releases 37th Annual Forbes 400 Ranking of the Richest Americans," forbes
      .com, October 3, 2018, https://www.forbes.com/sites/forbespr/2018/10/03/forbes-releases
      -37th-annual-forbes-400-ranking-of-the-richest-americans/#1912696e5cb1

h   Uirimchi Pillutla, Hannah Maslen, and Julian Savulescu, "Rationing elective surgery for
      smokers and obese patients: responsibility or prognosis?," BMC Medical Ethics, Volume 19,
      Issue 28, 2018, doi:10.1186/s12910-018-0272-7

i   Kevin Pham, "'Socialist' Nordic Countries Are Actually Moving Toward Private Health Care," The
      Daily Signal, June 13, 2019, https://www.dailysignal.com/2019/06/13/socialist-nordic
      -countries-are-actually-moving-toward-private-health-care

GRAPHIC
CALLOUTS

----

1   Kelsey Bolar, "'The Squad' Is Only the Beginning of Nancy Pelosi's Problems," The Daily Signal,
    July 22, 2019, https://www.dailysignal.com/2019/07/22/the-squad-is-only-the-beginning-of
    -nancy-pelosis-problems

2   Jennifer Bendery, "Bernie Sanders: What's Wrong With America Looking More Like Scandinavia?,"
    HuffPost, May 3, 2015, https://www.huffingtonpost.com/2015/05/03/bernie-sanders
    -campaign_n_7199546.html

3   Kerry Jackson, "Denmark Tells Bernie Sanders It's Had Enough Of His 'Socialist' Slurs,"
    Investor's Business Daily, November 9, 2015, https://www.investors.com/politics/commentary
    /denmark-tells-bernie-sanders-to-stop-calling-it-socialist

4   2018 Index of Economic Freedom, The Heritage Foundation, accessed November 29, 2018,
    https://www.heritage.org/index/ranking

5   Ibid.

6   Ibid.

7   Anthony B. Kim and Julia Howe, "Why Democratic Socialists Can't Legitimately Claim Sweden,
    Denmark as Success Stories," The Heritage Foundation, August 10, 2018, https://www.heritage
    .org/international-economies/commentary/why-democratic-socialists-cant-legitimately
    -claim-sweden-denmark

8   John Stossel and Tanvir Toy, "Sweden Is Not a Socialist Success," Reason.com, October 23, 2018,
    https://reason.com/reasontv/2018/10/23/stossel-sweden-not-a-socialist-success

9   Free To Choose Network, "Sweden: Lessons for America?," September 21, 2018, https://www
    .youtube.com/watch?v=jq3vUbdgMuQ&t=1444s

10 Per Bylund, "Stagnating Socialist Sweden," mises.org, Mises Institute, January 11, 2011,
    https://mises.org/library/stagnating-socialist-sweden

11 See Per Bylund, "Stagnating Socialist Sweden," mises.org, Mises Institute, January 11, 2011,
    https://mises.org/library/stagnating-socialist-sweden, citing Bjuggren and Johansson in
    Swedish Economics Association's Journal Ekonomisk Debatt, 2009.

12 For source, see: https://archive.org/details/TheMagicLantern-BiographyOfIngmarBergman

13 Atlas Network, "The Story of Sweden Is About Markets, Not Socialism," atlasnetwork.org,
    September 17, 2018, https://www.atlasnetwork.org/news/article/the-story-of-sweden-is-about
    -markets-not-socialism

14 Niv Elis, "Democrats Give Cold Shoulder to Warren Wealth Tax," The Hill, August 9, 2019,
    https://thehill.com/homenews/administration/456739-democrats-give-cold-shoulder-to
    -warren-wealth-tax

15 Taylor LaJoie, "Senator Sanders Proposes a Tax on 'Extreme' Wealth," Tax Foundation,
    September 25, 2019, https://taxfoundation.org/bernie-sanders-wealth-tax

16 Adam Sabes, "Joe Biden and Kamala Harris Agree on One Thing: Raising Taxes," atr.org,
    Americans for Tax Reform, July 3, 2019, https://www.atr.org/joe-biden-and-kamala-harris
    -agree-one-thing-raising-taxes

17 Rocky Mengle, "2020 Election: Tax Plans for All 24 Democratic Presidential Candidates,"
    Kiplinger, updated August 1, 2019, https://www.kiplinger.com/slideshow/taxes/T043-S001-tax
    -plans-2020-democratic-presidential-candidates/index.html

18 Kyle Pomerleau, "How Scandinavian Countries Pay for Their Government Spending," Tax
    Foundation, June 10, 2015, https://taxfoundation.org/how-scandinavian-countries-pay-their
    -government-spending

19 Alexandra Hudson, "School Voucher Systems Across the Globe Make the Case for School Choice
    in the U.S.," edchoice.org, July 19, 2016, https://www.edchoice.org/blog/school-voucher
    -systems-across-globe-make-case-school-choice-u-s

20 Bernie 2020, "A Thurgood Marshall Plan for Public Education," berniesanders.com,
    accessed August 9, 2019, https://berniesanders.com/a-thurgood-marshall-plan-for-public
    -education

21 Greg Forster, A Win-Win Solution: The Empirical Evidence on School Choice (Fourth Edition),
    EdChoice, May 2016, http://www.edchoice.org/wp-content/uploads/2016/05/A-Win-Win-Solution
    -The-Empirical-Evidence-on-School-Choice.pdf

22 Tommy Schultz, "National School Choice Poll Shows 67% of Voters Support School Choice," American Federation for Children and Beck Research, January 17, 2019, https://www.federationforchildren.org/national-school-choice-poll-shows-67-of-voters-support-school-choice-2019

23 Norwegian Petroleum, "Production Forecasts," norskpetroleum.no, accessed August 9, 2019, https://www.norskpetroleum.no/en/production-and-exports/production-forecasts

24 Rob Davies, "Norway's $1tn Wealth Fund to Divest from Oil and Gas Exploration," The Guardian (U.K.), March 8, 2019, https://www.theguardian.com/world/2019/mar/08/norways-1tn-wealth-fund-to-divest-from-oil-and-gas-exploration

25 See Nerijus Adomaitis, "With Energy High on Agenda, China's No.3 Leader Visits Norway," Reuters, May 15, 2019, https://www.reuters.com/article/us-norway-china/with-energy-high-on-agenda-chinas-no-3-leader-visits-norway-idUSKCN1SL0ZK; "Norway's New Crude a Threat to Rivals in Prized Asia Market," Bloomberg News, October 23, 2019, https://www.bloomberg.com/news/articles/2019-10-23/norway-s-new-crude-a-competitive-threat-in-prized-asian-market

26 See AFP, "China Irked by Norwegian Nobel Peace Prize Nomination for Hong Kong," October 17, 2019, https://www.thelocal.no/20191017/china-irked-by-norwegian-nobel-peace-prize-nomination-for-hong-kong

27 Organisation for Economic Co-operation and Development, Better Life Index, accessed August 10, 2019, www.oecdbetterlifeindex.org

28 Lydia Saad, "Less Than Half in U.S. Now Say Their Taxes Are Too High," Gallup, April 16, 2018, https://news.gallup.com/poll/232361/less-half-say-taxes-high.aspx?g_source=link_NEWSV9&g_medium=LEAD&g_campaign=item_&g_content=Less%20Than%20Half%20in%20U.S.%20Now%20Say%20Their%20Taxes%20Are%20Too%20High

29 Quentin Fottrell, "More than 44% of Americans Pay No Federal Income Tax," MarketWatch, February 26, 2019, https://www.marketwatch.com/story/81-million-americans-wont-pay-any-federal-income-taxes-this-year-heres-why-2018-04-16

30 International Energy Agency, "World Energy Prices 2019," iea.org, accessed August 10, 2019, https://www.iea.org/statistics/prices

31 Veronica Stracqualursi, "Postal Service Reports $3.9 Billion in Losses for Fiscal Year 2018," CNN.com, November 15, 2018, https://www.cnn.com/2018/11/15/politics/postal-service-losses-fiscal-year-2018/index.html

32 Kathryn Watson, "Comptroller General Declares Medicaid Waste Worse Than Official Estimates," The Daily Caller, February 15, 2017, https://dailycaller.com/2017/02/15/comptroller-general-declares-medicaid-waste-worse-than-official-estimates

33 Marissa Laliberte, "11 Bizarre Things the U.S. Government Actually Spent Money On," Reader's Digest, accessed November 26, 2018, https://www.rd.com/culture/wasteful-government-spending-examples

34 Laura Sullivan, "Government's Empty Buildings Are Costing Taxpayers Billions," npr.com, March 12, 2014, https://www.npr.org/2014/03/12/287349831/governments-empty-buildings-are-costing-taxpayers-billions

35 Curtis Kalin and Sean Kennedy, Prime Cuts 2018, Citizens Against Government Waste, 2018, https://www.cagw.org/reporting/2018-prime-cuts

36 Charles Blahous, "The Costs of a National Single-Payer Healthcare System," Working Paper, Mercatus Center, July 2018, https://www.mercatus.org/system/files/blahous-costs-medicare-mercatus-working-paper-v1_1.pdf

37 American Hospital Association, "American Hospital Association Underpayment by Medicare and Medicaid Fact Sheet," January 2019, https://www.aha.org/system/files/2019-01/underpayment-by-medicare-medicaid-fact-sheet-jan-2019.pdf

38 Kyle Pomerleau and Huaqun Li, "How Much Revenue Would a 70% Top Tax Rate Raise? An Initial Analysis," Tax Foundation, January 14, 2019, https://taxfoundation.org/70-tax-proposal

39 "Forbes Releases 37th Annual Forbes 400 Ranking of the Richest Americans," Forbes, October 3, 2018, https://www.forbes.com/sites/forbespr/2018/10/03/forbes-releases-37th-annual-forbes-400-ranking-of-the-richest-americans/#f4995ae5cb1f

40 Justin Haskins, "Estimating the Income Tax Hikes Required to Pay for Bernie Sanders' Medicare-for-All Plan," Policy Brief, The Heartland Institute, August 2019, https://www.heartland.org/_template-assets/documents/publications/Medicare4AllJK2.pdf

41   Bacchus Barua, David Jacques, and Antonia Collyer, Waiting Your Turn: Wait Times for Health Care in Canada, Fraser Institute, December 4, 2018, https://www.fraserinstitute.org/studies /waiting-your-turn-wait-times-for-health-care-in-canada-2018

42   Merritt Hawkins, Survey of Physician Appointment Wait Times, merritthawkins.com, 2017, https://www.merritthawkins.com/uploadedFiles/MerrittHawkins/Content/Pdf/mha2017wait timesurveyPDF.pdf

43   Laura Donnelly, "GPs to See Patients in Groups of 15," The Telegraph (U.K.), October 5, 2018, https://www.telegraph.co.uk/news/2018/10/05/gps-see-patients-groups-15

44   Donovan Slack, John Kelly, and James Sergent, "Death Rates, Bedsores, ER Wait Times: Where Every VA Hospital Lags or Leads Other Medical Care," USA Today, February 7, 2019, https://www .usatoday.com/in-depth/news/investigations/2019/02/07/where-every-va-hospital-lags-leads -other-care/2511739002

45   Anne Kauranen "Finland's cabinet quits over failure to deliver healthcare reform," Reuters, March 8, 2019, https://www.reuters.com/article/us-finland-government/finlands-cabinet -quits-over-failure-to-deliver-healthcare-reform-idUSKCN1QP0R6

46   Jeffrey Cimmino, "Finnish Government Collapses Due to Rising Cost of Universal Health Care," Washington Free Beacon, March 8, 2019, https://freebeacon.com/politics/finnish-government -collapses-due-to-rising-cost-of-universal-health-care

47   Anne Kauranen, supra note 45.

48   Organisation for Economic Co-operation and Development , supra note 27.

49   Centers for Disease Control and Prevention, "Deaths and Mortality," cdc.gov, accessed August 12, 2019, https://www.cdc.gov/nchs/fastats/deaths.htm

50   NCD Risk Factor Collaboration, "Trends in adult body-mass index in 200 countries from 1975 to 2014: a pooled analysis of 1698 population-based measurement studies with 19·2 million participants," Lancet, Volume 387, Issue 10026, P1377-1396, April 02, 2016, https://www.the lancet.com/journals/lancet/article/PIIS0140-6736(16)30054-X/fulltext

51   See Emma Beswick, "Which country has the highest average BMI in Europe?," Euronews, May 10, 2019, https://www.euronews.com/2019/05/09/which-country-has-the-highest-average-bmi-in -europe

52   "Automobile History," History.com, August 21, 2018, https://www.history.com/topics/inventions /automobiles

53   World Health Organization, "Road Traffic Deaths Data by Country," Global Health Observatory Data Repository, last updated February 28, 2019, http://apps.who.int/gho/data /node.main.A997

54   "Who was Alfie Evans and what was the row over his treatment?," BBC, April 28, 2018, https:// www.bbc.com/news/uk-england-merseyside-43754949

55   Robert Moffit, "The Sad Case of Alfie Evans: A Sordid Lesson in Government-Controlled Health Care," The Heritage Foundation, April 26, 2018, https://www.heritage.org/life/commentary/the -sad-case-alfie-evans-sordid-lesson-government-controlled-health-care

56   Helen Pidd, "Couples Being Denied IVF on NHS Over Man's Age or Weight," The Guardian (U.K.), October 28, 2018, https://www.theguardian.com/society/2018/oct/29/couples-being-denied-ivf -nhs-mans-age-or-weight

57   Alex Matthews-King, "Obese People Unfairly Denied IVF by Cost-Cutting NHS, says Oxford Academic," Independent (U.K.), April 14, 2019, https://www.independent.co.uk /news/health/obesity-ivf-fertility-treatment-pregnancy-nhs-funding-crisis-ccg -oxford-a8868676.html

58   Chris Smyth, "Elderly Go Blind as NHS Ignores Eye Surgery Rationing Advice," The Times (U.K.), April 6, 2019, https://www.thetimes.co.uk/article/elderly-go-blind-as-nhs-ignores-eye -surgery-rationing-advice-bp5x77t0g

59   Angie Drobnic Holan, "Lie of the Year: 'If You Like Your Health Care Plan, You Can Keep It,'"

60   J.B. Wogan, "Cut the Cost of a Typical Family's Health Insurance Premium by up to $2,500 a Year," PolitiFact, August 31, 2012, https://www.politifact.com/truth-o-meter/promises /obameter/promise/521/cut-cost-typical-familys-health-insurance-premium-

61 Jason Pye, "Watch ObamaCare's Architect Brag About the Deceptive Tactics Used to Pass the Health Law," FreedomWorks, November 10, 2014, http://www.freedomworks.org/content/watch -obamacares-architect-brag-about-deceptive-tactics-used-pass-health-law

62 Marissa Laliberte, supra note 33.

63 Hadley Heath Manning, "Massachusetts Shows Rationing is Inevitable when Government is in Charge of Healthcare," October 20, 2017, https://www.washingtonexaminer.com/massachusetts -shows-rationing-is-inevitable-when-government-is-in-charge-of-healthcare

64 Tax Policy Center, "How Do State and Local Soda Taxes Work?," Briefing Book, accessed August 19, 2019, https://www.taxpolicycenter.org/briefing-book/how-do-state-and-local-soda-taxes-work

65 Janelle Cammenga, "How High Are Cigarette Taxes in Your State?," Tax Foundation, April 10, 2019, https://taxfoundation.org/2019-state-cigarette-tax-rankings

66 Associated Press, "San Francisco Schools Ban Chocolate Milk: It's 'a Bummer, but Whatever,'" Chicago Tribune, July 10, 2017, https://www.chicagotribune.com/nation-world/ct-san-francisco -schools-ban-chocolate-milk-20170710-story.html

67 Gary Price and Tim Norbeck, "Direct Primary Care Trumps the ACA for: Value, Quality And Satisfaction," Forbes, June 28, 2017, https://www.forbes.com/sites/physiciansfoundation/2017/06 /28/direct-primary-care-trumps-the-aca-for-value-quality-and-satisfaction/#7a141f8b1dad

68 Matthew Glans, "Direct Primary Care, A Viable Solution to Pennsylvania's Primary Care Shortage," Research & Commentary, The Heartland Institute, May 30, 2018, https://www .heartland.org/publications-resources/publications/research--commentary-direct-primary -care-a-viable-solution-to-pennsylvanias-primary-care-shortage

69 Docs4PatientCare Foundation, The Physician's Prescription For Health Care Reform, accessed August 19, 2019, https://d4pcfoundation.org/about-us/the-physicians-prescription-for -health-care-reform

6. BUILDING A 21ˢᵀ CENTURY SOCIALIST ~~PARADISE~~ NIGHTMARE

a   Sidney Fussell, "Why Hong Kongers Are Toppling Lampposts," The Atlantic, August 30, 2019, https://www.theatlantic.com/technology/archive/2019/08/why-hong-kong-protesters-are -cutting-down-lampposts/597145

b   Jacqueline Alemany, "White House Considers New Project Seeking Links Between Mental Health and Violent Behavior," The Washington Post, August 22, 2019, https://www.washingtonpost.com /politics/2019/08/22/white-house-considers-new-project-seeking-links-between-mental -health-violent-behavior

c   Ed Feulner, "Assessing the 'Great Society,'" Heritage Foundation, June 30, 2014, https://www .heritage.org/poverty-and-inequality/commentary/assessing-the-great-society

d   Richard Best, "How the U.S. Dollar Became the World's Reserve Currency," Investopedia, October 1, 2019, https://www.investopedia.com/articles/forex-currencies/092316/how-us -dollar-became-worlds-reserve-currency.asp?

e   World Bank, "GDP [current US$]–Japan, United States," accessed September 26, 2019, https:// data.worldbank.org/indicator/NY.GDP.MKTP.CD?locations=JP-US, citing data from the World Bank national accounts and OECD National Accounts.

----

1   George Orwell, 1984, 60th Anniversary Edition, [New York, NY: Berkley Publishing, 1983].

2   iRobot, "iRobot Reports Record Fourth-Quarter and Full-Year Revenue," media.irobot.com, February 7, 2018, https://media.irobot.com/2018-02-07-iRobot-Reports-Record-Fourth -Quarter-and-Full-Year-Revenue

3   Jane Barratt, "We Are Living Longer than Ever. But Are We Living Better?," STAT News, February 14, 2017, https://www.statnews.com/2017/02/14/living-longer-living-better-aging

4   Interview between Glenn Beck and Ray Kurzweil, Glenn Beck Program, CNN Headline News, May 30, 2008, http://transcripts.cnn.com/TRANSCRIPTS/0805/30/gb.01.html

5   June Javelosa, "Robo Revolution: A Factory Cut Labor Costs in Half, Thanks to Tiny Robots," Futurism, April 22, 2017, https://futurism.com/3-tiny-robots-help-cut-chinese-warehouse -labor-costs-by-half-kelsey

GRAPHIC CALLOUTS

6   Charlie Campbell, "'AI Farms' Are at the Forefront of China's Global Ambitions," Time, February 1, 2019, https://time.com/5518339/china-ai-farm-artificial-intelligence-cybersecurity

7   Evan Andrews, "Who Were the Luddites?," History.com, updated June 26, 2019, https://www.history.com/news/who-were-the-luddites

8   Encyclopaedia Britannica, "Xinjiang," accessed September 23, 2019, https://www.britannica.com/place/Xinjiang

9   Encyclopaedia Britannica, "Uighur," accessed September 23, 2019, https://www.britannica.com/topic/Uighur

10   See Encyclopaedia Britannica, "Xinjiang," accessed September 23, 2019, https://www.britannica.com/place/Xinjiang

11   Dominic Nardi, "Religious Freedom in China's High-Tech Surveillance State," U.S. Commission on International Religious Freedom, September 2019, https://www.uscirf.gov/sites/default/files/2019%20China%20Surveillance%20State%20Update.pdf

12   Ibid.

13   Ibid.

14   Ibid.

15   Ibid.

16   Ibid.

17   Ibid.

18   Chris Buckley and Paul Mozur, "How China Uses High-Tech Surveillance to Subdue Minorities," New York Times, May 22, 2019, https://www.nytimes.com/2019/05/22/world/asia/china-surveillance-xinjiang.html

19   Ellen Halliday, "Uighurs Can't Escape Chinese Repression, Even in Europe," The Atlantic, August 20, 2019, https://www.theatlantic.com/international/archive/2019/08/china-threatens-uighurs-europe/596347

20   Ibid.

21   Ibid.

22   Associated Press, "China's Uighur Policy is Human Rights 'Stain of the Century'–Pompeo," July 19, 2019, https://www.theguardian.com/us-news/2019/jul/19/chinas-uighur-policy-is-human-rights-stain-of-the-century-pompeo

23   Dominic Nardi, supra note 11.

24   Simina Mistreanu, "Life Inside China's Social Credit Laboratory," Foreign Policy, April 3, 2018, https://foreignpolicy.com/2018/04/03/life-inside-chinas-social-credit-laboratory

25   Joe McDonald, "China Bars Millions from Travel for 'Social Credit' Offenses," Associated Press, February 22, 2019, https://www.apnews.com/9d43f4b74260411797043ddd391c13d8

26   Mike Elgan, "Uh-oh: Silicon Valley is Building a Chinese-Style Social Credit System," Fast Company, August 26, 2019, https://www.fastcompany.com/90394048/uh-oh-silicon-valley-is-building-a-chinese-style-social-credit-system

27   See Bruce Sterling, "Chinese Planning Outline for a Social Credit System," Wired, June 3, 2015, https://www.wired.com/beyond-the-beyond/2015/06/chinese-planning-outline-social-credit-system

28   Joe McDonald, supra note 25.

29   Dustin Volz, "Spy Agency NSA Triples Collection of U.S. Phone Records: Official Report," Reuters.com, May 4, 2018, https://www.reuters.com/article/us-usa-cyber-surveillance/spy-agency-nsa-triples-collection-of-u-s-phone-records-official-report-idUSKBN1I52FR

30   Laura Hautala, "NSA Surveillance Programs Live On, In Case You Hadn't Noticed," cnet.com, January 19, 2018, https://www.cnet.com/news/nsa-surveillance-programs-prism-upstream-live-on-snowden

31   Andrew Liptak, "President Donald Trump Has Signed the FISA Reauthorization Bill," The Verge, January 20, 2018, https://www.theverge.com/2018/1/20/16913534/president-donald-trump-signed-fisa-amendments-reauthorization-act-of-2017-section-702

32 Laura Hautala, supra note 30.

33 Patrick Toomey, "The NSA Continues to Violate Americans' Internet Privacy Rights," ACLU, August 22, 2018, https://www.aclu.org/blog/national-security/privacy-and-surveillance/nsa -continues-violate-americans-internet-privacy

34 See, for example, Derek Hawkins, "The Cybersecurity 202: Privacy Advocates Are Back in Court Fighting NSA Surveillance. It's an Uphill Battle," Washington Post, September 4, 2018, https:// www.washingtonpost.com/news/powerpost/paloma/the-cybersecurity-202/2018/09/04/the -cybersecurity-202-privacy-advocates-are-back-in-court-fighting-nsa-surveillance-it-s-an -uphill-battle/5b8d69f21b326b3f31919f29

35 See "EFF Urges Supreme Court to Take On Unconstitutional NSA Surveillance, Reverse Dangerous Ruling That Allows Massive Government Spying Program," Electronic Frontier Foundation, August 10, 2017, https://www.eff.org/ko/press/releases/eff-urges-supreme-court -take-unconstitutional-nsa-surveillance-reverse-dangerous

36 See Orin Kerr, "9th Circuit Upholds Warrantless Email Surveillance of Person in the U.S. Communicating with Foreigners Abroad when the Foreigners are the 'Targets,'" Washington Post, December 5, 2016, https://www.washingtonpost.com/news/volokh-conspiracy/wp/2016 /12/05/9th-circuit-upholds-warrantless-email-surveillance-of-person-in-the-u-s -communicating-with-foreigners-abroad-when-the-foreigners-are-the-targets

37 Patrick Toomey, supra note 33.

38 Joseph Mann, "Exclusive: Yahoo Secretly Scanned Customer Emails for U.S. Intelligence Sources," Reuters, October 4, 2016, https://www.reuters.com/article/us-yahoo-nsa-exclusive-idUSKCN1241YT

39 Dustin Volz, "Spy Agency NSA Triples Collection of U.S. Phone Records: Official Report," Reuters, May 4, 2018, https://www.reuters.com/article/us-usa-cyber-surveillance/spy-agency -nsa-triples-collection-of-u-s-phone-records-official-report-idUSKBN1I52FR

40 Mike Elgan, supra note 26.

41 Scott Jaschik, "New SAT Score: Adversity," Inside Higher Ed, May 20, 2019, https://www .insidehighered.com/admissions/article/2019/05/20/college-board-will-add-adversity-score -everyone-taking-sat

42 Ibid.

43 Lauren Camera, "College Board Backtracks on 'Adversity Score,'" U.S. News & World Report, August 27, 2019, https://www.usnews.com/news/education-news/articles/2019-08-27/college -board-backtracks-on-adversity-score

44 U.S. Census Bureau, "Historical Poverty Tables: People and Families–1959 to 2018," census.gov, accessed September 25, 2019, https://www.census.gov/data/tables/time-series/demo/income -poverty/historical-poverty-people.html

45 U.S. Debt Clock, https://www.usdebtclock.org/

46 Eliza Relman, "Alexandria Ocasio-Cortez Says the Theory that Deficit Spending is Good for the Economy Should 'Absolutely' Be Part of the Conversation," Business Insider, January 7, 2019, https://www.businessinsider.com/alexandria-ocasio-cortez-ommt-modern-monetary-theory -how-pay-for-policies-2019-1

47 "About Stephanie Kelton," stephaniekelton.com, accessed September 26, 2019, https:// stephaniekelton.com/about

48 Jordan Malter, "Bernie Sanders' 2016 Economic Advisor Stephanie Kelton on Modern Monetary Theory and the 2020 Race," CNBC.com, March 2, 2019, https://www.cnbc.com/2019/03/01/bernie -sanders-economic-advisor-stephanie-kelton-on-mmt-and-2020-race.html

49 Ibid.

50 Ibid.

51 Matthew Klein, "Everything You Need to Know About Modern Monetary Theory," Barron's, June 7, 2019, https://www.barrons.com/articles/modern-monetary-theory-51559956914

52 Jordan Malter, supra note 48.

53 Veronica Stracqualursi, "Postal Service reports $3.9 billion in losses for fiscal year 2018," CNN.com, November 15, 2018, https://www.cnn.com/2018/11/15/politics/postal-service-losses -fiscal-year-2018/index.html

54 Associated Press, "Amtrak Cuts Operating Losses to Lowest Level in Decades," apnews.com, November 15, 2018, https://www.apnews.com/d229959ca1334fb6bc0fb5780f0dcae0

55 Patrick Gillespie, Marilia Brocchetto and Paula Newton, "Venezuela: How a Rich Country Collapsed," CNN Business, July 30, 2017, https://money.cnn.com/2017/07/26/news/economy/venezuela-economic-crisis/index.html

56 Valentina Sanchez, "Venezuela Hyperinflation Hits 10 million Percent. 'Shock Therapy' May Be Only Chance to Undo the Economic Damage," CNBC.com, August 3, 2019, https://www.cnbc.com/2019/08/02/venezuela-inflation-at-10-million-percent-its-time-for-shock-therapy.html

57 Sally Helm, "Modern Monetary Theory," Planet Money, podcast, NPR, September 26, 2018, https://www.npr.org/templates/transcript/transcript.php?storyId=652001941

58 Hans Sennholz, "Hyperinflation in Germany, 1914–1923," October 27, 2006, Mises Institute, https://mises.org/library/hyperinflation-germany-1914-1923

59 Iain Burns, "When Money Was Worthless," Daily Mail, November 16, 2017, https://www.dailymail.co.uk/news/article-5088405/When-cash-worthless-Germany-World-War.html

60 Ibid.

61 MacDonald Dzirutwe and Karin Strohecker, "Zimbabwe Inflation Almost Doubles, Stirring Memories of Economic Chaos," Reuters, July 15, 2019, https://www.reuters.com/article/us-zimbabwe-inflation/zimbabwe-inflation-almost-doubles-stirring-memories-of-economic-chaos-idUSKCN1UA0Q0

62 Ibid.

63 Kimberly Amadeo, "US Inflation Rate by Year from 1929 to 2020," The Balance, updated July 21, 2019, https://www.thebalance.com/u-s-inflation-rate-history-by-year-and-forecast-3306093

64 Megumi Fujikawa and Kosaku Narioka, "For Some in Japan, Another Day Older and Deeper in Debt Doesn't Sound So Bad," Wall Street Journal, March 30, 2019, https://www.wsj.com/articles/for-some-in-japan-another-day-older-and-deeper-in-debt-doesnt-sound-so-bad-11553947202

65 World Bank, "GDP (current US$)–Japan, United States," accessed September 26, 2019, https://data.worldbank.org/indicator/NY.GDP.MKTP.CD?locations=JP-US, citing data from the World Bank national accounts and OECD National Accounts.

66 Pavlina R. Tcherneva, "MMT is Already Happening," Jacobin, February 27, 2019, https://jacobinmag.com/2019/02/mmt-modern-monetary-theory-doug-henwood-overton-window

67 Levy Economics Institute, "Scholars: L. Randall Wray," accessed September 26, 2019, http://www.levyinstitute.org/scholars/l-randall-wray

68 L. Randall Wray, "Response to Doug Henwood's Trolling in Jacobin," New Economic Perspectives, February 25, 2019, http://neweconomicperspectives.org/2019/02/response-to-doug-henwoods-trolling-in-jacobin.html

7. SAINTS, SINNERS, & SOCIALISTS

a   See History.com, "Khmer Rouge," updated August 21, 2018, https://www.history.com/topics/cold-war/the-khmer-rouge; Hobert C. Tucker, "Stalin and the Uses of Psychology," Project Rand, U.S. Air Force, March 10, 1955, https://www.rand.org/content/dam/rand/pubs/research_memoranda/2006/RM1441.pdf; Zhipeng Gao, "Pavlovianism in China: Politics and Differentiation Across Scientific Disciplines in the Maoist Era," History of Science, Volume 53, Issue 1, April 2015, https://www.researchgate.net/publication/275240414_Pavlovianism_in_China_Politics_and_differentiation_across_scientific_disciplines_in_the_Maoist_era

b   See R.J. Rummel, Statistics of democide: genocide and mass murder since 1900, Transaction Publishers, 1997; Jean-Louis Panne et al., The Black Book of Communism: Crimes, Terror, Repression (Cambridge, MA: Harvard University Press, 1999).

c   Thomas Sowell post on Twitter, July 19, 2019, https://twitter.com/thomassowell/status/1152262592221601792?lang=en

d   See Office of U.S. Sen. Rand Paul, "Waste Reports," paul.senate.gov, accessed September 10, 2019, https://www.paul.senate.gov/wastereport; Curtis Kalin and Sean Kennedy, Prime Cuts 2018, Citizens Against Government Waste, 2018, https://www.cagw.org/reporting/2018-prime-cuts

GRAPHIC CALLOUTS

e   See Josh Sanburn, "Paul Krugman: An Alien Invasion Could Fix the Economy," Time, August 16, 2011, http://business.time.com/2011/08/16/paul-krugman-an-alien-invasion-could-fix-the-economy

f   Emily Birnbaum, "Tulsi Gabbard Sues Google over Censorship Claims," The Hill, July 25, 2019, https://thehill.com/policy/technology/454746-tulsi-gabbard-sues-google-over-censorship-claims

----

1   Randall Hoven, "Liberal Myths vs. Reality," New York Post, December 19, 2010, https://nypost.com/2010/12/19/liberal-myths-vs-reality

2   James Madison, "The Structure of the Government Must Furnish the Proper Checks and Balances Between the Different Departments," Independent Journal, February 6, 1788. Later compiled in the Federalist Papers, Essay No. 51, made available by the U.S. Library of Congress, https://www.congress.gov/resources/display/content/The+Federalist+Papers

3   See Herbert J. Walberg and Joseph L. Bast, How to Use Rewards to Help Children Learn—and Why Teachers Don't Use Them Well (Arlington Heights, IL: The Heartland Institute, 2014), https://www.heartland.org/publications-resources/publications/rewards?source=policybot

4   Samuel Stebbins, "The Cities Hit Hardest by Extreme Poverty," 24/7 Wall St., April 25, 2019, https://www.msn.com/en-us/money/realestate/the-cities-hit-hardest-by-extreme-poverty/ar-BBWg7PK

5   Michael B. Sauter, Thomas C. Frohlich, and Michelle Lodge, "25 Most Dangerous Cities in America," 24/7 Wall St., https://247wallst.com/special-report/2018/10/17/25-most-dangerous-cities-in-america-4, citing statistics from the FBI's 2017 Uniform Crime Report.

6   Leon Trotsky, Literature and Revolution, originally published by Leon Trotsky, April 11, 1924, made available online by Marxist.com, https://www.marxist.com/literature-and-revolution.htm

7   History.com, "Russian Revolutionary Leon Trotsky Assassinated in Mexico," This Day in History, updated August 19, 2019, https://www.history.com/this-day-in-history/trotsky-assassinated-in-mexico

8   See Palash Ghosh, "How Many People Did Joseph Stalin Kill?," International Business Times, March 5, 2013, https://www.ibtimes.com/how-many-people-did-joseph-stalin-kill-1111789, citing multiple studies.

9   BBC News, "Khmer Rouge: Cambodia's Years of Brutality," bbc.com, November 16, 2018, https://www.bbc.com/news/world-asia-pacific-10684399

10 See Investor's Business Daily, "The Fidel Castro Myth Debunked: The Death of a Tyrant, Not a Hero," investors.com, November 26, 2016, https://www.investors.com/politics/editorials/the-fidel-castro-myth-debunked-the-death-of-a-tyrant-not-a-hero, citing research by R.J. Rummel, University of Hawaii.

11 See Council of Economic Advisers, The Opportunity Costs of Socialism, Executive Office of the President, October 2018, p. 8, https://www.whitehouse.gov/wp-content/uploads/2018/10/The-Opportunity-Costs-of-Socialism.pdf

12 Ibid.

13 Barnini Chakraborty, "California Bullet Train Project on Track to Blow Through Billions of More Dollars," FoxNews.com, August 31, 2018, https://www.foxnews.com/us/california-bullet-train-project-on-track-to-blow-through-billions-of-more-dollars

14 Ralph Vartabedian, "Newsom's Shorter California Bullet Train Plan Likely to Run Out of Money Before Completion," Los Angeles Times, March 3, 2019, https://www.latimes.com/local/california/la-me-bullet-plan-challenges-20190303-story.html

15 See Alex Dobuzinskis, "Seattle Employers Cut Hours After Latest Minimum Wage Rise, Study Finds," Reuters, June 26, 2017, https://www.reuters.com/article/us-seattle-minimumwage-idUSKBN19H2MV

16 See Sarah Ferris and Ian Kullgren, "Minimum Wage Bill Could Eliminate 1.3 Million Jobs, CBO Says," Politico, July 8, 2019, https://www.politico.com/story/2019/07/08/minimum-wage-bill-eliminate-13m-jobs-cbo-says-1400531

17 Congressional Budget Office, The Effects on Employment and Family Income of Increasing the Federal Minimum Wage, cbo.gov, July 2019, https://www.cbo.gov/system/files/2019-07/CBO-55410-MinimumWage2019.pdf

18 Bill and Melinda Gates Foundation, "Annual Report 2018," gatesfoundation.org, accessed September 10, 2019, https://www.gatesfoundation.org/Who-We-Are/Resources-and-Media/Annual-Reports/Annual-Report-2018

19 Office of U.S. Sen. Rand Paul, "Waste Reports," paul.senate.gov, accessed September 10, 2019, https://www.paul.senate.gov/wastereport

20 Curtis Kalin and Sean Kennedy, Prime Cuts 2018, Citizens Against Government Waste, 2018, https://www.cagw.org/reporting/2018-prime-cuts

21 See Lucy Handley, "Amazon Beats Apple and Google to Become the World's Most Valuable Brand," CNBC, June 11, 2019, https://www.cnbc.com/2019/06/11/amazon-beats-apple-and-google-to-become-the-worlds-most-valuable-brand.html

22 Forbes, "Forbes Releases 37th Annual Forbes 400 Ranking of the Richest Americans," forbes.com, October 3, 2018, https://www.forbes.com/sites/forbespr/2018/10/03/forbes-releases-37th-annual-forbes-400-ranking-of-the-richest-americans/#1912696e5cb1

23 Todd Spangler, "YouTube Now Has 2 Billion Monthly Users, Who Watch 250 Million Hours on TV Screens Daily," Variety, May 3, 2019, https://variety.com/2019/digital/news/youtube-2-billion-users-tv-screen-watch-time-hours-1203204267

24 Aaron Smith and Monica Anderson, "Social Media Use in 2018," Pew Research Center, March 1, 2018, https://www.pewinternet.org/2018/03/01/social-media-use-in-2018

25 Danny Sullivan, "Google Now Handles at Least 2 Trillion Searches per Year," Search Engine Land, May 24, 2016, https://searchengineland.com/google-now-handles-2-999-trillion-searches-per-year-250247

26 Nitasha Tiku, "Survey Finds Conservatives Feel Out of Place in Silicon Valley," Wired, February 2, 2018, https://www.wired.com/story/survey-finds-conservatives-feel-out-of-place-in-silicon-valley

27 FoxNews.com, "Google Fires Employee Behind Anti-Diversity Memo, Reports Say," last updated September 26, 2017, https://www.foxnews.com/tech/google-fires-employee-behind-anti-diversity-memo-reports-say

28 Christopher Carbone, "Google Employee's Anti-Diversity Memo Goes Viral, Prompts Response from Execs," FoxNews.com, last updated September 26, 2017, https://www.foxnews.com/tech/google-employees-anti-diversity-memo-goes-viral-prompts-response-from-execs

29 Planned Parenthood, "What Are Puberty Blockers?," plannedparenthood.org, accessed September 11, 2019, https://www.plannedparenthood.org/learn/teens/puberty/what-are-puberty-blockers

30 See Jane Robbins, "Why Puberty Blockers Are A Clear Danger To Children's Health," The Federalist, December 14, 2018, https://thefederalist.com/2018/12/14/puberty-blockers-clear-danger-childrens-health, citing Jim Strickland and Sheila Schutt, "'My Body Is on Fire': Ga. Woman Blames Drug for Pain, Sues Maker," Atlanta Journal-Constitution, October 29, 2018, https://www.ajc.com/lifestyles/health/body-fire-woman-blames-drug-for-pain-sues-maker/SXiOzDSFL694I7LcT4Ra0O

31 Michael Gryboski, "YouTube Blocks PragerU Ten Commandments Videos, Restricts to 'Mature Audiences,'" Christian Post, August 21, 2019, https://www.christianpost.com/news/youtube-blocks-prageru-ten-commandments-videos-restricts-mature-audiences.html

32 Carlos Garcia, "YouTube Responds to Vox Writer's Campaign to 'Punish' Steven Crowder, and He is Not Happy About It," The Blaze, June 4, 2019, https://www.theblaze.com/news/youtube-shut-downs-campaign-against-crowder

33 Interview of Steven Crowder by Glenn Beck, Glenn Beck Radio Program, Blaze Media, June 6, 2019, https://www.theblaze.com/glenn-radio/crowder-youtube

34 Section 230, U.S. Communications Decency Act, 47 U.S.C. § 230, 1996. Text made available by the Electronic Frontier Foundation, accessed September 11, 2019, https://www.eff.org/issues\/cda230

8. ECO-SOCIALISM & CLIMATE CHANGE

a   See Emily Ekins, "68% of Americans Wouldn't Pay $10 a Month in Higher Electric Bills to Combat Climate Change," Cato at Liberty, Cato Institute, March 8, 2019, https://www.cato.org/blog/68-americans-wouldnt-pay-10-month-higher-electric-bills-combat-climate-change

GRAPHIC
CALLOUTS

b   Maggie Astor, "Pete Buttigieg Calls Climate Change 'a Kind of Sin,'" New York Times, September 4, 2019, https://www.nytimes.com/live/2019/democrats-climate-town-hall/pete-buttigieg-climate-change; Gabriel Hays, "'Agnostic' Sarah Silverman Calls Climate Change Girl the Second Coming of 'Jesus,'" NewsBusters, September 16, 2019, https://www.newsbusters.org/blogs/culture/gabriel-hays/2019/09/16/agnostic-sarah-silverman-calls-climate-change-girl-second

c   Robert Bryce, "Vacant-land Mythology Impedes Serious Energy Discussions," The Hill, February 25, 2019, https://thehill.com/opinion/energy-environment/430992-vacant-land-mythology-impedes-serious-energy-discussions; Robert Bryce, "San Bernardino County Says No to Big Renewables," National Review, March 7, 2019, https://www.manhattan-institute.org/html/renewable-energy-land-use-san-bernardino-county

d   U.S. Environmental Protection Agency, "Global Greenhouse Gas Emissions Data," epa.gov, last accessed December 12, 2019, https://www.epa.gov/ghgemissions/global-greenhouse-gas-emissions-data

e   Lindsey Bahr, "New Michael Moore-Backed Doc Tackles Alternative Energy," Associated Press, August 8, 2019, https://apnews.com/933b49681b0d47d3a005d356f35251ab

f   Isaac Orr, "Capitalism is Saving the Planet Part 1: Wealth Makes Health, Eventually," Center of the American Experiment, July 12, 2019, https://www.americanexperiment.org/2019/07/capitalism-saving-planet-part-1-wealth-makes-health-eventually

g   Andrew McAfee, "The Economy Keeps Growing, but Americans Are Using Less Steel, Paper, Fertilizer, and Energy," Reason, October 9, 2019, https://reason.com/2019/10/09/the-economy-keeps-growing-but-americans-are-using-less-steel-paper-fertilizer-and-energy

---

1   Naomi Klein, This Changes Everything: Capitalism vs. the Climate (New York, NY: Simon & Schuster, Kindle edition, 2014, pp. 23-24).

2   Ibid., p. 177.

3   Ibid., p. 23.

4   See Justin Haskins, "Alexandria Ocasio-Cortez's 'Green New Deal' is Actually an Old Socialist Plan from Canada," FoxNews.com, January 19, 2019, https://www.foxnews.com/opinion/alexandria-ocasio-cortezs-green-new-deal-is-actually-an-old-socialist-plan-from-canada

5   The Leap, "Frequently Asked Questions about the Leap Manifesto," leapmanifesto.org, accessed September 19, 2019, https://leapmanifesto.org/en/faq

6   NaomiKlein.org, "Advance Praise," accessed September 19, 2019, http://tsd.naomiklein.org/shock-doctrine/reviews/advance-praise

7   The Leap, "Who's On Board?," leapmanifesto.org, accessed September 19, 2019, https://leapmanifesto.org/en/whos-on-board

8   ThisChangesEverything.org, "This Changes Everything-The Book," accessed September 19, 2019, https://thischangeseverything.org/book

9   John Nichols, "The Democratic Platform Committee Now Has a Progressive Majority. Thanks, Bernie Sanders," The Nation, May 24, 2016, https://www.thenation.com/article/sanders-picks-and-allies-could-write-a-boldly-progressive-platform

10   EPIC News, "New Poll: Nearly Half Of Americans Are More Convinced Than They Were Five Years Ago That Climate Change Is Happening, With Extreme Weather Driving Their Views," Energy Policy Institute at the University of Chicago, January 22, 2019, https://epic.uchicago.edu/news-events/news/new-poll-nearly-half-americans-are-more-convinced-they-were-five-years-ago-climate

11   Emily Ekins, "68% of Americans Wouldn't Pay $10 a Month in Higher Electric Bills to Combat Climate Change," At Liberty, Cato Institute, March 8, 2019, https://www.cato.org/blog/68-americans-wouldnt-pay-10-month-higher-electric-bills-combat-climate-change

12   CNSNews.com, "Elizabeth Warren: 'Climate Change is an Existential Crisis,'" August 30, 2019, https://www.cnsnews.com/news/article/cnsnewscom-staff/elizabeth-warren-climate-change-existential-crisis

13   Naomi Oreskes, "The Scientific Consensus on Climate Change," Science, Volume 306, Issue 5702, December 3, 2004, https://science.sciencemag.org/content/306/5702/1686.full

14 Joseph Bast and Roy Spencer, "The Myth of the Climate Change '97%,'" Wall Street Journal, May 26, 2014, https://www.wsj.com/articles/joseph-bast-and-roy-spencer-the-myth-of-the-climate-change-97-1401145980

15 Peter Doran and Maggie Kendall Zimmerman, "Examining the Scientific Consensus on Climate Change," Eos, American Geophysical Union, Volume 90, Issue 3, January 20, 2009, https://agupubs.onlinelibrary.wiley.com/doi/epdf/10.1029/2009EO030002

16 Ibid.

17 John Cook et al., "Quantifying the Consensus on Anthropogenic Global Warming in the Scientific Literature," Environmental Research Letters, May 15, 2013, https://iopscience.iop.org/article/10.1088/1748-9326/8/2/024024

18 See Joseph Bast and Roy Spencer, "The Myth of the Climate Change '97%,'" Wall Street Journal, May 26, 2014, https://www.wsj.com/articles/joseph-bast-and-roy-spencer-the-myth-of-the-climate-change-97-1401145980, citing David Legates et al., "Climate Consensus and 'Misinformation': A Rejoinder to Agnotology, Scientific Consensus, and the Teaching and Learning of Climate Change," Science & Education, Volume 24, Issue 3, April 2015, https://link.springer.com/article/10.1007/s11191-013-9647-9#page-1?mod=article_inline

19 Edward Maibach et al., A 2016 National Survey of American Meteorological Society, Center for Climate Change Communication at George Mason University and American Meteorological Society, March 2016, https://gmuchss.az1.qualtrics.com/CP/File.php?F=F_cAA91W0HjZaiVV3

20 Steven Koonin, "Climate Science is Not Settled," Wall Street Journal, September 19, 2014, https://www.wsj.com/articles/climate-science-is-not-settled-1411143565

21 Nongovernmental International Panel on Climate Change, "Lead Authors: David R. Legates," accessed September 19, 2019, http://climatechangereconsidered.org/lead-authors

22 Nongovernmental International Panel on Climate Change, "Chapter Contributing Authors," accessed September 19, 2019, http://climatechangereconsidered.org/nipcc-scientists

23 Scott Waldman, "Adviser Who Applauded Rise in CO2 to Leave Administration," E&E News, September 11, 2019, https://www.eenews.net/stories/1061113085

24 Office of the Faculty, "William Happer," Princeton University, accessed September 19, 2019, https://dof.princeton.edu/about/clerk-faculty/emeritus/william-happer

25 University of Alabama in Huntsville, "Dr. John Christy: Biography," uah.edu, accessed September 19, 2019, https://www.uah.edu/science/departments/atmospheric-science/faculty-staff/dr-john-christy

26 The Heartland Institute, "About Us: Roy Spencer," accessed September 19, 2019, https://www.heartland.org/about-us/who-we-are/roy-spencer

27 See John Christy, "The Tropical Skies: Falsifying Climate Alarm," The Global Warming Policy Foundation, 2019, https://www.heartland.org/publications-resources/publications/the-tropical-skies-falsifying-climate-alarm

28 John Christy and Richard McNider, "Satellite Bulk Tropospheric Temperatures as a Metric for Climate Sensitivity," Asia-Pacific Journal of Atmospheric Sciences, Volume 53, Issue 4, https://link.springer.com/article/10.1007/s13143-017-0070-z

29 Nate Silver, The Signal and the Noise: Why So Many Predictions Fail-but Some Don't (New York, NY: Penguin Books, 2015), Reprint Edition.

30 See Myron Ebell and Steven Milloy, "Wrong Again: 50 Years of Failed Eco-pocalyptic Predictions," Competitive Enterprise Institute, cei.org, September 18, 2019, https://cei.org/blog/wrong-again-50-years-failed-eco-pocalyptic-predictions, citing George Getze, "Dire Famine Forecast by 1975," Salt Lake Tribune, November 17, 1967.

31 Institute for Energy Research, "Climate Change Overview," accessed September 20, 2019, https://www.instituteforenergyresearch.org/climate-change/climate-change-overview/2

32 See Myron Ebell and Steven Milloy, "Wrong Again: 50 Years of Failed Eco-pocalyptic Predictions," Competitive Enterprise Institute, cei.org, September 18, 2019, https://cei.org/blog/wrong-again-50-years-failed-eco-pocalyptic-predictions, citing Robert Reinhold, "Foe of Pollution Sees Lack of Time," New York Times, August 10, 1969.

33 HumanProgress.org, "Global Hunger Index," Cato Institute, accessed September 20, 2019, https://humanprogress.org/dwline?p=585&yf=1992&yl=2016&high=0&reg=3&reg1=0

34 Victor Cohn, "U.S. Scientist Sees New Ice Age Coming," Washington Post, July 9, 1971, https://
    web.archive.org/web/20160805020812/http://pqasb.pqarchiver.com/washingtonpost_historical
    /doc/14808530 3.html?FMT=ABS&FMTS=ABS:AI&type=historic&date=html+%2C+&author=By
    +Victor+Cohn%7C%7C%7C% 7C%7C%7CWashington+Post+Staff+Writer&pub=The+Washington+Post
    %2C+Times+Herald++%281959-1973%29&desc=U.S.+Scientist+Sees+New+Ice+Age+Coming&pqatl
    =top_retrieves

35 Anthony Tucker, "Space Satellites Show New Ice Age Coming Fast," The Guardian (U.K.),
    January 29, 1974, https://www.newspapers.com/image/259696938/?terms=new%2Bice%2Bage

36 Time, "Another Ice Age?," June 24, 1974, http://web.archive.org/web/20060812025725/http:
    /time-proxy.yaga.com/time/archive/printout/0,23657,944914,00.html

37 See Myron Ebell and Steven Milloy, "Wrong Again: 50 Years of Failed Eco-pocalyptic
    Predictions," Competitive Enterprise Institute, cei.org, September 18, 2019, https://cei.org
    /blog/wrong-again-50-years-failed-eco-pocalyptic-predictions, citing Walter Sullivan,
    "International Team of Specialists Finds No End in Sight to 30-Year Cooling Trend in Northern
    Hemisphere," New York Times, January 5, 1978.

38 Walter Sullivan, "Climatologists Are Warned North Pole Might Melt," February 14, 1979, The New
    York Times, https://www.nytimes.com/1979/02/14/archives/climatologists-are-warned-north
    -pole-might-melt-another-projection.html?searchResultPosition=1

39 Walter Sullivan, "Increased Burning of Fuels," New York Times, November 20, 1979, https://www
    .nytimes.com/1979/11/20/archives/increased-burning-of-fuels-could-alter-climate-change-in
    -climate-is.html?searchResultPosition=7

40 Associated Press, "Researchers Renew Warning of Effects of Global Warming," July 21, 1982,
    https://www.nytimes.com/1982/07/21/us/researchers-renew-warning-on-effects-of-global
    -warming.html?searchResultPosition=53

41 See, for example, Reuters, "Global Temperatures on Track for 3-5 Degree Rise by 2100:
    U.N.," November 29, 2018, https://www.reuters.com/article/us-climate-change-un/global
    -temperatures-on-track-for-3-5-degree-rise-by-2100-u-n-idUSKCN1NY186

42 See Myron Ebell and Steven Milloy, "Wrong Again: 50 Years of Failed Eco-pocalyptic
    Predictions," Competitive Enterprise Institute, cei.org, September 18, 2019, https://cei.org
    /blog/wrong-again-50-years-failed-eco-pocalyptic-predictions, citing Edward Stiles,
    "Prepare for Long, Hot Summers," Gannett News Service, December 12, 1988.

43 Myron Ebell and Steven Milloy, "Wrong Again: 50 Years of Failed Eco-pocalyptic Predictions,"
    Competitive Enterprise Institute, cei.org, September 18, 2019, https://cei.org/blog/wrong
    -again-50-years-failed-eco-pocalyptic-predictions

44 Associated Press, "Rising Seas Could Obliterate Nations: U.N. Officials," June 30, 1989.

45 Charles Onians, "Snowfalls are now just a thing of the past," The Independent (U.K.), March 20,
    2000, https://web.archive.org/web/20150912124604/http://www.independent.co.uk/environment
    /snowfalls-are-now-just-a-thing-of-the-past-724017.html

46 CBS and Associated Press, "Gore: Arctic Ice May Soon Vanish in Summer," CBS News, cbsnews
    .com, December 14, 2009, https://www.cbsnews.com/news/gore-arctic-ice-may-soon-vanish-in
    -summer

47 Michael Bastasch, "Polar Bears May Have Quadrupled In Number Despite Melting Arctic Ice,
    Book Says," Daily Caller, March 19, 2019, https://dailycaller.com/2019/03/19/polar-bears
    -arctic-ice

48 See Justin Haskins, "An Inconvenient Commentary: 5 Times Climate Alarmists Made Horribly
    Wrong Predictions," TheBlaze, July 30, 2017, https://www.theblaze.com/news/2017/07/30/an
    -inconvenient-commentary-5-times-climate-alarmists-made-horribly-wrong-predictions

49 Doug Hardy, "Greatest Snowfall on Kilimanjaro Glaciers in Years," GlacierHub, April 4, 2018,
    https://glacierhub.org/2018/04/04/greatest-snowfall-on-kilimanjaro-glaciers-in-years

50 National Interagency Fire Center, "Total Wildland Fires and Acres (1926-2018)," nif
    c.gov, accessed September 20, 2019, https://www.nifc.gov/fireInfo/fireInfo_stats
    _totalFires.html

51 See Bigad Shaban, Robert Campos, and Michael Horn, "Federal Government to Blame for Faster,
    More Destructive Wildfires in California, Scientists Say," NBC Bay Area, May 15, 2019, https://
    www.nbcbayarea.com/news/local/Federal-Government-Blamed-for-Faster-More-Destructive
    -Wildfires-509928871.html

52   See Roger Bezdek et al., *Climate Change Reconsidered II: Fossil Fuels* (Arlington Heights, IL: Nongovernmental Panel on Climate Change, 2019), Figures 2.3.1.1.1 and 2.3.1.1.2, citing data from the National Oceanic and Atmospheric Administration and Environmental Protection Agency, respectfully, p. 190, http://climatechangereconsidered.org/climate-change-reconsidered-ii-fossil-fuels

53   See Doyle Rice, "Study: Cold Kills 20 Times More People than Heat," *USA Today*, May 20, 2015, https://www.usatoday.com/story/weather/2015/05/20/cold-weather-deaths/27657269

54   P. J. Klotzbach et al., "Continental U.S. Hurricane Landfall Frequency and Associated Damage Observations and Future Risks," *Bulletin of the American Meteorological Society*, Volume number 99, Issue 7, pp. 1359-77, https://journals.ametsoc.org/doi/pdf/10.1175/BAMS-D-17-0184.1

55   Susan Jones, "U.S. Major Hurricane Drought Ends at Record 4,323 days," *CNS News*, August 26, 2017, https://www.cnsnews.com/news/article/susan-jones/major-us-hurricane-drought-ends-after-record-4323-days

56   Benjamin Freed, "These Maps Show What Washington Will Look Like When Antarctica Melts," *Washingtonian*, March 31, 2016, https://www.washingtonian.com/2016/03/31/these-maps-show-what-washington-will-look-like-when-antarctica-melts

57   Sydney Pereira, "How Long Before All of Florida Is Underwater?," *Newsweek*, November 3, 2017, https://www.newsweek.com/how-long-all-florida-underwater-700835

58   Thomas Frohlich and Michael Sauter, "30 US Cities that Could Be Underwater by 2060," *Business Insider*, October 3, 2018, https://www.businessinsider.com/30-us-cities-that-could-be-underwater-soon-2018-10#25-west-ashley-south-carolina-6

59   See Craig D. Idso, David Legates, and S. Fred Singer, "Global Sea-Level Rise: An Evaluation of the Data," Policy Brief, The Heartland Institute, May 2019, https://www.heartland.org/_template-assets/documents/publications/SeaLevelRiseCCRII.pdf

60   For definition of "land subsidence," see National Ocean Service, "What is Subsidence?," U.S. National Oceanic and Atmospheric Administration, accessed September 20, 2019, https://oceanservice.noaa.gov/facts/subsidence.html

61   See Craig D. Idso, David Legates, and S. Fred Singer, "Global Sea-Level Rise: An Evaluation of the Data," Policy Brief, The Heartland Institute, May 2019, https://www.heartland.org/_template-assets/documents/publications/SeaLevelRiseCCRII.pdf, citing A. Parker and C.D. Ollier, "California Sea Level Rise: Evidence Based Forecasts vs. Model Predictions," *Ocean & Coastal Management*, Volume 149, November 15, 2017, pp. 198-209.

62   Ibid.

63   Judith Curry, "Special Report on Sea Level Rise," *Climate Etc.*, accessed November 27, 2018, https://judithcurry.com/2018/11/27/special-report-on-sea-level-rise

64   Hana Alberts, "Barack and Michelle Obama are buying a $15M estate in Martha's Vineyard," *New York Post*, August 22, 2019, https://nypost.com/2019/08/22/barack-and-michelle-obama-are-buying-15m-estate-in-marthas-vineyard

65   Barack Obama, 2015 State of the Union Address, January 20, 2015. Made available by CNN.com, https://www.cnn.com/2015/01/20/politics/state-of-the-union-2015-transcript-full-text

66   See Peter Hasson, "Climate Change Could Leave Obama's Possible New Mansion Underwater, According To Researchers Funded By Obama Admin," *Daily Caller*, August 26, 2019, https://dailycaller.com/2019/08/26/obama-marthas-vineyard-mansion-climate-change

67   Denis Slattery, "The Wolf of Belize: Leo DiCaprio to Turn 104-Acre Belize Island into Eco-Resort," *New York Daily News*, April 3, 2015, https://www.nydailynews.com/entertainment/gossip/leo-dicaprio-turn-104-acre-belize-island-eco-resort-article-1.2173108

68   National Geographic and RatPac Documentary Films, *Before the Flood*, October 23, 2016, https://www.beforetheflood.com

69   Lauren Beale, "Indisputable: Gore Buys Montecito Villa," *Los Angeles Times*, May 8, 2010, https://www.latimes.com/archives/la-xpm-2010-may-08-la-hm-hotprop-20100508-story.html

70   Rachael Rettner, "Al Gore's movie 'An Inconvenient Truth' Says Sea Levels Could Rise Up to 20 Feet. Is This True?," *ScienceLine*, December 1, 2018, https://scienceline.org/2008/12/ask-rettner-sea-level-rise-al-gore-an-inconvenient-truth

71   See James Taylor, "A Famine of Fact at U.N. Climate Panel," *Wall Street Journal*, August 30, 2019, https://www.wsj.com/articles/a-famine-of-fact-at-u-n-climate-panel-11567201352;

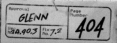

Food and Agriculture Organization, "World Food Situation," United Nations, accessed September 21, 2019, http://www.fao.org/worldfoodsituation/csdb/en; HumanProgress.org, "Crops, Net Production," accessed September 21, 2019, https://humanprogress.org/dwline?p=689&yf=1961&yl=2016&high=0&reg=3&reg1=0

72 NASA, "Carbon Dioxide Fertilization Greening Earth, Study Finds," nasa.gov, April 26, 2016, https://www.nasa.gov/feature/goddard/2016/carbon-dioxide-fertilization-greening-earth, citing Zaichun Zhu et al., "Greening of the Earth and Its Drivers," Nature Climate Change, Volume 6, April 25, 2016, https://www.nature.com/articles/nclimate3004

73 See NASA, "Human Activity in China and India Dominates the Greening of Earth, NASA Study Shows," nasa.gov, February 11, 2019, https://www.nasa.gov/feature/ames/human-activity-in-china-and-india-dominates-the-greening-of-earth-nasa-study-shows

74 Marlo Lewis Jr., "Climate-Related Deaths Are at Historic Lows, Data Show," Foundation for Economic Education, June 7, 2019, https://fee.org/articles/climate-related-deaths-are-at-historic-lows-data-show

75 Chris Cillizza, "Nancy Pelosi Just Threw Some Serious Shade at Alexandria Ocasio-Cortez's 'Green New Deal,'" CNN.com, updated February 8, 2019, https://www.cnn.com/2019/02/07/politics/pelosi-alexandria-ocasio-cortez-green-new-deal/index.html

76 House Resolution 109, Recognizing the Duty of the Federal Government to Create a Green New Deal, 116th Congress, February 7, 2019, https://www.congress.gov/bill/116th-congress/house-resolution/109/cosponsors

77 Senate Resolution 59, Recognizing the Duty of the Federal Government to Create a Green New Deal, 116th Congress, February 7, 2019, https://www.congress.gov/bill/116th-congress/house-resolution/109/cosponsors

78 See text of House Resolution 109, Recognizing the Duty of the Federal Government to Create a Green New Deal, 116th Congress, February 7, 2019, https://www.congress.gov/bill/116th-congress/house-resolution/109/

79 U.S. Department of Energy and BW Research Partnership, U.S. Energy and Employment Report, January 2017, https://www.energy.gov/sites/prod/files/2017/01/f34/2017%20US%20Energy%20and%20Jobs%20Report_0.pdf

80 Ibid.

81 Benjamin Zycher, The Green New Deal: Economics and Policy Analytics, American Enterprise Institute, April 2019, http://www.aei.org/wp-content/uploads/2019/04/RPT-The-Green-New-Deal-5.5x8.5-FINAL.pdf

82 Office of U.S. Rep. Alexandria Ocasio-Cortez, Green New Deal FAQ Sheet, February 7, 2019, https://www.heartland.org/_template-assets/documents/Green-New-Deal-FAQ-Fact-Sheet-Feb-7-2019.pdf

83 Ibid.

84 House Resolution 109, supra note 76.

85 See, for example, Global Carbon Project, "Global Carbon Atlas," accessed September 21, 2019, http://www.globalcarbonatlas.org/en/CO2-emissions

86 See Brady Dennis and Chris Mooney, "'We Are in Trouble.' Global Carbon Emissions Reached a Record High in 2018," Washington Post, December 5, 2018, https://www.washingtonpost.com/energy-environment/2018/12/05/we-are-trouble-global-carbon-emissions-reached-new-record-high

87 See Benjamin Zycher, The Green New Deal: Economics and Policy Analytics, American Enterprise Institute, April 2019, http://www.aei.org/wp-content/uploads/2019/04/RPT-The-Green-New-Deal-5.5x8.5-FINAL.pdf

88 Reuters, "China Plans 226 GW of New Coal Power Projects: Environmental Groups," reuters.com, September 19, 2019, https://www.reuters.com/article/us-climate-change-china-coal/china-plans-226-gw-of-new-coal-power-projects-environmental-groups-idUSKBN1W40HS

89 See Samantha Gross, "Coal Is King in India—And Will Likely Remain So," Brookings Institution, March 8, 2019, https://www.brookings.edu/blog/planetpolicy/2019/03/08/coal-is-king-in-india-and-will-likely-remain-so, citing Rahul Tongia and Samantha Gross, "Coal in India: Adjusting to Transition," The Cross-Brookings Initiative on Energy and Climate, March 8, 2019, https://www.brookings.edu/research/coal-in-india

90 World Bank, Poverty & Equity Data Portal, "India," accessed September 21, 2019, http://povertydata.worldbank.org/poverty/country/IND

91 House Resolution 109, supra note 76.

92 Office of U.S. Rep. Alexandria Ocasio-Cortez, supra note 82.

93 House Resolution 109, supra note 76.

94 Ibid.

95 Ibid.

96 Ibid.

97 Ibid.

98 Ibid.

99 Office of U.S. Rep. Alexandria Ocasio-Cortez, supra note 82.

100 Douglas Holtz-Eakin et al., The Green New Deal: Scope, Scale, and Implications, American Action Forum, February 25, 2019, https://www.americanactionforum.org/research/the-green-new-deal-scope-scale-and-implications

101 David Montgomery, "AOC's Chief of Change," Washington Post, July 10, 2019, https://www.washingtonpost.com/news/magazine/wp/2019/07/10/feature/how-saikat-chakrabarti-became-aocs-chief-of-change

102 Mary Kay Linge and Jon Levine, "Feds Probing AOC's Chief of Staff Saikat Chakrabarti After Sudden Resignation," New York Post, August 3, 2019, https://nypost.com/2019/08/03/feds-probing-aocs-chief-of-staff-saikat-chakrabarti-after-sudden-resignation

103 Shawn Regan, "Socialism is Bad for the Environment," National Review, May 16, 2019, https://www.national review.com/magazine/2019/06/03/socialism-is-bad-for-the-environment

104 Mario Penton, "Pollution is Destroying the Environment and Livelihood for Residents in This Cuban City," Miami Herald, June 7, 2019, https://www.miamiherald.com/news/nation-world/world/americas/cuba/article212612094.html

105 Ibid.

106 Shawn Regan, supra note 103.

107 Greg Norman, "San Francisco Human Feces Map Shows Waste Blanketing the California City," FoxNews.com, April 23, 2019, https://www.foxnews.com/us/san-francisco-map-shows-human-poop-complaints

108 American Lung Association, "Most Polluted Cities," lung.org, accessed September 22, 2019, https://www.lung.org/our-initiatives/healthy-air/sota/city-rankings/most-polluted-cities.html

109 U.S. News & World Report, "Pollution Rankings," usnews.com, accessed September 22, 2019, https://www.usnews.com/news/best-states/rankings/natural-environment/pollution

110 U.S. Environmental Protection Agency, "The Origins of EPA," epa.gov, accessed September 22, 2019, https://www.epa.gov/history/origins-epa

111 World Health Organization, "Ambient Air Quality: Exposure Country Average," who.int, last updated May 16, 2018, accessed September 22, 2019, http://apps.who.int/gho/data/node.main.152?lang=en

112 Naomi Lim, "Yang Urges 'Vast Majority' of World to Go Vegetarian 'Immediately' for Climate," Washington Examiner, September 4, 2019, https://www.washingtonexaminer.com/news/yang-urges-vast-majority-of-world-to-go-vegetarian-immediately-for-climate

113 Susan Jones, "Harris Would Change Dietary Guidelines, Food Labels, to Discourage Red Meat Consumption," CNS News, September 5, 2019, https://www.cnsnews.com/news/article/susan-jones-harris-would-change-dietary-guidelines-food-labels-discourage-red-meat

114 Daily Caller, "Sanders on Being Pro-Choice and Climate Change," September 4, 2019, https://youtu.be/gC8x27PzQ84, citing Bernie Sanders answering question at CNN's "Climate Crisis Town Hall," September 4, 2019.

115 Ian Schwartz, "Maher: 'Falling Birth Rates Are A Good Thing'; World Is 'Too Crowded," Real Clear Politics, April 13, 2019, https://www.realclearpolitics.com/video/2019/04/13/maher_falling_birth_rates_are_a_good_thing_world_is_too_crowded.html

116 Jack Crowe, "AOC: 'Is It Still Okay to Have Children' in the Age of Climate Change," National
     Review, February 25, 2019, https://www.nationalreview.com/news/aoc-is-it-still-ok-to-have
     -children-in-the-age-of-climate-change

117 Wes Siler, "I Got a Vasectomy Because of Climate Change," Outside, November 21, 2019, https://
     www.outsideonline.com/2406087/pointless-cruelty-ticketing-cyclists

118 Damian Carrington, "Climate Crisis: 11,000 Scientists Warn of 'Untold Suffering,'" The
     Guardian (U.K.), November 5, 2019, https://www.theguardian.com/environment/2019/nov/05
     /climate-crisis-11000-scientists-warn-of-untold-suffering

119 William Ripple et al., "World Scientists' Warning of a Climate Emergency," BioScience, November 5,
     2019, https://academic.oup.com/bioscience/advance-article/doi/10.1093/biosci/biz088/5610806

120 Colin Hickey, Travis Rieder, and Jake Earl, "Population Engineering and the Fight against
     Climate Change," Social Theory and Practice, Volume 42, Issue 4, October 2016, https://www.
     academia.edu/19933914/Population_Engineering_and_the_Fight_against_Climate_Change

9. A BETTER WAY

a   Ed Krayewski, "Bernie Sanders: Don't Need 23 Choices of Deodorant, 18 Choices of Sneakers
     When Kids Are Going Hungry," Reason, May 26, 2015, https://reason.com/2015/05/26/bernie
     -sanders-dont-need-23-choices-of-d

GRAPHIC   b   Johan Norberg, "Globalization's Great Triumph: The Death of Extreme Poverty," HumanProgress,
CALLOUTS   October 15, 2010, https://humanprogress.org/article.php?p=1528

c   World Bank, "Hong Kong, China: GDP per capita (current US$)," data.worldbank.org, accessed
     September 12, 2019, https://data.worldbank.org/indicator/NY.GDP.PCAP.CD?locations=CN-HK

----

1   See Charles Francis Adams, The Works of John Adams (Boston, MA: Little, Brown & Co., 1850–56).
     Quote made available online by the University of Chicago Press, http://press-pubs.uchicago
     .edu/founders/documents/v1ch16s15.html

2   History.com, "Spanish Flu," updated February 22, 2019, https://www.history.com/topics/world
     -war-i/1918-flu-pandemic

3   Sam Staley, "The Rise and Fall of Indian Socialism," Reason, June 2006, https://reason.com
     /2006/06/06/the-rise-and-fall-of-indian-so-2

4   World Bank, Poverty & Equity Data Portal, India, accessed September 12, 2019, http://
     povertydata.worldbank.org/poverty/country/IND

5   World Bank, "India: GDP (current US$)," data.worldbank.org, accessed September 12, 2019,
     https://data.worldbank.org/indicator/NY.GDP.MKTP.CD?locations=IN

6   Arthur C. Brooks, The Conservative Heart (New York, NY: Broadside Books, 2017), Kindle Edition,
     p. 112.

7   Zuraidah Ibrahim, "Lee Kuan Yew Was Ahead of the Curve when He Predicted China's Emergence,"
     South China Morning Post, March 24, 2015, https://www.scmp.com/news/asia/article/1745715
     /lee-kuan-yew-was-ahead-curve-when-he-predicted-chinas-emergence

8   World Bank, "China: GDP (current US$)," data.worldbank.org, accessed September 12, 2019,
     https://data.worldbank.org/indicator/NY.GDP.MKTP.CD?locations=CN

9   The Heritage Foundation, 2019 Index of Economic Freedom, "China," accessed September 12,
     2019, https://www.heritage.org/index/country/china

10   The Heritage Foundation, 2019 Index of Economic Freedom, "Hong Kong," accessed September 12,
     2019, https://www.heritage.org/index/country/hongkong

11   Cato Institute, Fraser Institute, et al., Economic Freedom of the World: 2019 Annual Report,
     "Hong Kong," 2019, https://www.cato.org/economic-freedom-world

12   The Heritage Foundation, supra note 10.

13   World Bank, "Hong Kong, China: GDP per capita (current US$)," data.worldbank.org, accessed
     September 12, 2019, https://data.worldbank.org/indicator/NY.GDP.PCAP.CD?locations=CN-HK

14   Organisation for Economic Co-operation and Development, Better Life Index, accessed
     August 10, 2019, www.oecdbetterlifeindex.org